GW00356924

DIFFERENT AND THE SAME

DIFFERENT AND THE SAME

A Folk History of the Protestants of Independent Ireland

DEIRDRE NUTTALL

Eastwood

First published by Eastwood Books, 2020
Dublin, Ireland
www.eastwoodbooks.com
www.wordwellbooks.com
@eastwoodbooks

First Edition

Eastwood Books is an imprint of The Wordwell Group

Eastwood Books
The Wordwell Group
Unit 9, 78 Furze Road
Sandyford
Dublin, Ireland

ISBN: 978-1-9161375-6-1 (hardback)
ISBN: 978-1-8380416-5-6 (mobi)
ISBN: 978-1-8380416-6-3 (epub)

British Library Cataloguing in Publication Data.
A catalogue record for this book is available from the British Library.

The publishers gratefully acknowledge financial support from the Department of Foreign Affairs under the Irish Government's Reconciliation Fund towards the production of this book.

Typeset in Ireland by Wordwell Ltd
Copy-editor: Myles McCionnaith
Cover design and artwork: Megan Sheer, sheerdesignandtypesetting.com
Printed by: Gráficas Castuera, Pamplona

Dedicated to Arthur John Alexander, 1877–1932

CONTENTS

ACKNOWLEDGEMENTS

My sincere thanks to the many people who agreed to participate in the research for this book, who were very generous with their time, knowledge, and attention (and also with tea and sandwiches).

Thanks are also due to a number of people who were extremely supportive in the very early stages of this project, including Colette Colfer, Tracy Fahey, and Tony Walsh.

I have huge gratitude to the staff of the National Folklore Collection at UCD, in particular director Dr Críostóir Mac Cárthaigh, whose enthusiasm and help ensured that the work was brought to fruition, and that much of this research is now part of the National Folklore Collection; and to Claire Doohan, whose administrative work was enormously appreciated.

Funding for the Irish Protestant Folk Memory Project was provided in the early stages by Marsh's Library and, on two later occasions, by the Department of Foreign Affairs and Trade's Reconciliation Fund. Needless to say, this funding was invaluable.

Finally, heartfelt thanks to Giovanni Giusti, whose constant support has been immeasurable.

INTRODUCTION

Storytelling is at the heart of Ireland's sense of self and identity, as it is for each of us, individually, and for all of us, as families and communities. The stories we tell about who and what we are, where we come from, and where we are going, impact on everything we do, on how we are seen, and on how we see ourselves. However, some stories are more accepted than others; some are supported by the state-endorsed version of history, and others are not, and some are experienced as safe to air in public, while others are kept within one's intimate circles. Here, we are going to explore the stories of the 'old' Protestant communities of independent Ireland and how these stories have justified feelings of belonging, entitlement, estrangement, marginalisation, and more in the context of a state that they have sometimes historically perceived as hostile, or at least indifferent, to their interests. These stories combine history and mythology, fact, folklore, and aspiration. They have also shifted over time and will continue to do so as Ireland changes and their narrators engage in the natural process of re-organising their stories into a format that seems to make sense in the current context.[1] Formal history involves all of this too, of course, although not in exactly the same way. Historians have often been accused of presenting facts in a certain way to suit a particular agenda.[2] In general, recognised history is never a full account of the past; it is the small selection of stories that we have chosen to preserve as a public memory.[3] Much can be learned from the narratives that are not officially recognised.

This work aims to at least partially address the stories of Protestants, especially non-elite Protestants, and to provide insight into the diversity and richness of the counternarratives embedded in Protestants' stories. To this end, ninety-eight interviews and seventy-six responses to a detailed questionnaire were collected from individuals from all over independent Ireland over a period between 2013 and 2017, for whom brief contextual data is included in an appendix. While they discuss the remote past, many of their stories encompass their own and their parents' memories, and therefore collectively form a folk history of the period from the start of the twentieth century to recent times. This work is not intended to replace, challenge, or support work carried out by scholars of history, but to complement history scholarship by providing insights into subjective lived experience and collective memory.

What is an Irish Protestant?

'Protestant' is often assumed to mean 'Church of Ireland', which is the most populous of the faiths, but the term 'Protestant' encompasses various denominations, including Methodists, Presbyterians, and members of the Society of Friends (Quakers). For many years, the Church of Ireland was the state religion, and other Protestants were considered 'dissenters', for which they suffered discrimination to varying degrees at different periods. However, in independent Ireland, and even before independence, Protestants' sense of kinship was strengthened by the fact that they inhabited a country in which the Catholic Church was a dominant religious, cultural, and political force, making them collectively other. This made their position as Irish citizens often a somewhat uncomfortable one throughout much of the twentieth century,[4] especially if they did not belong to the social classes protected by insulating layers of wealth and business connections. The 'old' Protestants are united across the various denominations by shared experiences and extensive social fluidity (to the extent that some Protestants would shift denominations, depending on their circumstances at a given time). This unity is often compounded by a feeling that they are not always entirely accepted in their homeland and that the stories that they hear about the officially accepted Irish past are not completely relevant to them.

Most people understand that Protestantism in Ireland is a cultural identifier. Intermarriage between the various Protestant denominations has been generally accepted, and their members recognise each other as kindred, 'from the same foundation'.[5] Therefore, we can understand 'Protestant' in the context of independent Ireland as a cultural marker more than a religious one. One can leave a religion, after all, but in Ireland many will see you (and to some extent, you will probably see yourself) as 'Protestant', even if you have never been religiously observant. The Dean of St Patrick's Cathedral once described a mutual acquaintance to the artist Lily Yeats as

someone who 'has no religion but is an out-and-out Protestant in everything else',[6] and one can hear similar descriptions even now, as in the case
of Archie, one of the interviewees whose perspectives make up a considerable portion of this work,[7] who says, 'Although I have not had a religion or
been religious ever since [the age of 14] I still see the Protestant background
as being part of me.' As we are exploring Protestants as a cultural group and
not strictly in terms of faith difference – and because of the high levels of
Protestant intermarriage – denominational differences between Protestants
are only mentioned when they are specifically relevant.

A Diminished Group
Throughout much of the twentieth century, while wealthy Protestants remained influential, the Protestant community diminished. By 1926, about
26,000 Protestants from the Free State had migrated to the North,[8] while
many others had emigrated.[9] Emigration was generally high, but it was particularly high among Protestants. Between 1911 and 1926, the Protestant
population of Dublin fell from 45,896 to 27,506, a decline of 40 per cent.[10]
Nationwide (across the whole island) there was a fall of 106,000 between
1911 and 1926, with a rapid acceleration in the 1920s.[11] This was partly because of the dismantling of British garrisons and other elements of the administration;[12] about a quarter of the total decline during this period relates
to the departure of the security forces.[13] Simultaneously, Protestant communities experienced a low or negative natural increase, and a top-heavy
age structure.[14] As the Protestants were a smaller group, their numerical decline had a dramatic impact on their self-perception and their role in society.
   The relative number of Protestants continued to decline,[15] and the proportion of Protestants among the large farmers and professionals was also
reduced as more Catholics achieved higher levels of education and wealth.[16]
Census figures show that between 1926 and 1936 the relative fertility of
the Protestant population, at less than 55 per cent, was insufficient to replace
the population, even before factoring in emigration[17] (then at a higher rate
among Protestants) and the 'loss' of children in mixed marriages to Catholicism.[18] In 1938, McDermott and Webb wrote that the decline had led to
churches being abandoned and unmanageably large parishes being created
– and that there was a general narrowing of outlook.[19] In the south, where
Protestants had dominated public areas like the arts, politics, and influential

areas of society, they 'had fallen back onto the defensive'.[20] Between 1936 and 1946, their population had dropped by a further 13 per cent. In this context, Archbishop McQuaid (then very influential) and his friends dedicated themselves to reducing the influence of Protestant-run organisations. Joe Walshe, who would become Ambassador to the Holy See, remarked to McQuaid that 'From all sides I hear that the P's are very much on the run except in the higher economic spheres like the Bank of Ireland. So the time is ripe for action.'[21] Between 1946 and 1961, the Protestant birth rate was lower than the death rate and the population (like the majority Catholic population) was also being depleted by emigration. In the late 1950s, the Church of Ireland responded to this haemorrhage by publishing a booklet, *Careers in Ireland*, intended to encourage young Protestants to stay.[22] In 1991, the population in independent Ireland was a third of what it had been in 1911, eighty years earlier.[23] Despite a recent rebound in some areas (largely because of Protestant immigration),[24] there are still much fewer Protestants in the Republic of Ireland than there were before independence. In the 2011 census, 208,899 people self-identified as belonging to one of the major Protestant denominations, with the Church of Ireland recorded as the largest group at 129,000.[25] Higher numbers in places like the border counties (as much as 8 per cent in Cavan, Donegal, and Monaghan, for instance)[26] are balanced by extremely low numbers elsewhere.

Culture, Nationalism, and the Irish Free State
'The folk' in Ireland is often assumed to mean 'the Catholic folk', who were mostly rural, poor people. This idea was born from nineteenth century studies that defined 'the folk' as primarily rural, illiterate, and poor, assuming that a higher class or elite group, educated and primarily urban, did not correspond with the designation.[27] The exclusion of Protestants from the category of 'folk' was partly fostered by work carried out by noteworthy scholars from Protestant and Anglo-Irish backgrounds such as General Charles Vallancey and Charlotte Brooke in the eighteenth century,[28] and literary figures such as 'Speranza' Wilde[29] and W.B. Yeats[30] in the nineteenth. For scholars such as Yeats and Wilde, collecting, publishing, and treasuring the oral lore of 'ordinary' people could be a way of respecting them, but also of wishing to keep them in their place, and, perhaps, it was also a useful way to express feelings about Protestants and Irishness without having to

discuss more challenging topics such as the plantation era and the strife that followed the Reformation.

Increasingly, rural, traditional people were regarded as having retained information, stories, and beliefs from an ancient time when 'the folk' was an entity 'united by common ties of the soul'.[31] Before and after independence, traditional culture was used to promote the idea of the Irish as a Gaelic people and to act as proof that there had been a sense of nationhood in Ireland throughout a long and venerable past, despite many generations of occupation.[32] In this context, there was little interest in considering the traditions and lore of a people associated with conquest and colonisation as part of the national heritage. Folklore, tradition, and the concept of 'Irish culture' in general had become associated with Irish nationalism – not only in the romantic, cultural sense propagated by people like W.B. Yeats but also as an important device in the toolbox of political nationalism.[33] In 1922, when Protestants were very uncertain about their future, the *Church of Ireland Gazette* (6 October) stated plaintively that 'Irish Protestants have done signal work in maintaining the literary reputation of their native land' and that it was grossly unfair that they were now being portrayed by some as aliens while 'foreigners' – presumably they meant Éamon de Valera, who was deeply disliked by most Protestants – were being hailed as patriots.

An Cumann le Béaloideas Éireann (The Folklore of Ireland Society) was founded in 1927 by Séamus Ó Duilearga to save the traditions of Irish-speaking Gaelic Ireland, and to collect and publish folklore when the numbers speaking Irish, and the viability of many Irish-speaking Gaeltacht communities, were in a state of decline and crisis. Ó Duilearga could see that rural Ireland's linguistic richness, traditions and oral literature were on the verge of being lost forever.[34] The society started to publish a journal under the name *Béaloideas* ('Folklore').[35] In 1930, the Irish Folklore Institute (*Institutiúid Bhéaloideas Éireann*) was founded by Ó Duilearga to collect folklore, study it, and 'perpetuate native tradition and culture'.[36] Under Ó Duilearga, a gifted folklorist and scholar, and an advocate for the ordinary people of Ireland, it was heavily influenced by the scholarly approach developed in Scandinavia.[37] Folklorists often looked for 'survivals': material or social habits that linked today's 'folk' with the remote past. Thus, rural Irish culture was not considered 'backward' but as representing an ancient, purer past; anything that suggested English or urban influence was a contaminant.[38] The institute was required to collect and publish a substantial amount of material in Irish.

In 1935, the Irish Folklore Commission replaced the Irish Folklore Institute; full-time collectors were appointed to the commission and de Valera's government arranged an annual grant of £3,000 to collect the 'best of what remained' of Irish folklore.[39] In the academic year 1937/8, the commission embarked on an ambitious programme to use the school children of Ireland as folklore collectors.[40] In a booklet sent to participating schools, the children were invited 'to participate in the task of rescuing from oblivion the traditions which, in spite of the vicissitudes of the historic Irish nation, have, century in, century out, been preserved with loving care by their ancestors'. Schools from the cities of Dublin, Cork, Limerick, and Waterford could opt out, as the commission was primarily interested in rural folklore. The booklet, written by Seán Ó Súilleabháin, which included a huge range of possible topics organised under fifty-five separate headings, aimed to help the children gather the sort of information that the commission was looking for on issues including traditional narratives, material culture, and local history.[41] In 1942, Ó Súilleabháin published the vast *A Handbook of Irish Folklore*; it included 700 pages of questions that collectors could use, many relating to popular Catholic religious custom and belief. Non-Catholic Irish feature in the handbook literally as 'others'.[42] By the end of the 1940s, the Irish Folklore Commission had gathered one of the biggest collections of folklore in Europe, with a strong emphasis on material from Irish-speaking and rural areas. Ó Duilearga had clarified his views on urban and 'imported' culture in his introduction to Ó Súilleabháin's handbook in which he said that 'the shoddy, imported culture of the towns pushes back the frontiers of the indigenous homespun culture of the countryside, and the ancient courtesies and traditional ways of thought and behaviour tend to disappear before the destroying breath of the "spirit of the age".'[43]

Of course, when folklore collectors came upon Protestant informants in the field, they did collect from them. For instance, Seán Ó hEochaidh collected several folktales from Charlie Walsh in Donegal in 1936, noting that he was an English speaker but had 'every appearance of a Seanchaí'.[44] However, the typical informant was rural and Catholic, and Protestants were not studied collectively as a cultural or folk group even though they featured

as individual informants. Samuel, 9 years old at the time of the Schools'
Collection, remembers how the material was collected in the Catholic primary school that he attended. When the teacher instructed the children to
gather information from their parents and grandparents and the older people in the area for the Folklore Commission, they were all given special
books to write the material in; he, however, was told that (as a Protestant)
he was exempt from this homework. He was the only child who was not
asked to gather folklore. Looking back, he says, 'the fact that the schoolmaster didn't think, "I should get something from this family" strikes me
now.' In retrospect, he feels that this was because there was little interest in
how Protestants lived in the 1930s. In the context of a new state that was
building an identity predicated on the idea of a noble Catholic peasantry
(ideally speaking Irish and tuned into a Gaelic culture and past), the idea
that ordinary Protestants' collective views, stories, and thoughts were worth
recording was not generally held.

The political agenda of the Irish government *vis-à-vis* recording
information about Irish traditional culture exceeded the remit of Irish
researchers. When the researchers of the Harvard Irish Study came to Ireland
to do anthropological work in the 1930s, de Valera suggested areas of study,
people who could help, and situations to be avoided; he also arranged for
the scholars Conrad Arensberg and Solon Kimball to meet the Roman
Catholic cardinal. Arensberg and Kimball also met Catholic religious and
political authorities in the areas where they collected data so that they could
tell them about the aims of their research and enlist their support; they also
benefitted from contact with Ó Duilearga.[45] Thus, the cultural agenda of
researchers in the area of folklore was both influenced and legitimised by
the work of these researchers. Their work would depict rural communities
characterised by social cohesion, implicitly supporting de Valera's view of
peaceful Catholic rural folk at one with each other and nature.[46]

The highly political agenda of the Folklore Commission did not go unnoticed, and there were some contemporary critics of aspects of its work.
Irish language writer Máirtín Ó Cadhain questioned its obsession with the
lore of solely poor, Irish-speaking rural people, pointing out that folklore
was found among people of all sorts, 'in towns and cities such as Dublin,
London and New York, and across all the social classes'. He said that many
Irish folklorists and ethnologists were so obsessed with 'old ways in the

countryside' that they did not see new traditions emerging among contemporary populations or the vibrant folklore of city people.[47] Still, for most folklorists and ethnologists, generally middle class and educated, 'the folk' were not people like themselves; they were the poor and uneducated – and specifically the rural poor – that were also generally understood to be Catholic.[48] Writing in 2007, Guy Beiner comments that the research aims of the folklore collection[49] were typical of newly liberated countries in rejecting the traditions associated with their colonial rulers while promoting those of the newly emancipated population.[50] This approach to collecting folklore preserved a great deal of important information, in Irish and English, from people who had long been underrepresented. Only in retrospect can we see that an intense focus on collecting folklore from rural Catholic informants meant that information that could have given us an insight into the totality of Irish folk culture – incorporating more urban people from all backgrounds and the Protestant community as a distinct cultural group – could have been collected in much more detail.

A Cultural Group?

Diarmuid Ó Giolláin considers Irish society as having been broken into two broad ethnic categories following the seventeenth century, loosely categorised as 'Catholic' and 'Protestant'.[51] One can still view Protestants in independent Ireland as a cultural group characterised by ethnic qualities, although they have never been completely separate. Arguably, according to various definitions, Irish Protestants can be classified as 'ethnic': they are a people who identify with one another and understanding that they share a range of social and cultural characteristics, and a shared history. Irish Protestants felt that they belonged to a particular kind of cultural group that was significantly different to others. They experienced emotional attachment to a shared set of symbols and engaged in behaviours intended to keep their community together, retaining and defending actual and perceived privileges on the basis of community membership.[52] There was a clear sense of a social boundary[53] between Protestants and Catholics in Ireland that could accommodate friendship, business dealings, and activities such as cooperation around busy times of the agricultural calendar, but that otherwise was expected to be breached only in exceptional circumstances such as 'mixed marriage'.

Cultural groups can be considered to have boundaries between them even when there is 'a flow of personnel across them', provided there are 'social processes of exclusion and incorporation whereby discrete categories are maintained'. Across such boundaries 'stable, persisting and often vitally important social relations are maintained [...] frequently based precisely on the dichotomised ethnic statuses'.[54] Following independence, Protestant communities tended to become increasingly insular. 'Such voluntary segregation', says Michael Poole, 'is one of the classic hallmarks of ethnic identity', helping to maintain Protestants as 'a socially distinct community sharing a common history and culture'.[55] Despite this, according to Poole, they struggled to be recognised as a distinct group and not simply as 'non-Catholics' or 'a demographic blank space in Irish life'.[56] This feeling of belonging to such a group is exemplified by a comment from Andrew (another interviewee):

> the various Protestant denominations would have seen themselves as having much more in common with each other and being part of a small minority. My family would regularly attend the Church of Ireland service on a Sunday morning, go home for lunch, and then attend the Methodist chapel in the afternoon [...] Quite a few of our cousins and some of my friends in primary school were Cooneyites [a small Protestant group founded in Ireland with some similarities to the Amish], so we would have been very familiar with their distinct customs [...] Other cousins were members of the Select Brethren.

The Irish Protestant community encompasses great socio-economic diversity. However, the popular view of Protestants as wealthy and privileged is not unconnected to reality. Land certainly was taken from the Catholics during the era of the plantations, being given or granted to Protestants. While not all Irish Protestants were wealthy, for a long time a very disproportionate number of them were; they owned more land, occupied more professional positions,[57] and, on average, were significantly better off. The biggest division of Protestants, the Church of Ireland, occupied a very privileged position under British rule.

However, the popular understanding of the role of Protestants in Ireland's past overlooks the many shades of grey that do not fit the narrative, including the experiences of poor or lower-middle-class Protestants. At the time of the 1926 census, 7.4 per cent of the population of the Free State was Protestant, but only a small minority belonged to the gentry class.[58] David Fitzpatrick addresses this, pointing out that the 'ascendancy was never typical of Irish Protestants' and that non-elite Protestants 'gained little or no material benefit from supporting an "Ascendancy" to which they did not in practice belong'.[59] Eugenio Biagini points out that, post-independence, 'Southern Protestants did not attract much attention: they were too quiet to make headlines, and did not fit in with the dominant Irish national narrative, focusing on an 800-years struggle against English oppression, of which many Irish Protestants were (or were supposed to have been) the agents and beneficiaries.' He indicates that relatively little was known of the experience of 'those living in rural areas, the non-intellectuals [...] the working-class, and the shopkeepers'.[60] Martin Maguire notes that, despite the well-known image of the 'Big House', Protestants in Ireland are a group dominated by the middle and working classes – a society 'complex in its social organisation'.[61] While the landscape is still dotted with the Big Houses that feature so prominently in stories about history, injustice, and persecution, the humbler houses of ordinary Protestants look like anyone else's, and can easily be overlooked – just like their inhabitants and their stories, which pass on traditions, memories, versions of history and stories about the past.[62]

Protestants' Stories: Memory and Counter-memory

The stories within and told by a group condition its members in terms of what they should remember and what should be ignored or forgotten.[63] Together, these stories are a collectively owned store of knowledge that informs the community of its unique identity.[64] While Protestants do not look objectively different from other Irish people (although some do claim to be able to 'spot them a mile off' by the way they look, dress, or 'carry themselves'),[65] views of history, storytelling and shared experience define them as a cultural group. Added to this, engaging in a certain type of storytelling[66] can be understood to have a performative aspect, demonstrating to other group members that one is an insider while concurrently performing difference to outsiders.

In the storytelling context of a family or community, accounts of events can be handed down so vividly that we remember them as though we had seen and experienced them ourselves, even if we did not.[67] Groups, rather than individuals, generally arrive at a consensus that determines which aspects of the past should be remembered and how they should be related.[68] Through this consensus, individual memories, sometimes consisting of great detail, can be held by people and communities who have no personal experience of the events that they are recalling.[69] Collective memories can tell us more about a cultural group's aspirations and beliefs than statistics. Moreover, unlike statistics, they are not fixed or static, but in a state of continuous development; they are 'a history in which everybody portrays, in which everybody is portrayed, and in which the act of portrayal never stops'.[70] They are a way in which people engage with the impact of the past on the present.[71] The autobiographical memories of groups have an influence on society's present and future. Stories passed from one generation to the next are often simplified or modified. Details that were once important might seem less so to a subsequent generation, while other factors might become more important.[72] As our current realities change, so can our view of history, with elements conveniently dropped or forgotten.[73] Aspects of tradition can be used to express difference and even conflict.

Society tends to 'erase from its memory' everything that might cause discord. As Maurice Halbwachs says, 'people well know that the past no longer exists, so that they are obliged to adjust to the only real world – the one in which they now live.'[74] The process of forgetting is often managed by vested interests. Some events are made central to the historical narrative, while others (which might challenge or be inconsistent with the interpretation of the past favoured by the state or the majority) are marginalised or omitted.[75] What people believe to be the truth is often much more important than what actually happened, and we often believe very stylised, even simplified, versions of the past.[76] Remembering the past, individually or collectively, is not passive, but an active process in which memories can be reconstructed for greater coherence.[77] Collective memory forms today's reality by 'providing people with understandings and symbolic frameworks that enable them to make sense of the world',[78] often by referring to events beyond the reach of living memory.[79]

In independent Ireland, the collective memories of the majority were encouraged to develop in a certain direction, and the collective memories of minorities went largely unheard, particularly in the case of communities that were small, dispersed and not particularly powerful, like many small rural Protestant communities. For many Protestants, the complex feelings that they have around identity and the past are often manifested in the stories they tell to themselves, about themselves; stories that are often little heard outside family or community circles; stories that 'are just there, like life itself'.[80] Often, they do not fit neatly into the country's dominant narrative of a Catholic people long oppressed by a Protestant upper class who, through heroic struggle, achieved independence and the triumph of their faith: the 'story of a people coming out of bondage'[81] that presents Irish history as a 'coherent ordering of events along a strict narrative line serving as an intellectual and emotional backbone of national identity'.[82] The largely unheard stories of ordinary Irish Protestants, a group that has 'tended to get short shrift in the rush to enforce the dichotomy between Protestant landlords and Catholic peasants',[83] are often about people trying to maintain a sense of cultural identity in the context of what they might experience as indifference, or even a degree of hostility, from the majority. In a society in which the past is often 'read exclusively under the sign of trauma',[84] people who have often felt excluded from the national hagiography of victimhood have trouble asserting a sense of identity. Some Irish people have almost been deprived of their own memories, which are not validated in the 'official mnemonic discourse' of the public arena.[85]

Source Material
The material in this book comes from published and archival sources, including various memoirs, and, most importantly, a series of lengthy interviews with ninety-eight individuals aged between 20 and over 90 years old, with the vast majority over 70 years of age; the interviewees span diverse socio-economic and denominational backgrounds. In the transcribed interviews, italics are occasionally used to reflect any emphasis made by the interviewees. Equally invaluable were seventy-six responses to a questionnaire survey that was carried out with the support of the National Folklore Collection in UCD.[86] The responses, under the Irish Protestant Folk Memory Project, now form part of the permanent collection of the NFC.

Interviewees and questionnaire respondents come from urban, small-town and rural environments, and from various educational and socio-economic backgrounds. The focus on older interviewees provides us with stories about the difficult early decades of the twentieth century, which were related directly to these interviewees by people who experienced that time, and first-hand memories of less difficult, but still stressful, periods in recent Irish history. Subjects were mostly interviewed in their homes in a very informal way, with open-ended questions about memories of childhood, stories that were told in the family when they were growing up, and knowledge of local and community history and traditions. In recruiting interview subjects, an emphasis was placed on the need for 'ordinary' Protestants' voices to be heard – 'small house' Protestants[87], though people from wealthier backgrounds were not excluded. The questionnaire used in this research posed a range of open questions intended to invite reminiscence. Participants in this project were notably enthusiastic, with many commenting that only now that their parents and grandparents are gone do they feel comfortable discussing many issues that were previously immersed in silence, at least in public.

All these stories are subjective; they are not an objective historical record of the recent past, and they may not be reflective of everyone's experience. Because an overwhelming majority of interview subjects stressed that they wished to be interviewed anonymously, pseudonyms have been employed throughout, with brief biographical and contextual material of a non-identifying nature provided in an appendix.

Conclusion

It is easy for most of the people of Ireland to recall what they have heard about the lives, beliefs, and values of wealthy Protestant aristocrats in Big Houses and of the well-to-do Protestant communities of Dublin's leafy suburbs; these are characters who often appear in the story of Ireland, and people who have been very good at making their voices heard. They have been authors, politicians, artists, academics, and business people. The only people who really know the stories of 'ordinary' Irish Protestants, especially those in rural isolation and in urban working-class contexts, are themselves. Nowadays, the Protestants of independent Ireland tend to be absorbed by a larger, increasingly secular culture. Still, for many people, even today, being Irish seems to be intricately bound up with being Catholic – or, nowadays, with having rejected the teachings of the Catholic Church to a greater or a lesser extent. Anyone who does not fit into this mould is often still considered something of an outsider.

The 'old' Protestants have witnessed both the dilution of their traditions through a process of cultural absorption[88] and, in many areas, the reduction of their numbers. Added to this, they have observed the general trend towards secularisation. However, people still living today have vivid memories of a recent past in which Protestants often saw themselves as a people very much apart. Family and community memories relate stories encompassing the difficult years just prior to and after independence, and other stories reaching back into the distant past. As Ireland becomes more secular, and the religious buildings and calendar customs become less important – as the cultural differences between Protestants and Catholics become less pronounced – the Protestant minority is one whose stories are ready to be heard.

1. Stories of Origin

All cultures, and all individuals, tell stories about their origins. These can be mythological or historical, and frequently they are both. They can be for public consumption, a matter of private memory, or both. Historical events mingle with events that the narrator believes or wishes had happened. It can become difficult, or even impossible, to separate the historical from the mythological and the aspirational from the real. Even relatively recent events, firmly grounded in documented history, can acquire mythological status, as we have seen with how the events of 1916 – an origin story of the Irish nation – have become, in much of the public imagination, a 'sacred history'.[89] The origin stories of the Protestant minority similarly serve as 'sacred histories' in the Irish Protestant imagination.

What Are Stories of Origin?
Collectively, stories of origin justify a cultural group's presence and position in a particular place. Often, such stories provide 'proof' that this group is entitled to be there, possibly more so than others, by placing its origins in a semi-mythical past. All this can be as true of complex modern societies as it is of tribal ones – and it is also true of minorities within a larger group.

R obert Tobin discusses the Protestant community's interest in genealogy and their own origins as resulting from their perceived need 'to demonstrate the community's longevity and legitimacy as part of Irish life' and 'to preserve its fundamental otherness from and superiority to the Catholic majority'; it acts as 'a flexible rhetorical means by which to reclaim their own relevance'.[90] These stories help to give a sense of place and legitimacy to a group whose members, on occasion, have experienced the feeling that they are not always welcome, or that they are seen (or even see themselves) as less than authentically Irish.

Long-established Protestant communities constitute a group because of shared history and cultural traits. In this context, the stories that Protestants tell about who they are, and where they came from, can be read as an attempt to 'fit in' or to justify the fact that they do not fit in; to construct a narrative that is less in conflict with the dominant national narrative, and that can be told with pride, or at least without shame.

Where Did the Irish Protestants Come from?

Clearly, there were no Protestants at all before the Reformation. After Henry VIII created the Church of England in 1538, the official church in Britain changed. By extension, the official church in Ireland became the Church of Ireland, which was the state religion and was therefore legally entitled to support from the people. In the more accessible areas – in the east and in Dublin – monasteries were dissolved, and statues and relics were removed from the cathedrals, which now belonged to the Church of Ireland. The Anglican faith spread slowly. Most people did not attend any church at all by the 1570s,[91] but Catholicism remained the dominant religion. The British state went to great efforts to make Ireland more Protestant, attempting to consolidate its authority by means of a wave of 'plantations'. From the sixteenth century, British government policy engineered the 'planting' of Protestants on land seized from Catholics and also engaged in efforts to convert Catholics to Protestantism. Planters could purchase land at greatly discounted rates, with the agreement that they would improve the properties according to certain specifications.[92] These plantations have left their mark on Irish demographic trends up to the present day.

Catholics suffered terrible discrimination under the new regime. Irish Presbyterians and other 'dissenters' faced similar (although less severe) penalties.[93] Presbyterianism had come with the Ulster plantation, beginning in the early seventeenth century. According to the mythologised history of this group (their 'mythistory'), they found a land 'covered with bogs and forests, interspersed with patches of wretched and wasted tillage' and industriously reclaimed it for productive use.[94] By the 1630s, there were 30,000 Protestant colonists in Ulster (while there were just 8,000 in Virginia and New England).[95] Many saw Ireland much as America was seen then: a wild land where the enterprising could flourish. According to a contemporary clerical minister, the Protestants of the Ulster colony were a dubious sort, 'all of them generally the scum of both nations [Scottish and English], for whom debt or breaking or fleeing from justice of seeking shelter came hither, hoping to be without fear of man's justice.'[96] Protestant immigration had slowed by the 1660s, but a statute in 1662 encouraged more to come, and some French, Dutch, and German settlers arrived. In the 1670s, about 35,000 English immigrants arrived. By 1715, about 27 per cent of the population of the whole island was Protestant.[97] Various waves of settlers, and a certain amount of conversion, added to the picture of Protestantism over the years.

It is reasonable to assume that many (if not most) of the 'old' Protestants in Ireland today probably have at least some ancestors from among these earlier settlers. Some Protestants refer to lingering anxiety about their sense of identity and belonging in a country in which they might be identified as outsiders or even invaders. In this context, this cultural group – as a unit, and individual families and people within it – has generated stories of origin that lessen this anxiety, staking claim to a sense of belonging. The stories of origin that they tell, and those they choose *not* to tell, are revealing; they often tend to distance the narrator from the historic fact of colonisation, aligning them with tales of ancestors whom they consider to be viewed as more acceptable by most Irish people within the context of popular Irish history.

Saint Patrick as Ireland's First Protestant

An important collective story of origin posits the faith and, by extension, the community of Irish Protestants in the remote Irish past by claiming direct descent from the original church of Saint Patrick. The Church of Ireland considered itself to be the true 'Celtic' religion of Ireland, and to have been founded by St Patrick in the fifth century, thus making it 'one of the most ancient churches in Christendom'.[98] This idea crystallised in the eighteenth century (having been originally introduced by Archbishop Ussher in the seventeenth century)[99] in the context of a surge of intellectual interest in Gaelic culture,[100] when efforts were underway to bring Protestants of English and Scots origin together under a common figurehead.

In 1783, when the Knights of St Patrick was founded, Patrick was given a special place in the Protestant story, his name becoming popular for Protestant baby boys.[101] R.F. Foster writes of how, in response to the heavily politicised Gaelic revival, 'several Ascendancy intellectuals and underemployed Church of Ireland clergymen' embraced the revival of the Irish language as part of their quest to prove that St Patrick was a Protestant.[102] It was said of Christ Church Cathedral in Dublin that the cross on its screen 'was a facsimile of the old Irish cross in Cong [...] made long before Romanism was introduced'.[103] St Patrick's mission was said not to have occurred under papal direction – that Henry II introduced papal rule only in the twelfth century. According to this narrative, Ireland entered a dark period until the Reformation restored the Church to its 'primitive purity'[104] and re-established St Patrick's original form of Celtic Christianity. There are many examples in the *Church of Ireland Gazette* of how important this idea was to the Church's self-image, and how it had become embedded in popular Protestant thought. The *Gazette* printed a sermon given by the Lord Primate on 12 December 1923 (p. 697) stating that the Church of Ireland 'inherits a very ancient tradition' conceived of as a 'Golden Thread', running through the centuries, linking them directly to St Patrick.

Protestant antiquarians were prompted to focus on areas where Irish Christian practice had historically differed from that of Rome.[105] In 1885, a group of clergymen anonymously published a 'Historical Catechism', on the title page of which the words 'Erin Go Bragh' appear. Within, they state their hope for the text to 'establish the minds of the members of our old Irish Church as regards her antiquity, apostolicity, and sound Scriptural faith and to increase their affection for her, and to keep them from having erroneous views about her history'. The authors discuss their belief that Patrick essentially introduced Protestantism to Ireland, stating that the clergy at the time had wives 'by his sanction' and that he disagreed with the doctrine of celibacy, a tenet of Roman Catholicism; with the idea of Purgatory, dismissed as a 'Romish doctrine'; and with the notion of transubstantiation. They then proceed to claim numerous other Irish saints for the Church of Ireland, including Columba, Columbanos, and Aidan, and claim that the arrival of Catholicism in 1172 forced 'a series of calamities hardly to be equalled in the world' on Ireland, from which the Irish could only be saved by a return to the 'ancient [Protestant] faith'.[106]

During the evangelical Anglican missions of the nineteenth century, this history of St Patrick was an emotive justification for their work. For instance, evangelist Charlotte Elizabeth, an Englishwoman who had dedicated her life to trying to convert the Irish, wrote that Patrick had introduced 'pure Christianity' to Ireland. The Anglican evangelists believed that all of this meant it was time for a second Reformation, which would save the people while also making them more willing to pay obligatory tithes.[107]

The belief that the Protestant faith was the 'real' Irish faith facilitated the establishment of various societies dedicated to converting Catholics, including the Hibernian Bible Society, the Irish Society for Promoting the Education of the Native Irish Through the Medium of Their Own Language, and the Scripture Readers' Society. As well as training and supporting travelling preachers, many of whom spoke Irish, these societies established schools that taught literacy, scripture, and other skills for free, and established areas where converts could live.[108]

The Presbyterian Church in Ireland also claimed St Patrick. A history of Presbyterianism published in 1959 affirms that his teachings 'are in harmony with evangelical Christianity', and that Patrick's form of Christianity, interpreted as being close to Presbyterianism, was not subjected to 'Roman practice' until after the Anglo-Norman invasion of Ireland in the twelfth century. [109]

Of course, the idea that St Patrick had anything to do with Protestantism was infuriating to Catholics, who believed that theirs was the original, true version of Christianity. In 1929, celebrating the centenary of Catholic emancipation and still rejoicing in the recently acquired independence of the twenty-six counties, the Catholic Archbishop of Tuam hoped that 'they would hear no more about the laughable claims of the so-called Church of Ireland to be regarded as the descendant of the [...] Church of St Patrick'.[110] In 1932, the supposed fifteen-hundred-year anniversary of the foundation of the Christian Church in Ireland, the Primate of the Church of Ireland reiterated the claim to St Patrick and described the Church of Ireland as 'the most Irish thing there is in Ireland.'[111] This was a view epitomised by the words of Victor Griffin, a former Dean of St Patrick's Cathedral, who stated that the Church of Ireland represented a return 'to the ancient faith, freedom and spirit of independence so characteristic of the old celtic [sic] church of St Patrick, St Brigid and St Columba'.[112]

While the Catholic Church celebrated St Patrick by holding an ecclesiastic congress that year, the Church of Ireland countered with publications, a series of lectures illustrated by lantern slides, and a conference discussing St Patrick's Protestantism.[113] In 1943, two years after the celebrations devoted to St Patrick, Éamon de Valera weighed in, stating, 'Since the coming of St Patrick [...] Ireland has been a Christian and a Catholic nation [...] She remains a Catholic nation.'[114]

Although all this arguing (a 'mnemonic battle')[115] over whose origin story was true was mostly conducted by clerics, the belief of some Protestant families in their spiritual and cultural descent from St Patrick was very important. When a young Seán O'Casey asked his mother to reassure him that they were really Irish, she said, 'if your poor father was alive he'd show you in books solid arguments [...] that St Patrick was really as Protestant as a Protestant can be.' Writing of his boyhood in Cork, Lionel Fleming says that only one of his relatives, 'my old cousin Hatta', identified with Ireland through her belief in St Patrick as a Protestant; she played her harp at a special Protestant service on the Hill of Tara on St Patrick's Day. Cousin Hatta stressed that it was important to remember that 'St Patrick was both Protestant and Irish.'[116]

John, an interviewee, remembers that, as a child, he was told that the members of the Church of Ireland were the 'real' Catholics, in the proper meaning of the term. John was also told that their Church had 'come from St Patrick', and that the Roman Catholics were just 'part of the Roman error'. Ed explains the view of the Church of Ireland in precise detail:

> the Church of Ireland looks to the original church in Ireland, the church associated with Patrick, for its origins. Its full title [...] is 'the Ancient Catholick and Apostolick Church of Ireland,' which declares that it is both catholic and ancient. In addition to having its historical continuity with the early Christian church in Ireland, it can also show through its teaching to have more in common with the teaching of Patrick than other churches in the land, most particularly than the Roman Catholic Church. Thus, it can rightly claim to be the oldest Church in the land and to be at once both Catholic and Reformed.

Freddie was told that the fact that the oldest churches belonged to the Church of Ireland proved that it was the original Celtic Church; the Catholic churches were typically much newer – nineteenth century or even later. Evelyn remembers her discovery of the idea that St Patrick was really a Protestant, and her doubts that this could be true:

From the Protestant point of view, it was celebrated by Catholics, giving the impression that St Patrick brought the Roman Catholic faith to Ireland [...] at a special St Patrick's Day service [...] the Canon [...] explained that St Patrick brought the old faith to Ireland and it had much more in common with the Protestant faith [...] When I was about 13 or 14 an old lady was staying at our house [...] The subject of St Patrick came around and what religion he was. I said that I thought he was a Catholic when she rounded on me. 'He was a Presbyterian,' she snapped, 'and everybody knows it.' I tried to point out that there were no Presbyterians as such when St Patrick was around, but she would have none of it.

Hope remembers

going to one church [...] and they had a list of all the bishops and people down starting with St Patrick and [...] it was straight down in the Church of Ireland line, more or less [...] Because they reckoned in some complicated way that the Irish church broke away *to* Rome rather than breaking away *from* Rome, at the Reformation [...] the Protestant state of affairs was the right one.

Embracing the idea of St Patrick as a Protestant helped Protestants to reconcile their faith and heritage with their Irishness. In this light, Hugo, Grace, and Marcus, a group of friends who were interviewed together, discuss the origins of the Church of Ireland. 'A pal of mine would keep hot balling [teasing],' says Hugo, 'and saying, "The English queen is the head of your church." There was times it used to make me furious, and it still makes me a bit angry. We have to remember that the Church of Ireland is ancient.'

'We were there *before* the Roman Catholic Church', affirms Grace.

'Yes', says Marcus, 'The Church of Ireland [...] would trace its history back to the ancient Celtic church, or so we like to believe.'

However, this group of friends does not accept this theory of the Church of Ireland's origins uncritically, 'We almost like to use that as a – let's be honest – as a one-upmanship on the Roman Catholics, don't we?' says Marcus.

'*I* think it's to try to prove that we're Irish', says Hugo.

'Well, that, too,' says Marcus, 'but maybe as a one-upmanship.'

Protestants' Stories of Origin

Following independence, many Protestants suffered a decline in status (or worried that they had or would). They also felt a great sense of anxiety founded on the burning of Protestant homes,[117] the relatively modest number of sectarian murders (most notably in Cork),[118] and a feeling of no longer knowing who they were. Ambivalent as their relationship with mainstream Irish culture could be, the same applied to their relationship with Britain.[119] Many had felt proud to be part of the British Empire, and some had even felt British. Even in 1922, the *Church of Ireland Gazette* (24 November; p. 673) found pride in tracing the descent of many of its readers from Cromwell's 'ironsides' and claimed the Irish police force 'derived their vigorous physique and hardy qualities' from these ancestors; they asserted that the Irish were a 'mixed race' and all the better for the incursions of planters.

The Protestant gentry 'turned to genealogy and its evidence of generations of residence to locate themselves in Ireland as Irish'.[120] The origin stories of less wealthy Protestants tend to be overshadowed by those of the wealthy, whose accounts of themselves transitioned from narrative to literature and art. Many ordinary Protestants have felt that they have been invited to assume a collective sense of shame for awful events in the distant past, such as the massacre by Oliver Cromwell in Drogheda in 1649 when the streets are said to have run red with blood, or the clearance of Catholics from their land to be replaced with 'planters'. They have felt that they are expected to apologise for terrible things that some of their ancestors might have done long ago.[121] In fact, many of them report having been explicitly told that they should be ashamed of 'what we are' because they are descended from the antiheroes of Ireland's grand narrative.

In the process of Protestant reinvention following independence, many found new ways of telling their stories of origin. Adam was told that his ancestors were introduced 'as developers' to occupy land that had been devastated by the Elizabethan wars. They were invited to 'work the land, to keep it safe, put it in Protestant hands and that kind of thing', and 'to open mines, cut down woods, create industries, build lime kilns and so forth [...] that was the origin of the family [in this area] in the early seventeenth century.' In Adam's family, 'It was all part of history for which we weren't responsible and the fact that we were the product of one side and not the other was just a fact you had to accept. I suppose we took the good from the bad on our own side and we certainly concentrated more on the good.'[122]

Some Protestants tell the story of their family's arrival with the addition of caveats regarding how standards in the past were very different. According to Trevor, his family arrived in Ireland in 1485 when his ancestor was sent with one hundred soldiers to put down a local rebellion. They subsequently became 'more Irish than the Irish themselves', but only after they had 'killed the men and took the wives. Which was standard, in those days.'

Large numbers of Protestants arrived at the time of, or in the wake of, the Cromwellian wars in the mid-seventeenth century (when Ireland was conquered by the forces of the English parliament). Honora describes how her sixteenth century ancestor angered Charles I, after which he was 'driven' into the ranks of Cromwell and came to Ireland, where he was granted land.

Protestants have often heard stories of their family's arrival during the plantations. James says, 'My father's people came to Ireland in 1670 under Charles II. They got a grant of land in Limerick, about 5000 acres. This resulted from [an ancestor] being an Adventurer who collected money for Charles I to send an army to Ireland.' Aphra heard that some of her ancestors came with the plantations, 'Our family originated from Scotland, I think. During the plantation we arrived in Northern Ireland [...] then to [another area] where my grandfather bought a few acres of rocks.' Richard's ancestors were established in the late seventeenth century with the arrival of a legal advisor to the Duke of Ormond. This was a source of considerable family pride.

For many, descent from someone who was granted land because of their participation in Cromwell's army or the British plantation of Ireland could be embarrassing – Daphne's ancestor came with Cromwell and was given land, 'not proud of this, obviously'. But this was not always the case. Some remember Cromwell being discussed, rather covertly, as someone to be admired. Basil says, 'My father was a great champion of Cromwell! [...] But he would *not* have been broadcasting that.'

Even in families that can proudly trace their ancestry through the centuries (even back to Adam and Eve, in one impressive case), some appear reluctant to accept that they might have some ancestors among the planters, and many strongly deny any ancestral link to the period of the plantations.

Some state firmly that all their ancestors were *always* in Ireland and that they were Protestant from 'the start'. Others state that all their ancestors are 'the indigenous Irish' and that they became Protestants in the distant past for reasons 'lost to the mists of time', while many know when their family arrived and express a sense of embarrassment or shame about the actual or assumed circumstances.

Many Protestants appear most comfortable when they are discussing ancestors they consider innocent of direct involvement in the plantations – the German Palatines, the French Huguenots, the Quakers, and relatively humble ancestors who came to work on the big estates or in businesses later on. It was common for servants and other employees of big landowners and wealthier farmers to be disproportionately Protestant.[123] When ordinary Protestants tell their families' stories of origin, they often emphasise these aspects of their heritage, 'We're Huguenots, Palatines and that sort of a thing.' These stories lend a sense of pride and of ownership over what is considered a dignified aspect of history.

The Palatines were a group of Germans who suffered religious discrimination in their own country. In 1709, three thousand of them were invited by the Council of Ireland to settle.[124] The administration felt that they would make a positive contribution to society because they were Protestants and that 'they will serve an occasion of strength to the Protestant interests of this nation, especially considering the great disproportion between the Protestants and Papists of this Kingdom.' They were initially housed in Dublin as refugees. Some moved into different areas around the country, while others stayed in Dublin, and some returned to England, which had been their first port of call on fleeing persecution.[125] Today, Irish descendants of the Palatines maintain a website dedicated to preserving their history.[126]

The Huguenots were a group of French Protestants who faced religious persecution.[127] They were also invited to settle, and although some Huguenot regiments fought for William of Orange at the Battle of the Boyne (a crucial moment in Irish history), they seem to be remembered in the popular imagination primarily as refugees who made a positive contribution to society.

Robert is proud of his Palatine heritage, saying that his ancestors arrived in 1702 as refugees, fleeing religious persecution at the hands of Louis XIV in the Rhineland. Until the 1850s, they were still speaking some German and marrying exclusively within the Palatine community. Miriam explains that her family, also Palatines, came to Ireland with nothing but their superior, more scientific knowledge of farming, enriching the whole island. In fact, Palatine agricultural methods resulted in less devastation during the potato famine of the 1840s, and apparently Palatine farmers in the Limerick area were in a position to help their neighbours during this awful time.[128] They knew more about the 'scientific side of farming' than the Irish, Miriam says, and showed people how to plant flowers alongside their vegetables to keep away pests and to plough the fields with furrows rather than lazy beds. Moreover, Miriam says, they integrated fully with the local community so 'there was never any trouble down around that part of the world'. Martha's Palatine ancestors introduced raised beds for growing potatoes, along with different ways of growing apples and attending to various crops and types of farm animals. They kept themselves to themselves until the arrival of John Wesley, the founder of Methodism, in the eighteenth century, when many of them joined his groups, and some emigrated to New York and established America's first Methodist church. The stories of these venerable ancestors were often told during Miriam's childhood, 'It was always part of our background and heritage, and still is regarded as a great bit of history.'

While it is undoubtedly true that many of today's Protestants *are* descended from Huguenots and Palatines, because the migration of these peoples into Ireland is a matter of historical fact, these stories of origin are also the stories that people choose to tell at the expense of others that may be just as true. Ancestors who might have come to Ireland as opportunists, or who might have been involved in clearing Catholics from their land, or who might have been among the troops that marched across Ireland under the leadership of Oliver Cromwell are often left out or brushed aside. Or, as Albert (with eyes averted) says in the context of a recorded interview, 'Let's say we came over with Cromwell. No, delete that. No, it's OK, you can leave it, but you're not going to be using our name, are you? Only we tend not to say it.' Myrtle reports that 'Cromwell was almost as much a hate figure to [Protestants] as to Catholics. No one would admit their ancestor came over with Cromwell!' Mitchell says, 'I don't *think* [my ancestors] were directly connected with Cromwell. A bit before. Not *much* before. We [Protestants] are all trying to say that we had nothing to do with Cromwell.'

Travers's family has been living on the same farm since they were granted land for their service in Cromwell's army, 'We came over with the bold Oliver Cromwell from the UK. The family came across over the hills there. They were bow-makers in Cromwell's army. We had a family history with a crest [when I was growing up] and I knew all the details.' However, Travers offers in mitigation the fact that his family served the wider community as traditional healers until relatively recently. Though they were involved in the destruction of the monasteries, they saved the monks' knowledge of herbal remedies and used it for 'the betterment of everyone'. Until recent decades, one of his relatives was often seen gathering medicinal herbs in local hedgerows. For this family, their role as traditional herbalists was the most important thing about their past and compensated for the violence associated with their arrival.

The Society of Friends, also known as the Quakers, is a very small religious community in Ireland today. Many Protestants are proud of their Quaker ancestors, even if they do not belong to the faith. Quakers from England settled from the seventeenth century onwards, especially in Munster and Ulster, where they were typically 'smallholders, artisans and shopkeepers'.[129] Hubert describes his family as having 'been Irish since 1675', 'they had originally emigrated from England in 1654, having been subjected there to persecution.' Although other types of Protestants 'treated the native Irish very badly', he is grateful to report that the Quakers 'had become Irish long since'. Although he is also descended from other Protestants of diverse denominations, he only discusses the Quakers, whom he sees as a more legitimate source of pride. Daphne makes a similar statement about her own diverse Protestant background, which includes ancestors who came with Cromwell:

> I'd be ashamed of the history of [my Protestant ancestors], yes [...] Not the Quakers, obviously, because [...] they worked for what they had. They didn't take it from anybody [...] but the people who were part of the establishment here came with the British Army [...] they were either planted and took the land or [it was] granted to them as favour.

Ben says some of his ancestors arrived during the years of the great plantations and did well, partly because of their loyalty to Britain, but that the ones he chooses to remember and discuss whenever he is asked about his origins were Quakers, who arrived later and whom he can discuss without shame, 'because they did not steal land from anyone and treated the native people much better'. He tells the story of the arrival of the first of his Quaker ancestors to come to Ireland and 'leaves out the rest' (although he himself is a member of the Church of Ireland).

Relatively humble ancestors are easy to discuss. Rachel says her family came to Ireland in the seventeenth century, and that their surname means 'farmhand', indicating that they were probably tenant farmers rather than landowners. Sam has detailed information about his ancestors, who came to his area in 1613, 'anecdotally speaking', and worked as stonemasons and part-time farmers. Eunan reports that the first of his ancestors to come to Ireland was an orphan, accompanied by his sister, and that the children were adopted by an Irish family, establishing his family line. Barney's ancestor was sourced as a servant in Scotland and brought to Ireland to work for a large tenant farming family, into which he married.

Among rural Protestants in coastal areas, there are stories about ancestors who arrived in Ireland as a result of shipwrecks. One family that has lived in a rugged coastal area for over three hundred years traces its ancestry to three Scottish brothers, all of whom are said to have arrived in the area when their ship was destroyed in a terrible storm many years ago, around the time of the Cromwellian wars, or shortly afterwards. Mark affirms that they were not planters, as all the planters, many of whom were employed as land stewards, stuck to the areas with the most fertile land and 'would not come this far'. The families who claim descent from those brothers still form the core of the small Protestant community in the area, and there are townlands with names that are supposed to commemorate the fact of their dramatic and difficult arrival. This family history is something that everyone, as children growing up, was 'very, very aware of'. Other local families with the same name are supposed to be descended from men who came over to fight in the Battle of the Boyne, but 'they have nothing to do with our lot'.

Martha explains that her family also arrived in Ireland because 'They were bound for America and something happened to the ship they were travelling on, it did not get going, and they ended up in West Limerick and south Tipperary [in the mid-seventeenth century]'. Marion was often told how her Huguenot ancestors 'washed up' as refugees on a windy beach in

DIFFERENT AND THE SAME

the south-west and built a humble, productive life as small farmers in that area, where they still are today. This story of origin was often referenced during her childhood, and her family was aware of the exact spot where the original ancestor was supposed to have landed. Matthew explains that his surname, which evokes the sea, was given to his ancestors because they had been with the Spanish Armada when it was wrecked in 1588 and subsequently integrated with a Protestant community in Ireland, settling in a particular area shortly after the Cromwellian wars; they are the 'flotsam and jetsam' of the doomed Armada and have nothing to do with the plantations.

Many families also trace their descent from relatively recent arrivals. 'The official story', Ian says of his ancestors, 'is that they were builders who came over here [in the nineteenth century] to build a school.' Helen's ancestors came for work in the early nineteenth century – on one side they were Scottish Presbyterian 'journeymen' who were poor and followed work around until they eventually settled in Ireland; on the other side, miners in Wales who settled in Cork, where there were mines in which they could deploy their skills.

May discusses her family's origins in the context of its surname, which is a very common one in Ireland – and usually Catholic. 'My father claims they were *always* Protestants', she says, 'but I am not so sure.' She had wondered if they might be descended from 'soupers' (those who converted to Protestantism in exchange for free food, probably during the Great Famine of the 1840s; they are discussed in more detail in Chapter Two) but family history maintains that they were Protestants from a time before that period. However, there was a degree of 'mixing' in the late nineteenth century, and one relative was a Catholic bishop. This family was very staunchly Protestant and, while insisting that they had 'always been' Protestants, they also kept a portrait of the Catholic bishop hanging on their living room wall.

Dublin is home to a relatively large population of 'old' Protestants, many well-to-do, who have worked in the areas of business, law, medicine, and so on for generations. The origin stories of this group are often less complex, because they frequently claim descent from the Anglo-Irish families who contributed greatly to Dublin's development, and point out that many of Ireland's great writers, artists, business people, and philanthropists come from this background; such associations can provide a sense of pride and belonging. But even some members of this community tell stories of origin that appear to distance them from Ireland's colonial past, aligning them with a more palatable origin story, such as descent from the great Gaelic tribes. Constance explains that some of her husband's family converted to Protestantism to keep their land, and Grace recalls her family's pride in being descended from one of the noble Gaelic families. Hillis traces his family's descent from a noble Catholic family; their branch is said to have converted to Protestantism in the early eighteenth century in order to retain their land, subsequently maintaining a symbiotic relationship with their Catholic relatives. The Catholic branch of the family was much wealthier but was subject to the Penal Laws, so their Protestant cousins bought and sold land and other property on their behalf.

Conclusion

A glance at how people discuss and mediate the matter of how their families came to be is fruitful ground for research and gives some insight into how it is also cause for certain anxieties and concerns. Although some families can trace their history on both sides with considerable historical accuracy, other families know little about their origins in Ireland – and some have heard stories of dubious veracity, sometimes only about one side. Surely, however, the historical accuracy of any family's story of origin is usually the *least* interesting and important thing about it. Much more than the accuracy, what is really important is that the stories that people choose to tell over the alternatives available, partial as they can be, reveal a vast richness of information about who we want to be, how we see ourselves, and how we tell stories about ourselves and our people. Profound social truths can be gleaned by reading between the lines of stories that might be impossible to prove (or disprove). Protestants' stories of origin reveal something of how they see themselves in the context of Irish society, Irish history, and their collective and individual aspirations. As a minority group, the 'old' Protestants, and especially the relatively unknown 'ordinary' Protestants without special wealth and prestige, continue to use these accounts and interpretations to position themselves within a society that does not always accept their stories as part of Ireland's grand narrative.

2. STORIES OF THE PAST

All peoples tell stories about the past that appear to make sense of the present and provide a narrative that flows logically from 'the beginning' to the current status quo: 'the end'. The past becomes a screen onto which different groups can interpret their own understandings.[130] It is important to record these stories from every element of a population; otherwise we lose one or more of our windows into the past,[131] and an important factor in understanding the present.

Informal histories are subjective, but formal histories can be too.[132] Formal history can be considered the inculcation of collective memory with a basis in 'state-approved civic truth'.[133] Moreover, as our view of what is admirable change and context shifts, so can our accounts of the past.[134] Folk history allows us to glimpse the experience of 'ordinary' people whose stories are often unrecorded or must be assembled from statistical data such as what is gathered in a census. These stories tell us 'not just what people did, but what they wanted to do, what they believed they were doing, and what they now think they did'.[135] The oral histories of minorities will differ, to varying degrees, from those told by majorities, but neither is necessarily more likely to be 'true'. Nevertheless, the accounts given by minorities are often downplayed or even overlooked.

Social groups tend to maintain that if a historical event is remembered in a particular way, then that is how it must have happened.[136] Over the course of one person's life, or across generations, the interpretation of historical events, and the remembered details of those events, can shift. Individual memories become historical narratives as they are told and retold by both the original narrator and those who have heard the story and passed it on. In the retelling, the subjective reality experienced by each narrator influences their own interpretation. These stories help to create social memories that give meaning to the lives and traditions of individuals, communities, and nations.[137]

In popular discussions of history, Protestants are often conceived of as either villains or heroes. The villains are the bad landlords and their employees, who had land that was stolen from Catholics, treated tenants abominably, and, during the Great Famine of the 1840s, left them to starve or sent them to America in 'coffin ships' that often sank. The heroes made their mark in nationalist politics or uprisings, or excelled in some other way that is seen as reflecting sufficiently well on the Irish. To this end, their Protestantism becomes irrelevant. When Protestants discuss the same events, they often offer a counter-narrative.

Forgetting and Remembering

Many of the chapters in Ireland's dominant narrative seem to have near-total consensus at popular level. When 'everyone' agrees that something happened in a certain way, it can be easy to assume that this version of events is completely correct and that dissenting views are simply wrong. Collective memories are never complete, but they are compelling, and 'a partial (and usually interested) account of the past [that] summons consensus is a sign of its strength and vitality.'[138]

Nation-building efforts incorporated the 'active forgetting' of elements of Irish cultural heritage that referred to the colonial period, even in university programmes.[139] Thus, most Irish people, being led by the state, engaged in efforts to align the past with the desired present and future[140] by creating a suitable national narrative. The education system was designed to create a 'strong, reasonable and enthusiastic national feeling' with a simplified version of history, resulting in the establishment of 'myths' in the national psyche.[141] The idea, according to Foster, was to 'stress the continuity of the separatist tradition' and the movement towards independence; to emphasise the idea that British rule always took the form of 'oppression and exploitation of a people struggling rightly to be free'; and to ignore aspects of history incongruent with this pattern by seeing them as 'deluded' or 'un-national'.[142] This was partly a response to how history had been taught before independence, when Irish history was presented as very unimportant[143] and the history of Britain and 'her glorious empire' were stressed.

The national school system, founded in 1831, had propagated the ideals of empire, and its textbooks were so admired that Irish national schoolbooks were exported for use elsewhere in the empire.[144] Throughout the nineteenth century, Protestant educators removed the systematic teaching of Irish history from schools on the grounds that 'the less they know about history, the better.'[145] When Irish history was taught, it was with a unionist slant and a focus on the 'constructive work and cultural achievements of the invaders and settlers'.[146] Interpretations of history with a nationalist slant, or that discussed the sufferings of the native Irish at the hands of the English, were avoided in case they aroused nationalist sentiments. One of the few history books considered acceptable was George Petrie's *Essay on the Round Towers of Ireland*.[147] Petrie's focus on the round towers, 'memorials of our early Christianity',[148] was a way for all students to take interest and find pride in Ireland's past without being exposed to ideas that challenged Britain's right to rule.

The absence of Irish history from schoolbooks prompted many complaints from nationalists in the late nineteenth century.[149] By 1905, the Christian Brothers were teaching from a firmly nationalist viewpoint, using the *Irish History Reader*, which dwelt, 'with pride, and in glowing words on Ireland's glorious past, her great men and their great deeds'. Popular histories were also circulated by nationalist organisations, and students establishing libraries were reminded that they should only stock books recommended by 'a good Catholic Irishman'.[150] History thus became a 'sacred, tribal narrative' that justified current political aspirations and nationalism.[151]

With independence came the task of creating a common story for the people of Ireland to share. A new school curriculum was assembled. One book was *Irish History for the Junior Grade Classes: The Defence of our Gaelic Civilisation, 1460–1660,* written by Helena Concannon, which 'reinforced the idea of the exclusivity of the Irish race, differentiating the Gaels from the Anglo-Irish and the Saxon, and outlined the narrative arc of nationalist history for young readers'.[152] History was often taught through Irish as part of the state's programme to extend the use of the language, fuelled partly by 'the belief in an inner spirituality of the Irish people, demonstrated by their abiding fidelity to the twin ideals of Catholicism and political freedom.'[153]

Where Catholic students once studied the 'glories' of the British Empire and knew little about Irish history, Protestant students were now expected to study an intensely nationalist narrative in which their antecedents featured largely as antiheroes.[154] In response, they initially used pre-independence publications that the Board of Education considered acceptable.

Protestants wanted history books that portrayed them positively.[155] In 1939, the Church of Ireland's Board of Education held a competition for a new history book that would depict Protestants palatably. The resulting volume was *A History of Ireland* by Dora Casserley,[156] which is still remembered by former students as telling a story of Ireland that did not show Protestants as villains. Casserley's book incorporated Protestants into a version of nationalist history in which the antiheroes were the colonisers of the twelfth century rather than the Protestant settlers of the sixteenth and seventeenth centuries. The assessor from the Department of Education, P. Breáthnach, gave the book a glowing review and it was approved for use in national schools in 1941/2.

Despite Breáthnach's approval, there were many complaints from Protestants. W.E. Kenny, a rector in County Laois, complained that the Church of Ireland's claim to St Patrick had been contradicted by an assertion in the book that Patrick had been sent by the Pope; a John L. Gough Meissner complained that the book might as well have been recommended by the 'Roman Catholic authorities'. Many Catholics also disliked the book, feeling that it portrayed Protestants too positively.[157]

Today, some Protestants remember using Casserley's book or being told that their parents were taught Irish history from special 'Protestant' history books (sometimes citing Casserley's book specifically). They recall their own ambivalence to studying history, while others remember feeling marginalised by books that did not seem to represent Protestants fairly. Matthew learned history in the Catholic national school that he attended from a book that provided a 'really one-sided story [...] inclined to derogate the Protestant community'. Richard says that he studied Irish history from 'an awful little book' by James Carty. Anyone who wanted to do well in the Leaving Certificate had to study Carty's *Class Book of Irish History*,[158] so studying a 'Protestant' version of events, or criticising Carty's interpretation, was out of the question. Lisa comments that Carty's book was considered 'biased in the extreme'. Neil, who attended Protestant schools, remembers a childhood friend's experience of studying history, 'she went to the Loreto convent, and she told me about history classes, and they absolutely humiliated her.' Ursula, teaching history as a substitute in a Catholic secondary school in the 1960s, found, to her surprise, that, rather than the standard text, she was supposed to use a handwritten version of Irish history penned by a local nun, 'the history textbook was an ordinary copy book, written in longhand by a nun, and there were things in it that I didn't like [...] Bad things about Protestants.'

In Roberta's Protestant primary school, they studied almost no Irish history but focused on topics like Gaelic myths and legends; she felt it was a deliberate way to teach historical matter without threatening Protestants' self-image. 'Partly a choice', she says, 'without wanting to be too outspoken.' Eadry says that because Protestants felt that the history curriculum was biased against them, 'we didn't have many history books.' Subjects thought to be uncomfortable, such as the Cromwellian invasion, were 'glossed over'.

Trevor attributes his own much more nationalist viewpoint, compared with that of his relatives, to his study of history in school, 'my mother's family called me "the Protestant nationalist" [...] I was more nationalist in outlook [...] I always figured England were milking Ireland, because in school I learned the commercial history of Ireland.'

Ian remembers a sense of frustration in secondary school when his classmates did not seem to recognise the leading role of Protestants in the history of Ireland as it was discussed in his home, 'I loved history and knew more Irish history than anyone else in the class [...] the Nationalist story was led [...] by Protestants. And almost *every* revolution, all the way down [...] was *all* Protestant-led, and I knew this, and most of my schoolmates didn't.'

In the 1960s and 70s[159] new textbooks were introduced that encouraged students to look at history more critically. However, Florrie, who attended school in the 1980s, remembered feeling uncomfortable, 'there was an atmosphere of [...] blame? and the odd comment from a classmate about being a Protestant.'

Some Protestants describe a feeling of having been written out of 'the only acceptable version of Irish history' or that the stories about the past that are available through popular channels do not really apply to them. Martha, who joined a local history course, says, 'They've been looking at the Troubles [around the period of independence in 1922] and that sort of thing, and I find myself removed from it. It's not *my* history.' Protestants were mentioned only in terms of invaders; Cromwell is said to have spent a night in a house in Martha's area, and many local homes were once used as barracks. The course Martha joined discussed the local origins of one of the signatories of Ireland's Proclamation of Independence, and the great pride in him. It never mentioned the reaction of the relatively sizeable local Protestant community. Hugo attended a lecture about the nationalist movement and met a friend who questioned what he was doing there, 'I walked in and he said, "What's *your* kind doing here?" That hurt [...] I accused him of it later on, because it hurt. He just said he was sorry. He half didn't mean it. It still came out.'

Protestants' Stories about the Past

Protestants' stories of important historical periods, such as the era of the Penal Laws (enacted in the seventeenth century), the Great Famine of the 1840s, or the years that led to independence are sometimes difficult to discuss because they can challenge the dominant historical narrative or because the families who tell the stories are painfully aware that their ancestors were on what is now considered the wrong side. Protestants can be keen to present their stories of the past in a way that mitigates what is now seen to be villainy.

Stories of 1641, Cromwell, and the Aftermath

In 1641, the Ulster Catholics reclaimed the province from Protestant settlers in a 'bloodless coup' that began when the Catholic gentry reacted to the English government's anti-Catholic policies by trying to seize control of the English government in Ireland. Then violence erupted across the region, leading to the deaths of up to twelve thousand Ulster Protestants at a time when the overall Protestant population was around thirty thousand.[160] Marianne Elliott compares the killing to the massacres of Rwanda, 'rumours of retaliatory massacre prompting neighbours to pre-emptive murders.'[161] John Gibney describes the 'widespread and often gruesome attempts to eradicate the physical, cultural and religious presence of the colonists in Ireland', and the vast exaggerations that occurred in the subsequent propaganda war.[162]

One of the effects of this massacre was that it helped to solidify a sense of Protestant cultural distinctiveness. Now the Protestants believed themselves to be 'culturally civilised and progressive', unlike the barbarous, Catholic native Irish.[163] As stories of the massacre became embedded in Protestant folk history, the number of victims grew within the context of such stories until it was many times greater than that of Protestants actually living in Ireland at the time.[164] The Protestants directly compared themselves

to the ancient Israelites in a narrative in which the Catholic Irish featured
as Canaanites, the Protestants eventually delivered from evil just as the Children of Israel had been liberated from Egypt.[165] A special day of commemoration was established on 23 October, which was the date when a Catholic
plot to seize control of the government failed and the massacre of Protestants in Ulster started. The annual celebration of these events captured a
sense among Protestants of being specially chosen by God. In the latter years
of the seventeenth century, when they were concerned about levels of unrest, public celebrations around this date, often featuring bonfires, helped
them to channel a sense of defiance and togetherness, and provided a focus
for anti-Catholic feeling.[166]

The political value of stories about the dreadful events of 1641 was
recognised for generations. In 1753, a senior fellow of Trinity College speaking to the Irish House of Commons on the anniversary of the start of the
rising stated, 'The uses which may be drawn from the memory of this extraordinary event are many, both political and religious.'[167] A popular source
for stories about the uprising was *The Irish Rebellion* by John Temple, who
had written hyperbolically that the Catholics, led by their priests, had done
things so awful that '[they] cannot be paralleled in the History of any other
Nation from the beginning of the World to this Day.'[168] Temple depicted
the Irish Catholics as traitors who rose against the Protestants; the Protestants, for their part, he described as 'peaceably settled and securely inter-
mixed among them'. He says the Catholics seemed happy with Protestant
'improvements' and paints an idyllic picture of life under the planters, whom
he describes as an industrious people who worked hard and who had 'en-
tertained' the native Irish with 'great demonstrations of love and affection'.[169]

In this account, the ungrateful Irish had then turned on them, killing
them viciously ('their childrens brains dasht out before their faces'). Temple
said that parents were told that if they dug graves for their dead children,
they themselves would be buried too, so dead bodies were left 'exposed to
ravenous beasts and fowls'. He describes Protestant women being murdered
by Irish women and children, while affirming that the Catholics had been
told by their priests that the Protestants were worse than dogs, 'that they
were Devils, and served the Devil', and that killing them was a 'meritorious
Act and a rare preservative against the pains of Purgatory'. The lengthy book

provides many examples of alleged atrocities, describing children being 'cut into gobbets and quarters' and 'hanged on a Clothiers Tenterhook', human fat being used in the making of candles, and a man being forced to disembowel himself. Temple also provides stories of encounters with sorrowful or vengeful Protestant ghosts.[170]

Versions of Temple's account became important narratives and fodder for Protestant propaganda throughout Ireland, especially Ulster; they were used to justify ongoing plantations and anti-Catholic discrimination.[171] Such written histories could combine with oral accounts and mingle with folklore and contemporary prejudices. In 1902, Charles Hanna wrote dramatically of how, in 1641, 'the brains of children were dashed out before the eyes of their mothers, some were thrown into pots of boiling water and some were given to the pigs that they might be eaten', while a Protestant minister is described as having been executed, and people were said to have been told that they would be saved if they executed their own loved ones.[172]

The events of 1641 acted as a decisive shift for those who considered themselves the 'native Protestant population'.[173] Unsurprisingly, given the passage of time, few narratives about it were gathered from contemporary interviewees, but Kate knows that her family benefited from contacts they made during the period. Her family is said to have come to Ireland in the early seventeenth century to work in copper mines, and that when the battle of 1641 came about, they were able to help English families to 'flee'.

The rebellion led, in turn, to the Confederate Wars. This was also a struggle along ethnic and religious lines around the issues of land ownership and control of government. The rebel leaders were mostly Gaelic lords and descendants of the Anglo-Norman settlers. In 1642, this group had declared itself the Catholic Confederation, aligning itself with the monarchy in their efforts against the parliamentarians. By the time Oliver Cromwell arrived in 1649, there was plenty of will in England to support a vicious retaliation and the forceful ejection of Catholics from the more fertile parts of the island. Under Cromwell, the Catholic share of land dropped from 60 to 22 per cent. The Catholic Confederation had been defeated by 1653. During the 1650s, vast swathes of land were distributed among about 35,000 planters. While many were drawn by economic opportunity, some also felt themselves to be involved in a struggle 'in the front line where Protestantism battled against Catholicism, civility against barbarism, reason against superstition, England against Ireland'.[174] This defeat set the scene for a prolonged period of anti-Catholic discrimination.[175]

Cromwell's army had largely destroyed many churches and ecclesiastical buildings, creating ruins that are still significant mnemonics for stories about the past. After Cromwell died, the finest churches were returned to the Church of Ireland, which remains a sore point for some. James remembers:

> I kept my bike in the shed in the grounds of the Cathedral, picking it up to cycle to the Deanery [where his family lived]. One day the [local] Roman Catholic curate, who lived opposite the Cathedral stood at the little gate, keeping it closed. He then said, 'You should tell your father that this Cathedral is stolen property from the Church of Rome. It should be given back.' Then he opened the gate and I fled [...] it became Anglican at the time of the Reformation and the local [Catholic] people say the stones in the nave weep to this day.

Of Ireland's 7.5 million profitable acres, 5.2 million were forfeited for redistribution among Protestants, New English settlers, and Cromwell's soldiers. About 2 million acres were returned to Catholic ownership after Cromwell's death. By 1691, 'the population of English or Scottish stock had grown from virtually nothing to over one quarter.'[176] By the eighteenth century, Ireland was ruled over by an Anglican elite, the Protestant Ascendancy,[177] who never represented more than 12 per cent of the population.[178] For the next three hundred years, Irish land was largely in the hands of this Protestant minority (which, itself, was a minority among Protestants). As a child, Barney, who is a Presbyterian, was told that while there was resentment among the Catholics because so much land had been granted to Protestants, over time they came to respect the Presbyterians, in particular, as working people far removed from the aristocracy:

> the Catholics, well they knew that [the Presbyterians] were on their land, or they thought they were on their land, but anyway, they seen [the Presbyterians] were mighty farmers. They seen [the Presbyterians] were great, great workers and they looked after their stock. And if you were a man of the land, you liked people who could look after the land and take care of it and do good in the land [...] they had great, great respect, to be truthful, for all the Presbyterians, and the

Presbyterians never really bothered or, you know, went the one way of insulting them, calling them bad names or anything. That was totally against the rules.

Throughout the period of the Penal Laws, the Catholic majority was subject to a wide range of restrictions. Catholics were prohibited from inheriting land from Protestants by marriage or descent, and could not hold public office, vote, or carry weapons. Although there were some attempts to evangelise through Irish,[179] many Protestants were apparently content to enjoy the benefits of belonging to a privileged in-group, while many believed that they were the Irish favoured by God.

By the early eighteenth century, the Church of Ireland largely succeeded in having a monopoly over the clergy, officerships within the army, and the legal profession (although some of the best jobs in these areas were off-bounds even for Irish Protestants and reserved for men from England).[180] Government positions, too, were mostly reserved for Protestants. By this stage, however, some of the Protestants felt much more 'Irish' than 'English' and became involved in nationalist movements. Later, this incipient Protestant 'Irishness' would become increasingly important.

1798

The 1798 Rebellion, primarily organised by the United Irishmen – a group comprising both Catholics and Protestants with republican revolutionary ideals – lasted from May to September 1798. Much of the violence occurred in the south-east, with battles in towns including New Ross, Enniscorthy, and Wexford. Further north, Presbyterian United Irishmen had initially risen in 1797, pikes and muskets in hand, only to be quickly suppressed.[181]

In the south, the rebels were trying to fight the British forces with home-made pikes. When possible, many destroyed Protestant homes. The rebel leaders soon found that they were struggling, not just with the fight against the British but with maintaining order among the rebels. Even if the rebel leaders had been motivated by lofty revolutionary ideals, many of the ordinary rebels were also motivated by anger, fuelled by the privilege that many Protestants enjoyed at a time of systematic anti-Catholic discrimination. In Wicklow and Wexford, while rebels attacked property indiscriminately, they burned only Protestants' houses. When they held Wicklow town in the first three weeks of June, they killed Protestant clergymen. Although several of the rebel leaders in Wexford were Protestants, most of the rebels were Catholics. Propaganda full of lurid stories about the massacres of 1641 was circulated among Protestant circles, making Protestants fear that the rebels' aim was the extermination of Protestants and strengthening their resolve to support a brutal suppression. Many leaders in the British forces behaved with hideous brutality, summarily executing rebels and raping women and girls; the rebels did likewise in areas that they had seized, such as Wexford town. The uprising, doomed from the start, ended just a few months after it had begun.[182]

As time passed, the story of 1798 tended to be recorded in one of two distinct ways – by the nineteenth century, loyalist narratives recalled it as a 'bloodthirsty religious war for the expropriation of Protestants, led by priests', while nationalist writers 'established the nobility of the enterprise'.[183] Presbyterian involvement gradually became a source of embarrassment to Presbyterians. A century after the uprising, leading Orangemen implored their comrades to forget the rebellion, as they were now loyal to Britain.[184] In 1959, a chronicler of Irish Presbyterian history wrote that the 'principles of the United Irishmen counted for little' in Wexford, where the peasantry, 'led by priests like Father John Murphy of Boolavogue', got control of most of the county, which led in turn to the Scullabogue atrocity in which Protestants were burned to death in a barn. This, he says, made the Presbyterians begin 'to think it better to bear the oppression of rectors and landlords than to be piked and burned by papists'.[185]

Scullabogue was the biggest massacre of 1798: 126 women, men and children, almost all Protestants, were burned to death in the barn.[186] About forty men were executed on the grass outside.[187] A few of the victims were Catholics (who had worked with, or for, Protestants), but most were Protestant farmers and their families, who were gathered from the surrounding area – probably after news of the defeat of the Battle of New Ross, at which about 2,000 rebels under the weak leadership of Bagenal Harvey had been killed.[188] Even by the standards of 1798, Scullabogue was particularly vicious, especially because so many women and children were killed.[189] Moreover, most of the victims were of modest means; they were tenant farmers and artisans whose lives would have been much more like those of most rebels than that of the big landowners.[190]

Historian Tom Dunne refers to two narratives about Scullabogue. One stemmed from the great Irish Folklore Commission collection of 1937, which gathered folklore from all over Ireland and cleverly used older primary school children as collectors who set out to gather tales from their grandparents, parents, and neighbours. The other narrative was related to him from within his own family (Dunne is from Wexford). The former narrative explicitly blames the burning of the barn on people from another parish, 'twas no one from this place that put 'em into the barn. Aunt Nelly said that the way they tested them to see if they were Protestants was if they couldn't say a Hail Mary.' The other version, which Dunne heard from his own great-uncle, maintained that 'there was a barn there where Cromwell burned the Catholics.'[191] In this story, the victims and perpetrators were reversed; the revised version was congruent with Ireland's dominant narrative in which Protestants can never be victims.

The people who died at Scullabogue were a tiny fraction of those that died during the rising, which amounted to about 30,000 in total. This was a huge number on an island of around 5 million. When the rebellion was quashed, the leaders captured in the Wexford area were dealt with brutally; their severed heads were displayed above the courthouse in Wexford town. Afterwards, many on both sides were horrified by the slaughter; 'selective amnesia about aspects of it' was a feature of subsequent discussions.[192]

After 1798, descriptions of the rebellion tended to be written in a way that enforced the writer's views. Catholic commentators and historians tended to stress the heroic aspects of the rebellion, presenting it as a compelling David-and-Goliath narrative in which dispossessed peasants revolted against the might of the British Army, minimising the occasions when the rebels had been less than noble. Writing in 1803, Edward Hay, the author of *History of the Insurrection of the County of Wexford*, blamed the events at Scullabogue on 'lower-class criminals and cowards'.[193] Beiner reports that antiquarians and travel writers in Ireland during the nineteenth century noted some stories about the rebellion as told by Protestants, saying, 'it is apparent that in certain Protestant circles there was great interest in loyalist recollections and traditions of the rebellion.' However, 'These traditions did not sit well with a predominantly Catholic folk history and so were not collected systematically in the early twentieth century.'[194]

At the end of the nineteenth century, when centenary celebrations occurred amid the huge growth in power of the Catholic Church, Father Patrick Kavanagh's *A Popular History of the Insurrection of 1798* downplayed the role of the United Irishmen and presented them as a 'corrupt secret society' while describing the uprising as an insurgence of noble Catholics against ignoble Protestants. Catholic nationalists used the centenary as an opportunity to press for home rule, a burning issue at the time. In 1948, the year of the Republic of Ireland Act, the one hundred and fiftieth anniversary of 1798 was marked with military pomp by a state focusing on the consolidation of power.[195] In 1998, the bicentenary, great commemorations were held – one feature of which was the 'skimming over' of certain events and motivations.[196] A government minister described the rebellion as 'non-sectarian, democratic and inspired by the French and American revolutions'.[197]

Stories about the Scullabogue massacre became such that they were not just details of a bloody historical period but an important element of Protestant folk narrative, just as the idea of the invariably honourable and noble rebel of 1798 became a hugely important motif in the folk history of the majority. Protestant narratives remembered it as even worse than the reality; while there had been some children who were about 12 years of age in the burning barn, stories told later recalled very small children managing to escape from the inferno only to be tossed back into the flames on the end of the rebels' pikes.[198] On both sides, this selective forgetting and remembering meant that a very partial version of events was recalled. In fact, nationalist efforts to deflect responsibility for the Scullabogue massacre had started soon after the uprising.

Tom Dunne, invited to discuss the massacre on the radio in 1998, was accused by another professional historian of 'playing the Orange card'.[199] Dunne had pointed out that the widely held explanation that the massacre was a retaliation for the burning of a hospital containing wounded rebels could not be true, because the only atrocity that approximated that event occurred in Enniscorthy two weeks afterwards.[200] The term 'scullaboguery' was coined to describe someone expressing the idea that sectarian atrocities are an unavoidable theme in Irish history.[201] For the bicentenary, a memorial stone was erected in the Church of Ireland graveyard in Old Ross, a few kilometres from the scene of the incident. Initial plans for the text were that the victims would be described as 'prisoners', with the implication that they were prisoners of war rather than civilians, but this was changed 'after some public protest [...] and private representation from [Protestant] Church leaders'. Still, the text focuses on the 'remorse' of the United Irishmen in 'a tragic departure from their ideals' in a way that seems to suggest that the United Irishmen themselves were also victims. The local vestry of the Church of Ireland approved the inscription because 'they felt they had no choice'. Dunne describes this half-hearted memorial as proof that the Irish are 'incapable of acknowledging even the basic facts about a 200-year-old tragedy'.[202]

Stories about the Scullabogue massacre still resonate for Protestants. Philippa recalls the moment she first heard about it, 'I remember that affecting me like the Hiroshima bomb.' She had always heard a very nationalist version of history, which sometimes made her feel uncomfortable with her heritage (she describes her experience of being Protestant as being like belonging to a 'dysfunctional family' and not knowing all the unwritten rules of society in consequence). Learning that Protestants were sometimes victims made her start to think that maybe all the other things she had been taught, like the official narrative of 1916, were not always completely accurate.

Stories of 1798 linger in the family lore of some Protestants. Winnie relates, 'of my father's great-grand uncles, there were three brothers who lived together [...] two were killed by the pike-men; one got away, eventually going to Canada. He became a wealthy man; he built an Anglican church in Italy.' Francis states that his great-grandfather was thrown down the stairs during a raid in 1798 and broke his hip ('This didn't stop him having 14 children!'). Barton asserts that the landlords in his area were popular, and consequently, although the rebels of 1798 camped on their land, they left them in peace. Juliet recounts learning about her family's role in 1798 at a meeting of the local historical society:

> we were preparing to commemorate 1798. I spoke up saying [my family] were [in the area] then but we had no memory of it. A Catholic member corrected me saying '[your family] foddered the horses of the Fermanagh Fusiliers in 1798!' [In other words, they supported the British forces putting down the rebellion.] That put me in my place [on the wrong side of history], but he was just correcting the facts, as related by his grandfather.

Quentin relates, 'My great-great-great-grandfather [...] had a raid on his house in 1798 by the rebels but, having heard a leak that a raid was planned, he secreted some soldiers in his house and outwitted the rebels and one was shot and another captured and hung.'

Walter grew up hearing stories about his fourth great-grandfather's involvement in the battles of 1798, 'He was in the Wicklow Yeomandry [sic] rebellion in 1798. I have a sword upstairs, as a matter of fact. It was handed down. Passed down all through the history.' This is a source of pride to Walter, who has strongly unionist views.

Ursula remembers a local event commemorating the rebellion of 1798 in which it was suggested that one of her uncle's horses might be used in the parade, holding someone dressed up as a rebel. Objections were made on the grounds that the horse was a Protestant, while the rebellion itself and the commemoration were identified as Catholic events.

Representing another perspective, Sam says, 'I don't know if any of my ancestors took part in the 1798 rebellion, but I would be very proud of any [...] since Catholics and Protestants fought alongside each other as equals. It was just unfortunate that the rebellion was unsuccessful.' Clive describes his joy at learning about his family's involvement in 1798 – on the 'right' side:

> I can't remember precisely when I made the discovery that my ancestors [...] led a rebel group against the crown forces in 1798 at the Battle of Granard [...] but I recall feeling a sense of satisfaction or validation. Not that I didn't feel Irish, but that now I had a credible tradition and context [...] I often found myself, in political discussion with friends, making every effort to outline the nuanced and crucial distinctions [...] and to lay claim to a republican tradition.

It is interesting to note that Dora Casserley, who wrote the 'Protestant' Irish history textbook discussed above, describes the rebellion as 'a melancholy and painful' story, and states firmly that 'nothing is to be gained by dwelling upon its details.'[203]

The Famine

The Great Famine of 1845–49, when the potato crop failed and the population was halved through starvation and emigration, was a defining period.

During and after the famine, Protestant missionaries were actively involved in feeding and converting victims of hunger. Some learned Irish to carry out missionary activities in Irish-speaking areas,[204] particularly Achill Island in Mayo and Dingle in Kerry.[205] The missions here were part of an evangelical movement that aimed to use Irish to convert the people of the Atlantic seaboard.[206] They believed they were saving people from the 'error of Romanism', and some earnestly believed that the famine had been sent by God to punish Catholics for rejecting the 'true faith'. Even the home secretary, James Graham, felt that the famine was a divine judgement.[207]

It suited Catholics and Protestants alike to characterise the famine as a Catholic problem. For Catholics, it was proof that the British state did not care about them: Britain had given extraordinary powers to absentee landlords and failed to deliver effective disaster relief. For Protestants, it seemed to show 'the superiority of their society and its work ethic', and even suggested that God was casting judgement on 'an indolent and unself-reliant people'.[208]

In fact, statistics show that the famine had a disproportionate effect on Catholics, but that Protestants were also affected. Before the famine, the Catholic share of the population on the island was 80.9 per cent, while 10.7 per cent were Anglicans and 8.1 per cent were Presbyterians.[209] Between 1834 and 1861, the Catholic population declined by 30 per cent, while the Anglican and Presbyterian population declined by 19 per cent.[210] In Bandon, Cork, the death rate among Protestants was three-fifths higher than its pre-famine rate during the years 1846–48, and registers in Dublin also show a (smaller) rise in the Protestant death rate.[211] While the population loss of Catholics was higher, Protestant loss was also significant.[212]

Despite relatively low levels of conversion during the famine years, the Irish Church Missions organisation claimed success, suggesting that the famine had made Catholics realise, as they broke the bonds they traditionally had with their priests, that their faith was an 'error'.[213] Apparently, however, those who remained Protestant tended to emigrate and those who stayed behind tended to revert to their original faith.[214] Catholics who converted to Protestantism during these years were known as 'soupers' on the understanding that they exchanged their religious allegiance for food. Myrtle says, 'Sam McGuire [a footballer and republican for whom the Sam Maguire Cup for Gaelic football is named] was a Protestant and they said, "Well, his ancestors must have taken the soup!"'

The 'soupers' have long been a very popular motif in Irish folk history, with stories about them amply represented among the collections of the Irish Folklore Commission.[215] The term also seems to have been current in Protestant folklore. An item in the *Church of Ireland Gazette* on 20 March (p. 234) discussing the sporting situation in Ireland in 1914 describes a scene in which members of the Gaelic Athletic Association were supposed to have justified their anti-'foreign sports' stance with the claim that the organisers of non-Gaelic games engaged in 'athletic souperism'; a humorous anecdote published in the *Church of Ireland Gazette* on 21 August of the same year (p. 715) describes a man being taunted by children who shouted 'souper' after him. He shouted 'stition' back at them to make the point that he regarded their Catholic faith as superstitious.

Converts were generally regarded with derision, and popular anger often manifested as local boycotts.[216] A diary written by a man who grew up in Knock during the famine discusses the many points of conflict between the local citizens, some of whom had converted to Protestantism. Eugene Hynes, on the topic of the man's diary, indicates how the man 'presents those local people who became Protestant as not really Knock people at all'. Hynes gives the example of a man who converted to Protestantism and verbally abused a priest during Mass, ultimately committing suicide in a particularly violent way; the implication was that this was somehow God's judgement. A schoolmaster who had used his position to disseminate Protestant material 'was spoken of publicly and denounced by the priest from the altar. He was to be excommunicated unless he made public reparation for the scandal given.' Among the ordinary people of Knock, 'To be a Protestant was to be not just an outsider to the community but an exploiter and persecutor; in becoming a Protestant one was becoming an outsider.'[217]

The hatred shown towards proselytisers who took advantage of the famine victims' vulnerability is also captured in works of fiction that were published later in the nineteenth century,[218] and it left a lingering legacy of suspicion and resentment.[219] When the Irish Folklore Commission collected famine memories in the 1930s, proselytism and souperism were recalled even in areas where they had not occurred;[220] in 1967, the parish priest of Kilrush erected a monument in honour of the 'numerous heroes of west Clare who died of hunger rather than pervert [become Protestants] during the Great Famine', although there is no evidence of Protestant missions having been active in his parish.[221] As late as the 1980s, 'the Dublin Christian Mission [an evangelical charitable organisation] was accused of "souperism" and picketed by the Legion of Mary',[222] while in 1985 outrage ensued after the Abbey Theatre showed a play by Eoghan Harris, *Souper Sullivan*, set in the Famine era, that depicted a Protestant rector positively.[223]

Honora's father told her about their family's experiences of the famine, 'My dad told me that his grandfather was a big, tall man and that during the Famine he used to carry the dying people on his back up the steep hill to the hospital. Our family was fortunate in being closely connected to the land and were able to grow food to feed their families and livestock.' Sam comments that stories of the famine impacted on his grandmother's behaviour many years later, 'My grandmother was born in 1876, which was thirty years after the Great Famine, and she grew up with a great fear of another famine. No food was ever put to waste; if she was walking along and a potato fell off a passing cart, she picked it up and took it home so as not to waste it.' Freddie grew up hearing about a local spot where famine victims are said to have died; it was linked to a strange phenomenon that he was told was related to the famine days:

> I heard tell of a few fellas dying all right, at, we'll say, the [local land-mark] [...] Kind of famished with the cold or something [...] *Féara gorta* [*sic*][224] [...] *Féara gorta* is supposed to be where you pass it and you get, you feel very hungry or something, somebody is supposed to have died on the side of the road at that particular point. You've got the *féara gorta* from them.

Some Protestants are eager to assert that the Protestant community has been unfairly pilloried for its behaviour during the famine, and that even some families from the Big House demographic did their best to help. For example, Esther states:

> Bord Fáilte [the Irish tourism authority] in their campaign of the Ancient East [...] appear to suggest that all Big Houses caused hardship to their tenants and employees or were absentee landlords. This was not so [...] my great-grandmother contracted typhoid as a result

of manning the soup kitchens, she never properly recovered and died early as a result [...] It has been said that the Protestants forced the starving Catholics to change their religion. I do not have any evidence of this.

Myrtle's testimony suggests that Protestant storytelling about the famine may have taken a different point of view, 'The Famine stories [related in her community] often involved tales of how Protestant clergy or merchants helped the sick and starving.' Eleanora discusses how a local gentry family in a Big House ('they would have been Irish chieftains and then changed their religion to hold onto their lands') helped more than others, trying to assist their tenants by providing them with passage to America or Canada and by feeding people in big soup kitchens. She opines that, because some of the landlords behaved dreadfully, all of them – and by extension humbler Protestants like her own ancestors – were seen in a negative light. She says that while it is true that *some* ships sank, that does not necessarily mean that the ships were inadequate or that any inappropriate deals had been made. Still, 'Roman Catholics would definitely say that that was deliberate rather than an unfortunate accident or whatever.' She also points out that while most landlords in her area were Protestants, some were Catholics, and they were reputed to have treated their tenants just as badly.

Natasha attended a Protestant secondary school where she feels they were taught history impartially. She says they were taught about 'good landlords and bad landlords and the Famine and all that sort of stuff', and contrasts that with what she has heard about how history was taught in Catholic schools, 'in the Catholic schools [the landlords] were all bad, and of course they never said that some of them were Catholic. They always said they were Protestant landlords. Whereas there were a lot of wealthy Catholic landlords who were as bad, if not worse.' Charlotte reports that a local Protestant rector died heroically, 'There is a young clergyman buried in the local graveyard. He died during the Famine. He gave his food to the hungry. He caught a fever and it killed him.'

Heather heard that her community had been devastated by the potato famine in the 1840s, and she had seen for herself the remains of old, ruined cottages which suggested that the area had once been more densely populated. In secondary school, her teacher assured her that the famine had been 'done to' the Catholics by the Protestants and that the stories that she had heard were lies. Years later, a local historian gave a lecture about the famine and she learned that her area had suffered badly. This historian explained that the famine had been a 'social famine' and that all the poor had been affected, including poor Protestants. This possibility was not recognised by her teacher because it was inconsistent with the story he knew of evil Protestant landlords, which did not entertain that some of the peasants who died might also have been Protestant.

Morality, Missionaries, and the Drift Towards Independence
In 1838, shortly before the famine, a Reverend Irvin preached at St Werburgh's church in Dublin's inner-city about the importance of a Protestant education. He referred to 'the wretched [Catholic] peasantry' and described them as 'wretched because vicious, vicious because irreligious, irreligious because untaught the truths of pure Christianity'.[225] Reverend Irvin believed that Catholic peasants were poor and wretched *because* they were Catholics. By implication, the better-off and educated deserved their good fortune because they were, so often, Protestants. Protestant evangelists believed that Catholics were 'the congregation of Satan and the vehicle of the antichrist', who could be saved if they converted to the 'true church'. They were puzzled as to why more Catholics had not converted, as it seemed obvious to them that God favoured Protestants. The evangelicals noted that there were fewer working-class Protestants than working-class Catholics and, fretting about the state of Catholics' souls and the relative paucity of Protestant numbers, started to actively evangelise. They became intensely interested in the Irish language and in creating and disseminating material that would help their mission. They established various missions and had a special interest in the west, but they were disappointed by the results. Catholics who converted often faced so much hostility in their communities that they emigrated.[226] Celeste, whose great-grandparents converted to Protestantism in the 1840s, recalls the family story of why it happened and the local response:

> My grand grandparents, both Roman Catholic and both teachers, married in 1848 and both became Protestants [...] That generation were rampant 'Prods'; the zeal of the convert set in. Going through

their village in West Cork to the C of I church in 1848 they met with a hail of stones as they passed the Catholic church through their conversion. They got the front seat in the C of I church and still have it to this day.

In 1834, a census had revealed that 'of an Irish population of 7.9 million, Catholics made up 6.4 million, the Church of Ireland only 852,000 and the Presbyterians just under 650,000.'[227] With growing numbers of educated Catholics, and increasing political awareness, change was inevitable. A contemporary 'address to Protestants' on the nationalist movement stated that it 'broods over our country retarding its social improvement, injuring its commercial prospects, and preventing the investment of capital, or the development of our resources'.[228]

A major blow to the position of the Protestants, especially the Church of Ireland, was the disestablishment of the Church of Ireland in 1871 following the Irish Church Act of 1869.[229] Many feared that they would see 'the results of three hundred years of toil melt away like the fabric of a dream.'[230] With disestablishment looming, the number of educated Catholics increasing, and the sense of an inevitable decline in their privileged position growing, wealthy Protestants started to suspect 'a sinister attempt' on the part of Catholics to remove them from public positions.[231]

The move to reconfigure the Church of Ireland as a 'self-governing voluntary body'[232] was ardently opposed by the bishops in the House of Lords. 'The church identified itself very much with the British presence,' says Griffin, 'and accordingly looked on Protestant home rulers as misguided romantics or troublemakers.'[233] The Dean of Cork railed against the measure in his maiden speech at the House of Lords, saying that Irish Protestants, 'ever the faithful and devoted servants of England', were about to be cast off 'without even a kind word of gratitude for old deeds of service and faithful and devoted loyalty', and were 'sorely, and naturally, irritated'.[234]

However, disestablishment was inevitable. An 1861 census had provided accurate information about the demographic breakdown of Ireland for the first time. Across the whole island, with a population of 5.75 million, 4.5 million were Catholics and just under 700,000 were Church of Ireland, with the rest belonging to diverse Protestant faiths. Given such numbers, and given the British government's desire to placate the growing Catholic middle classes, it was ridiculous that the Church of Ireland should continue to be considered the 'state religion'.[235] The Church of Ireland had effectively long been an element of the state as much as, or more than, it was a communion of believers, gathering for its own use 'the equivalent of local taxes', and 'peopling the magistry, and mingling religious with state ceremonies'.[236] The tithe-gathering was essentially a tax on agricultural produce, excluding pasture, that supported a Church which served the religious needs of a minority while railing against the religious views of the majority, often blaming them for all their own problems.

Soon after disestablishment, people rallied to pay for the upkeep and construction of churches with an enthusiasm, according to Archbishop Trench, that matched 'the return of the children of Israel from their captivity in Babylon to the land which God had given them'.[237] But many Protestants felt bitterly betrayed.[238] Cecil Frances Alexander, a famous author of hymn lyrics and the wife of a prominent cleric, wrote the following lines to sing after 1 January 1871, when the new law would come into effect:[239]

Look down, Lord of Heaven, on our desolation!
Fallen, fallen, fallen is now our Country's crown,
Dimly dawns the New Year on a churchless nation,
Ammon and Amalek tread our borders down.[240]

Ammon was a God worshipped by the ancient Egyptians; the Amaleks were members of a tribe of Arabs engaged in constant warfare with the ancient Jews, and they were therefore represented in Scripture as terrible people.[241] Conversely, the Catholic hierarchy was delighted. Cardinal Cullen reported that 'the Protestants will find themselves without any privileges [...] the poor Protestants are all very irritated. They never did imagine that England would have abandoned their cause.'[242]

William, who volunteers as the sexton of his local church, enjoys reading the old minute books in the church in the tiny parish where he grew up, as they give him a glimpse into his community's past and the concerns of his ancestors. Around the time of disestablishment, he says, the local community held many meetings and they 'did a lot of giving out' about Gladstone, then the Prime Minister of the United Kingdom. He says that the parishioners were very scared and upset and that this is abundantly clear in the minutes of their meetings. 'They were concerned, really, they felt that the end of the world had nearly come', he says.

The blow to the Church of Ireland community (which was extensively connected to the other Protestant communities through intermarriage) went beyond seeing the structures of their faith diminished in importance; it was also understood as a blow to their important role in society, and a portent of losses yet to come. In 1886, the First Home Rule Bill was mooted following a brief period in which the home rule movement united some Protestant and Catholic activists and politicians in a 'shared, moderate, secular and conservative vision' of what Ireland could be like.[243] Gladstone had asked the churches for their opinion, and the Bishop of Limerick proposed that the Church of Ireland, which then numbered about 600,000 followers, should affirm its 'constant allegiance to the throne and [its] unswerving attachment to the legislative union now subsisting between Great Britain and Ireland'.[244] Many Protestants worried that they would be victimised if home rule was passed.

The old stories about 1641 – still very much alive in Protestant folk history – were evoked. One opponent to home rule, writing in 1886, claimed that in 1641 a third of the Irish population had been killed or exiled, the fields were uncultivated, the sky was filled with birds that ate human corpses, and the number of wolves in the country was greatly increased. The suggestion was that the same could happen again if a Catholic government gained power.[245] There was also concern that if Protestant landlords did not receive rent from their tenants funds to the church would dry up. The bill failed.

Although Protestants had been very dominant within the early home rule movement, and despite the leadership of Charles Stewart Parnell (who was a Protestant), as Catholicism became more closely linked with nationalism, the movement became largely a Catholic one.[246] Many Protestants still remembered the huge upset that had followed disestablishment, and Protestants of all denominations worried that home rule would mean their disappearance as a potent political force. Members of the Church of Ireland and the Presbyterian and Methodist churches signed up in favour of continuing union with Great Britain.[247]

The First World War

Protestants sent proportionally more young men to fight in the First World War than Catholics and, of course, many died. By late 1915, there were about 53,000 Irish Protestants and 80,000 Irish Catholics fighting on the British side and in 1917, when 150,000 were enlisted, 60,000 were Protestants and 90,000 were Catholics. These figures refer to the whole island and indicate that while Protestants represented about 25 per cent of the total population they contributed about 40 per cent of the soldiers.[248] In fact, the total number of Protestants who fought in the First World War might be underestimated; usually the figures are taken from the Irish regiments, but many enlisted in British regiments.[249]

Many Protestant churches have monuments to fallen soldiers. Francis says, 'Our churches have many beautiful memorials to soldiers killed in the 1st and 2nd World Wars.' Francis recalls what he had heard of the First World War in his area:

> Many young men joined up. Some thought it would be a way to see the world at 'His Majesty's' expense. Others out of loyalty to the Crown. White feathers were placed in church seats of families with young men. On the other hand, some would not stand up for 'God Save the King' [when they came back] when played in church as they felt they were treated badly by England.

Gerald heard that the Boys' Brigade, a sort of Boy Scouts group organised along military lines with a strong scriptural element,[250] recruited heavily among its former members. His uncle was killed in the war, apparently a victim of his own social aspirations and the propaganda of the Boys' Brigade:

> I would say that was the influence of the Boys' Brigade [...] there was very strong recruitment, and I still have the recruitment leaflet. Amongst the better educated working-class [...] My father's family was moving upwards. The recruiting leaflet, which I have, says, 'You will be amongst your chums' [...] They don't say that, 'We're going to put them all together in the trenches where they're all going to be killed later on.' Really, it was, 'Come in here and this will be sort of a section of the Army that will be a higher social class.' He went off and joined. He lied about his age.

Evelyn recounts how her father and uncle fought in the First World War, and how upset they were afterwards when Donegal was part of the Free State, 'I think that the reason they went to war was to help ensure that Britain would not leave them or abandon Ireland.'

In her memoir, *I Also Am of Ireland*, Galway woman Frances Moffett wrote of buying red, white, and blue ribbons when the British victory was announced in 1918 (her father had served in the army as a vet) and being drenched with water by a woman who shouted 'Take that, you Orange dog!', saying something about 'the damned British' and 'My Paddy tortured in prison'. Her mother explained that 'The Orange Order is very bitter against Catholics' and said that the woman could not really be blamed.[251]

Katherine speaks of how her father returned from the war only to realise that he was no longer welcome in Ireland, with the result that he went to live in the UK; she herself only returned to Ireland permanently after retirement. Lisa states, 'We lost uncles in the 1914–18 war – went away to fight for King and Country – those who came back were deemed to be traitors.' Barton remembers, as a child in the 1930s, meeting a Protestant veteran who foolishly visited his home area dressed in his British army uniform, 'He was dressed up beautiful. Red hat and red jewellery.' He was run out of town very quickly, 'sure, the local boys turned him out as quick as they could […] he nearly was back by return.'

When Henry was growing up, there was still much discussion about family members who had been involved in the First World War. About six of his great-aunts and uncles had served. Two of his great-aunts were nurses and a great-uncle was a sergeant. Their stories were related with pride and he 'knows for a fact' that these long-ago people served in the British Army because of their loyalty to king and country. 'Up until the 1970s', he says, 'we kept old First World War Union Jacks in the attic […] so that when my great-aunts and uncles died, they were buried with the Union Jacks and with their medal.' One of his great-uncles joined the Dublin Metropolitan Police when he returned and stayed on when it became the Garda Síochána (Irish police force); apparently, he was the only garda to have a funeral cortege with a Union Jack on the coffin. Inspired by these family stories, and despite being told by neighbours that they were traitors for serving for the British, Henry's parents served in the British Army during the Second World War.

The Easter Rising and Its Aftermath

The Easter Rising occurred in 1916 when rebels seized strategic points around Dublin, including the General Post Office and St Stephen's Green. Many were extremely dubious about the rebels and the uprising, and most Protestants 'condemned the revolt unreservedly and heaped praise on the British troops [...] who put it down.'[252] By now, nationalism had become a largely Catholic movement (although some Protestants were involved). Within months of the rising's defeat, it was represented as an act of patriotism on the part of 'good *Catholic* Irishmen', while Protestants, although they could be nationalists if they wanted, were neither important nor necessary to the struggle for nationhood.[253]

Barney grew up with stories of how his recent ancestors and their friends, living in a border area, reacted to the events of 1916:

> there were nobody as close, we had to pull together when you were in a strange land with a different religion that [...] was hostile to you [...] We were building up a great relationship with our Catholic neighbours until the 1916 Rising. And then the fear came on us. Our religion's going to be swept away; our whole way of life [...] there was a savage fear [...] So, we rallied together [...] my grandfather, my uncle who was there before my father, all of them was in the Ulster Volunteer Forces[254] [...] All houses, Protestant houses in that time, was on the alert and armed. They had the armour of the Ulster Volunteer Force. They had the Lee Enfield rifle and they had plenty ammunition, but my father [...] got rid of all of that regalia and got rid of the [Orange] sash and got rid of some of this stuff. That regalia was all about our house, and everybody knew that if you went near a Protestant's house at that time at night, and you were any way hostile, you would have been fired at [...] It was a kill-or-be-killed attitude. There was no real bitterness, you would not go next day looking for someone, but if you had to defend your family, you would have killed.

Barney repeatedly describes his ancestors as feeling that they were living in a 'strange land'; it was a feeling that grew around 1916, in the years that followed, and into independence.

Betty's grandmother told her that one of the family had been injured and killed in the Easter Rising. She was excited, 'thinking I had a tale to tell'. But then she realised that he was on the 'wrong side' and so 'it would not do to tell that tale in history class.'

Violet recounts an anecdote she heard from her grandfather:

> My grandfather used to tell of an incident during the Rising when a very young, nervous volunteer came into the shop with a rifle demanding cloth. Grandfather told him to put the gun down – he was terrified it would go off by accident because the lad was shaking with nerves – and he could have whatever he wanted! So, he left the shop, laden down the bales of cloth, helped by my grandfather. During the burning of the Four Courts, Grandfather, and half the citizenry of Dublin, went down to the quays to watch – oblivious of the danger to themselves!

Harold remembers his grandfather, who grew up in poverty in Dublin's city centre, talking about 1916. His grandfather's memories were often prompted when the name of a street called after one patriot hero or another brought them to mind. His memories of that time troubled him in his later years. Harold recalls driving down a Dublin road with his father and grandfather. His father said that he had never heard of the man after whom the road was called and wondered why a road was named after him. His grandfather laughed bitterly and said, 'Probably shot some Englishman in the back and ran!' His grandfather often made little jokes like that, 'Protestant jokes'. Harold knows that his grandfather's childhood and adolescence after 1916 were difficult, 'I just got the overall impression that he had suffered all kinds of abuse […] I don't know if he was ever physically abused, but definitely verbal abuse, most certainly.' That was when the family started to feel like outsiders in the city that had been their home for as long as anyone knew.

After the rising, most southern Protestants were opposed to partition. They were concerned about being a small minority in a Catholic-dominated land. In July 1916, the *Church of Ireland Gazette* stated, 'We believe that home rule without Ulster would have been thoroughly bad; home rule with Ulster would have been less bad.'[255] Gerald discusses the long-term impact of 1916 and its aftermath on his mother:

> My mother was a staunch Protestant West Briton all her life […] She

was living on Arran Quay [in inner-city Dublin], next to the Four Courts during the Rising [...] Her father, as a rural policeman, would have had local status during her childhood. In 1916, the first casualty was a policeman and a major event was the siege of a north Dublin police station twenty miles from their home. Policemen were targets in the 20s, and her family must have been fearful. Her father did not remain on in the police service of the Free State but had a pension in Britain. The family moved to a small house in Harold's Cross [a suburb near the city centre] and he died in 1928. My grandmother had a small widow's pension. The overall position of the family changed from being part of the ruling class and regime to one of being part of a minority who may have felt under attack. [For my mother] Irish nationalism and Catholicism were synonymous, and we were not encouraged to embrace anything Irish.

Protestants started to leave. By 1920, the Bishop of Killaloe warned that numbers in his diocese had slumped by two-thirds from its peak a few decades before.[256]

The War of Independence and the Civil War
The Irish War of Independence occurred between 1919 and 1921, and ended with the signing of the Anglo-Irish Treaty on 6 December 1921, which provided for the establishment of the Irish Free State, within a year, as a self-governing dominion within the British Commonwealth of Nations. The Irish Civil War began on 28 June 1922; it was fought between those who supported the treaty (signed by Michael Collins, among others, and which had resulted in the partition of Ireland) and de Valera and his supporters, who opposed it. When Collins was killed in an ambush on 22 August 1922, the *Church of Ireland Gazette* wrote that 'Ireland has lost a son whom she will not be able to replace.'[257]

During this period, many Protestants found themselves identified by their Catholic fellow citizens as an ethnic minority. Having often considered themselves to be 'Irish in one of the best possible ways', they were increasingly 'treated in the newspapers, in political speeches, and in polemical pamphlets as strangers in their own land', in a philosophy 'that cast Anglo-Ireland in the role of alien persecutor'.[258] Sinn Féin and the IRA talked about their 'religious inclusivity' but relatively few Protestants were active political nationalists, individual republicans sometimes made bigoted statements, and it could be difficult for nationalist leaders to remain consistent with the pluralist message they theoretically espoused.[259]

On the ground, prejudice and discord around issues such as land ownership contributed to numerous outbreaks of local violence. In Monaghan, a Protestant farming family, the Flemings, managed to chase would-be IRA raiders off their premises. Later it was said that they had shot one of the IRA men dead, and that he had been quietly buried by his comrades. In reprisal, about fifty armed men told the Flemings that if they surrendered, their home would be spared from being burned to the ground. They surrendered, but father and son were executed. Also in Monaghan, a woman called Kate Carrol was murdered on suspicion of passing information to the RIC. In both cases, it is thought that the impetus to carry out the killings came from the grassroots of the IRA, not its leadership. Official IRA policy stated that women should not be executed but were to be told to leave the country. In these cases, it seems that local IRA policy was dictated 'by a desire to extract revenge at a local level'.[260]

Many Protestant families retain stories about this period. Sometimes self-censorship prohibited them for years from speaking of these events openly. Eadry knew families in which memories of the violence of the time were still very vivid, but says, 'you didn't talk about it because it would bring up sores that you didn't open.' Hope grew up in a family where a memory of violent times was a constant backdrop; it presented a challenge to her experience of the comfort of rural life in her locality, which was otherwise one of mutual friendship and co-operation:

> my grandfather was a justice of the peace, and he'd been [...] a hunting and shooting man, and farmer [...] he was coming back across the fields and he disturbed a group of the rebel army [...] practicing or manoeuvring or something [...] later on, he was seen going into the army barracks in the town, and then a while later a number of them were arrested and [...] it was presumed that he had reported on them, but my father and his brother certainly said no, that he didn't. [My father] was there the first time [the IRA] came out [...] my grandfather was told he must leave immediately, and [...] they were going to execute him, and one of the men apparently spoke up, and that upset my grandfather very much [...] because, when he

spoke up, he realised that he knew who he was [...] Their faces were all blacked and I think they were all masked. I've always just heard about their black faces [...] And they came right into the house and right into her bedroom [...] And he was brought out and put up against the wall, the kitchen wall of the house, apparently, and the children were all told to stay on the stairs in the centre of the house [...] houses had been put on fire, and they were afraid this might happen [...] and my father described it, that looking down, from the window [...] once the man spoke up [...] they said, well, he could leave, but he had to leave immediately, and then they blackmailed the family [...] they had to leave money in a certain place down in the wood, and they got sort of orders to do this every so often, and they didn't have much money at that time.

Having grown up hearing this story and its epilogue – when her grandfather was allowed to return after four years, he became severely depressed and alcoholic, and ultimately died of suicide – Hope has often wondered about what really happened. She was always assured that her grandfather had not reported on the IRA. On the other hand, it is hard to be sure, 'if he was a justice of the peace, one wonders [...] He certainly would have had unionist sympathies, because some members of the family [...] had been in the British army, and it was after the 14/18 war, and they must have been feeling quite loyalist, but [...] they were also interested in [...] Irish nationhood and in the Irish.' For Hope's father, the event was a milestone that marked him for the rest of his life, 'He talked about his father very cheerily, and praising him always, on ordinary occasions just talking about things his father had done, and the kind of man he was [...] but if ever he started talking about "the '22 business," as it was always called, he got very sad, because really it was the end of his home life.' Hope's family has long assumed that the IRA man who spoke up for her grandfather was a neighbour, but even now, after almost a hundred years, she prefers not to know for sure:

I've felt it was a neighbouring farming family probably [...] in recent years, a lot of information has become available, and I haven't gone to read it [...] I've debated with myself and one of my cousins to whether I should go and look it up [...] and then one man in whose judgement I would trust [...] he said, 'Well, you can go and look it up, but you'll find it upsetting [...] 'A nasty, dirty business,' was the way he put it [...] I really wondered if I wanted to and I still haven't made the decision.

Myrtle says her grandfather, a farmer and traditional healer, 'also practiced as a justice of the peace and for this reason the IRA came to his house during the War of Independence. He expected to be shot, but a local man in the group spoke up for him and probably saved his life.' Myrtle's grandfather had a traditional cure for horses and had used this to heal a horse belonging to one of the IRA men; this was what saved his life. Daphne heard a similar story about her grandfather, a fishmonger, 'my grandfather had gone [away] for the day, and he wasn't home, and my aunt told [the IRA this]. Eventually, they kind of accepted it and one of them said, "He's a decent man. We go. We leave."' The story was that they had come to take him out to either beat him up or shoot him, or both. Daphne surmises that her grandfather would never have been a collaborator, but that he probably supplied a local British army garrison with fish. Sylvia tells a similar story about her family, but the villains are the Black and Tans (the forces sent by the British to subdue the fighting in Ireland, mostly recruited from among former soldiers and notoriously vicious and cruel). In the story, her own grandfather is said to have saved his Catholic friends, 'they came to attack some of the [neighbours] and take out one of these men, and grandfather is supposed to have said, "You're not to touch him, he's a decent, hardworking fella." And ever since [...] when they came home, they visit [...] as a sort of thank you.'

During the War of Independence, Thomas's uncle was in 'the forces' (against the insurgency). Afterwards, he hid his ammunition by burying it underneath an apple tree. Gradually, the lead from the ammunition leached into the soil and killed the tree; its steady decline was a constant reminder of the secret underneath it. The corresponding rifle stayed in the attic of the old family home until the 1990s. Thomas had heard other stories about his family during this time too. His father worked as a postmaster, and the post office was raided by various members of the local IRA, all of whom were known to him personally. They even called him 'Master Sam' during the raid. One of the raiders started stealing cigarettes, but his leader 'let a roar at him' and paid his father, 'Jesus, me father got an apology for all [...]

"Oh," he says, "no," he says. "No need to pay." He says, "That's good enough," he says, "it's gone, it's gone."' The man was court-martialled afterwards for stealing. His father told this story to illustrate that these men were acting honourably; they simply wanted the government's money. But not everyone in the area was treated so well. Another man with a brother in the police force was taken from bed at night and brought to a bog where he was threatened with execution. Eventually, one of his persecutors, a neighbour, said, 'We'll let him go this time.' After independence, many Protestants in this rather poor rural border area moved to the other side of the border, where they felt safer.

Grace `was told of her family's experience with the IRA:

> They were banished out to the outhouses to sleep while the Free Staters took over their home. And my grandfather used to be [...] made drive them to [a town some distance away]. And at one stage, there was a trench over across the road, and the car went into it [...] And my second grandfather, he was made use a pony and trap. And they tied a body onto the back of it [...] he was alive when they tied him on [...] [they] made the horse drive to [the town] which would have been about six miles.

Honora's family was deeply affected by the actions of the IRA:

> [1921] was a particularly devastating year for my grandmother's family. Her brother and her brother-in-law were shot by the IRA, and when her nephew came home for his father's funeral he too was shot. The remains of their families (except one) fled to England. Their farms had to be sold off at ridiculously low prices. In one instance, the auction was boycotted by the IRA. They did get some compensation, but not enough. Nothing could compensate for the loss of loved ones.

Eunan has a similar account, 'My mother's people [...] suffered at the time of the Troubles in April 1922 [...] My understanding is that one of her uncles was shot dead in his bed and the other two had to leave the farm and flee to Devon [...] That left an unspoken grief, which was never mentioned until recent years.'

Eileen remembers eavesdropping on her parents, 'When my parents talked at night with visitors in the kitchen, my sister and I lay awake listening. Much of the talk was about "The Troubles" […] A horrific account stays with me, of two elderly Protestant women stripped naked and tied to a gate while their home was set on fire.' Eileen also remembers hearing about a disliked local character who was targeted at this time:

[He was known as] 'Billy the Divil' from his stern judgement as a magistrate […] Sometime during the Troubles, the local lads hatched a plan to go out and burn down [his house]. 'Billy the Divil' got wind of it and was ready for them. In a room high up at the front of the house he waited with loaded guns […] As soon as the lads arrived, he shot at them and continued to do so […] until they gave up.

Eustace recalls stories that his father told about this period, which focus on his own father's preparedness:

I was surprised to find that my grandfather […] had been a member of the Masonic Order in Cork, as nobody else in the family had been a Mason before or since. When I asked my father why grandfather had joined the Masons, he simply said that grandfather had expected to be killed […] and had joined to ensure that, in that event, his children would be looked after and could join the Masonic School in Dublin. My father did witness one possible attempt on grandfather's life. At the time the authorities ordered people to put a curfew notice on their front doors, naming all those in the house. If the Black and Tans came and those named on the notice did not coincide with those who were actually there you were in trouble. Of course, while the Tans wanted the notices on the doors, the IRA ordered people to take them off the doors. So, one evening a knock came to the door and grandfather answered it. A man demanded that he took the curfew notice off the door. Grandfather immediately ushered my granny and the children into the front parlour and closed the door. He kept talking to the man at the door and backed down the hall into the kitchen. My father had been getting coal from the coal-hole under the stairs off the kitchen and was not with the rest of the family. He heard the commotion and closed himself into the coal-hole

– but through a crack in the door he could see what was happening in the kitchen. His father backed into the kitchen followed by a man with a gun. Grandfather kept talking and got a bottle of whiskey which he put on the table. He offered some to the man with the gun [...] except that grandfather kept talking and giving the man whiskey for a long time. Eventually the man was drunk, and grandfather convinced him that he really had come to get the curfew notice removed and he brought him to the front door and removed it with a flourish, pushing the man outside [...] the IRA man must not really have wanted to shoot grandfather, otherwise he would simply have done it on the doorstep, as has happened so many times [...] grandfather must have known that something of the kind was going to happen, otherwise he would not have had a bottle of whiskey.

Eustace adds that the local IRA commander appeared to loathe members of the Masons. A local Mason was killed and, 'although he had been a home ruler, a note was attached to his body accusing him of being a traitor.' In response to the violence, the Masons 'had to stop holding their meetings for some time because they were being picked off on their way to them'.

Adam grew up listening to his mother's stories of that time, when she was in her teens. The IRA came to their house several times and took 'horses and whatever they wanted'. Although the family was not mistreated, they were terrified because other local people had been killed. His mother remembered the fear that they all lived with as much worse than anything she had experienced directly. The horses were taken and treated badly, but they were eventually returned. The fear lasted much longer than the violence.

Hillis grew up hearing how his great-grandfather, though a stern man and a unionist, had attempted to intervene on behalf of a local lad that was arrested during the War of Independence:

[he was] very conservative, but also very strongly [...] supportive of the community. I mean, when [a local youth] [...] was accused of murdering some British soldier or policeman [...] and he was caught and brought up to Dublin and he was going to be hung in Mountjoy [gaol] [...] My great-grandfather [...] went up and petitioned the British government that he was only eighteen years of age, and they

had no actual physical proof that he fired the shot, not to hang him. But anyway, they did.

Hillis also relates how, years later, he had a conversation with a local leader of the IRA at the time; the leader recounted how Hillis's great-grandfather had helped to keep the members of the IRA safe:

> they used to go up to the rectory and sit in the kitchen and my great-grandparents used to have the officers from the police and the army and the Black and Tan guys and [...] they used to interview them and draw them out as to where they were going to raid next, so that [the IRA captain] could get all the lads shifted out of the houses before they arrived. So, for that reason our family was very well in with the [...] nationalist side of things.

Years later, the IRA captain repaid his debt when Hillis's grandfather died. His second wife was Catholic, so the local Catholic priest insisted that the deceased be buried in the Catholic cemetery after a funeral Mass in the Catholic church, but the family brought the coffin into the small Protestant church. That night, the former IRA captain and his men stood guard to ensure that nobody interfered with the body – for which, Hillis says, they were excommunicated. He has always been grateful for their kindness at that time.

Eustace says his great-grandfather's car was requisitioned by the IRA and that his grandfather, still a boy, was thrown down the stairs. He thinks that they were targeted more because they had quite a big farm, and therefore could afford a car, than because they were Protestants. Samuel also says his father's car was used in the War of Independence, 'My father used to say that one night the IRA would have it and the next night the other boys [the Black and Tans] would have it and they would leave it back all right.' To facilitate both parties, he took to leaving the key in the ignition. He reports that both the IRA and the Black and Tans would leave the car back with a full tank of petrol, 'They weren't bad that way now.'

Norm tells his mother's story of the Irish War of Independence and the civil war. She and her first husband had a small grocery shop and a concession located in the village post office. During 'the troubled times' their shop was raided on five occasions and they suspected that they were targeted because they were Protestants. In one of these instances, her husband 'was brought out under the local railway bridge and shots were fired over his head'. He died young, leaving her with two children under the age of two; everyone felt that the shock had precipitated his death. She tried to keep the shop and post office concession going, but 'the community conspired to have the post office taken from her', and it moved a hundred yards up the road to the rival business, a small shop run by a Catholic family. She lived until the 1960s and often told her family about the terrible time when, as a young widow with two babies, her neighbours took her livelihood away, simply because she was one of the 'other sort'. The events affected Norm's mother for the rest of her life. They are one of the reasons why he knew few Catholics when he was growing up; he and his parents rarely went out, and when they did it was only to the homes of Protestant families that they felt they could trust.

Rachel's uncle was on his way out of the local town, the story goes, when he was met by two IRA men disguised in English uniforms. They came up to him and said, 'If you hear of any IRA activity, you'll let us know.' Her uncle, who had a reputation for being 'very loud', answered them by saying, 'Yarra, of course I'll let you know!' She comments that there is no way to know whether he meant this or thought, mistaking them as English soldiers, that he would be in trouble if he disagreed. 'What else was he going to say?' she says. Later, the IRA came to the house to kill him. He was not there, but his wheelchair-bound brother was, so the IRA men – his neighbours – executed him instead. Her uncle fled to England and the family put the farm up for auction. On the day of the auction, only one man bid, and they had to accept his low offer because 'nobody went against him'. People speculated that the mysterious buyer had set it all up just to get the land cheaply. When Rachel's aunt tried to take the family's furniture from the home after the sale, the buyer insisted that he had purchased this too, so she went to England with little more than the clothes on her back.

Rachel's grandparents were married during the troubles of the 1920s. They got married in a private house and returned home, without any celebrations, in a pony and trap, because 'In those days the Protestants in Cork were very, very nervous.' Rachel's family home had once been a dower house associated with a large, stately home that had been burned down. 'It was an old barn of a place and it was in bad enough nick, but it had the

Georgian doorways that you find in Dublin and that, and it had a certain look to it that was nice.' At one stage, a group of IRA men came around to the house during the night and said, 'Get out, we're going to burn the place.' They were expecting to find the men of the house, but there were no men there, and Rachel's grandmother, heavily pregnant, 'put her head out the window and said, "Listen, lads, go home to your mothers, they'll be worrying about you."' The men left without burning the house.

On another occasion, a group of IRA men came to the house looking for guns, 'My grandfather went up into the attic and he pointed his gun and he said, "Listen, I don't want any trouble, but I am not giving you my gun." The women of the house all went to the furthest bedroom and locked themselves in, and he […] trained his gun down through a trapdoor, saying "I am not giving my gun."' Eventually the men went away. After that, Rachel's grandfather's hair went white from shock and 'never grew straight'.

Despite this frightening experience, this branch of the family remained safe. Rachel attributes this partly to the fact that, although they were living in a house that had once been part of a big demesne, 'we were common stock. We weren't the ascendancy. We worked *mighty hard* to make ends meet […] We were never seen as big nobs.' Her grandfather's best friend was in the IRA, and when he asked her grandfather for cattle to feed the men, her grandfather refused, saying it was against his principles. The IRA man said they would take the cattle anyway; Rachel's grandfather said, 'Listen, let me know when you are taking them, and I won't bother looking for them.' The cattle were taken, but after independence he was paid for the animals by the government. Somehow, the two men could be friends despite everything. 'There was a sense of "my principles aren't yours, but you have to respect mine and I will respect yours."' She relates another story of her great-grandfather during the War of Independence:

> He was working up in the field and a priest came running by. He went one way at the crossroads. The Black and Tans came later, and they said, 'Which way did he go?' and he pointed the wrong way, because nobody liked the Black and Tans […] and because he was a Protestant and had sent them off the wrong way the priest came back afterwards and said he was going to bless him for three generations. Now, that missed my generation, but they were blessed for three generations.

Rachel says that it is only in very recent years, long after the deaths of all those directly involved, that people have started to tell these stories outside their families. For most of her life, there was a sense that they could never be discussed in public, 'for fear that it would be misinterpreted.' She says it takes a hundred years for such stories to become 'history' and something that one can discuss. She also points out that the grandsons of the man who acquired her uncle's land went to school with her own brother. While she suspects that their family knew the story of the auction, just as hers did, 'we would never have said to them and they would never have said to us.' When they tell stories of those terrible years, she says, Catholics tend to focus on the various local atrocities involving the murder of Catholics by the British forces, such as a massacre that occurred in a local pub 'for no good reason'. 'The thing is,' she says, 'if they were telling the story of the Troubles, that is the story they would tell. If I am telling the story of the Troubles, I would tell the story about my uncle. Both things happened.'

There are stories that show the IRA in a relatively positive light, or that at least show an understanding that, despite everything, they were sometimes dealing with friends and neighbours. Myrtle recounts her father's story of being a small boy during the War of Independence:

> what they called the Free Staters were in a house across the road from them, the street that they had their home in, over the shop, and then the IRA came into their house, and they had their guns out the window [...] and my father and his twin brother were running around and, you know, they knew these guys. 'Do you want to hold the gun?' they knew them, and they were being [...] friendly.

Freddie's aunt often told him about the night the IRA had come to his grandparents' home, when his father was a baby. Though the family was terrified, the IRA men treated them with courtesy:

> There was no choice in the matter [...] but they treated them well [...] [the IRA men] got breakfast in the morning [...] they were good to the children [...] the children at that time – and I suppose it will show you how poor things were – they were in horses' collars with just a blanket [...] to keep them from rolling around the floor [...] and the IRA men used to smile at them.

Emma's grandfather received a letter 'purporting to come from the IRA' that instructed him to leave the country. However, 'he took the letter to the local headquarters of the IRA in Cork and asked them straight out if this letter was from them', and they assured him that it was not, so he decided to stay.

Gay recounts her mother's memory of the War of Independence – when her mother was a teenage girl – and how the family was kept safe by their neighbours:

> the IRA broke into the house and at gunpoint demanded that the farm be handed over to Catholic farmers. Her father was in a wheelchair [...] Her memory was that 'he shook at the point of the gun.' Her three brothers fled across the fields to their Catholic neighbours. They had been warned that the local IRA were on the way [...] When the brothers returned the following day, my mother had a memory of them sitting on a kitchen chair with their feet in an enamel basin, whilst she and her sisters picked the thorns out of their feet. They had left in a hurry in their stocking feet and raced across the fields to safety.

Gay records her mother as saying that her family, a large, comfortably-off farming family, were kept safe by the young men who worked on their farm, 'They used to ride their bikes over to see us every day. We were very grateful. For a while some of them lived in the house with us for security.'

Bob's grandfather had unionist sympathies but was politically inactive. One day during the troubles, he went to retrieve a spade from a neighbour who had borrowed it:

> When he knocked at the door it was not answered straight away, but he could hear hurried movement within. When the housewife eventually answered, she turned around and said to those within the bedroom beside the kitchen, 'It's all right, it's only Joe.' A few of her sons emerged from the room. They were in the IRA and on the run and had, perhaps unwisely, come home for some rest and food. One of the sons chose to accompany my grandfather down the road, much to his discomfiture, as he would not have wished to have been seen with a gunman, any more than he'd have wished at that time to have

been seen in the company of a policeman. At the beech tree near our house, the gunman shot at a crow. Almost immediately an engine was heard—almost certainly a police vehicle in those times. The gunman fled up through the fields [...] Clearly, my grandfather was implicitly trusted not to betray the men.

Emma says:

> My paternal grandparents lived in a house between two roads. One night, the IRA lads arrived on her doorstep looking for shelter. She [Emma's grandmother] brought them in the front door and left them out the back and over the wall to escape down the other road – then calmly answered the door again for the Black and Tans telling them she was not sheltering IRA lads.

Miriam's family lived next door to an IRA man. On one occasion, the Black and Tans, having been tipped off, got the wrong house by mistake; they went to her family's and made an immense mess before heading next door and causing even more chaos.

Memories of the Black and Tans portray them as terrifying figures who terrorised Protestants as well as Catholics, or put them in the difficult situation of appearing to be collaborators – but who could also be more lenient with Protestants when they had been identified to them as such. Hugh Maxton, author of *Waking: An Irish Protestant Upbringing*, had a relative who told a story about travelling home from a job, blasting stones, and coming across the Black and Tans while he had dynamite in his pocket. His neighbour, who knew this, told them not to bother searching him as he was a 'fuckin' Protestant bastard' and 'one of yees', and so he escaped unscathed.[261] Robert's mother often told him about when her own father was seized in the middle of the night from his home, presumably by the Black and Tans. Nothing happened, but there were several agonising minutes while the family sat inside waiting to hear a shot. Robert comments that while some today envision the British forces at that time as targeting Catholics, they did not know the difference between Catholics and Protestants and did not care, because they were simply 'undisciplined'. Prudence remembers hearing about her father's experience, 'The Black and Tans pulled my father out of the bed, to look for guns under the mattress. But, he reckoned, because they knew it was a Protestant house, that they didn't feel the need to wreck anything; they just left.' Robert relates his grandfather's experience. When the Black and Tans arrived, he was 'approached [...] to allow his hayshed to be used for soldier lodgings one night [...] this put him in a very difficult position.'

Stewart tells a story of his grandfather providing help, under difficult circumstances, to neighbours with whom, on political matters, he might not have agreed:

> During [the troubled times] when the Black and Tans were on the rampage, my grandfather Paul hid a group of five Old IRA men in a hayshed for one week. I was never told about this, and only found out about this in the 1980s from [someone] who, at that time, was commandant of the IRA [locally]. He was amazed that I did not know this, and when I checked with my father [...] he smiled and said his sister [...] and he brought out food twice a day to the men in the hayshed, and he was shown how to use a rifle at the age of 5 years.

Olive's mother often related stories about the Black and Tans, including one about how their family helped to keep their neighbours safe from them. One of their neighbours was 'on the run' so they left a window open at night for him to sneak in and sleep on the sofa. One night he didn't come, but the Black and Tans did; someone had told them the family was hiding him. The family thought they were 'going to be burnt out', but instead the Black and Tans seized a new bicycle ('a big investment at that time').

Helen's family lived in an area of Dublin located near two barracks. One night there were snipers at the end of their garden, and the Black and Tans stormed into their house at a time when the children had measles and were sleeping on the floor beneath the window for fear of stray bullets, 'Granny had just baked cakes and they ate everything that was in the house and up-ended everything [...] looking for guns. She always said, "I hope they all got measles afterwards".'

While many Protestant families remained on friendly terms with their Catholic neighbours, between 1920 and 1923 harassment and persecution sometimes escalated to 'murder, arson and death-threats', which resulted in Protestants in small towns and rural areas living with great anxiety, waiting for and worrying about the 'next knock on the door'.[262] A total of 275 Big Houses were burned down during this period, most of which were owned by Protestants. According to some estimates, at least 400 Protestant homes and businesses were burned down overall.[263] Honora says, on the topic of a house belonging to the local gentry, 'The castle was burned by the IRA in 1921. [The owner of the castle] was taken capture and released after three weeks [...] he never got over it and went to live in England, as did many other Protestants at the time.' As well as Big Houses and ordinary homes, sometimes rectories and even churches were burned down.[264]

West Cork famously saw high levels of political violence,[265] including the burning of over a third of all the Big Houses burned in the whole country. Tom Barry, the leader of the IRA in West Cork at the time, wrote that their only fear was that they would run out of loyalists' homes to destroy. They felt that if the republicans were to suffer, the supporters of the British should suffer too, 'West Cork might become a barren land of desolation and misery, but at least the Britishers would have more than their full share of the sufferings.'[266] Between 1917 and 1923, in Cork, 747 people (of all religious denominations) were confirmed as deaths owing to political violence, and many more disappeared in situations that suggested that they had probably been killed too.[267]

In 1922, for example, seven Protestants were killed in the area of Dunmanway.[268] Over the course of a few nights in April 1922 (during a period of truce after the signing of the Anglo-Irish Treaty, two months before the civil war began) a spate of killings targeted an all-Protestant civilian group ranging from 16 to 82 years of age, perhaps because they were thought to be involved in anti-Sinn Féin activities.[269] Between 1920 and 1923, in that area, the IRA deliberately shot over 200 civilians, 'of whom 36% were Protestant: five times the percentage of Protestants in the civilian population', while 85 per cent of the homes burned in Cork belonged to Protestants.[270] The *Church of Ireland Gazette* claimed that 'a campaign of persecution is in progress', clarifying that Protestants did not feel persecuted by the government or most ordinary people, but that a republican minority was singling them out.[271] Panic spread among Cork Protestants and many went into hiding or fled, some apparently leaving without even their overcoats or handbags.[272] Trainloads of Protestants, convinced that a pogrom was imminent, flooded into Cork City and onto boats and mail trains leaving Cork for England. The killings around Dunmanway were quickly condemned by authorities both in favour of and against the Anglo-Irish Treaty, and a local IRA intelligence officer, Sean Buckley, stepped in to stop a reoccurrence.[273] While many of the 'refugees' returned a few months later, it was often just to sell their property so that they could leave permanently.

The events in Cork are probably the best known and were the most violent, but many Protestant communities and individuals were targeted; Gemma Clark points out that letters circulated during the civil war often threatened not just specific Protestant individuals but also whole families. The most vulnerable were families at either end of the social spectrum: wealthy landlords and working-class Protestants. Businessmen tended to fare well.[274] Lynne, who is from a business background, relates how her family's home was saved, 'there was a threat to burn down [the house] and my father pointed out that it would endanger the jobs in the brewery. That was the end of that.'

Some Protestants feel that the experience of their families in those troubled times is often overlooked or understated because it makes people uncomfortable. An obvious example is that of the massacres and intimidation around Dunmanway.[275] Matthew remembers his own family's part in this story, 'In 1922, my father was compelled to leave his farm in Dunmanway [...] a chap came up to him in the railway station [...] and said to him, "[...] if you are not gone by tomorrow morning, you'll be shot dead." And that night there were twelve people shot dead in Dunmanway, so he was gone, and my mother followed.' Matthew believes that his father may have been targeted because he fattened cattle and had them shipped directly to England. This may have led to people thinking that he was a spy and therefore an enemy target. Even before that point, his family had had a traumatic experience. Matthew's mother was pregnant with his older brother when one day, at two or three in the morning, a group of five or six IRA men came to the house and demanded a meal, 'and it wasn't a question of bread and butter and tea'. She had to get out of bed and cook them bacon, potatoes, and cabbage. She went into labour a few days later and delivered a premature child who died after three weeks; people assumed the shock had led to this loss. The family also had many of their animals stolen, as many did at the time, including cattle and their pony and trap, although the latter turned up a week later, many miles away.

Matthew is very proud that, although his parents were compelled to leave for several years, they returned and resumed farming in the same area. They had tried farming in England but were desperately homesick. As they had had to sell their first farm, they needed to buy another. But in one respect they were very lucky: whereas many Protestants reported being threatened by people who wanted to get their land for a low price, Matthew's family sold through an auctioneer and received a fair price. He says that many of the Protestants in this area either did not return or remained very bitter and angry towards Catholics; he gives the example of an uncle who chastised any Protestant who bought an important item, such as a horse, from a Catholic, 'He would say, "Do you *know* what you just did?"'. This uncle had lost eleven friends to sectarian violence, and he was left with an unforgiving 'fixed mind'. However, Matthew remembers his father's attitude towards the people involved in the deaths of his acquaintances and friends, 'I remember the day well [...] he was called to the [...] hospital to see this farmer who lived only two miles away from him [...] and the man said to him [...] "I want to confess to you that I killed a whole lot of your people. Will you forgive me?" And my father said, "Of course I will. You only did what you thought was right."'

Mariah says that, in recent years, the increased visibility in the media of stories about terrible things that happened to Protestants at that time opened a dialogue with the older members of her family, who had been told stories about events involving their relatives and who now found that the media coverage helped them to discuss these matters. She describes the murder of two brothers in the midlands, 'all simply because they had seemingly talked to somebody, but they hadn't really',[276] and contrasts this murder with the views of 'real extreme Republicans who still say, "Oh no, there wasn't a deliberate policy to wipe out" Protestants.' She says 'the facts are the facts' and points to the decline of the Protestant population. She says she was 'surprised but not surprised' to learn that the violence had affected her family and that stories about it had been suppressed for several generations.

Ed says many of the people who suffered at that time were targeted because they were considered 'informers', but insists that 'these people, far from being labelled in such a derogatory way, should have been regarded in the same way as "whistle-blowers" are today.' In fact, most Protestants were not informers during the War of Independence. While the police force and the army needed information on where IRA members were hiding, or what their plans were, 'with the exception of a few isolated individuals, Protestants did nothing to provide such intelligence, and generally avoided contact with soldiers and policemen'; one policeman stated that it was hard to get any information from Protestants 'because they were afraid to be accused of giving us news [...] they kept away from us altogether.'[277]

Ed states that he has 'come across families who still carry the scars of a grandfather or great-uncle who had been killed or attacked at that time. These families, for the large part, still live with the knowledge that not far from them are the descendants of the perpetrators.'

Although perhaps only a relatively small number of Protestants were directly impacted by serious violence during this period, the conflict that they experienced, directly or indirectly, or that they heard about from friends and neighbours, contributed to a polarisation in society. In these circumstances, the diminishing Protestant minority felt the need to stand together against a wider population often perceived as hostile or at least indifferent to them, or to leave and try to start a new life somewhere else.[278] The psychological impact of the Troubles lingered, 'It was not a question of living in constant fear, but of an anxiety that what had happened once could – in certain circumstances – happen again.'[279] Morale deteriorated to the extent that the bishops of Cashel and Ossory publicly appealed to their congregations not to emigrate.[280]

Stories about this awful time can be offset by stories of the positive relationships maintained between the local Catholic and Protestant communities. William says, 'We were one big happy family. Everybody. It was lovely. If you wanted your neighbour, you went to him. They came to you to help dig potatoes [...] It was just a fantastic community. No bitterness or anything like that.' Then he adds, 'I had heard it from my grandmother [...] at the time that the IRA were knocking around there was actually a meeting held to have my grandfather shot [...] Just because he was of a different persuasion.' 'Thank goodness' they did not shoot him, he says, 'because my grandfather [...] was a real gentleman. He was a lovely, happy man.'

For this family, and for many others, believing that things had always been fine, even in the face of compelling evidence to the contrary, became essential to continuing to live in their communities. After the bad times, they had to return to the co-operation and friendship that make sharing a rural area so much easier. William says that while it has not always been easy for him to read about history because of the things Protestants are said to have done, he has come to accept that much of it is true, and therefore that some of the bad things that happened to people like his family could be justified on these grounds. This has helped him to make sense of the conflicting stories of friendship and aggression that he had heard while growing up:

> I have to say this to you, I did realise that in fact the so-called [Protestant] baddies *were* baddies in lots of cases and, I mean, I am a great person to read and I love to read […] and I think that I grew up with a feeling and I still *have* this feeling that, in fact, the people who sort of, the people who were really natives of this country, and that's the Roman Catholic folk, that they had a good grouch, and they were entitled to make their grouch.

Early Decades of Independence

The Irish parliament, Dáil Éireann, ratified the treaty with Britain on 7 January 1922. When Éamon de Valera and his followers urged the IRA to continue its campaign because of their opposition to the treaty's terms, Protestants were left on the side of Michael Collins by default.[281] On 12 May 1922, the General Synod of the Church of Ireland sent representatives under Dublin's Archbishop Green to make a representation to the Sinn Féin provisional government, represented by Michael Collins and Michael Cosgrave, to request that the basic rights of citizenship be extended to Protestants in light of the new circumstances.[282] Collins assured them that they were welcome to stay and that his men would protect them.[283]

When the first senate was appointed, Protestants were very well represented, including sixteen members who had previously held unionist views.[284] The new government reassured Protestants that they would be regarded, 'not as alien enemies, not as planters', but 'part and parcel of the nation'. Twenty out of sixty seats in the senate were reserved for Protestants, a number vastly disproportionate to their numbers overall.[285] Those who had been affected by raids and thefts had the right to apply for compensation from the state. The Damage to Property (Compensation) Act was passed in the Dáil on 12 May 1923, after which those affected (who were not all Protestants, although Protestants were disproportionately targeted) could fill in forms and send them to the authorities. A successful application resulted in 'the decreed award, with adjustments and conditions'. The state was poor, so they could only compensate so much; it did not cover things like jewellery, art, or other personal valuables.[286]

Did the government's position on compensation do anything to address the concerns of Protestants from modest backgrounds? Clark writes of difficulties to the historian in exploring the experience of Protestants after the troubles of the 1920s, who were 'a small periodically persecuted minority [that] wanted to keep a low profile following this particularly intense period of political upheaval'.[287] There are stories about Protestant anger and their perception that the Catholic state appointed a few prominent Protestants to high office to give the impression that Protestants were treated fairly while, on the ground, ordinary Protestants often felt that they were overlooked. To add to this, many strongly disliked some of the nationalist leaders who had been instrumental in achieving independence. One group of friends, having observed the trend towards nationalism in Ireland in the 1890s, had decided to learn more about it and were in a good position to adopt a more nationalist stance after independence; they decided to stay in Ireland when so many of their peers were leaving. These efforts, in effect, were to pave the way for the next generation. Violet, whose grandfather was among this group, says:

> my grandfather and a group of his Protestant businessmen and Masonic friends, had joined the Gaelic League in the late 90s [1890s] to learn Irish and more about Irish heritage. Many of these people had no great interest in the nationalist cause but after the terrible executions in 1916 they re-evaluated their relationship with the nationalist cause. After the formation of the Free State, many Protestants upped sticks and left Ireland, terrified of the future – or perhaps more afraid for their finances. Grandfather felt strongly that the Protestants should contribute to the new state and my father was encouraged to return [from England, where he was working], to retrain as a chartered accountant, and to make his life in Ireland as an Irishman.

Protestants in the Free State remained a very small minority, although there were pockets (especially in border areas) where they were a large minority or even a local majority. Many (especially in Dublin and other areas with very established upper- and upper-middle-class communities) were better-off and better educated than average and thus were shielded from discrimination, but less well-to-do Protestants, in rural areas with small Protestant populations, were now in a difficult situation.

To assert its independence and culture, the new state focused on what most distinguished it from Britain, especially Catholicism, rural life, and the Irish language. For many people, to be Irish also meant being Catholic. For the Protestants who had been 'left behind', it could be hard to figure out what their identity was supposed to be now. Many still felt loyal to Britain[288] but this would start to change. Davina remembers hearing about people leaving the Free State and what her parents thought of it all, 'A lot of Protestants left [...] They were frightened of what would happen, you see. My father didn't agree with it. He said they shouldn't go. He said they should stay where they were and hold their own.' Eleanora says, although few of her own family members emigrated in early independence, in general the Protestant community was 'denuded' at this time. Many sold their farms and moved to the other side of the border.

In the Free State, it was hard for many Irish families to express pride in the sacrifices made by their young men in the First World War. In many Protestant communities, expressing pride and sorrow encompassed not just mourning but also a way of expressing feelings about their identity. While there was little fanfare about Remembrance Sunday in the small parish church William attended, those who had lost their lives in the First World War were mentioned by name, and there was one elderly gentleman in the congregation who had survived the war. William remembers, as a little boy, reading and rereading the plaques that had been mounted on the wall of the church in memory of the boys who had been killed, and one that always moved him greatly. The dead boy had been the son of a local land agent, and he had fought in India. The following words were inscribed on the plaque, 'If nothing else, there's some corner of foreign fields that is forever Ireland.'

Tensions eased but continued during the early decades of independence. The Protestants that remained were still vastly over-represented, statistically, in the professional and wealthier classes. In 1926, although just 7 per cent of the population was Protestant, they represented '40 percent of the lawyers, 20 percent of the doctors, and well over 50 percent of the bankers'.[289] The government was generous to the Protestant community in many ways (especially wealthy and influential business people, whom they did not wish to see leave, bringing their capital with them). Protestants were given a disproportionate number of important positions: Douglas Hyde served as the country's first president, and the first Free State Minister for Finance, Ernest Blythe, was also a Protestant. Both were cultural nationalists.[290]

At grassroots level, however, tensions were still felt, and Protestants from more ordinary backgrounds did not always find the change easy. Eustace discusses his grandfather's experience as a tailor's cutter:

> My father must have been off school because his mother asked him to take a message to his father, who was at his work as a tailor's cutter in the city centre. He always had his lunch at [a particular bakery] so my father set out to meet him there. As he got to [the] street he heard a lot of shouting. As he got nearer, he could see his father walking along [...] followed by a crowd of people who were shouting and jeering at him. My father was scared but thought that his dad would be safer if he managed to get inside [the] bakery. Grandfather did reach the door of the bakery but, instead of dashing inside, he stood at the door, faced the crowd and looked around as if there was nobody there. Then he reached into his pocket and took out his pipe; then into another pocket and took out matches. He lit the pipe, looked around, and then turned and went inside. It transpired that this scene had been going on for some time, with the crowd following grandfather each lunchtime. He had not mentioned it at home and continued going to work as usual. It appears that there were three Protestants among the larger number of people working in the tailoring establishment [...] the rest of the workforce had demanded that the Protestants be sacked. The management had refused to do so but asked the Protestants to stay at home for a while. The other two did so but grandfather would not [...] This resulted in the lunchtime scenes [...] It appears that neither the management nor grandfather gave in and the workers' protest eventually petered out.

Waning tensions continued to emerge on occasion. Ed recounts a story that his father used to tell:

when he was a young man in [a city in the south-west] in the 1930s he was in a pub one evening when he was roughly accosted by a man who invited him outside. He apparently took exception to my father simply because he was a 'Protestant.' My father accepted the invitation. As he told me, 'two of us went down the alley beside the pub, and only one walked out.' The physical nature of his work and general health meant my father was fit and strong, so he was the one that walked out.

Hugh discusses going to school in the 1930s amid the burnt-out remains of Protestant farmhouses, hearing and half-hearing stories about the things that had happened. His family had a local business and a rather nationalist outlook and no desire to leave. An acquaintance had also grown up hearing about the house-burnings but from a different point of view, as he was a Catholic. They worked in the same field and, together as adults, occasionally travelled on the train to Dublin. On one of their trips, they started talking about the burnings:

He seemed to have great respect for Protestants, but he said, 'When I was a boy, the parish priest used to get up every Sunday in church and he would denounce the Protestants and he would encourage us to burn them out,' and he said, 'Well, I was only a boy, I wasn't in-volved, but all the Protestants in [that area] were burned out and the [Protestant] church today is derelict.'

Hugh, a schoolboy in the south-west during 'The Emergency' (the years of the Second World War), says that people were anxious that the general unrest might spark anti-Protestant sentiment and violence like that of the early 1920s. One night it was rumoured that Germans had landed on the Irish coast near his boarding school. The local defence force gathered their men, who were told to collect guns and march down the street to a lorry that would bring them to the supposed landing. But, he says, as they went past the Protestant boys' school one of the men 'broke ranks and started march-ing up to [the school]'. The other men said, 'Hey, hey, you are going the wrong way, what are you doing?' and he said, 'I am going up to shoot the headmaster!' He had to be restrained from committing what would have been a sectarian act.

The Eucharistic Congress was held in Ireland in 1932. The main event was held in Dublin on 22–26 June; it was a very important, exciting year for Catholics, with celebrations all over the country. The congress was a matter of great pride to most Irish people, a triumph for Éamon de Valera,[291] and an exuberant celebration of Catholicism. It was also a clear illustration of the close bond between church and state.[292] The *Irish Messenger of the Sacred Heart* newspaper hoped that it would help 'to rid us of our national inferiority complex'.[293] An official *Handbook of the Congress* was published, urging 'all householders' to ensure that they had a lighted candle in 'at least one window' for the event. Businesses were instructed to illuminate their premises in honour of the occasion, and there was speculation that some Protestant-owned businesses might not and might therefore lose the patronage of Catholic customers.[294]

De Valera greeted the papal legate, Cardinal Lauri, by saying, 'we remain ever firm in our ancestral faith, answering unto death to the See of Peter',[295] and made it clear that, for him, 'Irish' meant 'Catholic', and that Ireland was an 'essentially Catholic nation'.[296] About a million people attended Mass in Phoenix Park, and the famous tenor Count John McCormack sang 'Panis Angelicus'.[297] It seems unlikely that most Irish people gave much thought, in this context, to their Protestant neighbours. After all, the congress had nothing to do with them.

But some of the Protestants who experienced the celebrations as outsiders remembered the Catholic celebrants 'rubbing in' the fact that they did not really belong. George Russell (also known as Æ), the writer, painter, and a key figure among Protestant cultural nationalists, was reported to have fled Dublin for the Wicklow Mountains, where he was supposed to have 'called on the heavens' for bad weather during the festivities.[298] Three young Protestant clerks from Bray were given stiff fines for interfering with papal flags as they returned from a dance.[299] Feelings of resentment were mirrored in actions taken by clergy and scholars in the Church of Ireland. A history of the Church of Ireland was commissioned to coincide with the Eucharistic Congress, with the idea of cementing the Church as an important aspect of Irish life even as many of its congregants continued to experience a sense of 'the erosion of standing, income and leisure'.[300]

Donald recalls a story he was told by a family friend, who was a young boy in 1932. He was walking home in his uniform from a Boys' Brigade meeting when he came across a large group of people going *en masse* to an event that was part of the Eucharistic Congress. In his uniform – and therefore clearly a Protestant – and walking in the opposite direction to everyone else, he felt that he was 'running the gauntlet'. He remembered that moment as a definitive one, when he realised that he would never really belong.

Living in a Republic

Ireland became a republic in 1948, building on the constitution of 1937 and ten years in which the president (the first being Douglas Hyde) had replaced the British governor-general. The constitution underlined the privileged position of the Catholic faith, using 'Gaelic, Catholic and nationalist symbols generously'.[301] Hubert Butler, a contemporary Protestant essayist, welcomed it, saying that the British crown had become like a 'fly on the nose' that stopped Ireland from focusing on what really mattered.[302] Butler felt that the new republic might provide a way for Protestants to develop a sense of belonging in a way that had so far eluded many of them. Opinions were divided. Hope remembers 'crossness' and a feeling that the split had been deeply foolish. Timothy remembers his parents, inner-city Protestants from unionist backgrounds, being upset and retaining a deep sense of loyalty for Britain that was bolstered by the excesses of Archbishop McQuaid, 'I suppose it was during the dominant period of Fianna Fáil, and Dev and all of that type of stuff, and John McQuaid, and stuff like that. "We're living here but, you know, it's not great, is it?" That sort of thing. They would have compared [...] classed the other side as always greener.'

James, whose father was a member of the clergy, remembers that 'My father prayed for the British monarch every Sunday in the three churches he looked after, and no one objected until the local ex-landlord suggested this was not wise in the Republic of Ireland [...] Then the President and 'all in authority' took the place of the monarch in Sunday prayers.'

Harry remembers the local Boys' Brigade making changes in 1948, 'the Boys' Brigade had a Union Jack, and they used to carry it on church parades. But when Ireland declared their break away from Britain, we had to roll up the flag. It was left in the church at the time, but I don't know where it is now.'

The Troubles

The Troubles in Northern Ireland erupted in the late 1960s. Although the Troubles might have felt far away to many in the Republic, for those in border areas they were very immediate. In the three 'other' Ulster counties, Monaghan, Donegal, and Cavan, the Protestant population had been high at the time of partition – up to 25 per cent in most areas and rising to 40 per cent in some pockets. They had found themselves on the wrong side of the border, and many had 'suffered decline in their economic prosperity, political power [...] the loss of their British citizenship and unionist political identity, and a profound sense of betrayal.'[303]

Billy's experience was that his family, and other members of the Protestant community in his border area, considered themselves oppressed. He was from a poor family and 'all we knew was survival.' His father had died at a young age, and he and his brother had a difficult childhood. If they had new wellingtons or shoes, they were not allowed to play in them in case they 'kicked out the toes'. His father had been a drummer in the local Orange Order band and they had abandoned the family when he died; his mother was still very hurt and bitter because of this. Knowing nothing of history, he assumed that Protestants in Ireland had always been badly treated. Later, when he studied history, he learned that Catholics had in fact suffered terrible oppression for centuries and that things had not always been as he experienced them. The historical perspective he acquired helped him to see the Troubles in Northern Ireland in a more nuanced way.

Heather had family members on both sides, including two cousins who served in the RUC throughout 'all those bad years'. One was very badly hurt in an explosion while trying to save a man's life and the other was caught up in a large bombing. Both were seriously damaged, psychologically. These episodes brought the violence in the North to life and although her family lived on the southern side of the border she felt it necessary to be very careful, 'We really did batten down the hatches. You kept your head down. You didn't talk about it.' Not being able to mention the terrible things that had happened to her cousins in the North was hard; for security and other reasons, she could never mention these incidents to her friends. Her family abhorred all the terrorist violence, but they were especially angry with loyalist Protestant terror groups that would 'take up arms and guns and bombs and murder in the name of Protestants'; they feared that there would be repercussions for them from 'the wider Catholic community round us' as a result of these crimes.

Reggie says local Protestants were anxious of the fact that they could be targeted if they travelled to the North, and that stories were told about frightening experiences that occurred on trips to the other side of the border, 'Protestants from here going across to the north, maybe just going visiting someone, and they'd be followed at night [...] in a car, and then the car would turn off, but it was sort of [...] an exercise in frightening them not to go back in here again.' Reggie also recalls that when IRA members died, local businesses were instructed to close on the day of the funeral as a sign of respect and that, out of fear, they all did – including Protestant-owned businesses.

Billy, living in the border area, says there are greater differences between Protestants in Northern Ireland and those in the Republic than between Protestants and Catholics in the Republic. Nonetheless, the period of the Troubles was very hard for him and his community, and there were many cases of intimidation and destruction of property. He is delighted that things are better now, but comments that people are being told they must just forget and that it is very difficult to forget a defining trauma of one's life. He feels that the Protestant community on the southern side of the border is the only one being asked to forget all the wrongs that were committed against it, while the Catholics can happily commemorate the many wrongs suffered by their ancestors, in music and words, in a public forum.

Further south, the most common reaction to the Troubles among the Protestant community seems to have been a redoubling of efforts to distance themselves from Protestants in the North. For Protestants who lived far away from the border areas, the Troubles seemed largely to have nothing to do with them. Robert says the general feeling in his community was that the Protestants in the six counties were irrelevant to them and that their sympathies lay much more with the Catholics, because the anti-Catholic discrimination was so egregious 'up there'. They felt confident that their Catholic friends and neighbours did not associate them with the highly politicised, often rather extremist Northern Protestants they saw on television. Beyond border areas, southern Protestants often regarded Northern Protestants with distaste, or at least irritation, while also being concerned that the Northern Troubles would have a negative impact on them. Daphne says, 'I think it's really difficult [saying that you're Protestant] because of what Protestants in Ulster have done. I think it's made the word almost toxic in some ways [...] Even at this stage with people, they sort of recoil if you say you're a Protestant.'

Arthur remembers that his parents ardently disliked both Protestant and Catholic people from Northern Ireland, 'They were all dismissed as bigoted trouble-makers [...] I heard my father say, "If there is anything worse than a Northern Roman Catholic it is a Northern Protestant. Have nothing to do with any of them." Quentin says that Protestants went to great lengths to distance themselves from Northern Irish Protestants, '[We] shared none of the hatred or fear of Catholics [...] We felt no affinity to them [...] we recognised the Troubles in the north to be a cultural issue caused by a genuine oppression of the Catholic population by the Protestant majority [...] We stopped travelling to Northern Ireland almost completely from 1968 onwards.'

Bob attributes the decline in the Protestant 'socials' (which are discussed in Chapter Four) at least partly to the impact of the Troubles, 'In one parish I know of, church socials ceased in 1971 when threats were made after the ejection or attempted ejection of a Catholic from a church social. This coincided with the imposition of internment without trial in Northern Ireland, when long forgotten tensions surfaced once again.'

Violet remembers how discussions of the Troubles highlighted a stark difference between the attitudes of her generation and the one before:

> after Bloody Sunday, there had been a sea change and had I not been stuck at home with small children I would have been at the burning of the British Embassy [in Dublin in 1972]! At the time of the hunger strikes, when Bobby Sands died, I was interviewed for RTE [the Irish national broadcaster] [...] asking my thoughts on how the Protestant South was viewing the Northern 'Troubles.' At that time Protestants were quite polarised – older people supporting the unionist side and younger the Civil Rights side – while abhorring the violence on both sides.

Luke comments that 'In the early days of the Troubles in Northern Ireland I was questioned about what 'my people were doing to RCs [Roman

Catholics]'. In 1972, *The Irish Times* reported rumours that Protestants in south and west Cork had only recently received threats; the same year, Protestants in Sligo suffered intimidation, including vandalism against their businesses. In 1974, following several attacks on prominent Protestants, one man contacted the Department of the Taoiseach to state his concern that he and his friends might need additional security; a Protestant Fine Gael senator was also killed by the IRA in Monaghan that year.[304]

Helen discusses her son's experience while attending a Protestant inner-city school in Dublin in the late seventies and early eighties. Everything was fine, she says, until a Northern Irish politician, Bernadette Devlin, a socialist and republican, came to Dublin. Many people living in the area became incensed when they heard her stories about the anti-Catholic discrimination in the North, and some of them decided to take it out on the Protestant school children in their area. Her son and his friends were beaten by youths who shouted 'Bobby Sands, Bobby Sands' in reference to the hunger striker who had died because of his protest. The youths beat them up and pushed them onto the road when they could; when they could not, they threw things over the wall at them. Once, her son was beaten so badly that he had to stay out of school for a week, and a girl in his class was 'nearly pushed under a bus'.

Ian attended a local Catholic secondary school. He remembers the nuns who ran the school as exemplary and fair, but that the Troubles in the North were ongoing at the time and the daily news reportage impacted on how his classmates saw him and his family. 'Maybe it was my paranoia', he says, but 'occasionally you'd get an uncomfortable feeling, especially after something really bad. They would associate the Troubles in the north with Protestants in the Republic [...] you switch on the TV and there's an atrocity 100 miles up the road and we have the same people in our community.'

Asserting Their Place

Famously, in his role as senator, W.B. Yeats described Irish Protestants as 'no petty people' and 'one of the great stocks of Europe' in an impassioned speech given on the occasion of the government's decision to ban divorce.[305] Another senator, Sir John Keane, made a less poetic but equally strong speech on behalf of his people, describing how they contributed to the nation's well-being, paid their taxes, and provided employment and succour to the poor.[306]

Some Protestants state a sense of grievance or disappointment that their role in Ireland's history is not recognised as they feel it should be.[307] Their stories of nationalist ancestors and Protestant deeds are sometimes related as a way of justifying and glorifying the Protestants' role in the past. Eleanora states that Ireland would not be independent today were it not for the efforts of Protestant heroes in the eighteenth and nineteenth centuries. She says that until Daniel O'Connell, the great nineteenth-century 'liberator' and parliamentarian, 'I can't think of any Roman Catholics who succeeded so well in setting up people and grouping them and, you know, bringing about change.'

Throughout the twentieth century, Protestant families appear to have gone through a process of change that has resulted in different stories about themselves coming to the fore — family stories about the past having been retold and reinterpreted. Today, many Protestants endeavour to associate their family with the 'heroes' and disassociate themselves from the 'villains'. They might boast proudly of an ancestor who participated in a nationalist uprising or qualify a story about a grandfather who felt loyal to Britain, served in the police, or was associated with another aspect of the colonial bureaucracy by asserting, 'lots of people felt the same way at the time, even Catholics', and will often conclude by saying, 'But he felt more Irish than anything else.'

Ian speaks of a great-uncle who had served with the Old IRA in the War of Independence. He was 'one of the Ultras' and had been imprisoned by de Valera. For his family, still loyal to Britain, this was shameful, but at least their house would not be raided by the IRA, like so many others. After independence, his great-uncle married a local Protestant girl and returned to the farm. His escapades were never mentioned again. After his death in the 1980s, an old man from the village requested permission to give him a military funeral with full honours. Permission was denied and the funeral passed quietly in the local graveyard. As the family walked away, several very aged men quietly emerged from the crowd to make a volley of shots over the grave. They were the deceased's IRA comrades — the few still alive after all these years — giving him the military send-off they felt he deserved, against his family's wishes and despite his Protestantism.

Protestants who can claim descent from one or another of Ireland's great nationalist heroes often seem to feel that this is a redemptive quality that compensates for their lack of 'proper' Irishness in other areas. Non-Protestant commentators reinforce this idea by praising qualities in Protestant public figures that exhibit how they distanced themselves from Britain. Daniel Corkery is described as seeing in Douglas Hyde, 'the exemplary Anglo-Irishman who cast off the derivative and exploitive culture of the Ascendancy to identify with the richness of Irish folk culture.'[308] A theme that emerges in many Protestants' stories is the idea that when Protestants were nationalists they were better nationalists than Catholics, and their nationalism also made them better Protestants. Eadry comments on how, as a young woman, she became deeply interested in the history of Protestant nationalists because she saw them as exciting – radicals who did not let their Protestantism 'rein in' their behaviour, as she felt many Protestants did. Norm asserts that:

> it's a common fact that all down through the generations the Protestants have boxed above their weight for numbers, so far as contributing to the future or well-being of our country. If you read true history, there have been Protestants prominent in various fields [...] who have really contributed to the well-being of the Republic of Ireland, all the way down through the generations. Yes, fair enough, a lot of Protestant households were royalists or royals but [...] it has been said more than once that the fiercest nationalist is a Protestant nationalist. There are a lot of Protestants who are fiercely loyal to the Republic in the true, best sense of being loyal to your country. We don't hear that very often.

Conclusion

Heather, who went to a Catholic community school in the early 1980s, remembers:

> I started to puzzle, and it really bothered me that I couldn't find one positive line about Irish Protestant people. And that saddened me. I thought, 'Where am I?' and all you could find were the Anglo Irish and the big houses and the way they behaved in the Famine and the way they did this and the way they did that, and I thought, 'Where's my people?' because they weren't there.

Many people comment on the wall of silence that was built around their recent ancestors' experiences and interpretations of difficult periods in modern Irish history. Everyone knew that bad things had happened but they were not discussed, especially in the case of rural people who were tied to the land and had to choose between 'making a fuss' or getting along with their neighbours, even if some of those neighbours might have been involved in aggressions against them or might have looked the other way while they suffered difficulties. While Marion knows that there were Protestants in her area who got caught up in the violence of the 1920s, 'they'd keep very quiet because they could be shot if they spoke out.' She only started to hear the full story when she was an adult, after those who were directly involved had died. For Marion's generation, the fact that most of the bitterness has receded means that there is finally an opportunity to tell these stories now, before they are gone. Protestant's narratives about the past sometimes carry the potential to challenge dominant motifs in Irish storytelling and help to form understandings of the present.

3. STORIES OF IDENTITY, LOYALTY, AND CULTURE

Protestants tell many stories in which themes of identity and loyalty are embedded, often in a social context in which Catholicism (or at least cultural Catholicism) is assumed. The version of nationalism that developed in the late nineteenth century and became integral to the emerging nation, denying the '"true" Irishness of Protestants',[309] lingers. By 1914, 'Irish and Catholic had become not just interchangeable terms, but Catholic had come to be the inclusive term.'[310] In the creation of this image of Irishness, history 'has been at best selective or at worst distorted', creating a sense of national identity that damaged Protestants' sense of belonging while independent Ireland became essentially a Catholic state 'in which the limits of law and of behaviour were set by Church orthodoxy and the beliefs of the Catholic bishops'.[311]

Irish Protestants and Identity in History

In the 1720s, Samuel Madden said that Protestants were 'envied as English-men in Ireland, and maligned as Irish in England'.[312] William Conyngham Plunket, Archbishop of Dublin from 1884 to 1897, railed against the idea that one had to be Catholic to be Irish and that Protestants were outsiders, complaining that Protestants were 'described at times as aliens', and reject-ing the idea that 'those who call themselves Nationalists ought to have a monopoly of patriotism.'[313]

With the onset of independence, ideas about nationalism were even more closely entangled with Catholic identity and the idea of an all-Catholic population of 'real' Irish people. According to this paradigm, the poorer, more rural, more likely to speak Irish, and more Catholic you were, the more Irish you were. State policy was to promote Ireland as a Catholic, Gaelic, predominately rural society in which Protestants, even those who were rural and poor, were considered different, with 'a consciousness and culture' representing 'different values and norms, different intellectual understandings [...] and different ideals of truth and reality that were diametrically opposed.'[314]

Shortly before his election in 1932, de Valera affirmed that he would give the Catholic Church a special position in his government, saying that, as most people were Catholic and believed in Catholic principles, 'it is right and natural that the principles to be applied by us will be principles consistent with Catholicity.'[315] De Valera was widely disliked by Protestants. Ed's grandmother 'had little time for de Valera'. She blamed him for the partition of Ireland and all the problems in the Free State, and referred to him as 'Eamonn *Devil*'. Liza recalls, 'Because de Valera was so anti-Protestant, he was hated by most.' Ursula's father said that when de Valera died he would dance on his grave.

The nationalist goal of restoring the use of Irish and a 'Gaelic' traditional culture was incorporated into the 1937 constitution. There was an immediate reaction to the new constitution from Protestants – a 'sudden rash of pamphlets' stressing that St Patrick's Christianity was preserved in Protestantism and expressing concern that they were heading rapidly towards extinction.[316] Letters to the *Church of Ireland Gazette* speak of the writers' anxiety that the Protestants would soon be no more (see for example 'A Letter to the Editor', 2 November 1923, p. 576). Famous Protestant institutions such as *The Irish Times* newspaper had to adjust. *The Irish Times* had long catered to the wealthier Protestant echelons of society and was 'the voice of the Irish Protestant gentry'.[317] It continued to cater to the reading needs, tastes, and prejudices of this group despite their dwindling numbers and influence.[318] After a time, however, R.M. Smyllie, editor from 1934 to 1954, could see that the paper had to change to attract more Catholic readers.[319] This Protestant institution, like Protestants in general, had to adapt.

The Decline of Unionism, Rejection of Britishness, and Being Other
When they realised that independence was approaching, Frank's family prepared for the inevitable, 'my grandfather, who had a certain amount of influence in the parish [...] went 'round from one family to another and told them to keep away from this rebellious [anti-independence] attitude, because eventually the Irish were going to get their independence, and there was no point in making a whip for your own back.' Others struggled to accept it and resisted the new reality for decades.

The Protestant gentry had the most to lose from independence in some ways, and their dismay was compared to that of white settlers in Africa contemplating 'government by black men'.[320] However, these wealthy Protestants were also protected by money, education, and property. If they wanted, they could live in a parallel world and rarely engage with Catholics. The state did not want their capital to leave the country and was not inclined to interfere with them. They could send their children to private schools, possibly in England, and avoid encountering the new national curriculum or anything that might challenge their worldview. Brian Inglis (a journalist, historian, and television presenter) writes that the wealthy Protestants of Malahide, a Dublin suburb, behaved just like British colonialists in India after the fall of the Raj, 'not out of calculated defiance but simply because they could not believe that their world could be overturned.'[321] Leland Bardwell remembers that the Kildare Protestants 'still imagined themselves superior, owned most of the richer farms and big houses, and maintained a haughty disregard for the disparagement in which they were held by the growing urban, and largely Catholic, population.'[322] F.S.L. Lyons describes the 'ex-unionists' of the 1920s and 30s inhabiting a 'stifling atmosphere' and engaging in 'an almost hysterical rendering of God Save the King whenever the British team won the Aga Khan cup at the horse show.'[323]

Protestants of every social class and financial means were surrounded by the emblems of the new state: the tricolour, the new national anthem, the new stamps with no monarch's head, the new coins, the new police force and army, the renamed streets, 'the lavish use of Gaelic in official nomenclature', and the politicians and other leaders with a Sinn Féin background.[324] In this context, the *Church of Ireland Gazette* wrote plaintively that it was 'all very well to say that loyalty can be transferred [...] but [loyalty] is an affair of the heart and it is not possible to force the heart to follow the hand.'[325]

In Lily O'Connor's small Protestant school, the children still finished the day by singing 'God Save our Gracious King'.[326] Ursula remembers that 'God Save the King' was still sung on Armistice Sunday in the rural parish church that she attended in the 1930s and 40s, and that this was beginning to become unacceptable; the schoolteacher sat down in protest for the duration of the anthem. Ireland was, of course, still in the Commonwealth then. Joe also remembers Protestants singing 'God Save the King' in the

1940s and comments that 'most Protestants felt different' then; they were a small minority 'in one of the most Catholic countries in the world' and 'would have been happier to remain in the United Kingdom'. He describes the period from 1916 to 1923 as 'disastrous' for Protestants, who lost their sense of belonging to a great empire so shortly after many of them died in the First World War. 'Protestants did not suddenly become nationalists', he asserts.

Heather recalls her grandfather's struggle to deal with the disparities between his days in the First World War and the 1960s and 70s, 'when partition came in, it wasn't encouraged to speak [...] of having British links or to speak about your war experiences [...] [now] it was a different place to be living, with different rules of engagement.' He struggled to reconcile his loyalty towards Britain with the new situation. It did not help that the new Irish state initially tolerated commemorations of the First World War but increasingly tended to suppress them, especially after 1932 (when de Valera came to power), as a way of 'denying legitimacy to any other political tradition'.[327]

Some Protestants were pragmatic. Jim says, 'when the crunch came, and this place became [independent] [...] you had a few choices, you assimilated, and you more or less buried [...] what your beliefs were, or you left.' Richard's family were unionists before independence and had flown a British flag on their roof. His father used to say that it was 'fortunate, in some ways', that his own father had died in 1913, because he would have insisted on fighting in the First World War, which would have made adjusting more difficult.

Richard's grandfather's widow was a nationalist and favoured home rule; she had let Michael Collins use their house, taking over 'the yard [...] and the trap and the pony and everything' for a week during the civil war. Long after that, the family remained loyal to Fine Gael and loathed de Valera. While many Protestants around them left during the difficult years, she and the next generation 'just realised that we were going to settle in Ireland and we weren't going to leave [...] it was where we *belonged*, and we were going to stick it out.'

Richard says that while Protestant numbers dropped dramatically after independence, the ones who stayed worked hard and were respected. If they had left, he says, it would have been to the detriment of the whole country.

His impression is that the 'the ones who left were slightly despised by everybody', while the families that stayed 'have actually contributed and become part of contemporary Ireland' and have been greatly 'respected in their districts'. Honora echoes those statements, saying, 'Those who remained in Ireland, to their credit, made up their minds to live peacefully and "to be the friends of all and the enemies of none" [a quotation from Wesley, the founder of Methodism].' Joseph Ruane and David Butler gathered similar testimony in Cork, 'If they couldn't stomach the changes', stated one interviewee, 'they went, and by and large, those who stayed were those who were quite prepared to give the country a chance.'[328]

Myrtle visited her mother's family farm every Sunday in the 1950s; at that time, they were still clinging to their unionist ideals. She viewed the portraits of King George and Queen Mary on the living room wall as a testament to the family's ongoing loyalist sensibilities. Doris's father continued to consider the 'English King' as the 'bee's knees' throughout her childhood. Remembrance Day[329] was significant in her family and in her school, and she remembers listening to the Remembrance Day service and the king's speech in London on the wireless and having to stand for the British national anthem. 'Imagine that!' she says today.

Iris remembers her father's struggle with his identity in the 1940s and 50s. He remained fiercely loyal to his unionist identity and the British monarchy. 'I mean, he was a fierce loyalist, and he was quite bigoted against Catholic faith', she says. 'A cousin used to send him newspapers from England [...] he used it as wallpaper in the old kitchen. Pictures of the queen and the king, and all the rest of them.' Later, Iris challenged his unionist views, 'I used to tell him why the hell didn't he go and live in England, if he felt like that about it.'

Kate says, 'My father's generation still had an age-old affinity with Britain that still exists, if I am honest, with older Protestants', and Wally comments that he remembers his father being 'almost anti-Irish to some degree [...] more anglicised, listening to the queen's speech on Christmas Day'. Despite his strong Dublin accent, Wally remembers feeling 'more English than Irish' as a child. Others, like Candide, make simple statements of identity that combine both a sense of Irishness and of difference, 'being a Protestant was being a little bit different [...] I also felt one hundred % Irish. We generally knew "who was who".'

Though many had been unionists – albeit, 'for the most part [as] a passive, unexpressed preference'[330] – they became 'ex-unionist', first abandoning
their political unionism and then, gradually, their emotional attachment to
Britain and the empire.[331] A 'trade' family in Dublin adapted quickly, says
Tim, '[They] were proud to take back anyone who had been on the streets
and had supported the Easter Rising.' Clive's family modified its surname
to sound more Irish for the sake of business, '[My uncle] was responsible
for the decision to place an "O" before the family name over the family
grocery shop [...] [he] wanted the family to be seen as Irish and not West
British or unionist.' In the 1930s, the headmaster of St Columba's College,
a Protestant boarding school for boys, opted to make some changes so that
the school and its students would be better integrated. George, who attended the school from 1940, explains:

> many of the families sending boys there would have had unionist
> views, some vehemently so, but the then Warden (headmaster) [...]
> saw that if the College was to survive it must be more Irish-focused,
> and to the horror of many, he invited de Valera to visit, stopped asking
> the British Ambassador to attend as Guest of Honour at St
> Columba's Day [...] and [stopped] the use of 'God Save the King.'

Lisa, who was a child in the 1930s and had quietly unionist parents, remembers, 'we were told to [...] keep your heads down and keep your mouths
shut and don't stir things up. We knew when not to say things [...] [Dad]
was a businessman [...] He'd to deal with the people of the town.' Other
families she knew remained 'West Brits in their hearts', although they too
'kept quiet here and there and they earned their bread and butter and everything'. Candide's parents raised her 'to never cause offence and remember
that our Catholic customers provided us with our bread and butter by supporting our shop'. Horace says that 'My dad would say that as a family we
very quickly became nationalist when the time came. And we also lay low
and lived our lives more quietly afterwards.' Jim's family was instructed to
'keep your head down, don't go into politics and don't rock the boat.' Adam
says, 'My father was very pragmatic [...] he certainly gave his allegiance to
[the new state] because it was pragmatic to do so [...] instead of dying for
Ireland, he felt the right thing to do was to work for Ireland.'

Vivienne remembers her parents' strong sense of Britishness, which waned as one generation succeeded another, resulting in them discarding certain points of view and the artefacts associated with them, 'they had a photograph [*sic*] of King Billy at the Boyne on his white horse [...] I think it's long since thrown out since my brother took hold. Now it's gone to the dump.' Donald remembers a generation gap in his family. On Christmas Day, the older generation felt that everyone should listen to the queen's broadcast on the radio, 'but the younger people felt this wasn't quite right. We felt that it wasn't really for us and I suppose we wanted to be part of the country we lived in, which had a different political setup.' He remembers his family's transition:

> Well, it says on my mother's passport [...] 'These children are not British subjects,' so we were aware from an early age that we were not British subjects, and I think my father was quite happy with that [...] What had the crown ever done for him? But I think he had a sense of exile, having been so close to the British time, having been born in the British time, himself. And grandfather having died for king and empire, and king and empire having then deserted him.

Eadry's family 'would have had great respect for England and the English way but they would not have been unionists' and they were 'very definitely Irish'. 'I mean yes,' she says, 'they all had family in England and relatives in England but then a lot of Catholics did too [...] I don't think that's where their sympathies were.' As a young woman, she worked for the British Army as a nurse. Her perception was that the Irish Army was a 'closed shop' that did not welcome Protestants. She and all her friends shared the impression that, in Ireland, *all* civil service jobs were 'for Catholics', so none of them applied to them. Frank has similar memories, 'Protestants always went in the British army [...] you had the old political divisions, England was the enemy [...] and the Protestants were in great sympathy with England, and everything English was good, as far as the Protestants were concerned.'

In Richard's community, there was much interest in, and loyalty towards, the British royal family, 'there were all these episodes of the film of the coronation being shown and people would organise parties [for Protestants].' A wealthy Protestant family in Hope's area threw a coronation party 'in their turkey house, which had been cleaned out, and we were sitting on bales of straw. It was rather prickly [...] I can remember [...] people being slightly cross [because we were in the turkey house]!' The party was held covertly, because of local IRA activity and because Protestants still felt 'a certain nervousness' and 'kept their heads down about things that they were doing that might cause offence [...] you just kept quiet.' Celeste remembers two films being shown secretly in her church hall – the life of Martin Luther and the coronation of Queen Elizabeth II, 'Parents were told not to tell anyone in advance. I was not told until we got to the church hall.' Gerald has a similar memory:

> In the summer of Queen Elizabeth's coronation, a 'film show' was held in many Protestant venues. The tickets did not say what was showing and the time and place were not widely advertised. It was the film of the coronation. Few people would have seen the event on television and it was not shown in the cinemas. There was always a police presence at the showings. At school, classes were suspended, and we assembled to listen to the BBC commentary.

Gerald describes the showings as 'clandestine' because of a fear that republicans might attack; he remembers the police showing up to keep the viewers safe.

Among many interviewees, the coronation of Queen Elizabeth is mentioned as a time when many young Protestants realised that their feelings of loyalty were quite different to that of their parents. Gerald made a quiet protest at school when the coronation was played on the radio and experienced a growing sense of nationalism as he reached adulthood; his parents, on the other hand, remained loyal to Britain and the crown. Trevor, a young man at the time of the coronation, had a similar feeling of irritation:

> in the 1950s, when the queen was crowned, and there was a *Woman's Weekly,* I think it was, on the counter of a shop down the road [...] a man was there, and he pointed to her and said, 'There's the person you believe in, that you [...] recognise as your leader.' And I said, 'What do you mean by that?' He said, 'There's the person you look after as your leader.' I said, 'That's nonsense!' [...] he thought that I was more subject to the queen [...] I was annoyed that he would think of me like that.

Violet remembers from the 1940s and 50s that 'Most of the Protestants I knew [...] would listen to BBC radio rather than RTE and so had a bias towards British values and outlook.' Albert says a sense of Britishness still lingers in him, although he would never discuss it, particularly with Catholic friends, 'I prefer to let it just quietly be', he says. This sense of Britishness was stronger for his parents and grandparents, who found Irish independence hard to accept; they had always been unionist in outlook and remained so for the rest of their lives.

Ian's family was deeply unionist on one side and 'leaning much more to the nationalist side' on the other. As a young man, he spent some time in Britain, where he learned that British people don't 'know or care' about Irish Protestants. Looking back over his family's history, he surmises that they accepted independence, 'OK, the Empire is gone. We came here because of the Empire and right, that's all over. What's next? What do we do now?' Hazel's family was similarly pragmatic, 'Irish history did not impact greatly on our family [...] crops had to be planted and cows had to be milked. Although my parents could have had British passports, they made a conscious decision to be Irish.'

Harry has learned over the years to question the unionism he grew up with:

> I question myself, what did England do for the Protestants or for the whole of Ireland [...] I don't think they were really interested in Ireland. Yet, I question why; *why* did the like of my parents want to be looking to England, because they were doing nothing for them? Most people [in our inner-city area] were poor, whether you were Protestant or Roman Catholic; in fact, maybe in some cases the Roman Catholics could have been a lot better off [...] I think the Protestants at that stage looked to Britain, even though Britain didn't give a tuppenny ticket about Ireland [...] a lot of Protestants of later periods possibly saw the wisdom of being Irish; if they were born in Ireland, they should be supporting the Irish government or whatever [...] I've come to realise that I'm Irish. I'm an Irish Protestant, and I asked myself, 'What has Britain done for me? What has Britain done for my parents?' On looking back, I say, 'Britain has done *nothing* for my parents and, therefore, has done nothing for me.'

May remembers pictures of British monarchs on the wall and how they were gradually disposed of as the family developed a strong sense of identity around their support for the Fine Gael political party:

> The king and the queen [King Edward VII and Queen Alexandra] were up in our living room but my mother took them down. My parents didn't go into history. They didn't want to talk about it. It was past, we're in the now, and this is the future [...] We were very much Irish in our house. [The political party] Fine Gael was the topic of conversation [...] In the other room we had a picture of [United States] President [John F.] Kennedy and his wife. And then after 1976 [...] my mother took down President Kennedy and put up the whole Fine Gael cabinet.

Feelings of Britishness lingered in May's extended family, but her parents preferred to cling to their sense of loyalty towards Fine Gael, 'if you were on your deathbed you had to get up and vote [for Fine Gael].'

Tim reported a similar sense of allegiance for Fine Gael:

> In local and national elections there was widely perceived to be a 'Protestant vote.' Votes of Protestants could go no. 1 to Fine Gael [...] This was regarded as 'normal' and people would refer to him or her as being 'one of ours.' Indeed, at one stage Fianna Fáil elected a lady who had been a Protestant as their candidate [...] to cash in on the Protestant vote.

Lisa comments, 'the Protestants would be Fine Gael, because they signed the treaty [...] My father [would] always fight the war with Fine Gael, because the treaty was signed.' Hope remembers, '[My father] always supported Fine Gael [...] they always collected at the church gate, and he would be told the week before [...] I remember there was sort of a little ceremony somehow when he was putting in the money for Fine Gael [...] he didn't like Dev.' Everett recalls, 'That was the one thing: "Oh, vote Fine Gael [...] the more Protestant party."'

For those families that resented independence, the association between Protestantism and nationalism was once considered shameful rather than a legitimate source of pride. Eleanora remembers that while the adults in her family knew that the history of Irish nationalism and Protestants overlapped, 'it wasn't acceptable […] you were just told not to say it and that's it.' Douglas Hyde, a Protestant and influential cultural nationalist, is a very important figure in the story of Ireland's cultural revival. His presidency is still a source of great pride to many Protestants, but he was considered a turncoat in Eleanora's community, 'There was no pride in him and his achievements. He would have been very unacceptable.' Gerald's mother had a similar view, regarding Hyde as a traitor because 'he spoke Irish and things like that'. However, as they continued becoming 'ex-unionists', many Protestants tended to look towards ancestors who had participated in nationalist movements or perceive connections with the great Gaelic tribes of the remote past, treating them as a source of reinvention and identity.

Constance discusses a relative who became intensely nationalist in early independence following a stay on the Aran Islands, where she had sought 'to rectify her ignorance' about traditional Gaelic culture. That relative's nationalism eventually took the form of a deep hatred for Protestant unionism and a degree of sympathy for the IRA's terrorist campaign of the 1970s and 80s, although she came from a landed gentry background, still spoke with an Anglo-Irish accent, and was culturally very Protestant. 'I found it very strange', Constance says, describing it as a sense of collective or ancestral guilt. Foster describes this sort of impulse – 'a sense of guilt and compensation' – as one of the factors that had prompted some middle- and upper-class Protestants to 'revolt against their backgrounds' and become involved in nationalism.[332]

Feelings of ambivalence and anxiety about the perception of Protestants as somehow British lingered. In 1977, Monk Gibbon wrote *Am I Irish?* and considered how he was 'only six generations removed from my Saxon forebears' (who had purchased land in Ireland in 1760) and that he was unable to trace an ancestor who was 'my only hope of genuine Irish descent'.[333] In 2012, Patrick Semple was dealing with the same issues. He wrote that as a Protestant he had often been assumed to be 'Irish but not the full shilling'. ('I am neither Gaeilgeoir nor Catholic – but I am still Irish' *The Irish Times*, 17 July 2012.) Neil says, 'I was made to feel an outsider. For so many people, both in Ireland and outside, Irish is synonymous with Roman Catholic.'

Vivian recounts two incidents when his Irishness had been queried. On a bus, a woman who had heard him speaking with the driver asked him if he was English (because of his Anglo-Irish accent). He assured her that he was not and, incredulously, she asked him when he had come over. 'Four hundred years ago,' he said. 'Ah sure, that's probably long enough,' she reassured him. On another occasion, his car was stopped on a country road by gardaí carrying out a routine inspection. Asked to identify his nationality, he said that he was Irish. The garda said, 'You're *not* Irish with a name like that.'

Adam is happy to consider himself 'Anglo-Irish' when the term is interpreted to mean 'people who were planted in this country regardless of their class or their success over the centuries', but he is careful to distinguish between his family and the gentry. William's family's sense of Britishness was very real but 'muted; it was kind of swept under the carpet you know.'

Henry describes his distress when he was confronted with the 2011 census, which asked him to classify his ethnicity. 'In the end,' he said, 'I wrote "NOTHING" in block capitals, because that is what the Irish state thinks people like me, the Protestants of the South, are.' He expresses pride in what he sees as his British heritage. 'I regard [...] the current queen [of Britain] as kind of my monarch,' he says, 'and the president [of Ireland] is my president. I have a president *and* a monarch.' Henry is very aware that this is now a minority view among Protestants. 'That's the thing being a Protestant in the Republic,' he says. 'You never really say anything. I said something once about five years ago, I only let myself get carried away once, and that's because I didn't really know the guy and I didn't really care about the fellow. Otherwise you just keep your mouth shut about politics and religion in mixed company [...] I would not call myself Irish, but I am an Irish citizen.' He is upset about what he sees as the deliberate erasure of Protestant cultural heritage. For example, he says, people are reluctant to refer to the Irish flag as being green, white, and orange, because the orange strip was originally supposed to represented Protestants. 'Senior journalists, very senior journalists, in RTE. They have got it wrong. Adverts on television, on bus stops. They all get it wrong. "It's amber"; "it's gold"; "it's yellow" [...] They don't want to use the word "orange".'

Like Henry, a few Protestants still report a sense of attachment to Britain and Britishness, though they are aware of their minority status (among Protestants) and are often reluctant to discuss it in public. Joe explains, for example, 'While I am a closet unionist my children and grandchildren have no such hang-ups!!'

Stories of Symbols and Signifiers

Rejection of Tradition

For some Protestants, Gaelic culture and tradition[334] were to be avoided. In the very early twentieth century, the Provost of Trinity College, then strongly associated with the Anglo-Irish gentry, stated that Old Irish Literature was 'degenerate' and 'filthy' and that Irish folklore was 'at bottom abominable'.[335] Elizabeth Bowen's mother did not believe in telling her fairy stories, 'for fear that I might confuse them with angels', and as a child she knew absolutely nothing about Irish fairy lore.[336]

Some Protestants continue to identify folkloric traditions as both Catholic and 'nonsense'. Davina says, 'About fairy stories and such, those things would not have been allowed in our house. My mother was very particular about nonsense.'[337] Ted reports, '[Protestants] looked on [tradition and belief] as pagan customs handed down by the druids and did not take any part.' Frances says, 'Protestants are usually against any sort of superstition and anything pertaining to the supernatural was very much discouraged.' Heather says that any talk of tradition was 'an absolute no-no […] if they talked about ghosts they'd be laughed at.'

Others report feeling less hostile towards their area's traditions and beliefs, but that these stories were irrelevant to them. Adam was aware throughout his childhood of stories of fairy forts, banshees, and so forth, but always knew that 'they belonged to the others, not to us.' He mostly heard these stories from the family's employees, and from the governess who taught the children.[338] Oliver remembers being told such stories while exploring the Irish landscape with his father and grandfather, who were keenly interested in archaeology; tradition was discussed as something that belonged to Catholics.

Some Protestants have a complex relationship with tradition and belief that sees them both rejecting it and engaging with it. Billy is disappointed when he encounters a Protestant who believes in 'superstitions'. For him, 'superstitious' Protestants are betraying their culture. He thought, 'What do you do with *this*?' when he was given a bottle of holy water from Lourdes by a friend, who suggested that he use it to cure a sick animal. 'To me it was nothing,' he says. However, so as not to offend her, he brought the holy water home and used it to make a drench (a cure, to be consumed) for the sick beast – which, he adds, recovered. He adds further that there are many beliefs regarding traditional cures in his area, and that these beliefs are held by both Protestants and Catholics. A 'very Protestant' woman he knows was said to have had a cure for bleeding. While he has 'no problem' with Catholics who believe in cures, because that is part of their tradition, Billy was annoyed with his Protestant acquaintance 'I felt that she was doing damage to the faith that she belonged to', he explains. He also explains that he was afraid of banshees as a child. He attributes his awareness of the tradition, and his fear, to the fact that he attended the local Catholic school, 'if everybody else believed it why would you not believe?'

Mabel remembers the Wren Boys who paraded on 26 December with a dead wren displayed on a bush and sang the traditional song about 'the wren, the wren, the king of all birds' in her area. She says that the Protestants never participated. She talks at some length about the bonfire night of 23 June, a widespread tradition in the west. 'In my young day,' she says, 'we were always led to believe that it was "burning out the Protestants" because the big bonfires were always set close to a Protestant area.' Because the Protestants felt that the bonfires were being lit 'at' them, they never attended the festivities, 'They would light the bonfires near a Protestant farm where people lived, usually at a crossroads or the end of the road and it was built in the middle of the road, basically.' Eleanora says that the June bonfire tradition remains popular in her area, and that few Protestants will attend even now. She learned as a child that 'It used to be to commemorate the burning of Protestants as happened in England in, was it [...] Cromwell's time or one of those.' She says Roman Catholics in the area 'would not want to hear' about whether the bonfires were used for intimidating Protestants, but that 'there could be an element of truth in it.'[339] Everett heard a similar account, 'We would never have been let to [the bonfire], because it's [...] "burning the Protestants" [...] that was their night for burning all the Protestants to get them out of Ireland.' Valerie says, 'There was a story that that was to burn the Protestants [...] I heard that said as I grew up.'

Marigold discusses the tradition of prayer at holy wells and having visited one that was considered to have curative powers, and how this was disapproved of by Protestants, who considered the tradition equivalent to praying 'to statues or idols or have anything that would make God second place in our lives'. When such traditions were mentioned, she says, it was in the context of 'something that Catholics do'. Billy relates his belief that traditions around holy wells originated in 'the times of the Famine' when Catholics were starving and discriminated against and had nowhere to worship. They were forced to assemble at places like wells, he says, because they had nowhere else to go. Moreover, he says, in the Catholic tradition, '*anything* can be considered holy [...] and I am totally not saying this as any sort of criticism, but there was blind acceptance.' He considers most aspects of Irish traditional belief as Catholic, superstitious, and embarrassing, and does not wish to be associated with them.[340]

Some mention that, even in families in which music was important, there was a feeling that traditional Irish music and popular ballads were not 'for Protestants'. In Samuel's family, hymn-singing was hugely important instead. All the children learned how to sing hymns and sang not just in church but also in the evenings around the fire, including when his grandmother played the piano on Sunday evenings. They learned classic Anglican hymns and modern numbers by American evangelists. Hope, for her part, remembers a degree of hostility towards Irish music in her childhood home, 'you'd be told to "turn off that jiggety jog" [...] on the radio [...] It was just felt that this [...] was just a noise, it wasn't tuneful, and Radio Éireann, as it was called at the time, was full of it.' May says that music was strictly 'for the glory of God', so young people studied piano in the hope that one day they would play the organ at church. There was little scope for attending musical events that were just for fun or getting involved with traditional Irish music, 'it wasn't to be entertaining yourself.' Harold states that songs were rejected partly because of their lyrics, '"Young Willie McBride" [a nationalist song] and stuff [...] I certainly wasn't encouraged to listen to this stuff. I couldn't relate to it either.'

Active Engagement with Tradition

At a glance, the testimony of many Protestants seems to confirm the idea that Irish tradition is really 'for Catholics'. Some interviewees, like Myrtle, describe 'ordinary' Protestants as 'too sensible' to believe in and recount stories of the supernatural, but they may describe the Protestant gentry as prone to believing in the supernatural. Evelyn describes the local Big House as having been haunted by 'all kinds of ghosts' but says these stories were 'in all probability [...] invented by the people in the Big House to keep the tenants away'. However, despite the relatively common view of 'ordinary' Protestants as 'naturally' less superstitious and 'more scientific', many Protestants also report sharing in a full range of Irish folk beliefs, legends, customs, and more. Sam recalls that 'Ghost stories were a common form of entertainment before electricity came. One person would try to outdo the other, with the result that people were often afraid to walk home in the dark!' Hazel says that the chief entertainments in her area were 'family gatherings and ceilís [when they met in each other's houses] to tell stories, sing, recite, and drink tea'. Barney says that while Protestants 'are not supposed to believe in superstition' many do, 'when you're [...] surrounded by a people steeped in superstition [...] you would stay away from [a fairy thorn]. You would *say* you didn't believe in it, but you would. Why, you don't bother bother till it bothers you.'

In fact, many Protestants often tell stories and subscribe (or used to subscribe) to beliefs, rites, and taboos that are all part of the standard repertoire of Irish tradition. The banshee, for example – the wailing woman who shrieks when certain people die[341] – is described by Mabel as 'following both Protestants and Catholics' and 'covering both traditions'. Mabel's whole family believed in the banshee 'very firmly', and that the spirit followed anyone with an 'o' in their name, regardless of their heritage. She describes two specific encounters with the spirit. Eleanora says that belief in spirits such as the banshee was widespread in rural areas during her youth, and no less so among Protestants. Her mother heard the banshee's eerie cries on the night that her own mother died. Thomas asserts that the banshee followed Protestant families as closely as she did Catholics, and that she was a 'genuine job'. He has heard her 'crying like hell' himself and saw a distant figure running across the top of the town as she did so. The next morning, a local Protestant had died. Joyce's father was followed by the banshee on his way home after visiting his brother-in-law who was ill. 'Something in the ditch' followed him all the way home, making a strange noise. His brother-in-law died the next day. To some, the idea that the banshee might not be 'for Protestants' is offensive and another way of telling them that they are less Irish than Catholics.

Many rural Protestants observed various well-known traditional taboos. They would not cut down hawthorn trees growing in the middle of a field for fear of bad luck, or because those trees were associated with fairies, or for reasons they did not know. Priscilla discusses her fear while walking to school as a child when they had to go past the fairy tree,[342] and how everyone carefully walked on the other side to avoid it. Millie comments that 'the fairy tree had to be respected.' Sam remembers that fairy trees 'would not have been cut back or interfered with [...] in case the stories about fairies were true and you would have bad luck afterwards', and he heard about people who broke the taboo and suffered problems in consequence. Evelyn remembers that 'the fairy bush or "skeag" [...] must be avoided at all costs, and never cut down and forts, of which there are many, must never be interfered with as they were the home of the fairies.'

Mariah says that folklore and traditional beliefs were part of the fabric of her life growing up in the countryside, with little difference between Protestants' and Catholics' views – according to her, Protestants 'would not knock it'. She knew how important it was not to interfere with ringforts, and that one should never cut down a hawthorn tree growing alone in the middle of a field. A local road had been constructed around a fairy tree to avoid damaging it. One year there was a big storm and the tree blew down. The following morning, 'There was horror: "What is going to happen to the parish now?"'

Honor's grandmother 'probably' believed in fairies, 'You couldn't not have drinking water in the house at night because the fairies would be very annoyed about that.' Also, 'My [mother's grandfather] drank a bit and when he was drunk there were two fairies who lived in the loft, with whom he would converse.' Daphne's mother not only believed in fairies but also saw them quite often; she would ask her husband to stop the family car when they were on a drive in the mountains to get a better look.

Edward often heard stories about ringforts, or raths, on various local properties and the terrible fate of those who interfered with them.[343] Protestant farmers agreed that if you had a rath on your land, you simply did not go near it. The attitude of people who formally scoffed at superstition was that it was better not to risk it, 'Why go near them? You're not gaining a whole lot, but you could lose a lot more.'

Thomas's father was 'very superstitious'. Many of his beliefs about the supernatural focused on butter and butter production. He assures me that 'they' (the fairies) used to take the butter. May Day, the first of May, was the fairies' day. Every May Day, when they were milking, his father gave the children a piece of silver Victorian money to put in the bucket; it had to be Victorian silver because 'ordinary' money had less silver in it.[344] This prevented the fairies from taking the milk for the rest of the year. Most Protestant farmers in his area observed this tradition. Thomas relates a story about a farmer from earlier times who found one day that the butter would not come. Eventually, although it was a frosty night, he went out in his bare feet and 'tricked the fairies' cows and brought the milk down and threw it into the churn and churned'. The results were clear, 'Oh, be the Lord God, they couldn't get the dash down, there was so much butter in it.' It did not stop there. The next Sunday, the local rector gave a sermon on witchcraft. As he was leaving, a single elderly lady known as 'The Fairy Howard' gave him a strange look. 'Hiya Reverend,' she said, 'do you see any green in me eye?' Everyone in the parish knew that the Fairy Howard was able to use witchcraft to take butter out of other people's churns and that the green in her eye had something to do with it. Stories about the Fairy Howard are still related in the community, and the ruins of her cottage can still be seen.

Iris recounts a story associated with the local Big House that may hint at resentments towards the wealthy family:

> there's always a wise woman in the locality. They couldn't churn the buttermilk down in [the local Big House] no matter what they did, it just would not churn [...] they got her down and she told them, 'A certain woman is going to come now and look for buttermilk, and you tell her to go, you're giving her nothing and you'll get your butter.' The [wise woman] came looking for it and they sent her off and the butter started churning again.

Ted, who reports that Protestants rejected tradition as they considered it pagan, was nonetheless familiar with the idea that 'a hare was to turn into a witch if chased and was bad luck running around your herd of cows and it was believed that a hare could take milk from your herd and take it to a neighbour's herd.'[345] In his area, the hare was associated with the tomb of a local member of the aristocracy – a 'Lady'. This is a great example of how supernatural lore often also refers to concerns and resentments about inequality.

Andy's family distrusted 'superstitions of all kinds', but his wife's rural family observed various traditional practices. They put hawthorn on their dung heap on May Day to bring luck and 'would never have used gorse to decorate the church as this was said to be unlucky for geese and their goslings'.

Although Natasha's parents were 'very staunch', she grew up knowing ghost stories and other legends. There is an old castle near her childhood home, and local lore maintained that it was haunted by a headless horseman. Her parents were returning from a Protestant 'social' on a pony and trap one night and the horse bolted as something crossed the road in front of them outside the castle. They immediately knew that this was an encounter with the headless horseman. She is inclined, she says, to give the story credence because her father was such a sensible, logical man, and (as a Protestant) not superstitious.

Travers says that a common practice in his area, believed in by Protestants and Catholics alike, was to put eggs in neighbours' potato drills. The person who put the eggs in someone's drills expected their own potato harvest to be enhanced at their neighbour's expense.[346] 'It was ridiculous', he says, but his family was 'very put out' when they found eggs in their drills. He also discusses treating lame animals by following them to see where they put the sore foot and then digging up the sod of turf in question, turning it upside-down.

William's family home was always known as a great 'visiting house' to which all the neighbours would come to talk and tell stories. His father owned a beautiful carved mahogany chair, 'I remember seeing as many as twenty people on that one chair. Well, that sounds like an exaggeration, but there would be one sitting above another.' His mother would make tea, some of the men might have a bottle of stout, and the talking would start; the children listened, wide-eyed, to tales told by the adults about fairies and banshees.

William also remembers a long, complicated story about a 'gentry' family from the area. He prefaces it by commenting that some gentry were very good landlords, but that this story is about a family of 'bad' landlords. Once, during a time of great poverty, a woman called to the Big House looking for alms and was turned away. As she left, she turned around and cursed the woman at the door, telling her that her first-born child would have the head of a pig. The child, a boy, was duly born with a pig's head. As proof,

William provides the fact that there was a picture of the child on a wall in one of the local Protestant churches. His father described it as a painting of a child with a pig's head eating from a golden trough. The child grew up, and to keep him out of sight, the wealthy family had a little house built on an island in the middle of a lake; that was where the unfortunate boy lived out his entire life.[347]

William still finds this story upsetting because, on the one hand, it has been reported as true by people he knows to be reliable and honest, and on the other, it is in stark contrast to his religious views. It makes no sense to him that 'God in his mercy would do that to somebody'. William also knows that stories like this, true or not, are sometimes told about wealthy families at least partly because of the huge historical resentment towards the Protestant gentry. While he feels that this story is probably true, he also understands that someone might want to tell it as a way of expressing resentment. He expresses concern that people might hear stories like this and think that *all* the Protestants deserved to be cursed, or that they were all capable of showing someone the cruelty that, in the story, was shown to the woman who issued the curse and the deformed child who resulted.

Traditional cures are found within the Protestant community in some areas; in some districts, they are even associated more particularly with Protestants. Lucy comments on how a relative had a cure for skin cancer, 'Protestants only went to him at first but, by degrees, everyone went. He was very successful and his relative is still carrying on this tradition.' Valerie gives the example of a local Protestant with a cure for bleeding, 'I used to suffer from terrible nosebleeds myself, and you'd ring him up and say, "Could you do the prayer?" and he'd do a prayer for you […] I don't know what it was, but it definitely helped me.'

Clara knows Protestants with cures for sprains and bleeding, while Myrtle's maternal grandfather 'used to cure horses with various lineaments and potions and was very popular locally'. Joan's family had a cure for the skin disease erysipelas that involved making a paste from butter and herbs and applying it while saying certain prayers. Barton reports Protestants having cures for 'warts, ringworm, convulsions in children'. Lydia's aunt had a cure for bleeding that took the form of a special prayer she had been given by her father-in-law.

Evelyn says Protestants in her area were keen to use traditional cures and often did so;[348] she says that her uncle had the cure for 'The Rose or rosacea'. She describes how her grandmother was cured of a badly sprained ankle by a traditional healer who prayed and tied a piece of string around it, 'She slept soundly all night and was able to get up the next day and get around with a little difficulty.'

Hazel grew up hearing lore about healers and the use of traditional cures. Frances says that Protestants routinely used cures for 'ailments such as mumps, measles, ringworm and burns', 'people would have been led three times round a well, or take three drinks of water from a cup or were led with a horse's blinkers on.'

Everett, the seventh son of a seventh son, is believed to have the cure for ringworm. Their family was poor, and although tradition did not allow them to accept money in exchange for the cure, the gifts that Everett received from grateful clients were useful, 'there'd be people queueing outside the house, and Mother was delighted [...] they'd bring you a bag of potatoes, turnips, things like that. I remember people bringing sugar.' As well as continuing to offer his cure for ringworm, Everett also makes use of the services of a variety of traditional healers; he describes how cures involving prayer can be adapted when the healer is Catholic and the patient is Protestant:

> She used to put a foot up on top of your leg like that [...] 'Now,' she says, 'say the Hail Mary with me.' 'Ah,' I said. 'No, I am not going to do that. I can't say this,' I says, 'I don't know the Hail Mary [...]' 'Oh,' she says, '[...] what kind of prayers do you say?' 'Oh,' I say, 'I'll say the Lord's Prayer. We'll all say the Lord's Prayer [...]' 'Right,' she says, 'I'll say the Hail Mary. *You* say the Lord's Prayer.'

Travers's family had traditional cures, mostly for animal disorders, since at least the seventeenth century (an ancestor, one of Cromwell's soldiers, is purported to have acquired them while helping to sack a monastery). Travers's own brother-in-law has a cure to stop bleeding, which he inherited from his father and has passed on to his son.

Sometimes traditions are marked in a similar, but different, manner. Every May Eve, Olive's father sprinkled salt on all the boundaries and gates of their farm 'to stop the pishogues [fairies] coming in'; otherwise they could 'take the cream off your butter or stop the butter from coming in the churn'. The Catholic farmers observed the same tradition, but they used holy water rather than salt. Olive states that salt was a Protestant – and therefore less superstitious – variation. Priscilla's family have always decorated May bushes (a tradition held on May Day) and she still does it, tying on 'little bunches of flowers or eggshells or the wrappings of Easter eggs'. She contrasts this with the local Catholics who had 'May altars' in their windows. Priscilla identifies May bushes as primarily a Protestant tradition in her area.[349]

Doris and her husband were invited to an event at a local holy well. Although this was 'unProtestant', they went and 'it was grand, [I] prayed with the rest of them and all.' It seems that there was a certain amount of thrill in transgressing a social norm: many Protestants seem to feel, or have felt, that attending rites at holy wells is not suitable for them. But this is one of the most persistent aspects of folk religion in Ireland, and often the rites and rituals have the flimsiest of relationships with official Catholic doctrine. For rural people, activities involving a local holy well can mean many things: they have an important religious element (often with roots in pre-Christian tradition) but they are also territorial rites associated with place, community, and belonging. Moreover, the meaning of a sacred space in the landscape can change and shift, or can be different to different people. By participating in rites rooted in the local landscape, even if they are usually associated with 'the other sort', one can convey the message that 'we belong here too'.

Honora reports that holy wells 'are places of prayer or pilgrimage for our Roman Catholic friends who have a strong belief in the healing powers of the water in these wells [...] I do know of Protestants who have had their warts cured by these waters too.' Travers says many of the Protestants in his area participated quite enthusiastically in local traditions that involved holy wells. The local holy well was marked out with white chains and there was a special day when all the locals attended a traditional ceremony involving prayer and a picnic that he remembers as 'a day out'. There was another holy well a few miles away and many locals went to it on pilgrimage annually. Some filled their shoes with hard peas and walked there in great discomfort. That was a step too far for the Protestants, who stayed at home for this one.

In some areas, Protestants identify aspects of traditional culture that are specific to them. Vivienne says fox hunting was important in her rural area and was strongly associated with Protestants across the socio-economic spectrum. She also pinpoints a local agricultural show as having been a major part of the rural social calendar and says that for many years it was always held on Protestants' farms; she estimates that 75 per cent of the participants have been Protestants. Millie comments that when she was a child some parishes still maintained the tradition of 'the beating of the bounds' at Rogationtide. This refers to a very old English custom that involved a formal procession around the boundaries of the parish on Rogationtide (the Monday, Tuesday, and Wednesday prior to Ascension Day, the fortieth day after Easter Sunday – always a Thursday) and that once included traditions such as whipping young boys or 'bumping' them against the boundary stones so that they would remember where the boundaries lay.[350] Others comment that the habit of gathering free wild food from the hedgerows for consumption was particular to Protestants, identifying this as a persistent element of traditional culture that is dear to them. Olive's family ate boiled nettles every spring, a habit that she identifies as particularly 'Protestant'. She says of Catholic neighbours that 'they'd come to see what you were doing.'

Gerald remembers the telling of sectarian jokes[351] – often very crude – as quite widespread when he was young. They were shared among schoolboys, members of the Boys' Brigade, and colleagues in Protestant-dominated businesses. Even the tamer jokes hint at underlying tensions and sectarian resentments that were current in some elements of the community:

> There was always the joke about the reunion of the Catholic girls' school and the Mother Superior talking to the girls and saying where were you and what were you doing, and one girl said to her 'I'm a prostitute,' and the poor Mother Superior … she said '*What*? You're a what, you're *what*?' 'I'm a prostitute.' 'Oh, thank God for that! I thought you said you were a Protestant.'

Jokes without sexual or obscene undertones but with a sectarian edge were also told in adult circles, including at some of the church socials Gerald attended. He gives an example, 'a woman coming in through customs with a bottle of gin and the customs officer said, "What's that?" and she says, "It's holy water from Lourdes," and the customs officer says, "That's gin," and the woman said, "'Holy Jesus, a miracle, a miracle!'" Jokes like this were also told by comedians at 'work dos', but as there were members of staff from diverse backgrounds at these events, this could be a source of tension depending on the comedian's religious background. The latter joke would have been acceptable for a Catholic, for example, but was offensive when related by a Protestant. Other jokes dealt with social issues such as contraception or the lack thereof; these jokes were sometimes told in a way that poked fun at Catholics, whose religious teaching informed government policy on the issue, 'The rhythm method? I'm not doing it with a ceilí band in the corner!' Hope also remembers joke-telling with a sectarian edge:

> I can remember people laughing at various foibles of clergy and people would have sort of stock parish priest jokes and snide remarks about nuns [...] When people were having tea, were socialising [...] while women were getting tea, men would say, 'Did you hear the one about ...?' [...] one friend of my father's [...] had a lot of these humorous jokes, and my father would quietly enjoy it. He didn't come out with it too much himself, but he would laugh appreciatively [...] They were a gentle humour. I am sure that there were some that perhaps weren't so gentle at all.

Over time, jokes like this 'lost their funniness', as Gerald puts it, and became socially unacceptable. However, Jonathan remembers that there was still a little sectarian joke-telling in his day, 'they used to call nuns [...] "mickey-dodgers" and they used to call priests [...] "fanny-dodgers" and they had nicknames [...] for Catholic people [and] they said, "If you are going to believe in something, you might as well believe in something good," meaning Protestants.'

At the folklore archives in the National Folklore Collection in UCD, one encounters quite a lot of sectarian material, often embedded in legendary narratives that associate Protestants with the devil and so forth. Considering that much of this material was gathered in the earlier part of the twentieth century, when many people had grandparents who had been born in the period of the Great Famine of the 1840s, when a Protestant aristocracy was more powerful than it is today, and when sectarian, racist, and sexist sentiments were less unacceptable, the sectarian element of these stories is easy to understand in terms of historical context. I am sure that the Protestant population told similar stories at one time; early published material aimed at a Protestant audience (such as the writing of John Temple, which is discussed in Chapter Two) certainly abounds in very sectarian, heavily mythologised versions of history that draw on a wide range of folkloric motifs. There might be echoes of a half-forgotten legendary narrative in the story Billy relates about his wife's experience at school when one of the teachers told her that nuns and priests had babies and drowned the infants in a local lake. Today, thankfully, most people are much less prejudiced than before. It is probably too late to gather much of this sort of material, and perhaps it is better not to look for it too carefully.

Tradition on the Border
An important aspect of tradition in some border areas is an involvement with the Orange Order, which marches on 12 July to commemorate 'the conclusive victory of the Protestant reformation in the British Isles': the Battle of the Boyne in 1690. Eustace remembers his border community as 'absolutely different' to that of the Catholics because of their avoidance of the GAA and Irish politics, and because of the membership 'of the Orange Order or associated bands'. Orangeism has been described as 'a mix of fact and fantasy, history and mythology'. Their marches incorporate Orange banners and link important historic events with what are popularly considered noble aspects of British heritage. Although it is rooted in mythologised versions of seventeenth-century events, the Orange Order emerged in the late eighteenth century, more than a hundred years after the battle it commemorates, at a time of considerable unrest among working-class people in the northern parts of Ireland.[352] While the Order is certainly rooted in an uncomfortable history of strife and sectarian conflict, Protestants in border areas often report their experience of it as primarily predicated on music, 'socials', and fun days out in rural communities where there was often very little to do. For many, the political and sectarian aspects of the organisation seem negligible, or even irrelevant. Evelyn remembers:

> On the 12th morning we would get dressed early and go into the
> hall to watch the band getting ready. All the [local] children were

gathered round. There was little or no bitterness in those days and the children of our Catholic neighbours were just as excited to see the bands as we were. When the colourful banner was unfurled, we would all ooh and aah with excitement [...] all the bands would assemble in a field at the station and march together down to the meeting point in another field beside the ocean. We followed behind holding the ropes of the banner [...] the Twelfth was the annual meeting place for friends and family to renew their acquaintance [...] in the evening, the bands could be missing members due to having spent too long in the pub. Others would weave along with their bands trying to look sober, it was hilarious [...] We still have our memories of those more innocent times and [...] can recall them with joy and laughter.

Jim's father played in an Orange band, although he was not a member of the Orange Order (which, he speculates, may have made it easier for him to get a job working for the council). Thomas says that when he was younger parties and events were held in his area on 12 July but that there was very little knowledge of the historical events that the day was supposedly celebrating. 'Down here with the Protestants,' he says, 'it was an opportunity to get out and celebrate and meet friends and everything else [...] you had a *different Protestant altogether* up the North.' Two of his uncles and many of the men he knew played in an Orange band and participated in local 'walks'. His only exposure to music as a child was what was played by the local Orange band, which played 'what the IRA call Protestant rebel songs'. When his own children were learning to play, the band was trained by a local Catholic, although few Catholics would come to listen to the band play at the various events in which it performed: the Twelfth, Remembrance Sunday, and Orange picnics.[353]

Davina reports that while the Twelfth was a Protestant tradition in her border area, it was welcomed in the area by Catholics, and that one Catholic-run local shop stocked 'flags and emblems and lemonade for the Twelfth and had a stall at the field [where the festivities were held]'.

Heather describes herself as coming from 'an Orange cultural background'. Her father was very committed to playing in an Orange accordion band, and all his children were introduced to music by learning to play gospel and other tunes in the band; they performed at church parades and attended 12 July events in Fermanagh. 'I would describe myself as being part of the Orange family,' she says, '[…] we play at 12th of July and at Protestant church services and at northern band parades and picnics which are unique to [this area].' In the past, 'picnics' were run by the various Protestant churches, and members of all the Protestant denominations were invited. They played games 'like catching a greased pig [...] or three-legged races or sack races or egg and spoon'. There were donkey races with 'contrary' donkeys and 'equally contrary young men'. Music was not important at these events; they were for the purpose of coming together as a community for entertainment and refreshments in the form of home-made baked goods and sandwiches. Everything was over by about five or half-past-five, when the farmers left to milk their cows. By the time she had grown up, the picnics were organised by the local branch of the Orange Order and had acquired a much stronger focus on music, with various bands invited to play. The picnics have continued in this format, and as many as twenty-four or twenty-five bands come to play, including bands from the Ulster Scots tradition.

Some point out that in some border communities before the Troubles of the 1960s and 70s, there were often good relations between local chapters of the Orange Order and the bands of the Ancient Order of Hibernians. Eustace reports that he heard of Orange and Hibernian bands that shared their instruments 'and draped them appropriately on different occasions'; Gavin comments that the local Orange Order lent their 'big drum' to the local Catholic band when the 'Catholic' drum was damaged shortly before an important event. '[B]ecause the name of the band was written on it', he comments, it 'must have raised eyebrows'.

For many youngsters in the border areas, learning to play in the local Orange band was the easiest, cheapest way to get a musical training, and it remains an important part of the local culture. Many years ago, Ulster Scots Presbyterians who left Ireland for America brought their music to America, where its influence is still felt – today marching bands play some traditional American tunes along with Scottish hymns. The love of Scottish music, embodied in the bands, is something that Heather identifies as having spanned generations, 'There's something deep within us that that appeals to.' She is clearly proud of her community's rich musical heritage, and is hurt by what she sees as its rejection, both locally and at state level:

It was made very clear to us that we were considered second-rate, that there was a kind of despising of our culture in the Republic of Ireland, that if you had any sense you would never admit in mixed company that you played in an Orange marching band [...] Out comes the absolute wall. You could almost touch it, this wall of silence that, 'OK, so you are a lesser culture, a lesser person than I am. I am good, and you are bad.'

While the Orange Order in the North often has a very political focus, Heather describes her local band as being firmly rooted in musical tradition and faith, and she says most Protestants she knows steer firmly away from politics, 'because of their experiences of history and the past'. Until very recently, most Orange bands in independent Ireland tended to keep their festivities and traditions within the community because they were regarded with suspicion and even loathing. Most people in independent Ireland only encountered the Orange Order when members of certain groups in the North appeared at politically divisive, sometimes violent, events. More recently, there has been some interest in the traditional aspects of Orange culture and music, especially from academics and locals who are interested in knowing more about their neighbours. One very encouraging sign was when the then Minister for Culture, Éamonn Ó Cuív, attended festivities for a particular band's fiftieth anniversary celebration, and even spoke on the stage. There is some hope that, with time, the Orange musical tradition in the Republic of Ireland will be celebrated as a valid aspect of folk culture.[354]

Work and Play on the Sabbath
For many Protestants, the view that the Sabbath is observed, known as Sabbatarianism, remains an important marker of identity as well as a key element of observing one's own faith. Sabbatarianism originated in early Christianity and held that Sunday should be retained as a day of rest and worship; in Ireland, it was historically observed much more strictly by the Protestant churches – some more so than others. Victor Griffin, relating his childhood holidays in Courtown Harbour in the 1930s, writes of the farmers who chatted happily on Sundays and feast days until dark, at which point many of the Catholics went to the cinema or for a dance. 'But for the Protestants,' he writes, 'no cinema or dance-hall. Such breaking of the Sab-

bath was frowned on [...] and any infringement was considered a lukewarm attitude to the faith and the first step on the road to a mixed marriage with the inevitable and dreaded consequence of capitulation to Rome.'[355]

Many remember how important keeping the Sabbath was, even when it caused problems. One of the reasons why Norm's family worked on Sundays was the fear of disapproval. On their small farm, they did the absolute essentials, such as feeding cattle, although it was painfully difficult to stay indoors and do nothing on a bright August day when the hay needed saving, they could see and hear their Catholic neighbours saving theirs, and it was likely to rain again on Monday. Mike remembers 'ripe fields of hay/corn being left idle on fine Sundays, although the previous weeks had been wet and cutting/harvesting impossible.' Bob remembers the same; his father often lost 'crops of hay' because he refused to work on Sundays. June, who grew up on a very small farm in a rocky area where it is difficult to eke out a living, says her family would also never save the hay on a Sunday, although they would often see Catholic neighbours doing theirs. Instead, they would stay in the house or go and sit on the local beach. This was because of the family's strict religious observance and because of the social penalties risked by Protestants who worked on Sundays, 'people would be giving out about them and talking about them, you know!'

Albert says, 'The hay could rot on the ground on account of not getting saved on a Sunday but that didn't count' because you simply did not work on a Sunday. His father had several employees, and he never asked them to do anything on a Sunday other than coming in to look at the stock and ensure that the animals were all right. William remembers how his father never saved the hay on a Sunday, although he and his children often worked late in the evening to do so on other days. Moreover, all the children had to polish their shoes on Saturday morning so that they were clean and ready for church the next day. Anyone who had forgotten to polish their shoes would 'go with them dirty and show yourself up in church'. Wallace remembers that Protestants 'abstained from working on a Sunday. Potatoes were washed, turf was brought in, and shoes were polished on the Saturday so that minimal work was required to be carried out on Sunday, apart from tending livestock.' This tradition was strictly observed in Heather's family, and it is still commonly observed in her area and – albeit less strictly – in her family to this day:

my parents would not turn on the TV on Sunday, or none of us would dream of washing a car, or mowing the lawn, or starting the tractor if it didn't need to be started. You certainly would not make silage or have a contractor or a workman in. We would respect the day as being set apart and would go to church and use the time to physically rest and spend time with family members.

Freddie remembers the first time the rule was breached in his family:

in 1961 or 62 there was Debbie Storm [Hurricane Debbie, 1961, an extremely powerful cyclone] [...] and we had [the farm] all in tillage. We had wheat, barley, and oats and it was in stacks that time. There was no combines [...] But it was all blown down in this hurricane. One of the worst storms going. The worst one I remember. Trees and sheds, and everything. It came out of a Saturday, and Sunday, Monday, Tuesday, Wednesday, they were all fine days and myself and my father were out. That was the first Sunday I remember out working.

Martha remembers an awkward moment early in her marriage when her mother-in-law came downstairs and saw that she had left the sewing machine on the dining room table on Saturday night. She was unimpressed, '"Oh, that should not be there on a Sunday!" so I got rapped over the knuckles for that!' Don's mother told him about the restrictions she faced in her youth, 'if she did any sewing on a Sunday [...] she would have to pick out every stitch in her afterlife – with her nose!' Frances remembers a typical Sunday as 'not a nice day for children', because 'no going to matches or cinemas [...] even going into shops playing games, gardening etc. was frowned on.'

The Sabbatarian rule was closely followed in Joe's family, 'No proper Protestant would ever go to dances, cinema, or the theatre on a Sunday, neither would they participate in team sports. When I played my first away match on a Sunday, my father – a very mild man – was very upset.'

One year, Samuel decided to do the hay on Sunday anyway. It was a very bad year and this was the first fine day. Unluckily, it was the very day the local rector decided to come for a visit. He was extremely annoyed with Samuel's family and said, 'There is no reason for that!'

Not everyone was so strict on the issue. Hope reports that her father 'felt that it was absolutely wrong to waste good weather! If you had had bad weather and you suddenly had a good day […] he would go to church, but he would most certainly and definitely cut the corn or whatever it was that needed doing.'

Mariah says one of her cousins, who was sent to a Catholic school, got involved with the GAA and started training on Sunday, which meant that he missed church, 'And I remember some of my uncles being very disgusted with him.' Neil recalls how his mother prohibited him from engaging in sports on Sundays, especially Gaelic games.[356] For her, 'that was only a Protestant attempt to be counter-distinct from Roman Catholics, who played most of their sport on a Sunday'. However, she considered cricket a perfectly acceptable Sunday activity. 'It's very tribal', Neil comments.

Christopher comments that his family had no interest in Gaelic games, partly because they were played on Sundays, which meant that they could not take place anyway; they also considered how 'at the All-Ireland finals at Croke Park, the ball would be thrown in by a bishop and "Faith of Our Father" sung. Not a welcoming place for a Protestant!' Percival recounts the harsh penalty a clergyman paid for his interest in the GAA, 'GAA games were not played by Protestants, ostensibly because they occurred on Sundays. A former Dean of Cashel lost the election to the bishopric (in 1950) because he attended a GAA final on a Sunday.' As late as the 1960s and 1970s, Everett and his brothers were not allowed to play Gaelic games because they were forbidden from playing on Sundays.

The taboo against working and engaging in sports on Sundays is more complex than it first appears. The observance of the Sabbath is also sometimes described as having been a 'convenient excuse' to facilitate some rural Protestants' active participation in their own exclusion, to varying degrees, from their local communities. Some rural Protestants who came of age in the fifties, sixties, and even seventies and eighties describe being isolated because Sabbatarianism ruled out participating in sports and other activities typically held on Sundays. While they often describe having an excellent relationship with Catholic neighbours, particularly when relating mutual help on farms, their inability or unwillingness to engage in community activities on Sunday inevitably had a distancing effect. Some feel that this was one of the desired effects of the ban, particularly because of anxieties associated with the prospect of courtship and marriage taking place outside of approved circles. Without offending Catholic friends and neighbours, the Sabbath rule enabled communities that were already very anxious about intermarriage and other ways in which their cultural and religious integrity might be compromised to avoid getting too closely involved in activities – which might include the GAA and local dances – in which young people might meet and fall in love with Catholics.

Visual Displays

One possible indication that a home was a Protestant one was the absence of religious iconography, such as the Sacred Heart, images of the Blessed Virgin, and so forth. However, some Protestant homes had their own distinctive religious items, such as embroidered samplers with religious phrases. Harry remembers being able to identify many inner-city Protestant homes through the display of such items. Photographs and images of members of the British royal family, while not religious, also served as cultural markers. Mostly in border areas, one could find images of 'King Billy' (William of Orange). Evelyn remembers that 'Most Protestant houses [in the rural area of the north-west where she grew up] had the usual pictures including King William crossing the Boyne on his white horse and the framed certificates of membership of the various [Protestant] organisations.'

In what might be interpreted as a gesture of defiance, some inner-city Protestants in Dublin displayed statuettes of white horses in the fanlights or windows of their homes, a discreet reference to King Billy and the Battle of the Boyne. Walter says, 'It was one of the inner-city things, in those days. It showed a house or the tenement where the people lived and up in the corner was a white horse. That was the symbol of a Protestant home.'

The use of poppies to mark Remembrance Day has been described as the characteristic rite of a still-loyalist minority.[357] Wearing poppies could be a striking visual display of identity and loyalty; marking Remembrance Day events en masse, particularly in public, was another way to achieve this. During the First World War, Protestants noted that they were contributing more soldiers to the war effort ('the Empire's call'), proportionately, than the Catholics,[358] and that this included many from the very privileged landlord class and from prominent families in church life.[359] The Church of Ireland primate noted that he knew of 'no clerical home' in his own diocese that had not sent at least one young man to fight, and that many clerical daughters also worked for the war effort.[360]

After independence, wearing poppies quickly became very contentious. In a context of heightened emotion, anxiety, and a sense of retreat, the poppies became important symbols to many Protestants; these Protestants felt that they had suffered disproportionately and that their great sacrifices were now being disrespected by a new state that many had never wanted. Between the two world wars, former servicemen and anyone wearing poppies in some areas were liable to be shouted at and possibly beaten.

Armistice Day (as it was known before the Second World War), or Remembrance Day (as it has been known since the Second World War), developed a sectarian edge. Protestants, especially urban Protestants, sometimes used it to express their dislike of the new regime and of Irish nationalism, and to experience 'an indignant, if muted, defiance' about the recent changes to Ireland.[361] In *Minority Report: The Protestant Community in the Irish Republic*, written in 1975, Jack White writes:

> Ironically, the poppies which were sold in aid of disabled ex-servicemen were themselves the focus of a petty war. Poppies were worn not only to aid the cause or to commemorate the fallen, but as a gesture of defiance. Trinity lads set a razor-blade in the lapel behind the poppy, so that anyone who tried to snatch it would slash his fingers.[362]

Don, who remembers attending Remembrance Day ceremonies in the 1940s, recalls that 'It was alleged that some participants embedded razor blades in their poppies to deter and injure anyone that tried to rip them off.' In 1945, students in Trinity College 'marked VE day [Victory in Europe Day] by flying allied flags over the college and burning the Irish tricolour'.[363] James stated, 'the state's refusal to remember those Irishmen who fell in two world wars on Armistice Day was deplored.'

Trev remembers, 'In my younger days in the 1930s and 40s it was unwise to wear a poppy openly on days centred on Armistice Day. This was objected to by nationalists.' In a parish in the north-west, says Jim, wearing poppies was generally understood to indicate that the wearer was pro-British; it was a risky practice and was frowned on until very recently. Thomas says that when he was a small child, he wore his poppy on Remembrance Sunday, but that as children grew older, they learned to remove the poppies before going into a shop (the local shops were all Catholic-owned) and that it was considered impolite to wear the poppy when visiting a Catholic house. Andy remembers a strong British element to observances in his area, 'It was marked by flags, such as that of the British Legion, and by the wearing of medals. Up to 1922, and in some instances up to the institution of the Republic of Ireland in 1949, the British National Anthem was played and sung at Remembrance services.'

Marigold remembers that all the local Protestant churches had services for Remembrance Sunday and marked the occasion strictly 'within the closed doors of the church'. She remembers singing 'God Save the Queen' at these events, which she found 'very odd'. For Shirley, Remembrance Sunday was important. She loved singing hymns in church and afterwards the whole family had a party together with other Protestant families at a Protestant working men's club. At some point, her father would make the children sing a hymn, 'with harmonies and everything', which she hated. But in general, she recalls that those were good days when her family and their friends felt that they could celebrate their identity without getting into trouble for it — as they often did in the inner-city area where they lived.

Ceremonies held on Remembrance Day were often discreet. Jennie remembers 'going to a service in Islandbridge at the Garden of Remembrance [in Dublin] with my parents and grandparents [...] it seemed to be sort of secret.' Jonathan remembers a certain amount of secrecy associated with uniformed individuals attending the Remembrance Day events at St Patrick's Cathedral, 'there were people over from Britain, and they would drive up in very, very large overcoats, and they would sneak round the side entrance, and they would sneak in and take their coats off inside.' Mabel's family wore poppies at church and at home that Sunday, but 'You probably didn't let your neighbours see you wearing them too much.' Vivienne remembers that poppies were put on as soon as they got into church and removed as soon as they came out, 'Because it was very anti-British [...] if you were seen wearing a poppy you would, well, who knows what, but it would not have been to your advantage. There was always a fear [...] we kept our head down and said nothing and got on with life.' Donald remembers an old woman who came out of her home to shout at him and his siblings, who were wearing poppies, "Yeh shouldn't be wearing them British things!" He was confused because he did not know that he was wearing something British, 'They were just things that were kept in the sideboard from one year to the next.'

Philippa's mother and grandmother sold poppies for Remembrance Sunday, and she has heard stories about her grandfather, who fought in the Second World War, wearing his, 'my dad's dad was a navigator and fiercely proud of his work. But he didn't flaunt it. He didn't put it out there. He would wear his full medals every Remembrance Day with a poppy, but he'd wear his coat over until he got to church and then he'd take the coat off [...] it was just easier to keep it hidden. Just "let's not ask for trouble."'

Lisa states that 'Remembrance Day was awkward. Wore a poppy to church, and the local cenotaph if there was a celebration there, but quietly, furtively, pinned it on when we got there, and took it off before we came back through the town to our home.'

Astra remembers wearing her poppy to St Patrick's Cathedral amid chants of 'Wear a poppy, be a Brit, become a lord like Gerry Fitt!'[364] Eleanora discusses anxiety and ambivalence around the use of symbols that might be interpreted as British. She describes a conversation with a Church of Ireland rector who found it hard to visit St Patrick's Cathedral in Dublin because there were British regimental flags there from various historical wars. He preferred not to celebrate Remembrance Sunday in his own church because he felt that it was associated with Britain. Under pressure from a parishioner, he eventually allowed poppies in the church for the special day because she argued that 'It's nothing to do with the Union Jack. It's about all the Irish people who died.'

Stories of Cultural Pride

Factors that Protestants identify as distinct elements of their culture are mentioned as sources of pride. Kate says, 'Deep down in every Protestant my age there is pride in the fact that we are different.' Davina says, 'My father told me that Roman Catholics looked on Protestants as being very honest'; James states that 'Protestants were reliable. A Catholic friend told me that they did not wind back the milometer in cars that they sold, nor cheat when selling farm animals.' Tom says, 'Protestants were perceived to be more honest [...] their word was their bond, and there was no grey area; they were always regarded as being more reliable.' Harold was taught about 'differences in attitudes and principles [...] Most Protestants would be more honest [...] the three 'Rs' in life: Reliability, Responsibility and Respectability.'

Ian says that the often-discussed Protestant work ethic is very real, 'Work is more important than relationships. The work ethic is real [...] it's the most real thing.' Doris and Samuel, a married couple of many years who were interviewed together, debate it: He says that it is real 'but she doesn't believe me', and she counters that many of the Protestants were 'not *nearly* as marvellous' as they thought. Samuel says Protestants are harder workers, and Doris says lots of Catholics worked hard too. He says then that the Protestants worked *better*, even if they did not work harder. They agree that, when they were young, Protestants never swore and never did anything 'crooked'. Barney attributes a good work ethic to Presbyterians ('they were *savage* for work ethic') above all other denominations:

> this is by no way a bragging – if you wanted men to break new land, you couldn't have got better people than Presbyterians. Because, idleness – we were taught that day in and day out by my mother – idle hands belongs to the devil! And if you're not working, you're in the devil's hands. You must keep working. Working, no matter what it is. Work ethic is deeply ingrained in the Presbyterian [...] work was not a toil to them. It was a joy, it was a joy. I would say maybe in all lines of work, Presbyterians love their work. They love it dearly [...] Farming especially. They're one with the soil and they love working with animals. That's their line of work. And they think they're doing God's work, which maybe they will be doing, they're doing God's work [...] my mother would have washed her hands, they could have been raw washing and carrying water [...] it was a joy to her [...] a woman around here, a godly woman, said, 'there'll be plenty of time to rest when you're dead.'

Billy says Protestants have a great work ethic and are 'tidy' and gives the example of a time when he was installing a sound system and did such a great job that someone said it was 'good and Protestant looking'. He adds that he can generally identify Protestant homes and workplaces by how tidy and well-kept they are, and that this cultural trait was one of the reasons why many Protestant families were previously reluctant to allow a family member to marry a Catholic. Rachel says although she feels that the famed work ethic had 'probably worn off' for her generation, it was very real before; she also affirms there was a 'tradition of being proud of your integrity'. She sees this as a function of being a small minority and a quality that made it easier to identify as a group. Honora feels that Protestants' hard-working self-image could sometimes act as a barrier between them and their Catholic neighbours, 'There was a distinct difference between us and our Catholic neighbours. The Protestant community viewed themselves as being very hard-working and thrifty, and sometimes felt that the Catholics could – and should! – tidy up their properties and farm with greater effort.' Hope says of the fabled Protestant work ethic, 'I always felt vaguely embarrassed by it because I was quite sure that I didn't have it.'

Stewart says Protestants are more inclined to free-thinking, so they 'did not automatically do what our bishop or clergy wanted without first thinking the subject through'. Conversely, some report a sense that Protestants seemed to take their faith particularly seriously. Tom asserts that 'Protestant people did not blaspheme or take the Lord's name in vain to the same extent as their Roman Catholic neighbours.' Eustace states:

> I think Protestants had a feeling that Roman Catholics were, in some vague way, duped by their Church. This would have come out in remarks about the pomp of the bishops or the 'fancy' churches being built from the pennies of the poor. There might also have been puzzlement at the loyalty of Catholics to their church contrasted with an apparent lack of seriousness in understanding the message. For example, in the 1950s, nearly all Catholics went to Mass on Sunday, but I remember [...] watching men playing pitch and toss at the open chapel door as the Mass was being celebrated inside – apparently feeling that this satisfied the requirement.

Bob comments that, in his parents' generation, 'some Protestants thought poorly of Catholic priests, believed they were less well-educated than Protestant clergy, and considered them also as petty tyrants with undue influence over their parishioners.' His mother told him that Catholics she had known as a child 'thought that if they disobeyed their local parish priest that he could turn them into goats'.

Roberta describes Protestants, and especially her parents' generation, as having 'a strong sense of civic responsibility', and as a 'practical, philanthropic group of people who would have used their background and their education'. She gives the example of Muriel Gahan. Despite her Anglo-Irish unionist background, Gahan was a 'progressive nationalist with a firmly pluralist outlook on Irish society'. She founded the Irish Countrywoman's Association (ICA) as a non-denominational group at a time when this was relatively rare, and she opened a 'country shop' on St Stephen's Green in Dublin, where items, including Aran sweaters and baked goods, were sold. For Gahan and other Protestants, who would today be described as social entrepreneurs, it was important to 'foster a sense of pride of making something for which you were paid'. Several people, including Roberta, have expressed a degree of hurt in their view that there is little recognition of the role played by Protestants in cherishing and protecting traditional arts and crafts.[365] Honora also mentions Gahan and her work in the ICA, which she sees as embodying a Protestant ethos, 'Before the Irish Countrywoman's Association came into being, I think there was more of this type of activity in the Protestant community than in the Catholic one.'

Protestants sometimes discuss having been taught that they were 'better' in some way, or they perceive that this view was one held by earlier generations. At times, this is related to social class and education (with Protestants historically having been more likely to be better-off). For the wealthy Protestants, who remained over-represented in the higher-status jobs for decades after independence,[366] wanting to marry within this still-privileged group must have been a motivating factor in maintaining feelings of difference, and of superiority. Particularly in large urban centres like Dublin, well-to-do Protestants could enjoy their membership of a substantial minority that was privileged in many ways. Don recalls, 'I was familiar with Protestants in a higher socio-economic class than many of the Catholics that I met or saw. Maybe I assumed that most of the poor people I saw were Catholics.'

In other cases, these feelings of superiority had no basis in economic difference. Eileen remembers her family's sense of being more fortunate than their neighbours despite the reality that they were not:

Although our social and economic circumstances differed little from those of our immediate neighbours, I think we felt ourselves 'better off.' My mother used to make porter cake at Christmas for the big family next door and this gave her satisfaction and to us as children made us feel well off – we could give something away! Also, I'm afraid, we had this notion the Protestants 'got it right' at the Reformation [which was] good for our morale.

Hazel remembers of the Protestants in her area that, although they were not wealthier than Catholics, they felt superior because of 'the supposed hedonistic ways of the Catholics. Some Protestants did not shop on Sundays or go to entertainments [...] giving us the moral superiority of not breaking the "work on Sunday commandment."' Consequently, 'Protestants may have felt superior in some way and didn't know how to relate well to Catholics [...] We did not invite Catholics to our parties, because it might look as if we were "showing off" and it might be embarrassing for them if they felt they must return the invitation. We kept apart.'

Homan Potterton – an Irish author, art historian, and genealogist, who served as director of the National Art Gallery – writes of growing up in a well-off farming family, recalling that the Protestants he knew growing up considered themselves thrifty and compared themselves favourably to Catholics, whom they saw as wasteful and extravagant.[367] Sam also discusses Protestants in terms of their notable frugality. He says that Protestants had to pay for everything upfront, 'so no hire purchase, getting things "on tick," borrowing money from friends. Also, we were not supposed to put money on horses or buy raffle tickets. The Irish hospital sweepstake was considered a bad thing.' Archie agrees that 'Irish Protestant values are based on thriftiness and an abhorrence of waste', a topic that 'frequently emerges when home baking, jam and marmalade are discussed'. The perfect day's golf for a Protestant, he says, 'is when you end the round with more golf balls than you started with and your blackberry jam has set before you get home.'

Prudence says she and her sister were made to feel that, as Protestants, they were better than others, 'We were made to feel that we were superior. Now it wasn't actually *said*, that we were superior, but we were made to feel that [...] I think it was generally felt, in the Protestant community [...] our houses were cleaner, and our yards were cleaner.'

Doris and her sister were taught to address everyone very formally, not

just as a way of being polite but as a way of indicating an underlying difference and maintaining distance between them and their Catholic neighbours. She gives the example of a neighbour whom everyone else called by
her given name but to whom they referred very formally; this was a way of
keeping everyone (including themselves) in their place.

Adam says, 'the Irish have a reputation for fecklessness [...] and we would
have concurred with that to a large extent.' There was a relatively big population of working-class Protestants in his area, and wealthier families, such as
Adam's own, preferred to deal with them as employees and contractors, when
possible, because they could be expected 'to be entirely honourable with their
dealings', unlike Catholics. He describes how these feelings leached into the
Protestants' political views. The older people disliked de Valera and Fianna
Fáil, seeing them as epitomising Catholic values. When people like Charles
Haughey and Albert Reynolds – former taoisigh ('prime ministers') – rose
to positions of power and showed 'that their word was not their bond', they
were thought to display Catholic values and 'they embodied some of the
worst traits of what we suspected as deeply ingrained in the Catholic community.' Horace also identifies political corruption with Catholic culture and
asserts that 'things might have been different if the Protestant community had
been more present in the civil service and in politics.'

Reliability is often identified as a Protestant characteristic. Martha says,
'The Protestants always seem to end up looking after money [in community
organisations]. They trust us more. We're not going to abscond with the
funds!' Priscilla, Martha, Vivienne, and Anne believe that Protestants tend
to outnumber Catholics on local committees because they like to get involved, and because they are trusted. Honora says, 'On the whole they
would have been honest, upright, hardworking and loyal. Protestants [...]
were highly thought of for their wisdom and integrity.' Bob says that 'Protestants were regarded as more reliable by both fellow Protestants and by
Roman Catholics [...] and my parents knew of some instances where
Protestants were used as arbiters by Catholics in disputes.' Bob believes that
Protestants' role as arbiters may also have been 'because they were considered
to some degree as outsiders'.

Protestant culture is sometimes described as particularly compassionate
and progressive. William tells the story of a local grave that belongs to a
young Catholic who died by suicide many years ago. Because suicide was

considered a mortal sin, the local parish priest told the family that he could not be buried on sacred ground. Fortunately, the rector told them that 'there's a place for him here', so he was buried in the Protestant graveyard. This story moves William every single time he works there. It gives him a 'certain pang in my heart', and he mows the grass around that area with special care because 'like, you know, only for the grace of God there I go, maybe'. For him, this story shows that Catholic culture could be 'very tough and very hard' – more so than his own.

Many Protestants proudly state that their group has long been more liberal about important social issues (while some state, with equal pride, that Protestants tend to be much stricter about the issues that *really* matter). Miriam says that she worked at one point in a Protestant children's home; she comments that unmarried Catholic mothers based in England would drop their children off at the home when they visited their families in Ireland, 'because they knew they would be given back their babies'. She contrasts this with similar Catholic institutions for unmarried mothers and their children: 'If the nuns got them, they certainly wouldn't get them back.'

Hugh points to the career of the politician Noël Browne,[368] whom he identifies as Protestant. He believes that Browne's conviction that women and their babies should receive free medical care was entirely linked to Browne's 'Protestant ethos and identity' and says, 'he was thrown out of office and had to resign because he wanted this for everyone whether they were married or not [...] he was forced to resign because he was going to give free medical aid to illegitimate children and mothers who weren't married and the Roman Catholics couldn't take that.' Archie attributes the opposition to Browne to 'the church's fear that Protestant doctors might be attending to Catholic mothers and children'. But Browne was not a Protestant at all; he had been born into a Catholic family and remained a Catholic in adulthood. However, he was married to a Protestant woman and attended Trinity College at a time when Catholics were not supposed to do so and few did.[369] His status as a Trinity graduate was one of the many reasons why Archbishop McQuaid, who was very conservative and very influential during much of Browne's political career, was so distrustful of him.[370] To Protestant observers of the mother-and-child affair, it seemed as though 'the Government, responsible to the electorate only, was taking its orders from the Catholic hierarchy.'[371]

Some see the growing liberalisation of Ireland as a matter of the Catholics finally realising that the Protestants were right all along: 'Our attitudes', says Adam proudly, 'have now been adopted by the main body of Irish society.'

Stories of Irishness

Although there are many stories about a sense of Britishness that lingered until recently or continues to resonate even today, many people also report that their families are well-integrated locally. Many also tell of a fairly quick adaptation to independence and of a strong sense of Irishness accompanied by a rejection of the idea that Protestants are linked to Britain in any way.

Matthew, growing up in the south-west in the 1930s, says that his parents made the unusual choice of sending him to the local school, which was not just Catholic but also Irish-speaking. Matthew grew up bilingual and considers Irish his first language. Although he is staunchly Protestant, this linguistic identity is very important to him, and he says that it has opened many doors that were typically kept closed to Protestants in independent Ireland. Because he was Irish-speaking, attended a local school where the headmaster ensured that there was no bullying, and learned how to play a traditional instrument, he was not even aware as a child of belonging to a minority. As he grew older, he gradually realised that his family was 'different'. Many of their neighbours had been 'burnt out' during the difficult years or had fled in fear. The move to secondary school, when he entered an all-Protestant environment for the first time, was a dramatic change. But he says that because of the way he was raised, and his ease in speaking Irish, he is not a 'foreigner in my country'. He says some Protestants still feel this estrangement, 'because of past history and what might have happened to their families and so on'.

Irish was also big in Ursula's life. As a schoolgirl, she was talented at Irish, and a local Catholic schoolteacher (a friend of the family's and not her own teacher) recommended her for a county council scholarship to University College Dublin, even sending in an application on her behalf. She won the scholarship, making her – she believes – the first Protestant to receive one in her area. Attending UCD was a mixed experience because of the assumption that all the students were Catholics, 'You would be asked awkward questions at times, were you going to the solidarity tonight [...] You'd have to be open and say, "Well, I am not a Catholic, you know …" The odd one would avoid you after that.'

Most Protestants today strongly reject any suggestion that they might be British, although this perception seems to linger in the general population more than they would like. They are typically very vocal on the issue and stress how proud they are to be '100 per cent Irish'. As Mariah says, she is 'not English at all – I *hate* it when they say that.' Philippa, who was taught Religious Education in a community school, was immensely offended when her RE teacher ('this *ignorant* woman […] whatever was she doing teaching religion?') asked, 'And do you still pray for the queen every week?' Rachel describes her daughter having a similar experience. Indignant and feeling as though her daughter was being told that she was not 'properly Irish', Rachel went to the school to assure the principal and the religion teacher that they were proud Irish citizens with no especial interest in any foreign monarchy.[372] She adds that 'yes, a lot of people have that perception that to be Protestant means you weren't a proper Irish person. [They believed that] you certainly had sympathies with England.' Rachel works in education and says she teaches the children at her school GAA games, 'because it's part of our culture', but that most Protestant schools play other sports. 'I am maybe pushing the boat out a little bit,' she says, '… but I think these things are two-way and I want my [Protestant students] to feel Irish, to feel the belonging to Irishness.'

Mariah has a distinctively English surname and, because of it, has often been told, 'Oh, you're English … you're not a proper Irish person.' She says, 'My husband's family would have come definitely in Cromwell times and it is an English-based name but that is going back 400 years at this stage […] I turn around and say, 'No, it is a *local* surname.' Sometimes she turns it into a joke, 'I put on a posh accent and say, "Oh *yes*."'

Conclusion

For Protestants in independent Ireland, understanding their own sense of identity has often involved comparing themselves to the perceived cultural and behavioural norms of the majority and creating a set of criteria that serve to define their own sense of difference. While in some areas there were large, affluent, and secure Protestant populations that were confident in their identity, in other areas Protestants were such a small minority that they have tended to define themselves almost entirely in terms of how their identities and loyalties differed from that of the majority's. Today, in an ever more secular Ireland, Protestants continue to discuss and mediate their identity in a way that is particular to themselves and heavily influenced by their shared history. While most Protestants today wholeheartedly assert their Irishness, others can be torn between feelings of Irishness and the knowledge that – still – some don't accept them as 'real' Irish people. Some also feel that aspects of their culture and heritage are insufficiently represented in depictions of Ireland.

4. Stories of Love and Marriage

Like everyone else, Protestants in Ireland have many stories about falling in love, courting, and experiencing long, happy marriages. These stories of love and marriage can also lead to discussions of family memories, difficult times, and issues of faith and cultural identity, each of which have been core motifs of Protestant storytelling for generations.

Ne Temere, 'Mixed Marriages', Resistance and Taboo

History of Mixed Marriage

From 1785, the Vatican recognised marriages performed by the Church of Ireland or by civil authorities.[373] Previously, under the anti-Catholic Penal Laws enacted after Oliver Cromwell reconquered Ireland in 1653, 'mixed marriages' were prohibited (although they still occurred). Bob recalls a family story about a mixed marriage in the nineteenth century:

> [My ancestor] was born in 1803 and died in 1901. He was said to have been a hedge schoolteacher […] he had the reputation of having had an extensive knowledge of the Bible, as well as being a fluent speaker of Irish – the only ancestor I know of who seems to have straddled both cultures […] That may possibly have been linked to the fact that his wife was Roman Catholic, the only Catholic that I'm aware of in my ancestry, and her family may still have been Irish-speaking in that part of [rural Ireland] in the mid-1830s. It is said that [he] was disinherited for marrying her.

After the partial repeal of the laws in 1785, mixed marriages were only officially recognised when they were carried out by a Church of Ireland minister. This remained the case up until 1870. Restrictions applied to other

Protestant denominations too. Until 1737, marriages conducted by Presbyterian ministers were unrecognised; until 1845, marriages between Presbyterians and members of the Church of Ireland were also unrecognised.

Throughout the eighteenth and nineteenth centuries, though mixed marriages with Catholics were not the norm (about one in twenty, according to some evidence)[374] or considered desirable, the tradition was for the children of mixed marriages to follow the religion of the parent of the same sex. Andy comments that this was driven largely by anxiety about land passing from one denomination to another and that the tradition had 'the merit of reducing friction in families'. Joe says, 'My great-grandfather [...] married an Irish-speaking Roman Catholic [...] they had one son and six daughters, three of whom became nuns. All the girls were brought up as Catholics, but my grandfather was raised a Protestant, as was usually the custom at the time.' Barney says the same tradition persisted in his area well into the twentieth century:

> There was a compromise – and I don't know if this were legal in the church or whatnot – but the boys were brought up Protestant [...] and the girls would be brought up Catholic [...] that covered the giving up of the land too [...] a perfect compromise.

It was more common for Protestant men to marry Catholic women than vice versa, so the sons who inherited land were generally also Protestants and represented no threat to the status quo in a community that prioritised keeping the land in Protestant hands.[375] Although some Protestants preferred marrying within their specific denomination, marriage between people of even very different Protestant faiths was generally not considered 'mixed marriage', as, in Samuel's words, they all 'came from the same foundation; there'd be no *feeling* about marrying them.' Samuel says intermarriage between different dominations was smiled upon, 'There was a certain mind of delight if John was fancying Jean [if he was Church of Ireland] and she was Presbyterian [...] because if a Protestant was going out with a Catholic girl, that was them lost to their denomination and their children.' This view is widely expressed among interviewees and questionnaire respondents.

Introduction of Ne Temere

On 19 April 1908 the *Ne Temere* decree came into force. Issued by the Catholic Church, it ruled that a couple in a mixed marriage had to raise their children as Catholics.[376] The Catholic Church would only recognise marriages performed by a Catholic priest. If a Catholic married someone from another faith without a Catholic priest officiating (who had received permission from the Vatican directly or through the bishop of the diocese), the marriage was considered void and the couple to be 'living in sin'. *Ne Temere* also attempted to legislate for the behaviour of anyone who had ever been Catholic, even if they had converted to another faith; it sought to direct the Catholic party to convert their spouse to the 'true faith'.[377] The decree was replaced in 1970 by the less stringent *Matrimonia Mixta*,[378] and it was formally put aside in 1983 – spouses in a mixed marriage were now expected to make an oral, rather than a written, declaration of intent to raise their children as Catholics.[379]

Ne Temere *as an Existential Threat*

Protestants were quick to identify *Ne Temere* as an existential threat. A young couple from Belfast – Alexander McCann, a Catholic, and Agnes Barclay, a Protestant – were married in a Protestant church shortly after *Ne Temere*.[380] In 1910, the couple was informed by a priest that their marriage was invalid. Alexander asked Agnes to marry him again in a Catholic Church, but she refused. In the ensuing breakdown of their marriage, Alexander whisked the two children away and Agnes never saw them again.[381] It seems that the Catholic Church supported Alexander; *Ne Temere* obliged him to have them raised as Catholics, and as Agnes refused a second marriage, he had good reason to think that she might interfere. Most Protestants were against home rule already; this case seemed to confirm their view that if Ireland became independent, the Catholic Church would threaten their rights.

In 1911, when census returns show that only 0.8 per cent of marriages on the island were mixed (although with considerable local variation),[382] Reverend Gregg addressed the Young Men's Association in Cork on the topic of mixed marriage. He admitted that 'if a certain mixed marriage had not taken place in County Clare three generations ago, I should not be here tonight', but quoted the pastoral letter of a colleague, Cardinal Logue, in saying that while 'such marriages' might sometimes appear to be 'quite successful', or at least 'tolerable', 'there is a want felt, a bar to complete happiness and perfection of the married life' that often leads to 'a world of misery, regret, black hopelessness and ruin, temporal and spiritual'. Along with this, he alluded to the 'imminent, pressing, palpable' risks of 'perversion [conversion to Catholicism], the danger of religious coldness and indifference in the parties themselves, [and] the still more probable danger of indifference in the children'.[383] While accepting that some of 'these marriages' were inevitable, Reverend Gregg urged Protestants to reject mixed marriage, which would lead to 'children who ought to be strengthening our community growing up as Romanists, giving their Protestant blood and brain and energy to a community which would drive us out of the land if it could'. He described Protestants who allowed their children to be raised as Catholics as traitors, insisted that they might be forced to convert on their deathbeds, and asserted:

> Mixed marriages tend to rob us of the next generation, and we need to band ourselves together to stop the leakage. Parents need not throw their children into unnecessary association with Roman Catholics [...] those who played together as children will quite naturally say when they grow up, 'If you let us play together then, why should we not marry now?' [...] Make it a first idea with your children that marriage with a Roman Catholic is not for them; that such a marriage cannot be entered into on fair and equal terms, but only on terms of shame and dishonour.[384]

The same year, John Ervine published *Mixed Marriage*, which discusses the love of two young working-class Dubliners, Hughie Rainey, a Protestant, and Nora Murray, a Catholic. The play, performed at the Abbey Theatre on 30 March 1911, describes Dublin Orangemen as being roused 'akin the Cathliks' and depicts scuffles on the street between Sinn Féin supporters and loyalists. Hughie's father, John, is unhappy about the prospect of the marriage:

> Rainey: What religion is she?
> Tom: (uneasily) A'm not sure.
> Rainey: She's got a Papish name. There's many a Fenian be the name o' Murray.

Tom: Sure what differs does it make if she is a Cathlik? She's a brave, nice wee girl.

Rainey: A wudden have a son o' mine marry a Cathlik fur all the wurl. A've nathin' agin the girl, but A believe in stickin' t'yer religion. A Cathlik's a Cathlik, and a Prodesan's a Prodesan. Ye can't get over that.

Young love wins out and Hughie tells his mother that he is going to marry Nora. When Mrs Rainey frets, he tells her, 'Aw, ma, half the religion in the wurl' is like a disease that ye get thrum yer father. A'm a Prodesan acuse you an' me da are Prodesans, an' Nora's a Cathlik acause her parents wur Cathliks.' Nora's father also takes the news badly, 'All yer own people'll cast ye off acause ye married a Prodesan.' An angry mob gathers outside the Raineys' door and the police come to disperse them. As things escalate and the police threaten to shoot at the crowd, Nora rushes outside only to be caught in the fire. As she dies, she says to Hughie, 'It wus right t' shoot me. It wus my fault. A'm quaren glad.'[385]

Ne Temere hardened many Protestants' attitudes towards both Catholicism and increased Irish autonomy.[386] All this excitement about mixed marriages was taking place in the context of the Third Home Rule Bill, which was introduced in 1912 (the first was presented in 1886; the second, in 1893). Anxiety about what would happen if Ireland was dominated by an increasingly powerful Catholic majority was galvanised by fears about being demographically swamped and losing their rights in mixed marriages.

Impact of Ne Temere *on Protestants*
Between the foundation of the Irish state and the early 1990s, the Protestant population of Ireland was reduced by half. Over a longer period, comparing 1861 with 1936, the population declined by 61 per cent.[387] While *Ne Temere* was only one of many reasons for this decline, it was a factor, and was often blamed by Protestants for their 'downfall'. The 1911 census (of the whole island) reveals that couples in mixed marriages tended to have fewer children. Fernihough, Ó Gráda, and Walsh speculate that this may have been a way to minimise problems over what religion their offspring would follow. They point out that 'the potential alienation and ostracisation experienced by mixed marriages could have removed the wider, non-nuclear family net-

work important for child rearing in historical societies.'[388] By the 1930s, many Protestants felt despondent, and some of them apparently preferred never to experience love and marriage if it was a question of marrying a Catholic. In July 1935, the Bishop of Ossory wrote, 'Many of our young men seem curiously reluctant to enter the holy state of matrimony. A leading clergyman said to me that in his parish there were several middle-aged men with good farms who seemed to have no intention of getting married.'[389] While relatively high numbers of both Catholics and Protestants never married in the mid-twentieth century, the 1946 census reveals that Protestant women in independent Ireland were less likely to marry than Catholic women.[390] When the fertility rate was low, generally because so many married late, it was lowest among Protestants.[391]

Mixed marriage remained undesirable. In 1947, Reverend Fletcher wrote that a Protestant man married to a Catholic was 'an outsider in his own home, forbidden to discuss religious subjects with his wife, or to teach his children his own religious faith, or to bring them to worship with him in the House of God', while a woman in the same situation was 'debarred from the most sacred right and privilege of motherhood: to teach her children her own religious faith'.[392]

Fletcher's pamphlet was one of many published by clergy who stressed the view that Ne Temere was dangerous to the individual and to society.[393] In 1951, Archbishop Gregg described mixed marriage as 'a grave injury to our church' and advised, 'We must create so far as we can such a deep-rooted prejudice, and such a community sense against such marriages on Roman Catholic terms, that even the thoughtless will know that they should not be entered upon.'[394] In 1952, Hubert Butler noted that three of the six Protestant families remaining in his Kilkenny parish had children who had married Catholics and complied with Ne Temere. He expressed anger and argued that 'we can't *stop* mixed marriages in a mixed community, but we can prevent them being made on unequal terms.'[395] In 1957, a group of young parishioners was advised to exclusively make friends within Protestant circles and was told that mixed marriage meant having to deal with Catholic standards, 'which are very different from, and lower, than our own', and losing the 'Protestant integrity' that was their 'birthright'.[396]

Stories of Ne Temere

Many of the people interviewed for this book discuss the direct impact of *Ne Temere* and interfaith marriages on their families and community, describing the widely held belief that the purpose of *Ne Temere* was to 'wipe us out', to 'get rid of us', to 'teach us a lesson'.[397] They also report that stories about couples in mixed marriages could be used as a form of social control to dissuade young people from becoming involved in relationships with Catholics; that mixed marriage was often discussed in very negative terms.

Joe remembers the day his uncle came to tell Joe's parents that he was going to marry a Catholic and the 'icy atmosphere this news created in our normally happy home'. He considers that 'the *Ne Temere* rule *always* had a negative effect on Protestants [...] when the Catholic Church was so powerful and arrogant, it put huge pressure on young people about to marry and at a very emotional time in their lives'. He refers to the rule as 'a subtle form of ethnic cleansing'. Hubert says that he reads the births, deaths, and marriages section in *The Irish Times* every day, 'just to see whether I'm still alive or not', and that he frequently notices 'a name where the service is a [Catholic] Mass and it's a name which is absolutely a Protestant name, it's a Protestant surname because they had to bring up their children as Catholics, in a mixed marriage'. He concludes that *Ne Temere* was 'devastating'.

William knew of nobody who married outside his tiny Protestant community when he was young because, although they had many Catholic friends, people 'didn't want there to be mixing'. When the topic of mixed marriage arose, his father banished the children from the room. Laura, who married a Catholic whom she had met through work (she was a nurse; he, a doctor), told her daughter about the dreadful outcome for her relationship with her family:

> When we got engaged, I went down to tell my family. Shortly afterwards I got a letter from one of my sisters and she said, 'My God, my God, why have thou forsaken us?' [...] They never met him [...] My aunt in Dublin and her daughter were the only ones at the wedding [...] I never went to see them after I was married [...] I didn't attend [my own church] any more. I wasn't allowed. In those days, it would have interfered with his practice. He often said to me that if he didn't go to Mass and if I didn't go to Mass then people might not come to the dispensary.

Stewart says the avoidance of mixed marriage was 'the most important' aspect of being Protestant in a land 'which was controlled by the Roman Catholic Church', because if the 'parents were not strict on this, we, as a people, would die out. So, it is correct to say we lived in a sort of a ghetto.' Frances states that *Ne Temere* 'nearly led to the extinction of the Protestants'. As she remembers it, 'Both sides obeyed the clergy then […] they hardly mixed at all socially, as a "mixed marriage" was considered a terrible thing, so even to go out together was not good.' Things 'changed overnight' in Sidney's family when his older brother noticed the pretty cashier in a butcher's shop and asked her out:

> They soon became a serious couple and that was when the trouble started […] Things became very strained between [my brother] and our father […] [My brother and his partner] became engaged to be married and eventually the date was set […] Our father refused to go, as did members of his family. Our mother went, bringing her four children with her […] When we arrived at the church, which is a large one, the left-hand side was very full of [the bride's] family and friends. The right-hand side was completely empty.

Don says the view (which also reflects the casual racism of the time) among the Protestants in his youth was that 'It would be better for you to bring home a black woman to meet the family than to bring an RC girl!' As children, Samuel and his siblings 'dreaded' mixed marriages and were 'taught to have nothing to do with that'. Doris always knew that 'it wasn't going to happen', and comments that *Ne Temere* was hard on young Protestants in many rural areas with small Protestant populations. 'It was a pity,' she says, 'because lots of girls probably fell for very nice fellows', but they couldn't marry them.

Hugh says that the more working-class Protestants in his area – 'tradesmen, carpenters' – married mostly Roman Catholics, which 'did a lot of harm'. Growing up in a small town with very few Protestants, Hugh and his siblings were mostly friends with Catholics; they were allowed to play with the Catholic children, although 'it was sort of an understanding that there would not be any marriage between us.' He reels off a list of 'Protestant' names from his town that are now associated with Catholic families and businesses as evidence that mixed marriages in his community 'wiped [Protestants] out'. One of his uncles married a Catholic and raised his children as Catholics. Hugh's father was eventually prevailed upon to attend his brother's wedding, which was held far from the homes of both bride and groom. Despite this initial display of forced acceptance, the brothers never visited each other in their respective homes over the forty years that followed, although they still worked together.

Ted recounts that *Ne Temere* caused problems in otherwise harmonious rural areas as a result of 'the constant bombardment from the Vatican to be on top of the pile' and describes the decree as 'dictatorship in the extreme' – something that 'won't be forgotten easily'. Craig remembers of his student days that he viewed *Ne Temere* as a 'breach of one's self' that meant 'the prospect of marrying a Catholic girl, even a TCD Catholic of one's own class, was therefore very disturbing.' Trinity College, still an almost exclusively Protestant stronghold, was a place where people (largely middle class and wealthy) met future spouses, 'It was a small enough group that they knew each other very well but not so small that they were marrying their first cousins.' Nancy, attending Trinity in the early 1960s, remembers friends' approaches to the dilemma of possible mixed marriages:

> girlfriends would say, 'Hm, I don't think I'm going to go further with this, because it will cause trouble if I really get attached,' and so, to a large extent, you didn't socialise very far. It was just too complicated. And I mean, I do know two or three girls at the time who […] made a very big sacrifice, I think, by saying, 'I love him, he's absolutely wonderful, and I would love to be married to him, but it's not worth it because my family would not want to know about it.'

Ostracisation, Threats and Social Control

While many families adapted to mixed marriages, others violently rejected them to the point of disowning or disinheriting their children and close relatives. Norman Ruddock, a Church of Ireland curate, writes of a cousin who married a Catholic, whom she loved, after becoming pregnant out of wedlock; he recounts how she was blamed for her mother's death, which happened shortly afterwards, and was disowned by her maternal aunt for years. Ruddock also relates the story of a businessman who had intended on leaving his business to a colleague of many years. Instead, when the man in question married a Catholic woman, he was 'shown the door'.[398]

Eric recalls the absolute disapproval of mixed marriage that prevailed. *Ne Temere*, he says, 'was all-invasive and poisoned relations in many families and in many areas [...] many families disowned any offspring who entered into such a marriage.' Gerald recalls learning about the estrangement of his paternal aunt when he was already grown up, 'When I enquired about her from my eldest uncle, he told me that she was not spoken about because she married a Catholic in 1928.' His mother's side had also experienced difficulties relating to mixed marriage:

> In 1888, my grandmother, at age 23, was working with a family in Carlow caring for a handicapped child. In July that year she married a policeman. She was 5 months pregnant [...] the marriage was mixed religion; my grandmother was Protestant and my grandfather Catholic. The girl children were brought up Protestant and the boys Catholic. When they left the house to go to school, they went in opposite directions. I was brought up with little or no contact with my uncles and cousins [...] my mother's brothers or their families never visited us or we them.

Juliet remembers hearing about a neighbour who married a Catholic man in about 1910 and observed *Ne Temere*. 'A very bitter man', the neighbour's father never spoke to her and would not acknowledge his six grandchildren. The marriage was also a loss to the community as the woman had played the harmonium in the local church.

An aunt of Eileen's who married a Catholic in the late 1920s 'was ostracised by her family as if she had died and in spite of living close by her family and having eight children'. Eileen learned of her existence only when the woman's daughter attended Eileen's mother's funeral in 1999. Tilly's relative disowned her daughter when she married a Catholic. When the young woman's father was dying, he called for her to say goodbye, 'and she was going upstairs and met her mother, who looked the other way'. Mariah discusses a first cousin once removed who 'married out'. Widowed young, with three children, she married the Catholic man from the adjoining farm. She was ostracised by most of the family, except for Mariah's father. The children of the first marriage were raised by Protestant relatives. Mariah met many of her relatives for the first time at the woman's funeral – she was buried in a different graveyard.

June says there was hardly any intermarriage in her area until at least the 1970s and that endogamous marriage is still considered desirable. When she was growing up, mixed marriages were 'swept under the carpet'. Only as an adult did she learn that there had been some mixed marriages in her family, in her grandparents' generation, but that the couples in question had been 'sort of, I think, ostracised'. Some had moved away and others had converted to Catholicism. Some emigrated to Scotland or America to escape from the stigma attached to their marriage and children. Colin comments that couples in mixed marriages often emigrated because of the 'disgrace' they brought on their families. Eleanora often heard stories about people who had married out; some were ostracised by their families for the rest of their lives. Most converted to Catholicism. She says, 'Marrying out was understood by us to be on par with committing a crime.' She further explains:

> People would talk about it happening in another family and their expectations of how that family should handle it, which was to put out that family member. They would do the same about criminal activity [...] where the family would feel the person who offended had got to get out, and the community would have expected that, and they would go to England or something.

Many who agreed to have their children raised as Catholics, converted themselves, or did both paid a huge price. Often, they became extremely isolated and 'very embittered and that type of thing'. Liza remembers that two of her first cousins married Catholics and were forced to observe *Ne Temere*. She remembers the decree as having 'alienated' Protestants and comments, 'my parents would have expelled me from the family if I had had an RC boyfriend.'

Grace recalls, 'If I had a date with a Roman Catholic fellow and my father found out, I was locked up.' Amy remembers that 'mixed' couples typically 'had' to leave the area, 'they would have maybe gone away, to England or someplace – eloped, we used to call it – and get married there, because the parents would have no wishes for them to stay around, if they were marrying a Roman Catholic.' Joyce's expectation in the event of marrying a Catholic would have been to be 'put out, disowned', and her mother often told her of couples who were made to 'disappear', presumably to England.

Donald recalls the stories he heard when he was growing up about babies of mixed marriages 'being smuggled out of the Rotunda Hospital [a maternity hospital] in Dublin to be baptised in the [nearby Catholic] Pro-Cathedral'. These stories indicate how the Catholic side of a family, worrying that the child would be raised Protestant, waited until the mother was distracted to sneak the baby out and have them hastily baptised. Looking back, he wonders if it was 'an urban legend; something that people talked about to explain why they were afraid or some way of articulating their fears'. He also says, 'the hospital policy was very much against it.'

Mabel was told that 'the Pope told [Catholics] that they had to repopulate and take over.' She attributes the *Ne Temere* decree with 'bringing our people down'. Myrtle states, 'I often heard it discussed as a way of wiping out Protestants.'

Frank remembers a young man who returned from fighting in the Second World War and became romantically involved with a local girl; the girl got pregnant. The local clergyman immediately took control, went to the boy's home, and informed his guardians of what had taken place. Then they all 'called the young lad up. He was maybe 22 or 3 at the time, and put the allegation to him, put the charge to him, and read it out and he agreed. It was true. This girl was pregnant. Well, the next order was, "You go upstairs, pack your bags, and get *out!*"'

Some report broad social repercussions for mixed marriage. Davina remembers just one man who married a Roman Catholic. 'Oh, it was awful!' she recalls. 'That was the way people looked at it. He was a man who used to visit the pubs and they would have him singing Orange songs.' Don remembers a friend who married a Catholic and subsequently had to transfer his bank account to a branch in Northern Ireland. Another married a Catholic girl, and when the young couple moved into their flat in suburban Dublin, they encountered Catholic bigotry rather than Protestant resentment, 'They were harassed by a group of people congregating outside their building and chanting, 'Prostitute, prostitute' – possibly because they had not had a Catholic wedding.'

Richard's grandmother died when he was about 6 years of age. One of his aunts had married a Catholic and, the day after her mother's death, when she came to the house to discuss the funeral arrangements, a vigorous dispute erupted between her and her daughter, a young Catholic woman of about 20. The daughter was very upset because her mother was determined to go to her own mother's funeral, which was banned, as Catholics were not supposed to step inside Protestant churches, 'My aunt was saying, "I'm not asking the priest for permission to go to my own mother's funeral!"' Richard remembers that 'the daughter was screaming back, saying things like, "You're imperilling your immortal soul!" [...] It was a huge row and [...] I was aware that it was terribly intense.'

Honora recalls that Protestants in mixed marriages were often 'excommunicated from the family' and grandparents frequently never knew their grandchildren, causing anguish on both sides. A woman in Eunan's extended family was completely omitted from family histories for generations. This was caused by her marriage, at 15 years of age, to a Catholic, 'She was left out of the family tree until recently and only recently was put back in when a large [...] clan in the US was seen to proceed from her.'

Olive remembers the awful scene that occurred shortly after her brother married a Catholic. Olive was working in a shop at the time and the local clergyman came in especially to see her, 'and he absolutely *devoured* me. Well, he just pulled me aside and gave out about our family and everything. It was awful. I can remember leaving that evening going home.' Ashamed and upset, Olive was unable to attend work for two days, 'it was hell in our house and everywhere else.'

Walter's aunt was in a mixed marriage, and she and her husband agreed that they would raise half their children as Catholics and half as Protestants. The first child was Catholic; when the second child was born, the father's sisters allegedly came and had the child baptised Catholic. 'A week later or two weeks later, or so,' he says, 'that woman died. Probably died of a broken heart or something like, you know.' An uncle also had a mixed marriage, and although he never converted, when he died the first the family heard of his death was when they read his notice in the paper; they learned that he had been given a Catholic funeral. When his mother died, she was also thought to have died 'of a broken heart, because of the way the family went'. Because of these family experiences, says Walter, 'My mother instilled [...] to make sure that you marry your own.'

Ethel recalls attending the wedding – 'the dreaded "mixed marriage"' –

of a close friend, 'Both churches put pressure on the couple right up to the night before the wedding, saying it was not too late to pull out. Both mothers wept the entire day.'

Henry discusses how important it was for him to find a wife within his own faith and culture, and the sense of threat he feels that mixed marriage represents to his people:

> my parents never said it, but it was always implied [...] well, you don't have to be a great genius to know that if you married a Roman Catholic woman almost certainly your children would be brought up as Catholic [...] perhaps from our late teens onwards, we realised that we didn't want that to happen to us [...] I think that if your culture is strong [...] to some extent you'll know the right thing to do or you'll know [...] if you want to keep your culture going, you'll know the right decisions to make.

He ascribes the low rate of marriage of the earlier generations in his family to their disillusionment after the First World War, and their consequent reluctance to continue the family line in Ireland. At least two great-uncles had fought and survived to return to a land that they felt they did not recognise – where they no longer felt welcome. 'Of a family of nine', he says, '[...] only two married in Ireland. One married in Britain, two died, four or five didn't marry [...] did you even want to have children in the new [...] Free State where perhaps you didn't feel very welcome?'

'Not Enough Protestants to Marry'
In the 1961 census, 60 per cent of Protestant men between the ages of 20 and 40 were unmarried; 40 per cent of women from the same demographic were also recorded as unmarried. Comparing the figures of 1971 with 1946, there was a 24 per cent decline in the number of Protestants living in Ireland, despite lower levels of emigration; this was partly because of their low birth rate. On the other hand, there was an increase in the number of Catholics.[399] Conor Cruise O'Brien stated that Protestants in the south who objected to being absorbed into the mainstream had generally either left or remained unmarried.[400]

The term 'under siege' is often applied to stories about demographic fears. It is a term that is identified by some interviewees as a defining factor of Protestant identity. This is the case for Myrtle, who reports, 'The Protestants did perceive of themselves as a people apart, because they felt a sort of siege mentality.' In some rural areas, there were so few Protestants that it was difficult to maintain endogamous marriage practices, especially for those on modest incomes who might have no car and no way to socialise with the nearest Protestants, who could be some distance away. Kate's uncle failed to marry until late in life, 'as there were no Protestant girls', and had no children as a result, causing 'the end of the line'. She believes that *Ne Temere* nearly led to their extinction. On the other side of the family, an uncle married a Catholic, 'This caused a lot of trouble with lingering effects to this day [...] Even when she died, she was not buried with her husband.' Myrtle's uncle waited until his mother died to marry the Catholic woman he loved, with the result that they also remained childless.

Many families in Samuel's rural area 'died out' because there weren't enough local Protestants to marry, he says. People did not talk about their disappearing community much – 'they just took it as it came' – but it was hard on everyone to see it diminish and the little rural churches become progressively emptier before finally closing. Thomas says his parents 'dreaded' their son or daughter 'getting in with a Catholic lad or lassie' because their children would have to be raised Catholic. He attributes the low rate of marriage among Protestants of his generation to *Ne Temere*, although they had 'Protestant dances every bloomin' place'. One man he knew, who had two 'big fine lassies', moved to Northern Ireland rather than risk seeing them 'get mixed married'.

There are many stories of elderly men and women who never married because they inhabited rural areas with no eligible Protestants – this was more often the case with men, who were left at home with the land while their sisters went to England. Mabel describes exactly this situation, 'There were very few mixed marriages at that time to take anyone away.' And although there had been a big community, 'Unfortunately, the men didn't get married so [the Protestants] dwindled down.' Andrew, referring to a recording of his grandfather's sister who emigrated in the early twentieth century, reports how 'she gave her reasons for leaving as the lack of eligible young Protestant men in the area as well as the lack of opportunities for educated young women'.

Heather says that women often had opportunities to leave rural areas and find work, leaving the men behind on the farms. These men, she says, are still there, 'These men I'm talking about are 70s, 80s; there's quite a lot of them about. They had a very limited outlook, they were anti-Catholic and they had little money. They didn't want to travel. They were not very educated or very open to different ideas. And there they sat. And there they sit today.'

Travers comments that in his area there have also been many bachelors who never married because they did not meet Protestant girls, 'I could read off three or four fellas who never got a partner.' As a young man, Travers was told firmly by his parents that when it came to Catholic girls he should 'steer clear if possible'. He met his Protestant wife through 'ingenuity and ways and means'. Morris reports:

> It was not always easy for Protestants to find a partner and they went on to live life with sisters and brothers [...] a lonely life of solitude [...] [A man I know] was maudlin from drink and what he was saying was that his parents stopped him marrying a Roman Catholic girlfriend and now he is alone and lonely. This is a story that could be repeated over and over again, particularly among the farming community.

Natasha also knows of marriages that were unhappy and suspects that the couple was pushed together when they were young because they were both Protestants and did not necessarily have much else in common. Rachel remembers the 1970s and 80s as a transitional period with respect to how people felt about mixed marriages. Overall, there was still 'an unease with it' and a feeling that they would lose something if a family member married out. She attributes mixed marriages at least partly to the loneliness associated with being part of a small minority:

> to be Protestant in a predominantly Roman Catholic society there is a sense of being separate that can be kind of lonesome, and different people did different things. I mean, some said, 'OK, I'll join your culture. I will go to your pub and marry within your community and I will become more fully Irish' [...] No, it's not that we didn't feel Irish, that's not right; 'I'll become more fully integrated into

Roman Catholic Irish style.' Because they didn't like the lonesome-ness. And others said, 'Well, what we have is special, we'll hang onto this. We won't go outside the little group because if we do, we will lose our identity.' There were two different ideas, two different ways of coping.

May's rural community was composed of three extended families, 'Now, we're not all first cousins but we're related. The other two are first cousins but we're second or third. In the actual church, everyone was related to somebody.' Of the very few people in the church who were not relatives, one was an elderly woman who had married a Catholic and raised her children as Catholics. Because her family had all 'gone the other way', she sat alone; she was an object lesson in what happened to girls who had not married suitable men.

Some have heard of Protestant families, usually in areas with relatively few Protestants, in which intermarriage with relatives 'happened too often', leading to health problems for their children. The issue of intermarriage, although not health problems specifically, is referenced by the historian F.S.L. Lyons in a lecture given in 1967. He speaks of the 'social isolation in which most of these people lived their lives', and how it got to a level that 'to this day the first ten minutes of conversation between any minority group who don't know each other personally is likely to be devoted to finding out which of them is connected to which'.[401]

Letitia remembers her father saying of a Protestant community in an isolated rural area 'that they were all intermarried up that way to keep land in the family'. He explained that intermarriage to this degree 'was a Protestant thing rather than a Catholic thing because there were fewer people to choose from and people didn't have cars'. Millie says, 'It was important for Protestants to marry Protestants, so it was not unknown for first cousins to marry. My husband's […] grandparents were a case in point.' Donald says many Protestant families in Dublin tolerated marriage between cousins (despite there being abundant potential spouses in the larger city community) and that his father, a science teacher, disapproved. He told his children the cautionary tale of an aristocratic family who had married their cousins so often that the heir to the estate was an 'imbecile'.

Many people in Doris's area married their cousins and extended family;

she adds that her paternal grandparents were first cousins, joking that 'It's no wonder we're all so mad!' Eadry, who grew up in Dublin, says that there was intermarriage with cousins in the rural branches of her family, and that the potential for negative health consequences was not originally understood. Fortunately, in her family 'it was just the occasional one [...] as my father said, there was sufficient to go around.' Edward remembers of his area that everyone was connected and 'often you could be related two different ways to the one person [...] at times there would have been marriages, they would have been closely related [...] because of the limits [...] it's not a big community.' Rachel remembers her community as being quite similar, 'I'd say the gene pool isn't huge. A lot of people would have ended up marrying second, third cousins. And the gene pool got fairly small [...] we would be one of the bigger communities, but it is still small.' Richard recalls his father talking about an acquaintance marrying a first cousin:

> everybody was very upset about that [...] they felt if there were children there could be great genetic difficulties and people were worked up about it [...] I don't know if it was him or my mother who said, 'It is not a good thing to marry a close relative and yet people do, because there is no one else to marry [...]' They would try to stop you having a relationship with a relative. But often there wasn't anybody else and a close relative would be better than a Catholic.

Natasha says with a laugh that there is a running joke (not taken very seriously) that the rugby teams in the big Protestant schools have improved since mixed marriages became common because, prior to this, the Catholics had 'a wider gene pool' while the Protestants had been weakened through intermarriage.

While the taboo against marrying Catholics was once stronger than the idea that one should try not to marry a cousin, now the opposite prevails. Mariah is 'aware of people my age and younger, and they married their first cousin'; such matches resulted in many 'raised eyebrows' at the time. She points out that, among Protestants, 'we do openly say, when you have to be in a room for 15 minutes, and it doesn't matter what part of the country you are in, you will know somebody who is related to somebody who is related to somebody. We're all half mad anyway.'

These stories about marriage between cousins among some Protestant communities, rather than an objective analysis of excessive intermarriage, are perhaps best considered as a way of expressing historic anxiety about a diminishing group that was anxious about its place in Ireland for many years after independence.

Marrying a Farm

Stories about love, courtship, and marriage are often also stories about the land, ownership of it, the desirability of keeping it in Protestant hands, and the anxiety of letting it pass out of the family or into non-Protestant hands. A farmer's preference for endogamy was closely related to ideas around land transfer; this was partly because of the fear of community disapproval should an inheriting farmer marry someone from another group. Richard O'Leary quotes a study from the 1970s which found that marriage customs in rural Ireland were 'very much bound up [...] with a tribal sense of land ownership'. A Leinster farmer said, 'if one of our boys or girls makes a mixed marriage, that's a whole family lost [...] Naturally we'll try to prevent that if we can.'[402]

Thomas goes through a litany of the Protestant families that used to own and work the land locally but who are no longer there. He attributes this fact to very low levels of marriage, and that some of those marriages involved intermarriage with Catholics:

> There was four brothers and a sister there. There was Dick, Sam, Willie and Johnny and the sister. None of them ever got married [...] Go up the lane then [...] well, Tommy humped off with a [Catholic] lassie [...] that's gone. That's no longer a Protestant area [...] Go up the, the lane [...] Ben was there, Tommy was there, and Robbie was there. Robbie had a place [...] Ben never got married, he was in the homeplace and the two sisters stayed there.

He names twenty families or so, relating the number of acres belonging to each of them. When he was born, he says, the small Protestant farmers in the area collectively had 'the guts of a thousand acres of land, but [...] All those families and all the farms are gone.' For him, the local landscape, including the derelict or Catholic-owned farmhouses that used to be home to Protestant families, has become a living memorial to his culture and way of life.

Nancy remembers discussions in the rural area to which she moved in the late 1960s about the importance of avoiding mixed marriage, particularly in the case of young women who expected to inherit land or of male heirs to a farm, 'if you didn't have a brother, in the end, the farm might go to your husband's family who were Roman Catholic, or if you were the young man, you married a Roman Catholic girl, your children were brought up Roman Catholic, and automatically the land went to them. And that was a great source of bitterness.' Andy states that *Ne Temere* led to a sense of insecurity among Protestant farmers, 'in rural districts land owned by Protestant farmers was sometimes lost to the community over a single generation.' Lynne comments that '*Ne Temere* was feared and dreaded and there was deep resentment that [...] farms passed out of Protestant families', while Millie recalls driving through a rural area with the local rector 'as he pointed out one farm after another' that had once been Protestant. Ed comments that many rural Protestants preferred not to marry rather than allow their farm to pass out of Protestant ownership, and Mike reports:

> Of course, many people felt that the Roman Catholic priests were interested mainly in getting more 'converts' and that the Protestants were more concerned lest their lands and property 'fell into' Roman Catholic hands [...] a running joke when I was young was that a Protestant farmer would marry his sister, if it meant keeping his land 'safe'!! In fact, my grandfather [...] married his first cousin [...] his father's sister's daughter. The long-term strategy there was to unite the [family's] lands.

Tom recounts his wife's memories from her rural background:

> Three of the lads in the family, each with their own farm but living in the family homestead, never married because they were unable to find a suitable Protestant girl. Mixed marriages were taboo as the older members could not countenance the farm going to 'the other side.'

Marcus recalls attending services in rural churches in the south-west in the 1970s and 80s and noting many unmarried older men:

> There used to be a lot of elderly gentlemen standing at the back of the church. I asked somebody, 'Who are all these men?' A lot of them are dead now [...] Because if they had married a local girl – a Roman Catholic girl – the land, which was very important, would have changed hands. Because the children would have brought up Roman Catholic [...] But, I suppose, it was very sad that here are these men, older men, who did not have the companionship of a wife for that reason.

Letitia's rural relatives were much more upset than city people would have been when one of their children married out, because of their anxiety about the fact that the land would be owned 'by descendants who were Catholics'. Mariah discusses a family in which the eldest brother married a Catholic girl and the farm was passed to the second brother. The mixed marriage may not have been the only reason for this, but 'it certainly didn't help'. Bob reports, 'One of my mother's cousins, an only son, fathered a child with a local Catholic kitchen girl in the 1950s. He had to leave his home farm [...] which his younger sister subsequently inherited.' While this reaction was harsh, he also comments:

> While one might not now admire attempts to close ranks, Protestant fears of the *Ne Temere* decree were very well founded: in many parishes, especially those a little further from the larger social centres, one by one Protestant farmers chose local Catholic brides and had to sign their unborn children to Catholicism; today the Protestant community has all but ceased to exist in those areas.

Martha reports having heard of 'economic matchmaking' among the Protestants in her community; the point was to bring two farms together or make strategic marriages that would be 'good for the land'. She gives the example of how the second or third son of a farm family would be matched to a woman, with no brothers, who was set to inherit a farm; in a small community, such a woman was otherwise considered vulnerable to mixed marriage, resulting in the passage of land into Catholic hands. Martha explains how, through carefully matched marriages, land could be brought together so that little enclaves of Protestants were maintained; the land itself was seen as sharing their Protestant identity. This happened in the area where Martha now lives, 'except for two fields, practically all our land is joined. It's Protestants around us [...] there are only two fields that aren't Protestant or Methodist.'

Natasha suggests how anxiety about the land leaving Protestant hands could have been fuelled by community pressure. In her conservative rural community, Protestant-owned farms were clustered in a tight-knit unit that did everything together, 'The whole road is Protestant [...] so the whole road went to the same church and the whole road went to the same primary school.' If someone sold outside the Protestant community, everyone in the immediate area would have felt that the integrity of the community had been compromised.

Mariah reports that her daughter married into another Protestant family in recent years, and that 'because he was the eldest son, the one getting the farm, they [his family] were quite happy; they wanted him to marry a Protestant'. His family would be much more accepting of a younger child, not due to inherit the land, marrying out. She feels that, for many Protestant farmers, it is still important to know that the land will continue to stay in Protestant hands in the generations to come. Flora reports that this is an attitude that lingers among older people, who still sometimes express regret when they hear of a mixed marriage involving a farm, 'I only heard the other day, "It's a shame, that farm now has gone out of Protestant hands."' Freddie similarly comments that, until very recently, the phrase used to describe land passing into Catholics hands was, 'well, there's another door closed now'.

The Fethard Boycott

Fethard is a small village on the Wexford coast. In 1957, a local Protestant in a mixed marriage, Mrs Cloney, changed her mind about the vow she had taken to raise her children as Catholics and left the family home, taking her two daughters with her.[403] Following her decision to send her daughters to the local Protestant school, Mrs Cloney had been visited repeatedly by local Catholic priests who insisted that her children would be educated in the local Catholic school, with or without her consent.[404] When she left, there were widespread suspicions among the Catholic community that the local Protestants, largely small farmers and shop owners, were complicit. At this time, the Protestant community of the Diocese of Ferns, of which Fethard was a part, was under pressure, with high levels of emigration, delayed and reduced rates of marriage, and ongoing financial difficulty.[405]

The local hardware shop and newsagent suffered a devastating loss of revenue as Catholics, at the behest of the parish priest, boycotted them. Nobody would buy the milk produced by Protestant dairy farmers.[406] Miss Knipe, a piano teacher, lost most of her pupils. The Church of Ireland primary school closed because the teacher (the only teacher in the small school) left, stating her intention not to return until the boycott had been resolved.[407] A Catholic woman, the primary school teacher had been warned by local Catholics that she should resign.[408] Owen Sheehy-Skeffington, a senator, asked the Department of Education what arrangements it would make for the education of the Protestant children; the department answered that it had 'neither the right nor the ability to intervene in a local dispute'.[409] The Catholic Bishop of Galway, Michael Browne, defended the boycott at the Annual Congress of the Catholic Truth Society, which was held in Wexford that year, saying that 'There seems to be a concerted campaign to entice or kidnap Catholic children and deprive them of their faith', and that most non-Catholics made 'political capital' out of a 'peaceful and moderate protest'.[410]

Norman Ruddock, the Church of Ireland curate, was invited to run the school at Fethard during the summer months. He found a sign pinned to the schoolhouse door that said, 'Scabs, beware of the boycott village' and reports having been extremely nervous, as 'there had been rifle fire on several nights outside Protestant homes.'[411] Protestants from nearby towns such as New Ross travelled all the way to Fethard to make purchases from the boycotted shops, despite their fear that the boycott might spread. Hope, who remembers first reading about the boycott in a newspaper at school, and initially feeling excited when realising that she knew the people involved, soon realised that it was causing upset and fear. She also perceived how it was also galvanising local Protestants to help, 'I can remember my mother telling me that they had a kind of agreement among a number of people in [the nearby town] that they would go down, different people would go down, and they would drive down a distance of about twenty miles, which at that time was a bit of a drive [...] and do shopping in the [boycotted] shop.'

The Protestant community in Wexford was encouraged by Hubert Butler and other activists to do what it could to buy supplies from the boycotted businesses,[412] but the Church of Ireland hierarchy described their actions as 'senseless provocation'.[413] The serving rector in Fethard was a young man called Adrian Fisher, who did not know the community well and was considered out of his depth. Reverend Edward Grant, his predecessor, who was now working in another parish, was called on to intervene and visited the local Catholic priest and his curate, Father Allen and Father Stafford, to discuss the boycott. He was shocked by their unfriendliness and left with the impression that the local priests strongly supported the boycott.[414] In fact, Father Stafford described the 'Parish Co-operation' (a euphemism for the boycott) as a 'grand, dignified, legal profession of our Faith'.[415]

The Fethard boycott occurred just seven years after another highly publicised case in which a Protestant man, Ernest Tilson, who had married a Catholic woman, had promised to raise their children as Catholics, only to seek custody of three of the four children when the marriage broke up.[416] The High Court and the Supreme Court had both ruled against Mr Tilson after his wife sought to remove the children from the Protestant children's home in which he had placed them; the general impression among Protestants was that the court had been biased against Tilson and that 'the courts had abandoned a rule of law which was impartial between denominations in favour of one which benefitted the Roman Catholic Church.'[417] Tilson's mother, Mitty, also claimed that her family had been boycotted and that her dress-making business had dried up.[418] The 'special position of the Holy Catholic Apostolic and Roman Church' in the Irish constitution was critical in the decision reached on the matter of custody.[419] When Justice Gavin Duffy ruled on the Tilson case in the High Court, he said:

> We are a people of deep religious convictions. Accordingly, our fundamental law deliberately establishes a Christian constitution; the indifferentism of our decadent era is utterly rejected by us [...] religion holds in the Constitution the place of honour which the community has always accorded to it in public opinion. The right of the Catholic Church to guard the faith of its children, the great majority, is registered in our fundamental document.[420]

In this context, in which it seemed to Protestants that the state was intrinsically Catholic and would not recognise their needs[421] (although the Tilson case was less clear-cut than it might appear for reasons that are beyond the scope of this chapter), there was great anxiety among Protestants about the likelihood of partisanship should the Fethard case come to trial. Andy reports that 'there was a feeling among Protestants that Catholic judges felt themselves obliged to conform to Catholic teaching in their judgements […] Protestants were only too aware of well-publicised cases such as the notorious Fethard-on-Sea boycott.'

The boycott was eventually resolved, partly because de Valera, the taoiseach at the time, denounced it, asking 'all who have regard for the fair name, good repute and well-being of our nation to use their influence to bring this deplorable affair to a speedy end'.[422] He described the boycott as 'ill-conceived, ill-considered and futile', and 'unjust and cruel'.[423] Mrs Cloney returned to her family home after the boycott was resolved. Although it remained an exceptional event,[424] in the aftermath it seemed clearer than ever to many Protestants that 'mixed marriages' were a bad idea. 'The events in Wexford', writes Broderick, 'impacted on the wider Church of Ireland community nationally, making it aware of its vulnerability.' [425] Arthur remembers:

> My father was very frightened by the Fethard on Sea boycott. He felt that if it spread it would be disastrous for all Irish Protestants. He was deeply relieved when Mr de Valera condemned the boycott and it collapsed. I remember his saying that he would never say a bad word about Dev again (and he did not). I subsequently heard him defending Mr de Valera and referring to his action on that occasion.

The Catholic Bishop of Ferns at the time, Bishop Comiskey, apologised for the boycott in 1998 at an event to mark the bicentenary of the 1798 rebellion.[426]

For many older Protestants, the Fethard boycott has become not just a fact of history but also an important folk narrative; it is also a way in which old hurts and anxieties can be discussed with reference to incidents within their own extended families and communities. Doris and her husband went to see a film about the boycott.[427] Aside from them, there were only three people in the cinema – a fact that makes her wonder if people were avoiding it on purpose 'because they knew what it was about, and they didn't want to know any more.' Seeing the film recalled the sorrow and anger that she remembers from the time. It was, she says, 'the saddest thing I have ever seen. It was ·terrible […] It was so cruel, so cruel.' It reminds her of her cousin who married for a second time after his wife died in childbirth; he married the Catholic nurse he had hired to care for the children. There was a great 'hullaballoo' about the mixed marriage. Looking back, she says, 'You think, "What was it all about, really?"'

Samuel remembers that 'everyone' was talking about the Fethard boycott at the time, and that there was concern that things could 'blow up' and start to impact on all the Protestants. Vivienne was very aware of the Fethard boycott as a child because her family used to visit a cottage in Wexford for the holidays. She remembers 'kind of understanding' and finding it very hurtful. The memory reminds her of another little girl whose father, a Catholic, was in the army. The child's mother had her baptised Protestant and 'there was a lot of trouble over that' locally; she attributes this to the fact that the local parish priest was a very difficult, bigoted man. She remembers this episode as being extremely upsetting for all the local Protestants, especially as it occurred shortly after the well-publicised Fethard case.

How to Get Married: Schools, Socials, Introductions, and Arrangements

One of the main reasons why Grace's parents felt strongly about Protestant children attending suitable denominational schools was the likelihood that they might meet their future spouse through the education system, 'The idea was you sent them to Protestant schools to mix with Protestant people and, hopefully, marry Protestant people.' Adam comments that the Protestant schools in Dublin were generally happy to accept Jewish students, who were not considered a demographic threat; however, they would never accept Catholic students because of the risk that friendships could lead to more serious relationships, either between the students themselves or, in the case of single-sex schools, with the students' siblings, 'there was a sense of "We'd better watch it, or we'll be wiped out."' Tom says one way of identifying potential partners in Dublin was to see what school scarf they were wearing, 'usually a school scarf was an indication whether the wearer was from a Protestant tradition.' When young people became romantically involved with Catholics, these relationships were often quashed. Elsie remembers, 'my mother often spoke of the Catholic boy whom she met and fell in love with [...] Her mother forbade her to have anything to do with him. They wrote to each other. His letters had to be sent to my mother's best friend. The relationship eventually fizzled out.'

There were social organisations and clubs specifically for Protestants where young people were encouraged to mingle. Maxton describes these events as 'preparatory courtship rituals within the declining Protestant population'.[428] Millie remembers 'various organisations for young people [...] which aimed to provide healthy and wholesome entertainment for the young *and* which might lead to "suitable" marriages'.

For teenagers and young adults, attending 'socials' was a good way of meeting other young Protestants. Kevin Dalton, a memoirist who wrote of his childhood and youth in the 1930s and 40s, recalls going to socials all over the Dublin area as a young man. The door was staffed by the local rector, 'to make sure only Protestants' attended, and in some areas 'you had to sign your name in a book and state which parish you came from.' The purpose, he says, 'was to avoid mixed marriages.'[429]

Robert attributes *Ne Temere* with having contributed greatly to Protestants trying to 'keep themselves apart'. He remembers that 'there was very much a concentration on Protestants marrying Protestants. We didn't go to dances; we went to parish socials where we would meet other young Protestants with whom, hopefully, we would become involved.' Honora remembers that 'Parents would have encouraged their young people to join these clubs as they were a good way for Protestants to meet'; Andy reports that 'tennis clubs and table-tennis clubs were a feature of many Protestant parishes, both rural and urban [...] The purpose was quite plainly to keep the young Protestant people in touch with each other and avoid "mixed marriages."'

Doris met her husband at a parish picnic organised by the local clergyman. 'There wasn't anyone else to meet', she says. There are many cases in her area of two sisters marrying two brothers; sometimes this has been considered a little embarrassing. Because communities in many rural areas were sometimes extremely dispersed, young people might have to travel for miles to attend parish socials. Doris says the local clergyman managed the parish's social life with socials that were Protestant-only in order to keep Protestant communities together. The socials were held in the school and the local 'RCs' [Roman Catholics] were banned. Trev reports that he was involved in running socials, 'and it was the norm that entry to them had to be by invitation only [and therefore Protestant only]. It also applied to a table tennis club I started.'

Candide remembers that she wanted to marry a Protestant:

> I wanted to live like my parents and share my beliefs with my husband. My parents wanted their children to marry Protestants. Our churches wanted us to marry within our tradition [...] We went to 'socials' [...] They were for Protestants only and you had to have an invitation with your name on it. Some of the men of the parish manned a table at the door and the invitations were taken in [...] There are many couples, including my husband and myself, who are very grateful to the parents of the parishes who facilitated our generation meeting each other thus.

Joyce discusses how she and her brother went to socials to meet other young Protestants, although they often had to travel very far, without a car, to get to them. Her brother and his friend rode their bicycles a great distance to attend socials where they could meet and dance with Protestant girls, and as the socials were usually far from their rural townlands, they generally stopped on the way home to sleep in a haystack until morning. Going to dances or pubs with the Catholics in their area was unacceptable, although they co-operated with Catholics in their farming work and their father often spent an evening playing cards with Catholic neighbours. The socials were great fun, with a 'full band and lovely music':

> the men all stood all along [...] by the door, and the women'd stay all down in the lower end of the hall. When they'd dance then, pick your partner or whatever, they'd all come droving up to the top [...] they used to say it was like a march [...] lots of times lots of the men, if they were slow about coming up [...] well, they'd walk up and there'd be no girls left [...] they'd have to go back to where they'd came from.

June reports family stories of her parents and grandparents travelling on their bicycles for a full day to attend distant Protestant-only *ceilís* and socials. Most of them met their spouses at such events, and most got married and raised families in the area. Basil remembers the socials in his area, 'They were parish dances, and it was a ticket [...] you had to have a card to get in, and that was to keep it segregated [...] the rectors would give out cards to their young people.'

Mabel remembers the Protestant socials, where so many happy matches were made, as 'beautiful events' held in church halls. Young people were brought by their parents at about ten o'clock at night and stayed until about two in the morning, with a break around midnight for tea, sandwiches, and cakes. Men would sometimes visit the nearest pub to have a pint or two in the course of the evening because alcoholic drinks were never served. After Mabel's marriage, socials died out in her area, largely because the young people who went to them now wanted to attend venues that served alcohol and had proper dance floors. For a while, socials were held in pubs or hotels, but that was 'the ruination of them'. They lost their unique atmosphere and they were much more porous, socially speaking; in the relatively neutral venue of a hotel or pub, anyone could turn up and you might take a fancy to someone before realising they were the 'wrong sort'.

Priscilla discusses travelling to quite distant areas to attend socials, and how they fostered a sense of community even among a very dispersed population. This, she says, gave rural Protestants like her family broader horizons. The young women were firmly told by their elders that they should get to a social to get themselves a husband, and she met and fell in love with her husband at one of them, 'we all socialised together and we didn't socialise outside of the Protestant tradition and it was inevitable you were going to find somebody that you fell in love with.'

Protestants in border areas, and in some cities, comment that it was much easier for them to meet potential spouses than in other parts of the country. Bob reports:

> It was relatively easy for Protestants in [my] area to marry within their own community in the 1950s/1960s and the majority did. There was still quite a robust Protestant population, and there was still a vibrant Protestant social life which comprised of badminton

and table tennis clubs, whist clubs as well as social dances which were run on exclusively denominational lines. The badminton and table tennis clubs usually had exclusively Protestant membership and ran competitive leagues which ensured members socialised beyond the parish [...] these clubs and activities all helped keep the community together, especially in the face of the detested *Ne Temere* decree, and [this] was seen as self-preservation.

Billy says, 'there were enough Protestant people around' his area for every-one to find a partner to marry. He tells the story of his father who found his first wife 'literally half a mile down the road'. After her death, their child was fostered out and 'meantime my father started romancing my mother who was half a mile up the road'. This shows the relative density of the rural Protestant population in the area. Hazel has a similar account:

> It was easy for Protestants to marry within their own community. We were so close to the border, there was even more choice, and young people travelled [across the border] frequently to play bad-minton/table tennis or attend socials in church halls and meet many young Protestants. I do not know of anyone in our area who was af-fected by the *Ne Temere* rule.

Liza remembers most courtships starting in the local Orange hall, 'Our main recreation was dancing every Friday night in the local Orange Hall. This was the meeting place for single boys and girls and how most courtships began.'

In Dublin, with a relatively high number of Protestants, quite a large number from affluent backgrounds, and a lively inner-city community, there was a wider range of venues for romance than in many rural areas. George remembers:

> [we] used to go to many dances, both dress dances for various soci-eties in TCD which would be in the Metropole or the Gresham, but we frequently went to 'hops,' less formal dances on Saturday nights in parish halls in Sandford or Harold's Cross, and there were partic-ularly good ones in the Boys' Masonic School in Clonskeagh. To get in you not only had to pay (5 shillings) but you also needed a 'ticket' which you got beforehand and showed at the door, which ensured that you were a Protestant.

Roberta describes the 'Protestant dances' and how they led to 'quite a lot of intermarriage [among different Protestant denominations], keeping the young people together'; she also describes how the local tennis club was a good place for young Protestants to meet one another. Jennie remembers that all-Protestant socials and clubs in Dublin were intended to ensure that young Protestants would 'make their friends and their future spouses among their own faith group', partly to keep the communities and congregations active, 'and also to avoid the heartbreak of mixed marriages and the choices that came with them'. She identifies the YMCA (Young Men's Christian Association) on Abbey Street as an important venue for these events. The Dublin branch of this worldwide organisation, which focuses on youth development and support of the young, was attended not just by Dubliners but also by young Protestants from all over the country who lived in YMCA and YWCA (Young Women's Christian Association) accommodation. Walter also remembers the YMCA on Abbey Street as the place where his parents met, and where he himself attended dances as a young man, 'They used to call it the Young Man's Courting Academy.'

Wally remembers travelling from Dublin to Greystones to attend socials; the events were not ticketed but the young people were quizzed on what parish they belonged to as a condition for gaining entry. He and his friends had to be prepared, because 'we'd have picked up a few Catholic girls along the way, and we'd say, "Now, when we ask you, say you're from Harold's Cross and the clergyman is such and such [...]" so we would get away that way!'

Protestant socials were closely regulated in Jim's home area. Catholics were not allowed to attend, and the dances concluded with a rousing rendition of 'God Save the Queen'; many of the border Protestants still identified closely with Britain. Jim's best friend was a Catholic and was eager to meet a new array of girls, so he was smuggled in; the most immediate Protestant social was out of the question, so they went a little farther afield, where he would not be known and could 'pass'. His Protestant friends referred to him as 'Billy' instead of his real, distinctively Catholic name. On one occasion, a suspicious rector questioned him about who he was and where he came from and hoped to catch him out by asking him the name of the captain of the Boys' Brigade in the area. 'Billy' didn't know for sure but managed to guess correctly. Jim says that he understood exactly why the Protestants wanted to exclude Catholics from the socials – it was because of *Ne Temere*. He says, 'the Protestant population would have been decimated, like it's decimated enough, but it would have been totally decimated, because as human nature being what it is, sure.' On the other hand, 'Billy' was his best friend.

Archie remembers, 'I once brought a Catholic friend to a dance [...] the vicar welcomed him in whereupon my friend said, "Thank you, Father" [the title given to Catholic priests].' The story does not relate whether or not the friend was barred subsequent to this revelation. Willy also remembers bringing Catholic friends to the Protestant socials in his areas; despite the fact that this was frowned upon, it was natural to him – most of his friends were Catholics:

> when I went to Protestant socials [...] You know, you went there, and a lot of people had a few drinks, and twelve o'clock you'd have tea and sandwiches and then it would go on till three o'clock in the morning, and it went on late, and I got approached by a lady who said, '[Willy], we don't mind you bringing one or two [...] Catholic friends, but *eleven* is a bit much!'

Myrtle remembers similar disapproval in her hometown, 'I had cousins who used to come, and they used to bring their Catholic friends, and that was really frowned on [...] They would not turn anybody away, but the people selling the tickets or giving out the tea would sort of, "Look at that, she's bringing so and so!"'

Eleanora remembers that 'sometimes someone would invite a Catholic friend or neighbour to a social, which was frowned upon. People would have to talk about it afterwards.' Marion remembers Catholic neighbours trying to access the socials, almost as a joke ('they would be laughing') but being turned away when someone recognised them. Thomas says that 'a shower of Catholic fellas' came to a Protestant dance and the dean himself had to go and talk to them and arrange to have them removed. They left without causing any trouble, leaving the Protestants to get their mugs of tea and sandwiches undisturbed.

As views began to lapse – that it was preferable for Protestants and Catholics to socialise separately, that Protestants should not drink socially, that mixed marriages were a taboo to be feared – the all-Protestant socials started to drift towards obsolescence in many areas. Morris says:

> many marriages between Protestants took place as a result of meeting up [at socials]. Alas, this changed when Protestants, feeling more re-laxed about Roman Catholics, began to bring partners of that reli-gion to the dances. Also, some members took to having a drink before the dances resulting in them starting two hours late. The dances gradually faded out in the 1970s.

The socials in Eleanora's area died out in the 1970s and 80s, and mixed marriages became more common after that 'because people started to go out to where traditionally Protestants would not have gone'. She attributes the death of the socials to two factors: Protestants wanting to drink more alcohol and local pubs becoming more accepting of women. May remem-bers being one of the last of her generation to attend socials in her area. Because there were few Protestants to be found locally, and she had attended a local Catholic school, her parents were keen for her to meet other young Protestants and started bringing her to socials when she was 15 years old. Her father taught her how to waltz and about the protocol, 'if a boy asked you to dance, you dance with him for three songs and then you say thank you, and then you sit down, and you don't ever refuse a boy to dance unless you think he's drunk, because it takes a lot of courage for a boy to ask.'

'The way it was,' May recalls, 'all my childhood my parents told me, "One day you will grow up and you will fall in love with a handsome Protestant farmer." Nothing else was presented to me as possible.' Everyone in her rural Protestant community assumed that they would grow up to marry someone who was not only Protestant but also land-owning; there was pressure on girls to choose someone from a similar-sized farm to that of their parents. While nobody was put under pressure to marry anyone specific, 'the seed would be sown in your mind very young' that young people were expected to marry someone very similar to themselves. If a young person did fall for someone 'of the other sort', they often tried not to let things go too far, 'you just didn't let it happen […] it just couldn't have happened.'

In some areas, it appears that arranged or semi-arranged marriages among Protestants occasionally occurred. This was in response not only to the relative scarcity of potential partners in those districts but also to the perceived need to 'keep land Protestant'. Wallace relates the story of his grandparents, and how his grandmother was proposed to his grandfather as 'a suitable wife', 'He made his way to the local clergyman [...] and they met for tea and decided to get married. That was in about 1910.' Trevor remembers local rectors getting involved in helping to set up marriages:

> Because I suppose the rector in [a nearby town] asked the rector in [Trevor's hometown,] 'Would you have a man? I have a good girl here and nobody to marry, would you have a man that needs a wife?' [...] And then we had a girl working for us, and she was invited one night out to a house [...] and she came back, and she said, 'I'm engaged!' She had met him, and they were given ten minutes outside the door.

Clara's uncle related the story of a local match, 'when he went to meet his future wife he went into the house and it was dark [as there was no electricity] so he lit a bush and put it in front of the girl's face and announced, "She'll do!"'

Hugh remembers of his own youth that arranged marriages still occurred at times, 'Protestant farmers in particular wanted their children to marry Protestants because they didn't want the farm to become Roman Catholic owned. I knew two or three cases where the parents on both sides got together and said, "I think our Willie should marry your daughter."' In Hugh's rural community, 'arranged marriages or at least marriages of convenience' were quite common. He gives some examples: a man with a big farm who married a woman young enough to be his daughter because he was a 'good prospect' for a girl from a poor family; and a couple from very evangelical backgrounds who did not wish to marry Protestants who were less pious than they were (let alone Catholics).

Samuel's grandfather had wanted to marry a particular girl – the second daughter in a suitable family – 'because she was better looking than the first one'. A marriage was arranged between him and the eldest daughter, as 'you had to start at the top and work down'. Although the bride was not his first choice, the marriage 'worked out' and they went on to have nine children. Honora reports that 'To keep Protestants from marrying Roman Catholics or their own first cousins, there were "made matches," often arranged by the clergy. They usually worked out well. Protestant young people were encouraged not to mix with Catholic young people for fear of mixed marriages.'

Doris says, while there was no formal system for arranging marriages between Protestants, there were older people, like her father-in-law, who liked to try to matchmake. He would say of a bachelor, 'Look at him. Couldn't he marry her? She's [got] children and all. A widow. Got a child reared and all; it's a great advantage!' She says these marriages lasted because 'once you were married you were married'. She also grew up with stories of her own parents' arranged marriage in the 1920s. Her father's sister, who had married a man from a distant area, met a nice young girl working in a local shop and decided that she would be just right for her bachelor brother. She arranged for them to meet and, despite a vast age difference of about thirty years, a marriage was arranged. It was a good marriage, partly because the wife was from a poor background and now had the security of belonging to a comfortable house and a large farm.

Mariah's grandparents' marriage was arranged, with the groom 'marrying into the farm'. This was a great prospect for him, as he was one of eleven with no expectation of inheriting land. Although the couple had only met once, briefly, before their wedding day, family lore remembers it as a happy marriage. Hubert says that one of the reasons why 'made marriages' were still relatively common in his childhood in the 1930s and 40s was that people were opposed not just to mixed marriages but also to excessive intermarriage between relatives, which was considered a risk in areas with a very small Protestant population. There were known matchmakers in his area, and arranged marriages were particularly common among Protestant farmers who wanted the land to stay in Protestant ownership. He says that while the tradition is unusual now, 'there could well be one or two here or there' among more traditional families.

Lingering Resistance to, and Growing Acceptance of, Mixed Marriages

The traditional preference for endogamy declined dramatically throughout the second part of the twentieth century. While in 1946 fewer than 2 per cent of married Protestants had married Catholics, this increased rapidly to 16 per cent in 1961 and about 34 per cent by the early 1970s.[430] As well as an abundance of stories that deal with sorrow and anger in relation to mixed marriage, there are also many stories of people coming to terms with mixed marriages, and most are keen to stress that mixed marriages are no longer considered a problem – that all that matters is that the young couple is happy.

Mabel says that although her parents had been 'a little upset' when her brother married a Catholic girl in the 1960s, they 'reunited shortly after'. The young couple dealt with a potentially difficult situation by marrying very quietly and living in England for a couple of years before coming home. Strikingly, although *Ne Temere* was still standing, the young man 'told the priest what to do with his paper' and would not sign.

By the 1950s, Donald says, most Dublin families accepted that 'marrying out' was here to stay, although each side preferred it when the young couple got married in 'their' church. Donald recalls mixed marriages were still 'very vexatious, and very much frowned upon' in his younger years, although they were becoming much more common:

> I remember a woman whose son married a Roman Catholic, which to her was a heartbreak. And next thing the child was baptised, as she said, 'in the chapel.' And she said to her son, 'That was very un-derhand,' and he told her to mind her own business. Being a Protestant, for him, was a protection against Catholicism. But he didn't feel the need to extend this protection to his children, who were raised as Catholics.

Protestants could be offended when mixed marriages occurred in the vestry or in a side chapel in a Catholic church. Donald remembers that one woman went to the parish priest and gave him a piece of her mind, later telling her own vicar, 'I told old father so-and-so my daughter will be married in no bloody vestry!'; whereas another young woman did not tell her Protestant mother that she was getting married until it was over because she would certainly have disapproved. But even the most disapproving parents generally came around in the end. They knew that 'there was no one else'.

Constance remembers the mixed marriage of a family friend. It was accepted but caused 'great consternation', and her mother was hugely upset when she attended the wedding in a local Catholic church at eight in the morning – a strange time for a wedding – in a side chapel, with no music, 'she said they all felt like criminals, they just scurried in and out the side door and it was all over as quickly as possible and she was upset by that.'

Robert's mother's first cousin had 'married out', which had caused a huge scandal in the family, but thankfully all had ended well, 'they lived to have the best daughter in law that they could ever have had. She turned out to be a really wonderful lady and looked after both of them in their old age.' The only downside was that all the children were raised as Catholics, 'Presumably the parents were forced to promise that when they were getting married.'

Edward remembers his father telling him that 'it would be better to find someone than no one', by which he meant that he should not limit himself to girls from the Church of Ireland community. There were still all-Protestant socials in his area, but by the time Edward was old enough to go to them, in the mid- to late 1980s, interest in them had waned considerably; the events were promoted more as a way of raising funds for repairing church roofs than as a way of introducing young people to one another.

Ian says his generation was the first in his extended family to have any mixed marriages, or at least any that were openly discussed. 'The older generation didn't take it well,' he says. 'People just discussed it in terms of, "The end of the world is nigh"; "It's all gone to hell."' For him, it was very important to marry within the community, and he married a woman from a similar background to himself. He says that although the taboo is of much less import than before, some older people struggle to accept mixed marriages 'because when you marry out, chances are the kids are raised as Catholics, so the Protestant community today is 90% of what it was 100 years ago [it is actually much less than that]. Do the sums and you'll see that in the next generation there's going to be very little left.'

As late as 1991, Risteárd Ó Glaisne, a scholar and enthusiast of both the Irish language and the place of Protestants in Ireland, suggested that one reason why Protestants had 'mixed marriages' was 'sheer laziness in seeking for a suitable co-religionist as partner, where one would have to go to some trouble'. He suggested that 'a Protestant can, if not without heartache, decide, after deep thought on the subject, not to marry a beloved Roman Catholic' and urged Protestants to consider the impact that marriage can have in terms of 'long term consequences affecting future generations'. He points out that one can fall in love with more than one person and suggests that, for Protestants, it would be better if that person were of the same background, because 'to be the cause of such an influence in a community as vulnerable as Protestantism is in Ireland carries with it a very great responsibility.'[431] In other words, his view was that it would be bad for the Protestant partner of a mixed marriage to come under the influence of the Catholic Church.

The sense of vulnerability Ó Glaisne alludes to was still felt by some families in the 1990s. Harold discusses one of his sisters who married a Catholic. Their parents, from an inner-city neighbourhood, were absolutely horrified at first, 'there was uproar is all I can say. It was madness [...] they were bigoted in their own way.' He compares his parents' community of working-class Protestants to a 'wounded animal' because of how depleted and powerless it had become, and he comments, 'I suppose a wounded animal thinks it's defending itself, but it is actually attacking.'

Rachel tells stories of parents who disowned their children for marrying Catholics. Although this had started to wane by the time she had grown up, she knows of a woman who was disowned as late as the 1990s, by which stage such a reaction had become very exceptional. Her own mother had advised her that it would be easier to marry within the Protestant community, saying, 'If you marry someone from outside your tradition you have to be a lot more versatile to cope. If you marry someone who is like you [...] marriage might be easier', but when her brother married a Catholic, his wife was accepted and 'loved as much as any of the rest of the in-laws'. However, the children were raised within the Catholic tradition.

Although many factors, especially the liberal and increasingly secular nature of Irish culture, have contributed to much higher levels of intermarriage between Protestants and Catholics, levels of intermarriage were, and have remained, closely aligned with the relative number of Protestants in a given area. In areas where the number of Protestants is higher, there are fewer mixed marriages, suggesting that marrying out, for many families, is still considered less than ideal. By the twenty-first century, mixed marriage rates were over 50 per cent in areas with fewer, dispersed communities of Protestants, but the rates were lower in areas like Cavan, Monaghan, and Donegal, where the relative number of Protestants was higher, and in Dublin.[432] Some, such as Jonathan, express impatience with those who still feel strongly about keeping marriage within the Protestant community. He says that when he meets former classmates who married within the community, 'I feel like saying "Crikey, you didn't get far, did you?" […] It was almost like a Jewish thing. You know, where they are required to marry Jews, Jews who marry other Jews […] I couldn't wait to get out of it.' His own experience was that 'There was a whole world out there. Let me out! This is just too claustrophobic for me.'

Marigold has pragmatic views on her aspirations for her daughters' marriages. Ideally, she says, they would marry Protestant men, 'but I know, being sensible, that's probably not going to happen. They are not going to meet them here […] I think it's got to the stage where you'd be happy if they just even met an Irish person!'

Conclusion

Themes of love, marriage, and the difficulties associated with them as a minority are prominent motifs in Protestants' storytelling. Many of them have stories about their family's experience of mixed marriage and *Ne Temere*, and the efforts expended in finding the 'right' sort of spouse. For most of them, the sense of relief associated with the relaxation of these rules and norms is tangible, although some of them miss aspects of the old days.

For some older Protestants who have never married, particularly those from rural areas, there is a sense of sorrow over opportunities lost. These are people who lived through a period where marrying out was considered intensely shameful in many families. They may have seen for themselves how 'mixed' couples were sometimes ostracised by both sides of the family, but now they often feel a little silly about the fears that stopped them, when they were younger, from taking the brave step that marrying out necessitated. For William, the fact that he and many of the men he knows never married is a source of grief and loss, not just because he is now living through a solitary old age but also because he believes that his small rural parish feels the lack of the children who never came. Neither he nor his brother ever married; three of his cousins, who live 'over that way', never married either. 'I hate to think about it,' he says. He continues:

> I can't see much future for the parish really […] it is hard […] and I blame myself as much for that but, when we were growing up, there

was a great shortage of ladies in the area. A great shortage. And you can understand that, and you would find if you looked through our parish that, in fact, quite a number of the people here would be related. There weren't that many people to marry, you see.

5. Stories of Feeling Different and the Same

Difference has long been central to the identity of Irish Protestants, whether it is an affirmation or denial of difference, or an aspect of how it has been negotiated. It is at the heart of many of the stories that Protestants tell about themselves. Feelings of difference can provide a sense of collective identity, while feelings of being very much the same as the Catholic majority in many ways help to assert a sense of Irishness.

Not Quite the Same

With the establishment of the Free State, 'the large Catholic majority was viewed as legitimating the uniform imposition of a Catholic ethos', tending, in turn, to alienate non-Catholics.[433] Catholics were considered 'pure and authentic' and others were 'inevitably cast as counter-types [...] targets of suspicion and hostility'.[434] The new government enacted policies that enhanced feelings of difference and peripherality.[435] Shortly after independence, a young don at Trinity College, who felt that Protestants should be 'loyal to Ireland before all other countries', said that Protestants had to endure the assumption that one had to be Catholic to be truly Irish.[436]

When he was a child, Hugh Maxton received two books from his mother: one that explained the difference between the sexes, and one that explained the difference between the Protestant faith and Catholicism. For years, the two issues were completely intermingled for him.[437] At around 7 years of age, Elizabeth Bowen realised that Protestants were a minority. She met few Catholics, '"the others" whose world lay alongside ours but never touched'. As the other two topics that were not to be discussed were sex and social class, she developed 'an almost sexual shyness on the subject of Roman Catholics'.[438] Writing of her working-class Dublin childhood in the 1930s and 40s, Edith Newman Devlin — an academic who wrote a memoir of her working-class childhood in Dublin — remembered profound

173

feelings of being 'unnoticed and accepted', 'not the genuine article [...] only playing at being Irish [...] not the real thing.'[439] Robert says, 'Ireland was very definitely a Catholic country. Everybody said it. We said it, the Catholics said it [...] we were slightly misfits.' Thomas discusses the day of his birth. It was St Patrick's Day, and he was born with the help of a local midwife, a Catholic woman, while the men, including his Uncle Bill, waited downstairs. 'He'll have to be called Paddy!' the midwife said. Uncle Bill retorted, 'There'll be no Paddies in this house!' It was important for the baby to be given a 'Protestant' name.

Some Protestants lived in what James describes as 'a form of self-imposed apartheid'. Some appear to have felt that public spaces – streets, parks, shops – 'belonged to' Catholics and Catholicism more than they belonged to Protestants, and that Protestants inhabited a sort of psychosocial fringe of society. Quentin remembers a sense of awkwardness around playing in public spaces, 'we might have felt just a little bit different and not necessarily entitled to be part of the games other children were playing.' He and his sister went to the local playground sometimes, where 'we always did feel like intruders', especially when everyone else left at six o'clock to say the rosary in a local hall. Eadry felt that her Protestant background was a 'restraint', as there were so many things one could not say, discuss, or even think, especially in public. On occasion, the widespread assumption beyond the constraints of the Protestant minority that 'everyone' is Catholic led to difficult situations. Ethel remembers 'attending a lecture in the town where I worked. In it the speaker alluded to the belief "of course Protestants and heretics cannot be saved and will go to hell." I was young and unable to object; I just did not attend the rest of the lectures.'

There is a sense of frustration among people who feel that they are still not always considered 'fully' Irish, or not Irish in the same way as Catholics. Ed recalls 'being regarded as not quite Irish' – 'perceived to be some class of Anglo-Irish' who recognised the British monarch as the head of their church. Dave remembers feeling hurt when he read a letter to *The Irish Times* 'that claimed that Irishness and Catholicism are synonymous, that to be truly Irish one has to be Catholic'. Archie finds it 'extremely annoying and even disturbing' that his family, which 'evolved from a Quaker background', can be seen as less Irish than others.

Mariah remembers hearing a radio interview with a man who was the first child in Ireland to be born to a lesbian couple and identifying strongly with him because of the 'difference' they share. She says it is because they are both from minorities and that, as a minority, 'you're more pronounced in your activities in relation to the minority viewpoint [...] You make more of an effort.' The interviewee described spending his life trying to be better behaved than everyone else, aware that people would point to his minority status if he did something wrong. She says that, as a member of a tiny rural Protestant minority, she has always felt the same. Henry says of his family, 'They knew who they were [...] and they found strength in being different.' Jennie remembers a sense of both difference and a strong sense of Irishness, 'everyone I knew was "something." The majority were Roman Catholic, some were Jewish and the rest of us were Protestants [...] we were "different."'

Eleanora asserts that while most Protestants are proud to be Irish and to contribute to the Irish nation, their efforts are often ignored or rejected, whether one is speaking of the patriots of the past or the everyday efforts of Protestant citizens today. She tells a story about Mary Kenny, 'that journalist in *England*',[440] who, she says, 'came on the radio' in the 1970s or 80s and said that you had to be Catholic to be Irish. 'I don't know if she still believes it or not', she says, 'but a *lot* of Protestants were offended by that statement of hers.'

Rachel describes her upset when anyone discussed the hostilities between the UK and Argentina during the Falklands War. She provides an example of a debate over whether Britain should have gone to the Falklands after Argentina invaded. Her Catholic friends said, 'Eh, they're only planters anyway!' She felt this was not just a comment on the conflict but also an indication of their views on Protestants in Ireland. She segues quickly from this story to another about the various people who have assumed that Irish is not taught in Protestant schools – she is a teacher. She is affronted and upset at the fact that they would even think that Protestant children follow a different curriculum. She says that while Protestants in her area were not quite considered foreigners, they were not accepted as completely Irish.

In response to being identified as 'others', Protestants often felt the need to 'keep the head down'. This reaction is often described as an essential feature of Protestant culture and identity, particularly where the relative population of Protestants is low. Letitia explains, 'You wanted to blend in and if you didn't talk about it [being a Protestant] it was easier to blend in. We must have felt anxious or something.' Roberta says, 'there was an atmosphere of not putting ourselves forward [...] being well-behaved, good members of society and not attracting special attention [...] being good citizens, but not making too much noise.'

Shirley says her lifestyle and outlook differ little from those of her Catholic neighbours, but that she never discusses her background or identity. 'I don't really tell people what I am,' she explains, 'I'm on Facebook and I have 700 friends [...] I don't want to get into an argument about it and I don't want to flaunt it. They'd still [...] "Oh God, she's one of *them!*" I still feel like that.' When he was fourteen or fifteen, Harold asked his parents, '*Why* are you Protestants?' They did not know how to answer him, 'I think their angle was more "We're not Catholics" rather than "We're Protestants."' Harold believes that a large part of his parents' identity came from their experience as young working-class Protestants in Dublin in the 1950s, 'it would have been heavy duty.' However, he was always aware of a keen sense of Irishness, 'If England were playing Ireland, we'd be screaming at the telly for Ireland most certainly.'

Getting an Education

In 1831, Edward Stanley, Chief Secretary for Ireland, established a state system of primary education that was intended to be non-denominational and integrated; however, it was quickly controlled on a sectarian basis in most schools.[441]

Although the Catholic authorities had initially been relatively positive about mixed education,[442] as the nineteenth century progressed, the bishops became concerned about the possibility of religious integration or co-education; they were opposed to the amalgamation of schools – too small to be viable as they were – because of the perceived risks involved in Protestant and Catholic children being educated together.[443]

The Church of Ireland also opposed integrated education. Its position as the church of state (until disestablishment in 1871) had given it control over the education system, which was a power it did not wish to relinquish. The Church Education Society ran schools in which children from the Church of Ireland would not come into contact with Catholic or Presbyterian teachers.[444] Presbyterians campaigned against the national schools system because it 'mutilated the Bible' and Presbyterian activists engaged in the burning of schools and the harassment of teachers, among other protests.[445] By the 1860s, the education system was almost completely denominational (with Protestant schools generally accepting Protestants of all denominations).[446]

The Catholic Church had thrown itself wholeheartedly behind the nationalist movement in the late nineteenth century, especially after Charles Stewart Parnell 'had offered to cede education to clerical control under any future home rule parliament' in 1882.[447] The Catholic hierarchy was respected at this point by the political establishment as an influential group whose views on denomination education were to be honoured. Denominational teacher training colleges were established in 1883.[448] In 1922, the new state announced the closure of the only non-denominational teacher training college.

The Catholic Church had associated itself intimately with the provision of state-funded education.[449] The Free State's first Minister for Education, Eoin MacNeill, and his successor, John Marcus O'Sullivan, decided on a policy of non-involvement on the part of the state in dealing with education, leaving it all up to the churches.[450] Catholic schools opposed hiring lay teachers, even devout Catholic ones, and only accepted them if the teacher training colleges remained under religious control.[451] While the Protestant denominations educated Protestant children, the Catholic Church 'insisted on having a monopolistic control of the education of young people in a Church-owned and state-financed school system'; the state used taxpayers' money to buy land and property, handing them over to the Church so that it might lay claim to that control.[452]

In 1929, the Catholic Church issued the decrees of the Synod of Maynooth, stating that it was a mortal sin for Catholics to attend non-Catholic primary or secondary schools, or the Protestant Trinity College Dublin.'[453] In the 1940s, Archbishop John Charles McQuaid reiterated that the Church forbade parents or guardians from allowing Catholic children to attend a non-Catholic school, stating that this was a mortal sin.[454] Hubert attributes Ireland's sectarian education system to lingering resentment about past injustice, '[the Protestants] treated the Irish people badly when they came over and just snaffled land left, right and centre, stole it effectively.' Consequently, Hubert feels, Catholics did not wish to be educated with them.

Protestant schools generally had a positive relationship with the state, which was happy to assist them in maintaining their separate education system. It provided generous funding and transportation to bring children to school – the transport in question often drove past several Catholic schools on the way.[455] Protestant families in Dublin and some other towns and cities had plenty of primary and secondary schools to attend and could progress to Trinity College if they were wealthy enough. Many affluent Protestants, however, still sent their children to boarding school in England.[456] All around the country there were Protestant children of medium and small farmers, shopkeepers, and others with few or no prospects of joining the elite. These less affluent Protestants were often a very small minority at a local level, and many of them believed strongly that Protestant children should be educated separately to Catholics.[457] In some areas, Protestant schools were small and economically unviable, but such schools could remain open with fewer children than what was accepted as the absolute minimum for Catholic schools – as few as seven.

In theory, all children had the right to attend schools that would educate them along appropriate denominational lines. In practice, especially in rural areas, Protestant children were often unable to attend the 'right' school. Nevertheless, the state continued to be extremely accommodating to Protestant schools when possible. In 1942/3 there were 573 Protestant schools, of which 400 had between just seven and thirty pupils. A state-funded transport system brought many Protestant children to schools otherwise too far from their homes.[458] When, in the 1960s, there was a shortage of Protestant teachers, the state allowed married women to teach despite the 'marriage bar' of 1932 that prevented married women from working in the public sector. The alternative was to hire Catholic teachers for Protestant children.[459]

Though free secondary education was introduced in 1967, a delegation from the Protestant community in Sligo stressed that they were 'poor Protestants' who could not afford fee-paying schools: Protestants in rural areas often did not have a local Protestant school and had to continue going to boarding schools if they wanted a Protestant education – and boarding schools still involved fees despite the recent changes.[460] The government established a system of means-tested 'block grants' that helped Protestants with fees, even if there was a vocational school (nominally non-denominational) operating locally.[461] While this was generous, Protestant pupils had, on average, a lower percentage of their overall fees paid than Catholics.[462] While 75 per cent of Catholic students could attend a free local secondary school with an 'ethos' compatible with that of their family, the same was true of only 7.5 per cent of Protestant students in the same age range, as the community and their schools were 'too widely and thinly dispersed'. The Minister for Education, Donogh O'Malley, told Dáil Éireann that the 'Protestant grant' provided 'equity of treatment with Catholic children'.[463] When free secondary education was introduced in Heather's border area, she says the Protestant community quickly fell behind because there were free local Catholic secondary schools but no Protestant schools. Many Protestant families were too proud to send their children to schools that had been established for 'the others'. According to Heather, some local Protestants, rather than send their children to local Catholic day schools, opted not to send their children to secondary school at all – even with the grant they could not afford Protestant boarding schools.

An inevitable result of the rigorously sectarian education system was to underline feelings and perceptions of difference – even where cultural, economic, and other differences were very slight. Many Protestants report that they first began to experience themselves as 'different' and 'other' at school, either because they were educated in a Protestant school and were thus different to most of the children where they lived, or because they were among a small minority of Protestants in a Catholic school and were excluded from many of the school's activities. Laura recalls her interactions with other children in the early years of the Free State while going home after school, 'people would open their cottage doors and yell, "Protestant bitches leapt over the ditches." We would reply, "The Catholic dogs leapt over the hog"' [...] it was a bit hard to grow up in that kind of atmosphere.' Jennie reports on how her first realisation that she was 'different' related to the segregated school system, 'One of my first memories is being told by the children walking to another school that we were going to hell! [...] Now and then, when a new group of nuns came [...] the children were told that they should not play with us because they would go to hell.'

Mabel attended the local Catholic school with her siblings and cousins. It was generally a positive experience, but they experienced their own difference during catechism and prayers when they were 'put out'. 'Other than that,' she says, 'there wasn't any hard feelings.' Albert and his sisters stood outside the classroom door when religion was taught. This was the beginning of a great feeling of difference that has persisted, 'it has lived with me quite a bit too, that I am quite aware of it […] you were almost different […] It wasn't a very nice feeling. You didn't altogether belong […] you knew that you just weren't quite the same.' When Albert was nine, his parents sent him to boarding school, where he was much happier, although he rarely returned. When he did come home, he was lonely. He did not play with the local Catholic children, and his father drove him quite a distance to reach the nearest rugby club; the local children did Gaelic games.

Samuel attended a local national school; it was a Catholic school, as there were insufficient Protestants to open a school specific to their faith in the area. He was happy but remembers having to leave during religion class and a sense of discomfort when the teacher read from a book that seemed to belittle people like his family. 'It wasn't a good thing to teach children,' he says, firmly. At 12 years of age, he was sent to boarding school. He feels that one of the most negative aspects of boarding school was that young Protestants were isolated from their communities. Their childhood friendships faded and they ended up knowing nobody. When they returned in their late teens, their parents were anxious for them to socialise mostly with 'their own sort' to avoid mixed marriage, often discouraging local friendships. In parts of the country with few Protestants, socialising with 'your own sort' could mean having few potential friends. Samuel spent his late teens and early twenties playing table tennis with his siblings. He says separate education contributed to a great feeling of difference and a lack of a sense of connection to the locality. His own children, educated in local Catholic schools, are 'better able to mix' and play an active role in community organisations.

Johnston identifies the issues around education for rural Protestants as a contributing factor to high levels of emigration. In areas where there were few Protestants, the catchment area had to be enormous to assemble enough children for a school, and when children went to secondary schools, boarding school was the norm. The inevitable result was that Protestant children had few friends in their home areas, did not have local contacts, and were more likely to leave.[464]

If there was no Protestant school nearby and the family could not afford boarding school, children had to travel to the closest Protestant school. This often involved spending a lot of time on the bus. Edward describes going to school on the 'Protestant mini-bus' and going around 'half the country' collecting children from the small, dispersed community. They had to get up an hour earlier than the other children and got home late in the evening, too tired to go out and play with the Catholic children in the area. The children whose parents could afford to send them to boarding school tended to have friends in distant parts of the country and few friends at home – they tended to be cut off from local leisure activities. Andrew reports, 'I didn't know the neighbouring children particularly well […] I travelled further than them to go to school […] Secondary school was even more like that. My older two siblings went to live with my grandparents in Dublin because the nearest Protestant school was a boarding-school.'

Pamela's first day at the local Catholic school was a day of contrasts; she was very badly treated by one nun and rescued by another:

> when [the nun who was initially assigned as my teacher] was calling the roll, when it came to my name, she just left her perch […] and came down, and gave me a fist into the head […] and my little nose hit off the desk and there was blood everywhere […] We knew what she did it for. She didn't want us [because we were Protestants] […] lucky for me, this other nun saw the whole thing happening […] and I can still see her face, it was pure red […] her handkerchief was a check handkerchief, home-made, and she put that to my nose and she lifted the little case […] and she said, 'You'd be better off in my class […]' so she brought me into safety.

Pamela says that another nun 'was nice to me in her own way' but that she also said, 'Your mother and father will be burned in the fires of hell', and she instructed the class not to shop in 'Protestant shops' and to tell their parents to do the same.

In general, Joyce says, Protestant children were not discriminated against in the Catholic school she attended. Only when there was an argument of some sort in the playground or you bumped into someone would it be 'thrown in your face'. Then they would say, 'You Orange dog!' As there was no Orange Order in her area, she did not know what they meant. Many years later, she found out what the Orange Order was when it was mentioned on the news in the context of the Troubles in Northern Ireland. Barney was also accused of being 'Orange', but being from a border area, he was familiar with the organisation and had a favourable view of it, 'you could have been called wee Orange folk or whatever [...] You always had this bit of a fear, and your mother would say, "Go on about your business and don't bother about them," you know.'

Joyce and her family had many Catholic friends and no problems with integration, she says, before adding that going to school was a source of stress because the Catholic children in the area had 'bits of stories on us' and a nasty rhyme that she doesn't quite remember about a Protestant dog looking over a ditch. 'We never said nothing [back] [...] my mother said take no notice.' She is philosophical about it, 'sure a child is a child, like.' Lisa and her sister were called 'dirty Protestants' but had been instructed by their mother not to respond, while some of their classmates had been given permission to call back, 'Proud to be one!'

Letitia attended a Protestant primary school. When the time came for secondary school, her parents could not afford boarding school and there was no local Protestant school, so she was sent to a local convent school where she was treated very differently, 'not by the teachers, not by the nuns, but by the other children. They would just stand and look at you and point at you and almost expected you to look different.'

Billy attended the local Catholic school. The priest used to come into the school twice a week and 'his first word was "put out the Protestants."' In retrospect, Billy says that although it was an unfortunate use of language, it was probably a way of 'safeguarding' the children. The four Protestant children 'stood out in a hallway [...] where coats were hung and the rain blowing in the door if it's a wet day.' The other students pitied them because in their minds the Protestants were going to go to hell: as they would have to suffer enough later, there was no bullying. When he was a little bigger, he read out the catechism questions to his classmates. When he was older again, he moved to the nearest Protestant school so that he could qualify for a subsidy from the Protestant Orphan Society fund. The local Catholic school was much bigger, so usually, when children met on the road, the Protestants were very outnumbered. At secondary school, they stood out even more. He attended a tiny Protestant secondary school in the middle of a housing estate with 118 houses; of these houses, only one belonged to Protestants. The students felt very vulnerable going to and from school because some of the people in the housing estate shouted sectarian abuse at them.

Travers was one of very few Protestant children in a Catholic school. Playtimes were awful. They called him 'you heathen' and bullied him. 'It was pretty serious stuff,' he says. He is not sure whether or not the teachers knew, because he just 'got on with it', but he was made to attend prayers in the local Catholic church and say, 'Hail, rain or snow, to the sodality [a Catholic confederation or guild] we must go.' He found this upsetting – it seemed like a betrayal of his people – but the Christian Brother told him it would do him no harm and to 'get on with it'. 'It's little things like that stick in your mind,' he says.

Emma always walked home alone from school down a tree-lined country road. 'One day when I was about 9 or 10 years of age,' she says, 'two girls from the Catholic girls' school followed me up the road calling me names and throwing cow dung at me [...] My mother decided the best thing to do was to speak with the [...] teacher in my school.' Emma was sent to identify the other children, who were then caned in front of her, 'I left feeling really sorry for them.'

Grace experienced feelings of difference in a positive way. As a Protestant in a Catholic school, she felt 'very special [...] It was like I had maybe two heads or something because they used to look at me', and her friends pitied her 'because I couldn't go to Mass'. When Grace progressed to secondary school, the nuns enjoyed dressing her up in a habit; she always left before the 'headgear' came out but remembers the dressing up as having been done 'in a nice way'.

Priscilla had many friends among her Catholic schoolmates, 'We used to walk to school with the children from the village and with the Catholic children. There was no problem at all.' The other children were jealous because the Protestant children were allowed to play during religious education, 'Those children were jealous about us then and used to call us names [...] we were called "Protestant dogs" and they had a rhyme about us.'

Edwin attended the local Christian Brothers school, where 'being different' was to his advantage, as he was singled out not to receive corporal punishment, 'when I held out my hand it was frequently brushed aside by the brother with the strap!' Ted was quite happy to sit on the porch with an unusual friend while the other children did catechism, 'My best friend at school was a mouse. I used to feed crumbs to it [...] as I was put outside while catechism was taught for a half hour [...] They were all good boys really, and it worried me to hear them beaten with a strap for so little as [not] having reams of manmade verses off by heart.'

In Hugh's area, numbers in the local Protestant school decreased until the government closed it down. They could have kept it open if they had agreed to admit Catholic students, assuming any Catholic families would have sent their children there. However, the local Protestant clergyman rejected this idea, so the few remaining Protestant children had to attend the local Catholic school or travel a great distance to have a Protestant education. Joyce left home early to walk two miles to school, although there was a Catholic national school just a field away. 'It was disgusting, like [...] I'm telling you, we were drownded [sic] [...] you see that time there was none of these raincoats [...] You'd just be wet and that's it.'

Richard was sent to a local woman's house to learn how to read and write. When he was about 8 years old, his father went to the local Catholic school to see if he could attend it, but his father told him afterwards that 'the principal there made it very clear that that would not be a good idea [...] he couldn't guarantee that I would not be bullied badly.' Instead, he was sent to boarding school at 9 years of age. Richard's family was middle class and could manage to pay school fees. Local Protestants who could not afford a private education sent their children to the same Catholic school that the principal had advised Richard's father to avoid. That, or they took a lengthy bus journey to a bigger town, which meant leaving home at 6.30 a.m. and getting home after 6.30 p.m., leaving no time to play with the local children.

The risk of Protestant schools closing in rural areas with small and scattered populations preyed on people's minds. Honor remembers, 'it was constantly touch-and-go, that the school was going to survive [...] a family of four or five coming into the area would be a huge boost.' A Protestant adoption agency, The Fold, sometimes arranged for children to be fostered into rural Protestant homes in order to keep small Protestant schools open; it did this without regard for how suitable the foster homes would be.[465]

When she was little, Doris's family – fairly well-off farmers – hired a governess for her. In those days, the view was that you had to 'mind your daughters', as they were considered more vulnerable to Catholic influences than boys. Doris also spent a couple of years at a Protestant primary school that took boarders. When a Protestant school some miles away risked closure due to insufficient numbers, the local rector insisted that all the Protestant children in the region be sent there to keep it open and Doris was removed from the local school. She and a number of other children boarded with a rector and his wife, who lived near the endangered school.

May attended the local Catholic school. At 6 years of age, a little boy called her a 'blank blank Protestant' ('blank' indicating the expletives that May did not wish to use in an interview setting), which she remembers as the first time she realised that some people disliked Protestants. All the other children went to the local Catholic church on Ash Wednesday to have their foreheads anointed with ash. May and her sister sneaked into a coal yard and anointed their own foreheads with coal dust. Their mother was annoyed because she felt that the children were 'being traitors to the Protestant church'. May experienced Protestant bigotry when she was sent to an all-Protestant boarding school and met many students who were unashamedly anti-Catholic.

Heather met Catholics for the first time when she went to secondary school. Suddenly, 'You were aware of yourself as a Protestant getting onto this overcrowded bus of strange children; most of them you'd never seen before.' Because the school was Catholic, her parents never attended anything there – no school concerts, no parent-teacher meetings. Heather felt that she could not ask the teachers questions very much, especially in history. The Protestant children waited in prefabs when the other children did anything relating to religion. There was also a blithe assumption that all students would understand certain cultural references. Her English teacher decided that the children would act a play based on a short story by Frank O'Connor called 'First Confession'. She and her friend did not know what a first confession was, but they were given lead roles. 'Imagine nowadays going into a Jewish school and asking them to do a play about Muslims!' she says. Reflecting on the events afterwards, she says:

> I wondered [...] did the teacher have any idea what he was asking of us. I don't think he had. I think, because Catholicism was just

something that just ruled everywhere, that minorities or their feelings or opinions were not considered. You suddenly started to realise that there was something totally different going on around you that you knew nothing about. 'Do you know what? You're going to have to learn it pretty quick, because this is your reality.'

Ireland's segregated education system was less problematic in larger urban areas, where the Protestant minority was big enough to fill schools; it was not really regarded as problematic at all in places like Dublin's affluent suburbs – Dalkey or Rathgar – with large well-to-do Protestant populations and an array of denominational schools. Nonetheless, urban children could still discover feelings of difference when they started going to school.

Shirley remembers having to travel outside her working-class Dublin community to get to primary school. One day, when she was coming home from school on the Feast of the Immaculate Conception, stands out. All the Catholic schools were closed for the religious holiday, but the Protestant schools were open. School children were not supposed to pay the full fare, but the driver would not let her on the bus without it because he insisted that all the schools were closed – she feels he was doing it on purpose because he disliked Protestants. Shirley was one of the very few children from her inner-city area who attended a Protestant school. This marked her and her siblings out as different, 'we were bullied going to school. Jeered and stones thrown at us and things like that. We'd be called "Proddy Woddy."'

Harold attended a Protestant primary school but a Catholic secondary school – the latter was not a positive experience, 'They thought all sorts of things. They thought you worship the devil […] just absolute madness that I couldn't get my head around. I was bullied for the first year or two […] I told them: "If I am English then you must be Italian, because you are Roman Catholic," but it didn't seem to register with anybody!'

Oliver suddenly realised that he was different when a group of children from another fee-paying elite school shouted 'Proddy dog' at him. It was an experience he found more puzzling than upsetting, as he had been unaware that anyone objected to Protestants. After that, and as he got older, this 'difference' became increasingly clear. His fee-paying Protestant school still had old maps on the walls showing the British Empire in red, although the British Empire had already lost many of its territories (including most of Ireland). Oliver knew that the display of maps and other items associated with British colonial history was considered a 'Protestant thing' in Dublin.

The general opposition to 'different' types of Irish people being educated together persisted beyond school. In 1848, the Catholic coadjutor bishop of Derry wrote that all the young Catholic people who had spent time at Trinity College returned home 'shipwrecked in faith and moral, wholly profligate', adding that Trinity was just as detestable as 'Paganism in its filthiest lycées, where Venus and Bacchus were deified'.[466] For those who attended Protestant schools at both primary and secondary level, there was often a revelation of 'difference' upon entering university or working life, although this could be delayed by attending Trinity College in Dublin up until the 1970s (when the official ban on Catholics attending Trinity was lifted).

Trinity is remembered by many former students as a sort of Protestant enclave in an otherwise predominately Catholic city. Edith Newman Devlin wrote that she never met one single student from the Catholic University of Ireland and that 'we might as well have been on different planets for all the encouragement we were given to meet each other.'[467] Craig remembers Trinity as a 'Protestant village' populated by students with distinctively Protestant accents and surrounded by a 'Catholic hinterland'. He was irritated by the deduction that he was somehow British because he was a Trinity lad, 'I have never felt myself to be English [...] it was something that always irked me. I had a colonial Ascendancy's disdain for the English part of Britain: the cosy English could not know what it was to be of settler origin.' Eleanora describes meeting other Protestant students and many students from the UK and various parts of Africa – but almost no Irish Catholics. It was possible to move seamlessly from an entirely Protestant rural community into an entirely Protestant urban community. She lived in a YWCA hostel; the staff and all the residents were Protestants and 'it was like moving to home'.

Rebecca attended University College Dublin and remembers that she was 'allowed to borrow some books in the library that were not available to Catholics. I think they concerned pagan Roman practices.' Bob attended University College Cork and was shocked to find himself feeling very different to the rest of the student population. 'You just couldn't get away from it', he says, '[...] but it was just something you couldn't get rid of [...] I probably didn't realise until then [...] how thoroughly the Protestant environment that I grew up in had sort of shaped me. I had really no idea.'

Natasha's parents kept her within Protestant circles to such a degree that it was only when she went to university that she realised she was different. She was aware of a vague sense of cultural superiority. She was not from a wealthy background, and neither were most of the people she knew, but this feeling came from her sequestered childhood. She had only ever mixed with families like her own: rural and Protestant.

Natasha moved into all-Protestant housing for female students and started to study for an Arts degree in University College Dublin. From the very start, she felt different; it was a very uncomfortable experience for someone who had never been outside her Protestant comfort zone before. Her distinctively Protestant name stood out among all the Gaelic names in the Irish department where she studied. Never before had she seen ash on people's foreheads on Ash Wednesday; she had never even heard of the practice. She felt that there was a certain 'cooling' towards her when she revealed where she had gone to school, and after that she was accused of speaking 'posh Irish'. She dealt with the strain by retreating to her all-Protestant boarding house and her Protestant friends. A defining moment occurred when she went to the Gaeltacht with a group of classmates and the *bean an tí* (woman of the house) announced that she hoped that there were neither 'pagans nor Protestants' among them. 'I realised', she says, 'that this was the Catholic equivalent of my mother.'

The Irish Language and Gaelic Culture

The Gaelic League was founded by Douglas Hyde[468] in the late nineteenth century to revive the Irish language.[469] When it approached the Church of Ireland and asked them to make Irish compulsory in their national schools, they refused. Gradually, the Gaelic League became increasingly political and focused on constructing a national culture that rejected anything considered English, which, in turn, implicated *anyone* associated with England.[470] The Irish language, already spoken by a small minority[471] – many of whom inhabited areas of poverty with high levels of emigration – was considered 'an essential wellspring' of a distinctive, unique Irish culture.[472] This view was inconsistent with the idea of Protestants also being truly Irish.[473]

From 1913, anyone who wanted to attend the National University of

Ireland had to have a pass grade in Irish. After 1922, Irish was made compulsory in primary schools. Many Protestants felt that learning Irish was pointless and seemed inconsistent with their identity; many resented the state's efforts to promote the language. Bishop Crozier felt that 'we would be doing an injustice to our [Protestant] children by compelling them to learn a language which would be of no practical value.'[474]

Many Protestants continued to resist learning Irish. Some of them did so because they were concerned that the language was a backdoor to Catholic proselytising. A.A. Luce, a professor of philosophy at Trinity College, Dublin and a precentor of St Patrick's Cathedral, Dublin, claimed that the language movement was also a cultural movement, and that if Irish was compulsory, 'in a hundred years' time half the Protestant population of the Free State will be converted to Roman Catholicism.'[475] On 9 November 1923, the *Church of Ireland Gazette* (pp. 604–5) published a letter claiming that the use of Irish hampered the progress of Irishmen and described it as 'useless', conflating the emphasis on teaching Irish with discrimination against Protestants seeking public sector jobs. The letter claimed that it would take young people five years to reach the minimum required standard, and that if Irish became compulsory, Protestants would 'dwindle away to vanishing point'. From 1926, knowledge of Irish was a prerequisite for a civil service job.[476] In 1929, P.L. Dickinson, a Dublin architect and one of the original members of the Georgian Society, scoffed, in *The Dublin of Yesterday*, that while 'Gaels' had certainly contributed something to western civilisation, they were a 'rung on the ladder […] which has long been overstepped', and that attempts to revive Gaelic culture and language were 'pathetic', 'comic', and 'useless'. He added that neither Irish nor independent Ireland would last for long.[477]

The provost of Trinity College at the time, John Mahaffy, described Irish textbooks for schools as 'either silly or indecent'[478] and believed Irish teaching was intended to marginalise Protestant schools. Irish was now a prerequisite for getting a county council scholarship, so fewer Protestants attended the National University than before. Third level education became even more segregated, as Protestants either went to Trinity or left to study in the UK.[479] The system of providing bonus points to secondary students who answered exam questions in Irish tended to act against poor Protestant families, as the teaching of Irish was consistently worse in Protestant schools.[480]

Protestants' frequent lack of proficiency in Irish contributed to greater numbers emigrating because they could not work in the civil service.

Many Protestant teachers were bitter about having to learn and teach
Irish,[481] and many Protestants worried that literature published in Irish, or
focusing on Gaelic culture, would be anti-Protestant, or at least pro-
Catholic.[482] Ultra-nationalist publications like *The Catholic Bulletin* did have
an established track record of impugning anything that came from Protestant or Anglo-Irish culture. *The Catholic Bulletin* described Anglo-Irish tradition and culture as a 'mongrel upstart' when compared with true
Irishness.[483] In 1933, the Department of Education published *Notes for Teachers: History*, stressing the government's view that Irish history was, above all,
the study of the 'the Gaelic race and Gaelic civilisation for a thousand years
of foreign domination', and that the Irish language helped to save the Irish
'from defeat and absorption by alien forces' and should therefore be used
to teach history.[484] In 1938, the principal of the Protestant Bishop Foy's
school in Waterford opined that Irish was about as useful as the languages
of the Aboriginal peoples of Australia, remarking that the Aboriginal languages 'had done little for the culture or nationality of the bushmen'.[485]

Following national conferences of educationalists that were held in 1921
and 1926, official policy determined that in the national schools only Irish
history was to be taught – with the specific intent of 'inculcating national
pride and self-respect' and of 'showing that the Irish race has fulfilled a great
mission in the advancement of civilisation'.[486] It was also agreed that the education system should function to 'revive the ancient life of Ireland as a Christian state, Gaelic in language, and Gaelic and Christian in its ideals'.[487] The
state consistently pushed the idea that learning Irish was 'for the good of the
nation'. Educational policy resolved that children, especially very young children, should be taught through Irish as much as possible, even when the
teacher was only 'marginally competent' in it. By the 1930s, schools had
dropped 'rural science' as a compulsory subject and reduced the level of instruction in mathematics to accommodate more instruction in Irish.[488]

Foolishly, some Protestant schools in the early years of the Free State –
some of them even as late as the 1940s and 50s – did not teach Irish, or
taught it wilfully badly. Nicholas Fitzsimons recalls how the families of the
students at St Columba's in the 1940s saw the study of Irish as 'enemy territory'.[489] Flora remembers the headmistress in her small private secondary

school instructing the students to pretend to be studying Irish in case an inspector visited:

> I didn't have to learn Irish, and it was very funny, because our head-mistress [...] there were two books, her Irish book would be there open, and on top we'd have, it could be French, it could be anything else on top, and we were warned that if ever the door opened, we were to immediately put that under our desk, so we were seen to be learning Irish.

In the 1940s, the Minister for Education, Richard Mulcahy, wrote of how 'stupid' and 'short-sighted' it was of Protestants not to embrace educational policy, describing their opposition to Irish as 'senseless'. He said that they had to decide if they wanted to be considered English.[490]

Views on Irish were by no means universally negative. For some it was an opportunity to identify more closely with Gaelic culture. When Rosamond Jacob, a writer and activist for the suffrage and other progressive movements, visited the Gaeltacht area of Ring, Co. Waterford, she found that Gaelic culture and the Irish language liberated her 'from the circles of polite Protestant society in Waterford' and experienced them as 'a rite of passage into an idea of Irish authenticity'.[491] Lisa remembers her (perhaps more typical) father being very cross about the Irish language, seeing it as a 'political football' of de Valera's; however, an enthusiastic teacher in her school assured the students, 'This is *your* language as well as other people's!'

The standard of Irish teaching in Protestant schools gradually improved, especially with the help of graduates of Coláiste Moibhí, a Protestant secondary school founded in 1926 that prepared students for teaching at primary level. To encourage enrolment, even those who had not reached the required standard of Irish could enter. Graduates of Coláiste Moibhí entered Protestant teaching training college and collectively contributed a great deal to the future of the Protestant community in the Free State by ensuring that Protestant primary schools, which fostered the sense of having a distinctive Protestant culture and helped children to form friendships with other Protestants, survived.[492] For some young people, a scholarship to Coláiste Moibhí could be a path to upward social mobility. One such person was Honor's mother:

all her life [my mother] expressed just enormous gratitude because [...] as she was 12 or 13 coming up for leaving school [she] had a dread that her fate would be to work in one of the local Protestant-owned shops and the principal of her school said, a new school had opened in Dublin for people to go and if they went through that school they could train to be teachers.

A great deal of consideration went into maintaining a Protestant-controlled network of schools, so even those who disagreed with mandatory Irish could accept the provision of graduates from Coláiste Moibhí as a factor that would help the community to survive and remain different.[493] Quentin comments on both the importance of Irish in his family, and their persistent feelings of difference, 'My parents were both National School teachers and my father was educated in Moibhí College, an all-Irish Protestant school to prepare children for a teaching profession. I myself had [...] quite a strong affiliation with the Irish culture, but I was still different, and I knew it.'

Questions about whether Irish was suitable for Protestants lingered for years. In 1965, Risteárd Ó Glaisne, a Protestant scholar of Irish, wrote that 'the more superior Protestants consider themselves to be [...] the less they understand the importance of Irish [...] such a "coarse language."'[494] Conversely, he wrote that the Protestant who knows the Irish language 'is welcomed as an Irishman in a way in which a Protestant who doesn't is not'. Ó Glaisne addressed the question of whether it is appropriate for a Protestant to feel a sense of loyalty to the Irish language and compared it to English, which he described as having 'a Protestant bias'. Rather defensively, he lists some of the great Protestant contributors to the Irish language and its scholarship, including Henry Flood and Eleanor Knott. However, he notes that some Protestants who were interested in Irish and Irish nationhood had subsequently converted to Catholicism, and he describes Prot-estant 'negativity and narrowness in spiritual things' as creating, at times, 'a loneliness and a longing in the individual which can pave the way to a conversion to Rome'.

Social Life, Clubs, Social Organisations, and Friends
For many years, some Protestant families tended to socialise separately, particularly where the local community was dense enough to allow for all-Protestant socialising. Neil remembers that his parents, although loyal to the

Irish state, had few Catholic friends in their provincial town. Their social life was saved by the arrival of several English families who arrived to work in local industries, whose children helped to keep the local Protestant school open, and who were considered a more natural fit for friendships.

There were many 'Protestant' social organisations, such as the Church of Ireland Mothers' Union and the Christian Endeavour (a Methodist organisation), and children's organisations such as the Boys' Brigade, the Girls' Brigade, and the Girls' Friendly Society (all of which still exist today), and there were also various all-Protestant sporting activities. Gerald has rather mixed memories of the Boys' Brigade:

> The Boys' Brigade was British-based and organised on military culture [...] we were taught marching, drill, saluting and how to polish the brass buckle on the uniform belt. [We had a] 10 days' summer camp where the juniors were kept in line by bullying seniors with the threat of being taken from bed at night, stripped naked, and 'blackened' with boot polish. We learned how to put up a bell tent and fold blankets. We also learned from other boys how to smoke, dirty jokes, and inaccurate sex education. There was also a Sunday Bible class with hymns, a long prayer and an address. Usually this was conducted by one of the officers, but there were visiting preachers. I remember one praying, 'That Ireland would once again become known as the Land of Saints and Scholars and not the Land of the Irish Sweepstake.' Another memorable time was when the Methodist minister talked to us about growing up as good Christian youths. He rubbished the Catholic doctrines of Confession and Transubstantiation and finished by warning us of the terrible evil of masturbation. We laughed all the way home.

Ian remembers that the Boys' Brigade was less about having fun and more about 'trying to hold a community together'. Lisa remembers a very active Boys' Brigade in her area, and that the children were told to remove their hats when walking in certain parts of the town to avoid attracting undue attention and being bullied.

Scouting organisations were organised along denominational lines. Roberta was in an all-Protestant Girl Guide group. All the girls were Protestants and the Girl Guides provided them with a social outlet that was not just Protestant but also slanted very much towards an English worldview. Mitchell describes the time when the scoutmaster of his Protestant troupe called all the boys together and told them, 'Now, next week we'll have a boy with us who is a bit different from the rest of us, so I want you to be very nice to him.' The children were all very curious. When the boy came in, 'we all looked at him and thought, "What is the difference? Has he two legs, four legs, what has he got?"' The little boy was a Catholic, 'He was a nice lad, but he was definitely different!'

Jennie remembers a wide range of Protestant-only activities in her inner-city parish, 'Every night in the week there were activities, meetings, Christian endeavour, table tennis club, first aid, brass band practice, PE, there was a cycling club, hockey club, tennis club, soccer.' George comments that wealthy Dublin Protestants were often members of clubs for tennis, sailing, golf, and other activities; they were often either explicitly for Protestants or, because aspiring members could be excluded by being 'blackballed', operated to exclude anyone who was not Protestant or of the 'right' social class.

Many rural Protestants played gaelic games informally, and some of them were involved in local clubs. Amy mentions Protestants in her community playing GAA, but stresses that they tended not to get involved competitively, 'Maybe they just had friendly games in what was called the local park [...] but they would not be going away for games or that type of thing.' Ida Milne, writing in 2019 in her paper, 'The jersey is all that matters, not your church', provides an interesting study of positive engagement with the GAA by Protestants. Kate, whose parents were in the service of a wealthy family (as a groundsman and a nanny or maid), commented that his family was unusual among Protestants insofar as 'they played camogie and my mother learned Irish dancing'. Her next comment is that the children walked barefoot to school, so perhaps she associates their relatively humble socio-economic position with their interest in Gaelic sporting activities.

Despite the involvement of some Protestants with the GAA, the perception of the organisation as Catholic, and even anti-Protestant, was common. The fact that GAA games occurred on Sundays is often mentioned as a factor that inhibited Protestant involvement; another factor was that Gaelic games were not taught in Protestant schools. Trevor, commenting on the GAA in his area, states that they 'didn't seem to want Protestants [...] we weren't courted in any way to join. We were never asked to join. We were never invited to join a Gaelic club, and they would always play games on Sunday, and […] Sunday sports were out for us.' Simon remembers that the GAA in his area 'didn't really want us', though 'We certainly weren't that interested in them either.' He comments on how Protestants disliked the fact that many GAA clubs were called after nationalist heroes, which he thought was provocative, and adds, 'At any sport that *we* play, like badminton or any other thing, it's just a badminton club. It's not the "King William Badminton Club" or anything like that.' Gavin remembers that the Protestants in his area '100% felt we could not play GAA […] we felt it was a Catholic game, run by priests with bishops throwing in the ball at Croke Park and teams named after IRA men like Sam Maguire [in fact a Protestant][495] and Catholic institutions.'

Protestants who might otherwise have been interested in playing on their local GAA team could still be excluded due to the GAA's ban on anyone who played 'foreign games' such as rugby, soccer, or cricket, which were often taught in Protestant schools and were, more generally, part of Protestant cultural tradition.[496] Celeste remembers how she used to 'smuggle' Catholic friends to rugby matches in disguise in case their GAA club found out and threw them out. Joe comments, 'There were no sports we could not play because of religion but we were, of course, banned from playing hurling and Gaelic football by the bigoted GAA [for] playing "foreign" games.'

The GAA has been important for Valerie's family, despite her parents' initial opposition to it, 'strangely enough, my two brothers played the Gaelic […] which was unusual for Protestants to do in that time [from the 1970s to the 90s].' When Reggie's uncle, who was born in about 1916, was elderly, he told his nephew that he had played Gaelic football under an assumed name so that nobody would know that he was a Protestant – both to prevent the family from finding out and because he also played soccer for the local grammar school, risking the GAA's ban. Reggie discusses his parents' initial opposition to their sons' involvement with the GAA, 'you were sort of on a slippery slope in the sense that you were socialising with the wrong people, and you probably would end up marrying them.' They considered badminton 'a better game'. Over time, however, they became more accepting. As Protestant players, he and his brother accepted that a certain amount of sectarian abuse was inevitable, 'everything is thrown at you, you know yourself. So, this is only another stick to beat you with, you know [...] if they can bring the religion into it, sure, why not [...]?'

Marcus regrets never having had the opportunity to do Gaelic games, 'my biggest regret in coming through school [...] I never played Gaelic games and I always regret it [...] I never kicked a football or hit a sliotar [a small, hard ball used in hurling] and I feel I've lost out somewhere in my culture that way along the way.'

Some report lingering issues around Protestants playing GAA. Mariah's son played Gaelic games but, 'if they were looking at five people in the field and four of them had only one hand, they would still pick them before him because he has got a Protestant surname.' Players who were Protestant or 'blow-ins' of some other sort (Mariah's family has been living there for hundreds of years) would be ignored, 'unless you happen to be exceptionally good and then they'll rave about you.' Protestants and blow-ins alike, she says, tended to be left out of GAA things and various elements of local life in her rural parish because they 'have the wrong surname'. 'But sure, that's life', she says.

In recent years, the GAA has become much less overtly nationalist and the taboo among some Protestant families against playing sports on Sunday has receded. Thomas discusses the dramatic change that he has seen in his lifetime in his locality. When he was a boy, he says, no Protestant in his area would have been 'caught dead' playing Gaelic games, and neither would they have been welcomed. Gradually, as the 'hatred' of Protestants receded, and Protestants' observations around working and playing sports on Sunday relaxed, a few of them started to play in his area. His own grandson was a talented sportsman and played for the local Gaelic football team.

Many Protestants have numerous stories about their close friendships with Catholics, despite what could sometimes seem like a great divide. On the day of Grace's wedding, 'a lot of my schoolfriends were dying to come in to see me being married, and they weren't allowed inside the gate [by the local parish priest].' In the 1950s, Trevor was active in the local community and had many Catholic friends. He remembers one friend from the mixed tennis club that he helped organise, 'we'll call her broad-minded [...] And she went to a Protestant wedding, had to get permission from the chapel [...] and another Protestant wedding was coming up six months later and she went for permission. "No, you can't have permission, you were at one already this year!"'

Hillis's family had many Catholic friends, although sometimes the wider social environment conspired against these friendships. This was especially the case for a close friend of his father's, who was a priest, 'Poor old Father – ran foul of the famous Doctor Brown in Galway for associating with Protestants [...] he got shifted then from his parish [...] the crawthumpers, as we knew them [...] the old women were complaining, letting the bishop know that the priest was associating with Prods.'

Timothy grew up in an inner-city neighbourhood of considerable poverty. Although daily relations between Catholics and Protestants were 'standoffish' – 'I only got beaten up once for being a Protestant' – when a family was down on its luck (as his was when his father died young), everyone rallied around to help and did not care that his family was 'different'.

Dave remembers friendship between the Protestant and Catholic communities emerging in an unexpected way, in the context of an attempted boycott a few years after the Fethard Boycott of 1957. A local priest called for a boycott of Protestant businesses in response to remarks made by a visiting Protestant preacher that were interpreted as offensive, but very few families complied. 'I am sure that the vast majority of Catholics would have been upset', he adds, 'if they had known that on one occasion Protestant shopkeepers received anonymous letters stating that, as Cromwell had made the blood of Catholics flow down the streets of Drogheda, so Protestant blood would run down the streets of this village.'

Freddie remembers a similar show of local resistance to the stricter elements of the Catholic Church. The area was noted for enjoying a wonderful sense of neighbourliness, and traditionally the parish priest and the local rector had always been friends. Then a new priest came and told the Catholics that they were not allowed to attend the funerals of their Protestant friends. This was resisted, 'the local blacksmith said, "Well, he's not going to boss *me*, I'm going to go one way or another," he said, "they're my friends," and he did!' Barton has a similar story of how Catholic members of the community defied their priest to support the local Protestant fête.

Ethel remembers her mother's delight in the friendships she had with Catholics in her area, including the local priest, 'She had a great relationship with the local priests and [was] very proud that the priest visited her every first Friday when he was bringing Communion to his own flock.' Hope remembers her mother's best friend, a devout Catholic, flouting the rules to attend her sister's christening, for which she had to 'pay some penance or other'. Mariah's family was extremely integrated in their community, and her father, as a Protestant, was chosen to 'lead the decade of the Rosary' at local wakes when the priest was not available; he was the perfect person to lead the prayer, as he would not be praying himself and he 'thought nothing of it'.

Many Protestants stress the close, loving friendships they shared with Catholic neighbours and colleagues, and they discuss how differences could be made apparent even in very close friendships. Lisa had a dear friend; the two women often cared for each other's children, but Lisa's friend refused to go with her to the local Protestant parish sale, 'in case the money might be used for proselytising [...] in case it would be used for promoting the Protestant Gospel', and she remembers close friends of her mother who made a point of saying that they would never buy the 'Protestant' *Irish Times* newspaper.

Death and Funerals

Differences in religion and allegiance were often on display at funerals. When Douglas Hyde, a Protestant, Gaelic scholar, and Ireland's first president died, Catholics did not enter St Patrick's Cathedral for his funeral service. A biography of Hyde describes how most of the official state mourners 'huddled in an alley near the cathedral' rather than going in.[497] Christopher says of Hyde's funeral that 'the Taoiseach, John A Costello and his cabinet and the opposition, led by Éamon de Valera, sat in their cars in the close [...] This would have been regarded as an insult.' Similarly, on the death of W.B. Yeats in 1939, none of his Catholic friends were allowed to enter the church for his funeral; his sister commented, 'now that they are "on top" and in the majority it seems so foolish.'[498] Tobin comments that while it is 'important not to exaggerate the significance of any one incident', such as the non-attendance of Catholic dignitaries at Hyde's funeral, 'neither should it be forgotten what a disproportionate effect even small slights could have upon so vulnerable a community.'[499]

The story of Hyde's funeral has been handed down in many families. People who were not yet born at the time can still talk vividly about the hurt and upset experienced by those who saw the photographs of the Catholic mourners standing outside the church and refusing to enter. They also remember, or have heard about, similar slights that have caused hurt to their own families. Joe says, 'Catholic clerics were viewed in a very negative light and the fact that they would not allow their flock to enter our churches for weddings and funerals was something we could never understand.' Liza remembers, 'A next-door neighbour, who had visited our house weekly for years, stood outside the church at my mother's funeral [...] Being an RC, he felt he couldn't go in. He actually stood at the gate, not to enter the grounds.' Christopher has a similarly upsetting memory of his great-uncle's funeral, 'some of the people who had attended stayed outside the church door with their fingers in their ears, as they were banned from attending.'

Harry remembers how a relative, adopted by an uncle when her parents died, would not attend her uncle's funeral, 'he took her in and looked after her like a daughter [...] it turned out she was practising Roman Catholic [...] she would not go into the church and it was very upsetting, because my mother was very fond of this person and would've done anything for her.' Winnie has similar memories of Catholic friends and neighbours who were not allowed to attend Protestant funerals, or were punished for doing so:

> The local RC priest went to the Catholic neighbours of the deceased, told them not to go to the funeral, unless they had permission from the bishop. Another memory of two Roman Catholic boys aged about 13 or 14 [...] who went to a Protestant funeral in the Cathedral to see what was going on. Somebody told the local schoolmaster; they got a flogging the next day in school, not with a cane but a chair rung, because they went into a Protestant church.

Trev remembers his grandmother's death in 1941, 'She was highly thought of by all our Catholic neighbours [...] all her Catholic friends and neighbours stood outside the church door as their presence in the church was forbidden.' Jennie remembers the tragic early death of her mother:

> I think the saddest day for me, and the thing that underlined our differences, was when my tiny 38-year-old mum died tragically

199

after having a stillborn baby at home […] I was eleven and my sister was eight. Mum was loved by all the neighbours, who came to our home where she was laid out in the parlour. On the day of the funeral, as we followed the coffin […] I can still see the neighbours in tears walking through the railings on the pavement. They were not allowed come into a Protestant church in those days.

Lizzie once arrived at a funeral and found that many the friends of the deceased were pacing up and down outside the door. 'Didn't the funeral come?' she asked. 'Well, the coffin has gone in,' they said. 'Why aren't you going in?' she asked. One person said that they would have to ask for the bishop's permission before doing something like that, and another added, 'We'd turn into a pillar of salt!' Lizzie asserts that the people in question literally believed that Catholics would turn into salt if they went inside the Protestant church. Hugo recalls how a friend of his deceased father 'gave me a hug […] in tears. Because he couldn't come into church and he said, "I'm terribly sorry […] I am not allowed in."'

Myrtle remembers Protestants feeling particularly grateful to Catholic friends who came to funerals, although they had to stand outside, 'if they came at all, and stood outside the church, it was reckoned that was very nice of them, you know. I think it was more appreciated, because they had […] been a bit rebellious to do it in the first place.'

An entertaining account of how the treatment of the dead differed between faiths tells of a Protestant woman who died and requested that she be cremated, which necessitated that her remains be transported to a crematorium all the way in Belfast:

The remaining sister was disappointed that the ashes were not immediately available and had to be satisfied with the promise that they would be promptly posted to her. Christmas was approaching, a busy time for the postal services and delivery was slow. The sister complained bitterly that her sister would be most unhappy to know that she was being carted all over Ireland in a postman's bag. Eventually the ashes arrived, and the local rector was to perform the scattering. He said he could not do this as there was no service in the prayer book for scattering […] the sister agreed to a burial after a family member advised her that, 'The Catholic neighbouring farmers might not like the idea of the wind blowing Protestant ashes onto their fields.'

One of the ways in which feelings of loss have been expressed is through stories – of which at least some may be apocryphal – about forced conversions and baptisms after independence. Donald relates the story of a man who had converted from Catholicism; on becoming ill and being confined to the Mater Hospital, he called for his rector and told him, 'They're after me!' Donald adds that 'the nuns had been sent in to get him back to the Church of Rome'. Allegedly the rector hastily started making plans for the sick man to be moved to a Protestant hospital, but in the meantime he died and 'they' won: the funeral was held in a Roman Catholic church.[500]

A friend of Gerald's family joined the army. There were so few Protestant officers at the time that he was sent in an official capacity to every Protestant funeral requiring state representation, as Catholics were forbidden from attending. Peter heard a similar story about a colonel in the Irish army who spent much of his time representing the army at Protestant funerals, 'he was worse than my sister'.

Sometimes the rules regarding Catholic attendance at Protestant funerals were flouted. Mabel discusses growing up in a very integrated, poor rural community where Protestants and Catholics were close friends. She was very upset when she asked a friend why she could not attend a Protestant funeral and learned that it was because the bishop 'would put horns on them – like, they were the devil!' However, she adds that other friends flouted the bishop's ruling and went anyway. Lisa remembers the very poor women of her town ('shawlies') defying the parish priest to attend the funeral of a beloved local doctor, a Protestant, who had often treated their children for free. Letitia's father often told the story of his own father's best friend, a Catholic, who dared to go against the rules and attended Letitia's father's funeral despite the fact that he was very active in the church and a Catholic men's organisation. Afterwards the local parish priest called him for a meeting and made it very clear that he was in trouble.

The Second Ecumenical Council of the Vatican (Vatican Two) addressed relations between the Catholic Church and the modern world. The council was opened in 1962 and closed in 1965, and resulted in a number of significant changes, including, for example, a greater focus on ecumenism and dialogue with other religions, as well as a switch from the Latin Mass to Mass in the vernacular, Mass now being given with the priest facing the congregation, and the revision of Eucharistic prayers. After Vatican Two, Catholics were formally allowed to attend the funerals of Protestant friends and neighbours in the spirit of increased ecumenism. A Catholic acquaintance of Mabel's had previously been forbidden from attending the funeral of his best friend and did as he was told. Six months later, after Vatican Two, he was livid, 'I can see him there hitting the table and saying, "Who came down from heaven to change the rules now?"' Frank remembers when he and his mother attended a Catholic funeral for the first time. His mother was reluctant to join him at first but he, having lived abroad, had become more broad-minded:

> I said, 'Well, you come along with me,' and she allowed me to persuade her to go up, and we went into the chapel, and it was full. We got inside through the vestry door [...] we stayed there. There was nothing I could disagree with [...] when it was over, a lot of the people recognised us, you know, as if we were intruders. But no! They extended the hand of welcome! And it was terrific!

Differences in the Workforce

Before independence, Protestants were disproportionately represented in higher levels of business and in state jobs. In 1913, for example, there were thirty-four Protestants for every thirteen Catholics on the Local Government Board; on the Board of Works, seventy-nine Protestant civil servants earned an average of £326 a year while their Catholic colleagues earned an average of £197.[501] This situation was defended by the view that Catholics were more likely to be disloyal to Britain.[502] After independence, Protestants were concerned that they would be discriminated against in the public sector. Leland Bardwell – an Irish poet, playwright, and novelist – reported that in the 1920s her father applied to the Shannon Scheme, a major hydroelectric project, and was turned down because they were only employing Catholics; she also stated that her uncle, a doctor, applied for a job at the Coombe maternity hospital and was turned down for the same reason.[503]

A famous case in Mayo in 1931 involved the removal of a librarian, Letitia Dunbar Harrison, by the Mayo Library Committee, with the support of the county council. Officially, it was because Harrison's Irish was poor. The Catholic Dean of Tuam stated that they were not appointing a 'washerwoman' but an 'educated girl who ought to know what books to put into the hands of the Catholic boys and girls of the country', and he queried whether it would be safe to entrust this important role to 'a girl who is not in sympathy with Catholic views'.[504] He asserted that 'Only a thoroughly educated Catholic man or woman, loyal to and energetic in the case of Catholic action, can be deemed fit for the highly responsible and influential post of County Librarian.'[505] The act was defended by P.J. Ruttledge, later the Minister for Justice, who pointed out that 'practically 99%' of the people of Mayo were Catholics and therefore the librarian should be too, because 'What might appear to a member of one religion as being perfectly all right may appear to a member of another religion as being completely wrong.'[506] Referring to Harrison's Trinity education, a Mayo newspaper thundered that the culture of Trinity was not the 'culture of the Gael' but 'poison gas to the kindly Celtic people', urging intolerance on the matter.[507]

The position of librarian was ultimately given to Ellen Burke, who had failed the Irish test but who came from 'very respectable [Catholic] stock'. The *Church of Ireland Gazette* commented that the case inevitably contributed to an increase in the anxiety felt by Protestants about their treatment by the state.[508] The government at the time (formed by Cumann na nGaedheal, which had supported Michael Collins's decision to sign the treaty that saw Ireland separated into north and south) dissolved Mayo County Council, a decision that was roundly attacked by Fianna Fáil. De Valera stated that if he ever had a vote on a local body and had to choose between a Catholic and Protestant, 'I would unhesitatingly vote for the Catholic.'[509] Myrtle remembers that the story of Miss Harrison was still being told with outrage in her childhood, twenty years afterwards; she also reflects on the lingering repercussions of the view that Protestants would not be treated fairly by the state, 'I think they had the attitude that [...] they would have to fight [in public sector jobs] [...] that the Catholics would be promoted ahead of them and that because of their religion [...] they would be at a disadvantage.'

In Gavin's area, where most Protestants were small farmers on fewer than thirty acres, the Protestant populace felt the need to 'look after' one another because of a sense that the state did not support them, 'We were conscious as non-politically aligned citizens, mistrusted equally by Fine Gael and Fianna Fáil, we had no "pull" for getting state jobs (in the post office, county council, etc.). And so, Protestants tended to employ co-religionists in businesses of all sizes. If we didn't look after our own post-partition, who would?'

Indeed, for many years, many businesses employed 'their own'. Laura found work through a nursing agency in the 1930s, 'I had no trouble [finding private patients] because the woman running the agency said that she had a lot of Protestant patients and they would not have anyone else but a Protestant.' Memoirist Lily O'Connor writes of how, in the 1940s, when a Protestant Dubliner was looking for a job, it helped to have a letter from a clergyman. With such a letter, she was able to obtain work in a factory.[510] *The Irish Times* ran advertisements for jobs which specified that candidates should be Protestants.[511] The 'gentry' tended to hire Protestants as a matter of preference and sometimes even got staff from England. Honora reports, '[The local aristocracy] brought most of their servants from England [...] only a small number of local Roman Catholics were employed there.' Winnie remembers of a local gentry family that, while they hired both Protestants and Catholics, 'Sometimes Protestants were given better positions in the house.'

In towns with sizeable Protestant populations, shops were often identified as 'Protestant' or 'Catholic'. 'There were Protestant shops', Mabel explains, 'and there were Roman Catholic shops. The customers did not matter, but [if you wanted a job] you could apply but you would not get it.' Many Protestant shops aspired to having all-Protestant staff but were not always able to achieve this. Sylvia explains that 'they would employ Protestants, all right, and they would employ Roman Catholics then, to fill in. It would not have been like discrimination; it would just be the done thing.' Winnie remembers, 'Protestant businesses tended to employ members of their own faith. Sometimes this did result in hostility or damaged relations.' Frances remembers that 'Protestant businesses employed Protestants as far as possible' and that Protestants only ever applied to Protestant businesses anyway. Local wealthy families hired 'RCs' for servant and labouring positions, 'as there were insufficient Protestant workers to go around'.

Upon leaving school, Sidney recalls, 'I was sent to the Protestant Employment Bureau, which had its office in Molesworth Street.' They arranged his first job at a Protestant solicitors' firm and for him to join the Protestant Abstinence Society. Eleanora explains that when Protestant people left school they tended to go and work for local Protestant-owned businesses. Most Protestant-owned businesses sought Protestant staff, because 'the feeling was that they should supply the jobs for their own […] that there should be a couple [of Protestants] on all staff.' Aphra comments that Protestant businesses tended to hire Protestants and held them to strict codes of behaviour, 'Protestant businesses hired Protestants who were expected to practise their religion and observe fairly strict moral rules. [The employees] were expected to socialise within Protestant circles.'

Trevor reports that business was heavily dominated by Protestants in his hometown, but he says this was because, 'With all due respect, we were trusted [more than Catholics]. If we said something, we'd look after it. I won't add any more to that because I'd only be damaging other people's reputation.' Tom remembers that 'it was common knowledge that Protestant-owned businesses would employ Protestant people as far as possible, mainly because their parents would be an indicator as to how their children had been brought up.'

Protestant hospitals used preferential hiring practices. The Adelaide had a reputation for being 'anti-Catholic'; in 1950, the taoiseach and other dignitaries were invited to a fundraising event at the Adelaide, but they turned the invitation down because of its reputation. The president attended, however, because things had started to change: Catholic patients could attend, and Catholic priests could visit. By 1980, the hospital had become ever more dependent on state support and eventually conceded to relaxing its remaining restrictions.[512]

Donald reports that having been a member of the Boys' Brigade made it easier for young Protestant men to get work:

> if you were known to be a member of the Boys' Brigade, or you had your BB badge on, you were definitely Church of Ireland, Presbyterian, Methodist. If you went for a job interview in a Protestant firm, they felt you were OK […] if you brought a reference from your BB Captain, that was very well received in cases like Parkers of the Coombe [a Protestant-owned business].

Sidney comments that he obtained his 'second and fourth' jobs through his Boys' Brigade connections. Through his Boys' Brigade connections, Jim was able to get quite a good job as a message-boy at a local Protestant business that preferred to hire young Protestants; the captain of the Boys' Brigade was one of the managers. As time passed, he was promoted ahead of considerably older employees; this was possibly, he believes, because he was a Protestant (although he says it was equally possible that it was because he was male and they were female). Although the work was poorly paid, it was considered a prestigious place to work – a place where Protestants could have a job for life. He also notes that there were some difficulties inherent in working for people of another faith:

> It was difficult for Protestants to ask RC employers for time off to attend the 12th of July [...] and many didn't feel confident doing so [but] when my mother worked in [a particular firm in a border area] in the 60s, all Protestants took this day off and, I am told, there were so many Protestants employed [in the factory that] Orange songs were played on the PA system with other songs of other traditions/themes.

Jennie's father was involved with the local Boys' Brigade and often used his connections to help out 'his' boys, '[Dad] had very good networks in the Protestant business community [...] Apprenticeships and office jobs were often available, and his recommendation was useful to give a young person a start.' Jennie's first job also came through Protestant circles, 'an old Protestant firm contacted my secretarial college and asked for a young [Protestant] girl to be trained as a bookkeeper.'

In Dublin, says Gerald, Protestant-owned companies that 'still had British connections' were seen as 'Protestant-friendly and a source of employment on leaving [Protestant] schools'. Mitchell says the young graduates of Protestant secondary schools tended to work in Protestant businesses because of an informal system that involved past pupils requesting recommendations from teachers. Recruiting staff this way was not considered discriminatory, but a case of looking for 'your own' first – a response to the feeling that Protestants were less supported by the state. Candide remembers that application forms for clerking jobs called for candidates to list where they had gone to school. 'Most schools were faith based', she explains, '[…] so firms picked their employees accordingly.'

Many people have memories of Protestant-owned companies tending to preferentially promote Protestants to managerial positions, even when the workforce was very mixed. Andy remembers, 'Some companies were known to have a strong preference for employing Protestants at their managerial and clerical levels.' Other companies were less rigid, and 'though they probably employed a greater proportion of Protestants than in the population as a whole, the majority of employees were Catholics.' He adds that 'This situation probably led to Catholic firms employing very few Protestants.'

Gerald went to work at Jacob's Biscuits – 'managed by Protestants for over 100 years' – in the late 1950s, when management and social aspects of the business were heavily dominated by Protestants:

> All the directors were Protestant. There were five women managers. Four were Protestant. The craftsmen, fitters, electricians, carpenters had Protestant foremen. The sales manager and sales representatives were Protestant. The superintendents of the male and female units of the St John's ambulance were Protestant. The boys' gym class was run by a man active in the Boys' Brigade. The girls' gym class was run by a lady active in the Girls' Brigade. The clerical staff and the staff Badminton Club were 90% Protestant.

Gerald also comments that there was a 'strong Masonic element' in the business, and that many of the managers were in the Masons. Masons were almost invariably Protestants, so when Masons helped each other out, they were also working to preserve high levels of Protestant representation in certain businesses, particularly in management.

Pat recalls that in Dublin Protestants 'were particularly good at business' and were among the largest employers. He comments that Quakers were known for treating their staff well in companies such as 'Jacob's, Cadbury's, Bewley's, Fry, Pym, Jenkins, etc.' and says that 'the two traditions worked happily in these companies although the Protestants tended to be in management while the Catholics were on the "shop floor."'

Joe, who worked in the insurance industry (considered a 'Protestant' sector), remembers, 'only one of the senior staff was a Catholic [...] Rather surprisingly, there was only one Protestant girl in the large typing pool.' Insurance firms even preferred to hire Protestant caretakers and janitors; Wally's father worked as a janitor for one such business.

As late as the 1970s, Everett says, the business that employed his father hired Protestant workers as much as possible and promoted them to more senior positions, 'All the managers would have been Protestants [...] Like, there was no way a Roman Catholic would get to the top [...] They'd have to be a Protestant. But they'd be better educated. That'd be the theory, you know.'

Large Protestant shops and department stores operated a system that recruited young Protestants and offered them apprenticeships, for which their parents had to pay, which included training in the retail sector, and room and board – and the opportunity to meet other young Protestants and possibly their future spouse. Some young people took apprenticeship positions far from their own home. Pamela remembers a large department store that took on young Protestants at the age of fourteen and fifteen. They were provided with dormitory education and cared for by a sort of matron, who kept a close eye on them and brought them all to church on Sundays.

William's older brother found work at a company in Dublin owned by 'the Protestant ascendancy'; they employed Protestant youths from poor backgrounds, who then lived in hostel accommodation exclusively for Protestant workers. The family was devastated when William's brother contracted TB and died. The hostel he lived in was probably the one known as 'The Ranch', which had been founded in 1878 to provide accommodation and training in a trade for Protestant boys. In his memoir, Kevin Dalton speaks of living at The Ranch for a period as a young man. There was a 'character' who drank in a pub across the road who used to shout 'abuse and obscenities' at anyone he saw coming and going, 'You Protestant bastards are finished. Your auld empire is bunched. You'll all be run out of it yet.'[513] Protestant firms who hired the boys who lived at The Ranch were known for providing work to unskilled Protestant boys and for paying them very badly.

By the mid-twentieth century, The Ranch focused on providing accommodation for Protestant boys from rural families, with limited incomes, who had found work in Dublin; the work was usually for 'Protestant firms' such as Parkers of the Coombe, an ironmonger's, Dockrell's, a hardware shop on South Great George's Street, and Brooks Thomas, a builders' providers. Of Dockrell's, Walter remembers, 'You could go along to your minister [of the church], say [...] and then say, "I'm looking for a job. Do you think you could fix me up?" or whatever. He might give you a reference to Dockrell's.' Elsie remembers her mother discussing hiring practices in their south Dublin suburb, 'She often spoke of the Protestant shops who only employed Protestants, usually "girls up from the country," who were uniformly badly treated and paid poorly [...] Protestants looked after Protestants, and there would always be a job for a Protestant.'

While many people report hiring practices that discriminated in favour of Protestants and businesses that tended to prefer to have Protestants at management level, there are also accounts of discrimination (and perceived discrimination) against Protestants. Robert Abbott, a marine engineer and voluntary Methodist preacher, wrote about the difficulty his father had in keeping work in Athlone. They were a poor family, and his father often lost jobs because the local priest would have 'a word' with a business owner and say, "You had better let him go. We don't need his sort filling scarce jobs here."[514] Barton reports, 'After we became a Free State, most government positions were filled by RC personnel, [there were] hardly any [Protestant] state doctors etc.'[515] In Dublin, Harry speaks of a local creamery in the north inner-city that posted notices saying 'No prods need apply' whenever they advertised for new staff.

Protestants report 'supporting' other Protestants when possible by shopping in Protestant-owned businesses. Gerald's mother, for example, avoided shopping in Cleary's Department Store in Dublin because it was Catholic-run, and it was where nuns and priests bought their habits. Bob says that 'Protestants were very likely to patronise Protestant professionals such as the doctor, vet, chemist, and solicitor', and that 'Some of these shops had accommodation for live-in staff [...] and up to the 1950s a couple of pews at the back of the [local] church were reserved for staff from the Protestant businesses in the town.'

Hazel states, 'Protestant businesses and shops employed mainly Protestants, and our family shopped there on a regular basis.' In rural areas and small towns, Protestants were also expected to support Protestant-owned shops and other businesses. Don remembers, 'When I went to work near a

small village [...] I was advised which were the Protestant-owned businesses, and that I should direct my purchases towards them, to support "our"
side.'

While most people report no problems with working in a 'mixed' environment, sometimes feelings of difference manifested. Eadry remembers
being the only Protestant girl in the nurses' home where she lived while
training. She got along well with the other girls, but there was one who
liked to tell her, 'We'll convert you before we're finished!' Although this was
said in a 'slightly jokey' way, it made her anxious, 'I said to her, "You will,
yeah. Over my dead body you'll change me!" I mean, I was telling her "forget it." And I just thought from then on, "Be careful."' Hannah remembers
that when she and her husband founded a company in the 1960s, their staff
was largely made up of Catholics. She was furious when the local Catholic
curate announced from the altar that none of his flock should work for
their business. Thankfully, she says, his edict was ignored.

Walter served in the Irish Army for a very brief period. While he disliked
the work, he has fond memories of how the army accommodated to people
of different backgrounds, 'Whatever religious persuasion you belonged to,
they can't stop you for going to church.' Walter was able to use this to get
frequent passes to leave and visit family and friends, 'There was a military
policeman that was on duty and I got to know him. I say, "Can I have a
pass out, please? I want to go to church." This could be on a Monday night.
Says he, "Certainly" [...] I'd get home to my parents and then back again.
Then, maybe the next week, I'd go out maybe on a Tuesday [...] One day,
he says, "Jaysus, you Protestants are really religious!"'

Quentin suggests that there was a correlation between the fact that some
Protestant businesses operated positive discrimination in favour of Protestants and the perception that the public sector preferentially hired
Catholics. When he graduated from Trinity College, he expected to find it
very difficult to find work in the public sector. However, he was hired upon
graduating and has never experienced any discrimination; if there was discrimination, he feels that it was over by the time he entered his career in
the 1960s. He suspects that the idea that Protestants were not hired for public sector jobs may have dissuaded people from applying, even if this was
no longer the case.

In 1963, a senator, Mr Ross, told Protestant school children in Dublin that they should not plan to emigrate because, although Protestants had once been right to worry that their employment prospects were limited to Protestant-owned firms, those days were now gone.[516] Nonetheless, in some quarters the suspicion that the state was anti-Protestant lingered. Bob remembers the headmaster in his school advising students not to join the civil service in about 1970, stating that they would be denied promotion because they were Protestants.

Marigold says that though the local work culture had already started to change when she was young, a few local Protestant-owned businesses still preferred to employ 'their own' because of the feeling that anti-Protestant discrimination lingered in other sectors. She says they did not actively look for Protestant shop assistants; it was just a case of giving work to young people they knew, usually after a parent had been into the shop to ask about any position that might be available. At one point a shop owner put up a sign in the window that read, 'Shop assistant required, apply within'; under the sign someone added another note on the outside of the window that read, 'Only Protestants need apply'. That shop was the last of its sort, and by the time Marigold was working, there was little evidence of anti-Protestant discrimination in the public sector.

Robert remembers everyone's surprise when a Protestant he knew became a guard, 'people probably thought he was sort of brave to go there because there wasn't a number of Protestants there'. Roberta remembers a university friend who was given a job in the Department of Foreign Affairs, 'everybody was quite amazed that they would have a Protestant in Foreign Affairs [...] there would still have been that sense in which they would not be accepted and that their Irish would not be good enough.'

Even when there was no longer any barrier to Protestants working in the public sector, the perception of state jobs as 'Catholic' lingered. Some workplaces that were nominally non-denominational nonetheless had Mass every so often; staff were expected to attend, and people who did not participate could feel conspicuously different. Eleanora worked in the public sector and states her view that Protestant civil servants were less likely to be promoted 'until well into the 1990s'. She remembers a department official, not realising that Eleanora was Protestant, scoffing, 'And would that *outfit* down there [the local Protestant community] have anything like confession?' There was an awkward silence. She left the room and later a friend told her that all the staff had been instructed that she was Protestant and that nothing was to be said about Protestants in front of her from now on. 'If you're accepted', she said, 'That would not happen'. 'It's, "You're an outsider," end of story. "You're not *one of us*."' From then on, she says, whenever there was an official function to which clergy were invited, the Protestant clergy and their spouses were put beside her.

Differences Among Protestants

The cultural 'sameness' of the various Protestant denominations tends to be stressed. By and large, intermarriage between the various Protestant groups was accepted, and they worked and socialised together, generally attending the same schools and belonging to the same leisure organisations. One could stop attending a Methodist church and go to a Church of Ireland or Presbyterian church without raising eyebrows. In this environment, Timothy explains, one couple in which the man was Methodist and the woman Unitarian raised their children as Church of Ireland 'as a compromise'. However, some issues relating to denominational difference are also discussed by the interviewees and questionnaire respondents.

While they were never treated as badly as the Catholics during the era of the Penal Laws, the Presbyterians were 'acutely aware of their religion as a source of exclusion from the highest circles of social and economic power'.[517] Guinnane says that they 'suffered the double difficulty of being both a minority religion and of not enjoying the established status of the Church of Ireland'. In the early eighteenth century, marriages carried out by Presbyterian ministers were described as 'licences for sin'; the couples were called 'fornicators' and the children 'bastards'. Presbyterian marriages did not receive full legal security until 1844.[518] Doris, whose mother was Presbyterian before marriage (she attended the Church of Ireland after marriage), often heard about how badly the Presbyterians were treated during the period of the Penal Laws, which discriminated against Catholics and 'dissenters'.

Presbyterians can still stress the distinctive qualities of their faith group and community, which is typically seen as stricter than other Protestant denominations. Hazel states, 'As our family was Presbyterian, there was no alcohol in the house. Whiskey was kept to cure an animal with a cough, or occasionally to cure my father's severe attack of "flu."' Despite widespread acceptance of marriage between people of diverse Protestant denominations, some strict Presbyterians preferred to stay among their own people. Barney's father spent almost two decades working in America before he was summoned home to marry a Presbyterian woman:

> you could not marry outside your religion. That'd be the whole point of him coming back from America. We've got to be perfectly truthful about this. To keep the farm and the Protestant name. And Presbyterian was the only system we knew […] Do you know, Church of Ireland was as bad as, as far as we were concerned, as bad as being Catholic. Presbyterian was our way.

Presbyterians are noted, by themselves and others, as being particularly strict in matters of religious observance and faith. Barney says:

> The Presbyterian system that's in the church was a hard, a hard religion to follow. It was a severe religion […] everything was a sin […] See, on a Sunday, when my father was living, you could not whistle, you could not kick a ball […] that was drilled into him when he was young, and my mother was the same. She had a deep, deep fear that if we'd tell a lie or anything she'd say, 'I'm telling yiz now, it's not me you have to worry about, you have to face your God if you done anything bad […]' People never showed emotions […] you did not show emotions. Not to nobody, you couldn't let the opposite side see you crying. Women or nothing would not bat an eye […] You see, you could not afford even for the women to be crying in front of the opposition […] You do not show emotion. That was one of the things. We're a hard, hard breed […] We are dour people.

Presbyterians in Barney's community were not supposed to engage with music at all. 'Some of them sorely, sorely loved it,' he says, 'but it would nearly be classed the devil's work.'

Eustace, the son of a Methodist preacher, comments on the 'itinerant nature' of the Methodist ministry and the enriching effect this had on his childhood, 'We would meet visiting preachers from different parts of the country and abroad. So as a small child in rural Ireland I can remember having a Chinese man for tea and being taught some words of Swahili by a missionary from Kenya.' He also reports that the Methodists were seen (and saw themselves) as particularly honest, among other virtues, 'I remember my father telling me about a dispute about money between two people [...] who were not Methodists. They agreed to lodge the money with a local Methodist until the dispute was resolved, knowing that it would be in safe hands.'

Basil grew up hearing about his 'low church' ancestors who, in the nineteenth century, objected to elements of Church of Ireland worship. They left the church in outrage when the local aristocrat wished to erect a memorial in the chancel. One of them became a Methodist and the other joined the Cooneyites.

In general, Protestants from border areas (whatever their denomination) tend to report stricter views around restrictions on activities such as playing cards and drinking alcohol. Sylvia remembers the cautionary tales she was told as a child with relation to card-playing, which was forbidden in her home:

> My father used to tell a story about [...] men out late playing cards, and they were coming home and there was four of them. And one fellow looked around, and he could see five. Four and himself. And each of them looked around and each of them could count an extra person, but they couldn't make out who it was [...] They believe it was the devil [...] There were always little stories about card players and an extra person around, and the devil, and a cloven hoof [...] and the Protestant houses didn't play cards much, or didn't like cards, and I remember my father [...] there was a bit of a row in our house about cards, and he threw them in the fire.

Popular perceptions regarding social class are frequently discussed in memoirs, and they were a recurring subject among interviewees and questionnaire respondents. Victor Griffin writes that during his childhood in the 1930s and 40s, the local gentry disparaged their Protestant and Catholic 'inferiors' with equal disdain, saying that 'no special degree of intimacy was extended to Protestants.'[519] Many stress that the Protestant community was very diverse in socio-economic terms. Non-elite Protestants often find it very annoying to be associated with a 'gentry' class that persists in Irish popular narratives, often in the role of the villain; they also find it irritating to be considered 'posh' when they have the same sort of financial struggles as other people.[520] Helen's family 'would have been what they would have called "the poor Protestants."' She explains that 'Money was very tight [in my mother's generation] and they lived on a shoestring. Mum will tell you now that she used to go to school in a pair of runners and the snow on the ground because there was no money to buy proper shoes for them.' She comments that she feels most Irish people, including historians and other scholars, have little interest in Protestants from poor families because of the common assumption that Protestants are all rich, and she compares poor Protestants in Ireland with poor white people in South Africa.

Everett discusses how people often assume that he is a Catholic and will talk about Protestants, in terms of class, in front of him, 'like, a lot of people would not know that I'm Protestant, like at work and different jobs, and they'd say, "Oh, look at that Protestant, he thinks he's above everybody."' Everett is from a labouring background and is used to people struggling to accept that he can also be a Protestant.

Frequently, very wealthy or aristocratic Protestants are discussed disdainfully by interviewees and questionnaire respondents because they are seen as having given a 'bad name' to all Protestants. Hugo says, 'They'd live on a big house, usually on the East Coast, and they'd be living on old money and they would not work. They'd be calling the locals "peasants."' Norm explains that because 'the Big House would have been Protestant', Protestants were resented, 'All you would do is mention the Big House and immediately: "Protestants! Protestants! They are all rich! They have everything, and we have nothing."'

Joyce was one of eleven children growing up on a small farm. She identifies the wealthy Protestants in her area as 'English-oriented', unlike her own family, which had 'always been Irish'. The wealthy families seemed to have an attitude that suggested that 'they'd think that they were above ye or whatever, you know [...] they'd be stepping off, like, and would not hardly see ye half the time.' Her feeling was that these people 'invited trouble' on the ordinary Protestants. Catholics resented them and assumed that the apparent views of these wealthy people applied to all Protestants, sometimes taking their irritation or anger out on poorer (and more accessible) Protestants.

Heather relates how an acquaintance learned that she was Protestant and said that she had a 'silver spoon background'. She was very indignant; she grew up in an area of considerable rural poverty, and her parents struggled to keep going on their small acreage:

> I said, 'Excuse me, anything but!' Wellie marks up the back of the legs and very little of anything. Running water was down the walls and coming up through the mud floor. We didn't have a toilet [...] When I was a little child there was no electric [...] no nothing, and that was our norm [...] There was only a few wealthy neighbours who had 200 acres. You know, the bigger houses. Country houses that would have had a different lifestyle.

Heather's father's generation had no education beyond primary school; her father remembers that many of the Protestants in their border area were still illiterate in the 1930s. Because everyone worked long hours every day to make a meagre living from the land, their lives were very rooted in the present. The land and the work it demanded, including the struggle to keep it within the community, was everything, and life was all about getting up early, working all day, eating a simple meal, and going to sleep.

Billy remembers that, in his community, 'there was no pride' in Protestants that worked in the senate or in other public offices, because they seemed completely irrelevant to them. By contrast, 'There might be pride in the [Protestant] man down the road who had twelve cows.'

Barton remembers the Protestant community in his area being strictly divided according to social class. After the annual Harvest Thanksgiving, there was a party where the 'nobs' went into the dining room of the rectory and the 'ordinary people' went to the sitting room. He comments that 'there was no social contact between the Big House and the ordinary Protestant community. The family had their own secluded part in the church. No one would enter the estates except on business.'

Doris explains that ordinary families had nothing to do with the local aristocratic families. According to her, these families would have served in the British parliament before independence and continued to mix and marry purely within their own ranks afterwards; they socialised with – and married – their own cousins or English people, but they were 'a very closed shop' with no interest in ordinary Protestants. Moreover, she says, the real distinction was between landlords and tenants – not between Protestants and Catholics. She knows a story about a big landlord family in the area that 'turned on some of its Protestant tenants' in the late nineteenth century. The tenant farmers had once owned a small patch of land; when they experienced financial difficulty, they got a loan from the Big House against their land, but when they tried to pay off the loan and get the land back, they still lost everything. This story indicates to her that the people in Big Houses only cared about their elite social class, and that the idea that small Protestant farmers somehow had it easier than their Catholic counterparts, or could be associated with the aristocracy, is false.

Jim is old enough to have heard stories from people of the days, going up to the 1930s, when it was expected that the local Protestants stand outside the church on Sundays and wait until the local gentry had taken their places. 'They would run down in their pony and trap or whatever it was, to church,' he says. 'Then the driver came back for them then after the service.' While the parishioners resented waiting outside the church, 'Nobody wanted to rock the boat' because they were afraid of the potential repercussions from a major local employer.

In the rural area where Gerald's family holidayed, the 'local gentry' were very much in charge at church, 'The family sat in the front pew of the church and the sexton would keep the bell ringing until they arrived. On a fine Sunday, many of the congregation stood outside until [the 'gentry family'] had gone in.' Gavin's community was 'not at all socially diverse. 90% of us were small tenant famers with holdings of less than 20/30 acres.' There was once a Big House in the area, although it was derelict by the time of his childhood. 'I was told', he states, 'that those attending church would have to wait until this family arrived for service before entering in their wake.' Francis recalls that there were several Big Houses locally, and 'little communication between them and us'. All of their staff were Protestant; many of them were English. Eric says that the local aristocrats had paid for a church to be built on their estate, and had a gallery erected in it, 'an excellent position from which to observe who was in attendance and who was not at Sunday Service.'

Often with a sneer, the gentry are designated as 'Anglo-Irish'; they are also considered Protestant, but less Irish than Protestants on lower incomes, especially if they were educated in England or had English employees. Robert describes these people as 'the landed gentry' and explains that 'They were socially way ahead of the rest of us, who were very lower middle-class and working-class people. They would have been Anglo-Irish.' Bob remembers his grandfather's story about his first car, a second-hand Model T Ford bought in 1929, and the reaction of the local 'gentry', 'He drove it to church [...] the following Sunday, and a local landowner, who had once been the landlord of what was then my grandfather's farm, said to him, "I see even the peasants are now driving cars!"'

Ian reports that his local church once reserved the front row for the wealthiest families, the back rows for their servants, 'and everyone else in between'. He also comments that local lore about these wealthy families belittled their purported origins, claiming that one family was said to have won their estate by swindling a Cromwellian soldier and that the other was descended from 'a servant who persuaded the original owner to lend him the deeds of the estate but then refused to give them back'.

Members of the gentry often had an influential role in the management of the local Protestant church (which generally belonged to the Church of Ireland); the construction of the church might well have been paid for by their ancestors. The gentry were often de facto vestry members with the right to make decisions about the parish. Robert describes a vestry meeting in the midlands in the 1950s or 60s, 'They [the 'ordinary' members of the vestry] were sitting there and nothing was happening.' The reason being, they were waiting for the local aristocrat to arrive – 'we're waiting for the lord to come' – as nothing could happen without him. Eleanora says that the wealthy family in her area was deeply involved in administering church issues, and 'the ordinary person in the pew had practically no say. They dominated the vestry and the diocesan synods and everything.'

Nancy has a favourable view of the aristocratic Protestants and comments that gentry families did a huge amount of work for their parishes. She believes that it is 'a great pity that the Anglo-Irish families have, by and large, died out or gone, because they had a great sense of [...] service to the church'. This was perhaps partly because they had more leisure time to serve on church committees. Myrtle comments on the role of wealthy Protestants in providing practical support for the Protestant community. While wealthy Protestants in her area did not mix socially with ordinary Protestants, 'they did, however, make a point of visiting the local Protestant national school, always went to Sunday services and let the parish use their grounds for the sales of work, etc.' Richard comments that the expectation in his area was that poor Protestants would receive charitable help 'in the form of cast-off clothes and food at Christmas time' from wealthy families such as these.

Sam comments on how 'Big House' people were often quite isolated because of their reluctance to socialise outside their class:

> There were several Big Houses in this area. The only contact people living in these houses had with the ordinary farmers was at church on Sunday. They just socialised with other people from Big Houses [...] I rented a field to grow potatoes from the people in the Big House. I went to ask if I could use their shed to store potatoes in as I had none of my own. It was the first time I had been in the yard or house and the lady of the house welcomed me in and gave me permission [...] and she exclaimed, 'We don't know what's going on in this area; we might as well be living in Inishbofin [an isolated island in the west].'

Penelope says that the Protestant community in the area where she grew up in the west was 'centralised' in a church in the biggest urban centre as, one by one, the rural churches closed. This church had been built by the wealthier members of the Protestant community, and they still 'ruled the roost' and disparaged the poor farmers who now worshipped with them. The latter felt very disrespected, 'We were very much little aliens who sat down the back [...] we did feel a little bit inferior to them because they were very much moneyed people.' Over the years, the wealthy Protestants have left, leaving an aging congregation tasked with scraping enough money together each year to keep the church in good repair. Barton comments that the same applied in his area, 'Because mostly the landlords had churches. They paid all the expenses. And then nobody put their hand in their pocket afterwards [when the gentry had gone].'

William tells a story about a local man from the Protestant community who worked as a farm hand for a wealthier family, also Protestant. The woman of the family was very unpopular. One day the man accidentally stuck a pitchfork in a pony's eye. The woman was very upset and asked him

what they should do to help the animal. He said that they should put some
whiskey in it; he persuaded her to buy a bottle of whiskey and that the best
way to put it in the pony's eye was to fill his own mouth and spit it at the
animal. In that way, he tricked her so that he could get 'a feed of drink' and
he had a great story to tell.

Many people go to considerable lengths to stress differences between
Protestants in independent Ireland and in the North. Heather speaks of growing up in a family that belonged to one of the more evangelical faiths, which
had links to churches in Northern Ireland. Her parents often hosted Northern
Protestants on their visits south and the topic of conversation frequently
veered toward talk of history, as her father had a great passion for it. Even as
a child, she was struck by how 'closed in' Protestants from the North seemed
to be compared to their southern equivalents. She felt that their attitude was,
'The border is there so we are only interested in the geography of the six
counties', and, 'We are not particularly interested in Irish history.' Her father
often challenged them because he was knowledgeable about history and of
the links between Irish Protestantism and Irish nationalism, and 'he could see
both sides'. In other words, he had some understanding of, and empathy for,
nationalists and their actions, and for the positions of unionists in the North.
They typically responded by quoting the Old Testament.

Representations and appearances of Northern unionists on television
have often been seen as problematic and annoying by Protestants in independent Ireland, giving people the impression that Protestants in independent Ireland have similar views. Some report the sense that Protestants in
the North have little interest in those in the south. Henry scoffs that the
Protestants in the North 'have written us off down here in the south [...]
As any kind of cultural offspring or off-post.' Honor's parents 'were particularly anxious to disassociate themselves from what they saw as the Protestants in the North'.

Public Expressions of Faith

Elsie remembers overt symbols of Catholicism as constant reminders of difference and minority status:

> Religious symbols were everywhere – holy pictures, Sacred Hearts,
> saints, Our Lady, the Angelus three times a day, and people stopping in

the street to bless themselves [...] people felt nervous of their minority status and did not feel that they belonged in the State. However, they also did not feel that they were British or English, and often expressed upset when people would accuse them of being 'English.'

In general, public expressions of faith and allegiance are often described as underlining difference. Andy remembers:

> We looked on Corpus Christi celebrations, processions and decorations as having no relation to us, and sometimes we were conscious of a certain triumphant emphasis [...] our house tended to look bare when contrasted with the decorations and banners which, with a strong competitive element, adorned the houses of our Catholic neighbours.

Henry says, 'I remember once watching what must have been a Corpus Christi procession coming down the street. It was a complete surprise to see the girls dressed in white with baskets and throwing stuff around.'

Lisa remembers how all the streets were closed during a religious procession, making it impossible for the Protestants to attend their church, 'You didn't get out if there was a pilgrimage going on. I don't think it occurred to the Catholic authorities that there was a service up there. In a way, we lay low and maybe didn't make our voice known.'

Eileen recalls public expressions of religious identity making her feel different, 'There was a feeling of being left out [...] The Catholics had Corpus Christi processions and events such as [local 'Patterns' or religious events] which I wanted to see, and my mother would not allow.'

Even ordinary Sundays underlined difference. Daphne remembers, 'this great sort of *tsunami* of people walking in one direction [for Mass] and us going the other direction [...] There was always that sense of great numbers on one side and being part of a very small group on the other side.' Bob remembers, 'standing there watching these people, of which I was clearly not [...] and my parents didn't belong, and they were just walking and cycling down for nine o'clock Mass [...] and I wasn't part of that.'

Stories about difference are told around issues such as the now-defunct Catholic ruling about eating fish on Fridays and fasting on certain days of the year. Eleanora remarks that '[Catholics] would never eat meat on a Friday and if they were going back to England on the boat and some neighbours saw a Roman Catholic going back and eating meat on the boat this would all be transferred back to the community: "Do you *know* who was on the boat and they were eating meat?"'

Many Protestant children also attended Sunday school which, particularly in rural parishes, made them stand out. Eleanora remembers how her Sunday school teacher had to walk her and the other children some of the way home after their Scripture lessons, 'because we would have been stoned and that by Roman Catholic children'. She believes that nobody ever remonstrated with the Catholic children, and that their parents knew what they were doing and turned a blind eye.

Even as Ireland progressively became more modern, more secular, and more liberal, certain public events reminded Protestants of being a minority. The visit of Pope John Paul II in 1979 was one such event. The whole country was excited, and huge numbers went to see the Pope and attend public Masses. Peter gleefully recounts how he had a vasectomy at the Adelaide – still the 'Protestant hospital' then – on the day of the Mass, 'because there was nothing on for the Protestants' that particular weekend.

Bullying and Social Antagonism

Of his childhood in a Protestant orphanage in the 1930s and 40s, memoirist Kevin Dalton writes that the other local children knew where the Protestant orphans lived and identified them as 'different', and that the two groups of boys would engage in a shouting match. The Catholic children shouted, 'Proddy woddy ring the bell, all the soupers go to hell', to which the Protestant children returned, 'Catholic, Catholic, go to Mass, riding on the divil's ass.' In response, the Catholic children would conclude, 'Protestant, Protestant, quack, quack, quack, go to the divil and never come back.'[521]

Norman Ruddock writes that in the year of his birth, 1935, 'Minorities were considered of no consequence [...] and were just about tolerated.' He also remembers how the bishop was present 'at every opening of the Irish Sugar Company',[522] while Protestant bishops were either not invited or did not accept invitations. He recalls feeling very different in his childhood (his mother, a widow, ran a small shop in Carlow) in the 1930s and 40s; he had little contact with Catholic neighbours, who were forbidden from entering

Protestant churches and who made fun of them for eating meat on Fridays. The Protestants resented the fact that everything closed on Catholic holy days and had a sense of keeping their heads down and feeling apologetic for not being 'papists'.[523] Trev remembers that there were negative feelings towards Protestants in his area, which manifested occasionally as nastiness, 'Interference was minimal [but, for example] when we went carol singing before Christmas it was common to find a gate festooned with barbed wire when coming back down an avenue.'

Hugh remembers, in the 1930s, the local landscape was still scarred by the events that had taken place, including 'the burning of Protestant houses and farmhouses'. He remembers feeling very 'different':

> Going to school in the thirties was not pleasant for a Protestant because there were a lot of boys out the [...] road, all Roman Catholics, and it wasn't long after the War of Independence and the burning of Protestant houses and farmhouses and [...] From the age of seven, I had stones thrown at me, and horse manure from the sidecars. And when I was going home from school, I had to hurry out at three o'clock and get as far down the road as I could, before the boys from the monastery [...] these boys, twelve or fourteen of them, they'd walk abreast down the road and they'd be calling out names and threatening me with castration. One of them had a penknife and he was going to cut me up. I had a companion who lived half way; he only had one mile to go. And he complained to his father, and his father used to come down the road in his motorcar [...] patrolling it and he spoke to some of these boys and it didn't make much difference, but I suppose it made a little. Now, I don't know whether they would have actually [...] you know [...] I think it was just bullying, I don't think they would have done me any harm.

There was one local man who singled him out and terrified him:

> If he ever came around and saw me, he was going to pinch off my nose. He had a nice little pincers and he was going to pinch off my nose [because I was a Protestant child] and as a 6/7/8 year old I was terrified [...] he used to drive a four wheel caravan in to meet the railway train at about half past three in the summertime and I would be walking out from school. It was horse–drawn. When he'd see me,

he would crack the whip across me, and he never actually touched me, but I used to shrink in against the wall, so I didn't get a cut of the whip on my ankles. And, you know, he'd be just gloating there on the wagonette, and I was always terrified of him.

Hugh's family had been very nationalist because they had 'never' been English or unionist and therefore, he says, did not deserve to be the targets of resentment. In fact, theirs was the first business in town to put the name of the shop over the door in the Irish language; they even wrote to a professor at the university to find out the best way to write 'unlimited' in Irish. His father was 'an armchair Republican'. They were not members of the gentry, but they were 'in trade'. All this made it doubly upsetting when their neighbours (and, it seemed to him, the state) refused to accept them as real Irish citizens, 'The policy generally was to get rid of the Protestants and that policy was very evident in the 30s and it was quite, quite tangible.'

Lizzie remembers that 'for years' the children who saw her and her siblings on the street chanted a 'nasty rhyme [...] a well-known rhyme' at them. She found it baffling, as 'where I went to school, I was never taught against anybody [...] We were never taught against any religion or anything.' At one point, she and her siblings were living with their mother on church grounds because her mother had a caretaking position. She had a good friend who came to visit occasionally, but her brother, a priest, could not visit because he would have to walk across Protestant holy ground to get there. Eileen remembers a neighbour telling her that 'there would be 3 dark days at the end [of the world] [and] Protestants would not have a light.'

William describes a childhood that was mostly happy, with all the children in the rural area playing hurling with sticks they had cut themselves from the hedge. There was one boy, who was older, who made him feel very different, and he and his brother dreaded being asked by their mother to go to the village for a few messages because he would 'call us old Protestants and all that sort of stuff [...] Really nasty, to be honest with you.' In those times, he said, no matter how well you got on with your neighbours, 'there was kind of an undercurrent of that sort of thing [...] we were always conscious of the fact that we were a different religion.' He says, 'It wasn't a nice feeling. It was a bad feeling, really it was, I think it's not good for young people to feel like that and we were conscious of it.'

Ed remembers 'a small gang of young lads of my own age, all Roman Catholic, in the next road to where I lived' who chased him and shouted slogans such as 'Proddy woddy green grass', as well as 'throwing stones at me and hitting me if they could get in reach'. Ashamed, he kept the experience to himself until he was referred to the doctor for stomach aches caused by stress. Robert, who grew up in 'widows' alms-houses' because his father had died young and his mother was poor, remembers, 'Somehow the children […] knew that we were Protestants and they used to stand outside the gate and shout in at us: "Proddy woddy ring the bell, all the soupers go to hell."'

Helen grew up in a 'brewery house' in Dublin that belonged to Guinness and was leased to brewery staff. Guinness had long been known as a good employer for Protestants, but they were a small minority in the cluster of brewery houses. She says the cultural differences between the Protestant and the Catholic families in that community of working-class homes were 'huge' and that they had a 'totally different outlook'. The Protestant children stood out on Sundays because they went to Sunday school and a special children's service in the afternoon; by the time of the service, the Catholic children had all been released from their Sunday obligations and were playing in the street. The Protestants were often bullied.

Wallace remembers that, when he was a child, 'I lived surrounded with Catholic boys and girls, but there seemed to be an agreement that I didn't go to their parties and they didn't come to mine.' Hubert remembers a distinct feeling of difference that he attributes to Protestants considering their past and concentrating more on the aspects of their culture that they found 'good'. As a small boy, he first became aware of his difference when other children accused him of being English, something that was 'tinged with insult'. At the time, this puzzled him because he had no sense of Englishness and had never been to England, but, looking back, he can see that they were identifying him as different because his family, and other people from their Protestant background and well-to-do social class, spoke with different accents and tended to have different sorts of names.

Ursula was in hospital having her tonsils removed when another little girl on the ward found out that she was a Protestant; the girl tried to convert her, asking her if she was aware that she was going to hell. Although probably well meant, the comment was hurtful. Quentin remembers, 'some Catholic boys on occasion shouted "Proddy dogs" at us but I'm afraid we replied with "Candlesticks."' Gerald recalls another exchange of insults, "Proddy, Proddy ring in the bell. All the Proddies go to hell" and "Cathy, Cathy go to Mass, riding on the Devil's Ass".

Eleanora recalls attending an exam together with teenagers from all over the area. One boy heard her giving the name of her school, a Protestant school, and said, 'Well, you know that the Protestant religion is a wrong religion?' Embarrassed, a girl said to him, 'You shouldn't say that', and he retorted, 'Well, doesn't the priest tell us every Sunday to say that?'

Stewart remembers:

> I never came across hostility [towards Protestants] except for being jeered and cat called in the 1950s [...] when I would leave [my school] and walk to my grandfather and grandmother's house [...] this was the norm at the time and my parents instilled in me 'not to engage' but to take the insults and keep walking. Many years later some of these children, now grown up, told me they were instructed and encouraged by the local elderly priest to do so.

Richard's father was very good friends with the local Catholic priest. One day he decided to hold a public fête in his garden to raise funds for the Protestant church and he invited the whole community. The priest responded by saying at Mass, 'There's an event taking place in this area next Saturday and none of you are to attend.' In the process, he was banning members of Richard's family who had 'married out' and converted. That was the end of a long friendship.

Morris got into a dispute with the owner of a neighbouring business, 'I was hit with vile comments about being a "West Brit" and go back to my own country.' And an otherwise friendly encounter with a neighbour took a sour turn, 'While out walking in a public wood/park I met a neighbour and his wife. We chatted before the wife came out with, "It's great your crowd no longer own the place."'

Attitudes to Social Issues

Protestants frequently consider themselves more liberal than the majority on a range of social issues, particularly relating to reproductive rights. Morris reports that, during his career in sales, Catholic customers often asked if he could obtain contraceptives for them, as the belief that Protestants had access to contraception was widespread, 'I would be greeted with, "You're a left footer" or some such comment, followed by a request to get them rubbers/johnnies etc. [...] one had only to scratch the surface to be treated as an outsider/someone who had wealth hidden away.' Gerald's workplace organised an outing every year to the Isle of Man; during the trip, Protestant employees were expected to purchase large quantities ('crates') of condoms for all their friends, who felt that the Protestants would find it easier to get them past customs.

Elsie remembers how it was stressed that, 'when having a baby, a C of I [Church of Ireland] woman should not go to a Catholic maternity hospital because if a choice had to be made [by a Catholic obstetrician or midwife] between saving the baby or saving the mother, the baby would be saved.' Basil also remembers discussions about the importance of 'Protestant' maternity care and how, 'if there was a balance between the baby and the mother at birth, [among] the Catholics, the mother was allowed to die, and the baby survived, and it was the other way around in the Protestant.'

Priscilla, Martha, Vivienne, and Olive stress how strongly women felt about attending Protestant hospitals such as the Adelaide. The Adelaide was opened in 1839, initially to treat poor Protestants in Dublin at a time when they were a sizeable community.[524] Unsurprisingly, it placed 'denominational restrictions' on patients, staff, and management, allowing only members of 'reformed Protestant churches' to work at the hospital or provide religious services there. By the 1860s, it had become a training hospital for Protestant girls who wished to become nurses, partly because of anxiety that dying Protestants might be attended by Catholic nurses with their 'dangerous influences'.[525] Protestants preferred the Adelaide because most of the staff were Protestant, and they felt that the ethos guaranteed better treatment, especially for women. They had heard terrible stories about the treatment of women in Catholic-run hospitals. Above all, 'you were in a place you knew'. Lisa, who spent some time working at the Adelaide, remembered that it provided sterilisations ('tubes tied and things') not just to Protestant women but also to 'ordinary Dublin people like, Stock and York Street and places like that with 10, 12 and 14 kids' who knew that they could be sterilised discreetly there.

Miriam, who married a Catholic and raised her children as Catholics, says that the private maternity hospital she attended insisted that the new-borns had to be baptised before leaving. This was partly, she believes, because she was in a mixed marriage (and therefore might be tempted to raise the child Protestant) and partly because it was hospital policy generally. Her baby was baptised there, 'I had no choice […] all this hoo-ha is quite sad when you think about it.'

It should be noted that, despite the widespread view of Protestants as more liberal on social issues, people also describe hypocrisy and poor treat-ment toward those who were considered transgressors of Protestant norms and ideals. For example, Gregory supplies his mother's account of the Bethany mother and child home and why conditions were so bad in the 1940s, 'When Catholic boys got Protestant girls pregnant, sometimes the boy in question or his parents would not want to be identified, and the girl's parents were threatened with retaliation by the boy's people if the boy's deed was made known, so the unfortunate girls were hidden away in Bethany homes.' The Bethany home was known for its poor treatment of young women and babies. Gregory explains that this was because 'the poor lady who ran the home was always under pressure from the girls' parents, the boys' parents, the Catholic Church and sometimes the Protestant Church, to keep the real reason for her charity's existence a secret, resulting in her never having sufficient workers or funds to run the place properly which meant the girls got neglected and some babies died.'

Embarrassment and Awkwardness
Protestants sometimes link feelings of difference with the idea that people associate them with well-known and reviled characters from Irish history. For example, Lisa remembers:

we were perceived by others as VERY DIFFERENT to our neigh-bours and townspeople […] We went to local dancing class etc but were called 'dirty Protestants' by the 'townies' children on the way to school […] Drogheda had SO SUFFERED from CROMWELL who could blame them, even if it was back in 1648!!!! We were pay-ing for the sins of our fathers as the Catholics viewed us – and they had a point. But they didn't consider us IRISH! Even in the 1930s – not REALLY Irish!!! […] we local Protestants genuinely were HORRIFIED by [Cromwell's] murderous action, and ashamed of

228

the later PENAL LAWS etc – genuinely ASHAMED!!! […] we were
ALL victims of HISTORY!!! [original formatting retained]

Hugo still feels guilty about the Penal Laws, because they were imposed by
'English Protestants' and, as he is a Protestant too, he feels in some way implicated and marked out as different.

Norm describes a visit to the local hospital when his Protestant status was
highlighted in a way that he found hurtful. He was visiting an elderly relative
when the hospital chaplain, a Catholic, was doing his rounds. 'What's your
name?' the priest asked him. He gave his name, a common one in the Protestant community. 'Oh,' said the priest. 'I never heard of a saint with that name!'

Penelope asserts that the younger Protestants she knows are 'embarrassed' and prefer to pretend that they are 'nothing'. She tells the story of a
young friend who married recently. Her parents insisted that she have a
church wedding but, because she did not want to be spotted emerging from
the local Protestant church, she opted to have the ceremony in a small
church out of town.

Henry (who is unusual for his generation in having pronounced unionist
views) says, 'It's only when you leave school you think "Oh my God, it's different out here! All these Irish nationalists and republicans!"' He suddenly realised that he was 'different' in his early teens when his mother sent him to a
summer course at the Gaeltacht, 'It might make a proper Irishman out of me!'
It had not occurred to the course organisers that some of the children might
not be Catholic, so they had organised compulsory nightly recitations of the
Rosary. 'I would literally say "rhubarb" a lot, both forwards and backwards. I
used to try to pass the time by saying "rhubarb" backwards.' When his scout
troop attended a national scouting jamboree in the 1970s, again, the assumption was that everyone was Catholic, 'There was a huge big outdoor Mass
held at this jamboree and again we turned up and […] the service started and
people started crossing themselves and we were very embarrassed and I think
we just walked off and decided to go back to our camp.'

Shirley remembers a sense of embarrassment whenever, as a young person in the 1980s, she had to tell someone her 'Protestant' name:

Protestants have funny names. I would go to discos and things and
it was hard to shout my name over the music […] they would say

'That's a funny name!' And if you told them you were Protestant then you would not see them again. They'd be scared off. They would say, 'Oh, you're one of *them!*' […] My sister had a few dates with a fella and then she told him she was Protestant and he left her.

Shirley often feels awkward about her identity as a Protestant. A friend brought her to a work party and announced to everyone there that she was a Protestant. 'Why do you feel you have to say that?' she asked, and her friend said, 'Well, I want to show you off!' She disliked everyone looking at her and realising that she was different. One day the staff of the nursing home where she worked as a cleaner in the 1980s or 90s were talking about a night out; one of the men said he had had a great time at a ball until a woman he had asked to dance told him she was Protestant. It was clear that he was absolutely horrified. He hadn't known what to do. That was too much to bear, so Shirley stood up and admitted that she was also Protestant. 'You're not, love', he said. It did not make sense to him because she was not wealthy, she was working in a relatively unskilled job, and she did not sound 'posh'. But she said, 'Yeah'. The room went quiet and everyone looked away from her.

Oliver describes how, as he moved beyond his Dublin childhood and the comfort zone of the almost all-Protestant social circle within which he had grown up and been educated, he began to feel that he did not have the 'secret script'. He spoke with an Anglo-Irish accent (though he is careful to distinguish himself and his family from the wealthy gentry with their more pronounced accents) and was sometimes mistaken for an English person, 'and made know by that response that I was an outsider.' In response, he says, he 'flirted with nationalist politics'. Years later, living abroad, he felt that he could understand scattered communities elsewhere after having grown up in a culture that saw him as 'other'.

Conclusion

As is the case with most minorities, stories of difference are a fundamental aspect of narratives about identity. However, the differences in question are complex; it is not just a question of being different to the Catholic majority, but also of how these differences are mediated. There are also issues of differences between social classes and differences between perception and reality. Moreover, many Protestants' stories stress sameness: the many ways in which Protestants experience the same things as everyone else and are no different to any other Irish person. In general, feelings of difference have greatly eroded, and there have been some landmark moments that signalled the realisation of change. Lisa remembers how her sister, who emigrated to the UK as a young woman, rang her in tears of happiness when the GAA allowed rugby to be played in Croke Park for the first time. With the passage of time and the steadily growing secularism of modern Ireland, feelings of difference are increasingly relegated to the past.

6. Stories of Land and Landscape, Rural and Urban

No cultural group can tell stories about itself without referring to the rural or urban landscape that surrounds its people. The landscape forms a backdrop to the narratives of their shared past, present, and their aspirations for the future. The landscape is a cultural construction and artefact, even though we may think of it as 'nature'. As a cultural artefact, it is 'the autobiography of society', a 'manuscript', or a 'palimpsest'; it is a repository of the collective memory of the people who inhabit it and a critical forum in which ideas about identity are forged.[526]

Inevitably, any landscape develops mnemonic associations. Features of the landscape, natural or constructed, rural or urban, are aligned with memories of the past and its people.[527] In the landscape, groups find the places, buildings, monuments, and other features that help to preserve and create collective memories.[528] Stories about land and landscape are often much more complicated than they first appear. There are many layers of meaning, often even within the narratives of an individual. Reminiscences that initially seem to be simple stories about country life, or scenery, or a family's personal relationship with the land, can also be full of statements regarding allegiance, loyalty, and territoriality.

The Human Landscape

During the plantations and the efforts of the British state to consolidate its position and that of Protestantism, the landscape was altered; sites associated with Catholicism, the indigenous Irish, and the Normans were destroyed.[529] These included churches, Norman tower houses, and structures around sacred spaces such as holy wells. There was a desire to destroy sacred sites and structures while also expressing 'an instinct to preserve mutilated residues of the vanquished past as enduring evidence of Protestantism's glorious triumph'.[530] Protestants regarded the ruined abbeys, sacred structures associated with holy wells, and monasteries as necessary reminders 'of our indignation and detestation against them',[531] although destroying buildings in places that attracted popular religious observance often failed to deter the faithful. In 1680, buildings on the holy island of Lough Derg were destroyed, but the pilgrims kept coming; in 1714, the authorities disrupted an annual event in the monastic site of Glendalough, destroying several crosses, and still popular devotion continued.[532]

For early generations of Protestants, their right to be in Ireland was very much predicated on their ownership and occupancy of the land, their economic power as a result of British dominion, and their belief that they represented a civilising force and were therefore the land's natural owners. In this context, the changes that the Protestant settlement created in the landscape, from the destruction of churches to the transformation of the agricultural landscape, created a sort of living monument to what Protestant rulers then considered the rightful ownership of Ireland by people who could really do something important with it.

Villages and small towns tended to form around big estates in a pattern that is still visible. In the early seventeenth century, for example, Richard Boyle, a planter, made the landscape around his new home conform to the English model, with a deer park, orchards, fish farms, stud farms, and so forth.[533] By the eighteenth century, the Irish landscape had become marked by the large estates, their stately homes, and all the trappings of the demesnes.

Wealthy Protestants – the ascendancy – while always a very small minority, had a visibility in the landscape disproportionate to their numbers, just like their influence on society. Even today, the relics of this privileged class remain very visible in the form of stately homes (often in ruins), gate lodges, impressive stone walls encircling the territory of former estates, and so forth. Surely the great visibility of the now-largely-toppled Protestant ascendancy contributes to the widely held idea that many, or even most, Protestants are wealthy. Humbler Protestants' homes and farms are not very visible because they look like everyone else's, while nobody can ignore the Big Houses that memorialise, through their presence, the long, contentious history of the Protestant ascendancy.[534] As well as featuring in many Protestants' oral narratives – and narratives about them – the Big House is an important motif in Irish literature, theatre, and the visual arts. This, as well as the visibility of Big Houses in the landscape, must have contributed to the story of Protestants as being rich, or formerly rich, and at risk of imminent extinction.[535]

Maps, which reduce the subtleties of the landscape to two dimensions and are, in theory, an objective rendering of a place to understand it better, are in Ireland (and in any country with a colonial past) a loaded issue. In the mid-seventeenth century, Sir William Petty produced a series of maps with place names in English and a view of Ireland 'filtered through English cultural lenses and assumptions'. Many of the native Irish objected to the work of Petty's cartographers (some of whom were soldiers), which they accurately viewed as part of the machinery of conquest. Despite the fact that the cartographers were protected by experienced soldiers, protestors executed eight of Petty's surveyors in Co. Wicklow in 1655.[536]

The detailed Ordnance Survey maps of Ireland, on which all subsequent Ordnance Survey maps were based, were created in the first half of the nineteenth century, starting in 1825.[537] British soldier-surveyors attempted to depict the landscape and thus bring it further under control, anglicising place names and redrawing boundaries in a way that made it easier to value property and expropriate more of it for the ascendancy.[538] The surveyors were trained in dealing with locals who wanted to sabotage their work, although the locals also told them stories about folklore, history, and tradition, including stories about historic dispossessions. The maps showed not just natural features of the landscape but also settlement and housing patterns that helped landlords and administrators to decide on matters such as rent. They also showed how the landlord class had already modified the landscape with their great homes and estates. Accurate maps could also be status symbols; many big landowners hired private surveyors to carry out detailed surveys of their properties and often displayed the resulting maps like trophies on the walls of their stately homes.[539]

Despite the 'conquering' aspect of the Ordnance Survey, it was an important contribution to understanding Irish culture. Among the two thousand or so employed to work on the project were several Irish scholars, including John O'Donovan, Eugene O'Curry, and George Petrie, who helped to record place names in transliterations of the original Irish, and recorded folklore and traditional knowledge.[540] Petrie's *Essay on the Round Towers of Ireland* drew heavily on his experience with the Ordnance Survey[541] and would remain a standard text for many years; it was widely studied in schools and considered to provide an uncontroversial glimpse of Ireland's past, suitable for Catholic and Protestant students alike.

Access to Land

In rural areas, where people tend to be much more 'fixed' to a specific part of the landscape than in urban areas, stories of people, families, and communities are inextricably linked to how the landscape is viewed and experienced. The land provides a livelihood and a link to the past and to a sense of community.[542] Francis says, 'The land and our heritage [were] important to [Protestants] to the point of obsession.'

Issues regarding ordinary Irish people's access to the land had already started to change before independence. In 1870, the Landlord and Tenant (Ireland) Act was passed and land started to be transferred to small farmers, most (but not all) of whom were Catholics,[543] and out of the hands of the landlord class, which was mostly (but not exclusively) Protestant.[544] As Irish nationalism continued to grow in strength, the land and issues of ownership became a powerful symbol of Irishness. The land had to be returned to the 'real' Irish people, and because most of the landlords had been Protestants associated with a foreign colonial power, 'real' Irish people could never be Protestants. Land in Protestant ownership tended to be considered stolen property. Elements of the human-made landscape associated with the once-so-dominant, mostly Protestant ruling classes 'came to symbolise English exploitation of Ireland and were excluded from the iconography of the newly ascendant narratives of nationalism that were created in the late nineteenth century'.[545]

At the time of the War of Independence, the land, as a symbol of what 'real' Irish people should have, and as a pragmatic good that retained value and offered a livelihood, was at least a contributing factor to many of the apparently sectarian incidents that targeted Protestant farmers,[546] famously in Cork, but also, to a lesser extent, all over the country. Because Protestants tended to have larger farms, up to and including large estates, they were often the source of resentment, which sometimes erupted into violence and livestock theft.

By 1920, many Protestant farmers from the west and south had started to sell and move north to buy farms in Co. Fermanagh, driving up the cost of land in the area.[547] Early in the War of Independence, when the IRA was burning evacuated barracks, the rumour spread that Big Houses whose owners were living in England would be pressed into service as barracks, and so the house-burning began[548] – although most of the Big Houses were actually burned slightly later on, during the civil war. Clark describes the house-burning as the reclaiming of a landscape, 'fire ripped off the roof, blackened the walls and literally opened the house to the outside, reclaiming the landscape from the landlord.' It 'reclaimed the landscape from the Protestant planter and opened these symbols of British social and economic power […] to the Irish sky.'[549]

The land could also be 'reclaimed' after the house was burned. For instance, two years after Tubberdaly House was burned in 1923, the Irish Land Commission made a compulsory purchase of 1,225 acres of land, which was redistributed to local families, including some who had been involved in the burning.[550] In a country obsessed with land, the political climate seems to have made it easier for anyone eager to acquire land to target people, officially because they were Protestant or loyalist and therefore disloyal to Ireland's true army, the IRA, but also (or sometimes only) because of a desire to access land. Two Protestant farmers were murdered in 1922, in Ballinamore, Co. Leitrim. One of them was killed because he was thought to have passed information to the police; the other, because he would not pay the IRA the levy it demanded. At the same time, while the IRA was involved in expelling some families – or 'encouraging them to leave' – some criminals pretended that they were from the IRA so that they could access land or other valuables.[551]

The shells of the burned houses served as monuments to the complex emotions their former inhabitants had once inspired. The sight of these Big Houses is still a mnemonic for storytelling about the past. People remember being taken for walks as children and being told how a house was burned down; by association, they were told other stories about how the Protestant community was treated during the turbulent early decades of the twentieth century. Depending on the backgrounds of the storyteller and the listener, different aspects of these stories could be emphasised to make diverse points. Eleanora vividly remembers how the sight of a Big House occasionally prompted recollections from Catholic friends and neighbours. Although her family did not generally discuss the past with Catholics, as during her childhood it was still too soon to explore events that might have involved some of the older local people, 'Very occasionally a Roman Catholic would acknowledge that something had happened that shouldn't.'

Rachel remarks that when she drives around, she can easily see which areas were once large estates, because there is invariably a very 'treed landscape' with many mature trees. She says that the native Irish were less inclined to plant trees, whereas the Protestant landowners, especially the very wealthy ones, liked to have a lot of trees, particularly deciduous oak and ash, on their property.[552] Despite the fact that the big landlords are almost all long gone, their impact on the landscape is apparent to Rachel every day because of the trees. And although her own family was never rich, the sight of a destroyed Big House, or of the trees around a space that once contained a Big House, recalls their tribulations during those difficult years.

To what extent violence against rural Protestants in those days was motivated by a desire to access their land remains a controversial issue. The belief that many incidents were engineered specifically to put 'Protestant land' into Catholic hands is widespread among rural Protestants. Stories about the land and the violence it sometimes inspired are often told in rural communities.

Rachel, who lives in an area where many Protestants experienced violence (including homicide) in the early 1920s, says that there is still huge local resistance to acknowledging terrible events of the past. She refers to her belief that one of the primary reasons for this resistance is the fact that some of the local farmers still work land that came into their family's possession around this time, and that might have been purchased in shady circumstances for a less than fair price. She says that it would be upsetting for these farmers to discuss these events. 'People would deny it', she says, 'despite any evidence to the contrary, simply because they wouldn't want it to be true.'

Is there a parallel between Rachel's statement and the many stories of origin, previously related, in which Protestants give all sorts of accounts about how 'they' came to be in Ireland and yet evade the possibility that there might be 'planters' in their family's distant past? We all deny things that we would prefer not to be true, often to ourselves as much as anyone else. Rachel, who works in education, goes on to recount her efforts to teach history impartially in the school where she works; she cites, unselfconsciously, her preference for teaching 'social history' over political history, avoiding the topic of the plantations and how Protestants were granted land, as this has led to tension between children in the past.

In the early years of independence, Ireland was still heavily dependent on agriculture and the iconography of the simple, peasant lifestyle – epitomised in paintings of humble thatched cottages in beautiful western landscapes – which came to symbolise, along with Catholicism, all that was authentically Irish. Because it was felt that 'true' Irishness was found in the lives, values, and beliefs of rural Catholic people, representations of the landscape that evoked these people and how they used the land became associated with a cultural ideal. With the growth of tourism, this image of the landscape, with depictions of picturesque country folk living simple, virtuous lives, was presented as the best Ireland had to offer. Together with the Catholic Church, successive governments sought to present an 'ideology of the rural' that evoked an imagined traditional model of Catholic family life in rural Gaelic-speaking communities.[553] In 1943, de Valera gave a St Patrick's Day speech that depicted the rural landscape, and its rural inhabitants, in accordance with this ideal:

> the home of a people who valued material wealth only as the basis of right living [...] who were satisfied with frugal comfort and devoted their leisure to the things of the spirit – a land whose countryside would be bright with cosy homesteads, whose fields and villages would be joyous with the sounds of industry, with the romping of sturdy children, the contests of athletic youths and the laughter of comely maidens.[554]

The Land Commission, Protestant Land, and Keeping the Land Protestant

The Irish Land Commission was initially established under the Land Act in 1881; the commission was to administer the transfer of land from landlords to tenants and to establish fair rents.[555] The Land Commission continued this process after independence and was hugely important to agricultural and rural policy.[556] Large landowners were sometimes obliged to sell their land, and small farmers were given incentives to buy the acres they needed. The Land Commission stopped acquiring land in 1983 and definitively ceased operations in 1999.

Between 1917 and 1923, land reform was muddied by an outbreak of agrarian violence that impacted on both Catholic and Protestant landowners. While one can understand revolt against a system that had been deeply unfair for generations, sometimes awful things happened. A landowner in Galway, Frank Shaw Taylor, told a group of men who wanted him to sell his estate that he never would, and he was murdered shortly afterwards. In 1922, in Luggacurren, Co. Laois, two Protestant tenant farmers were forced from their homes by armed gangs and, a few weeks later, sixteen more Protestant families were forcefully evicted. Similar events occurred in nearby Stradbally. These episodes were condemned by the local Catholic clergy,[557] but the hunger for land and the conviction that it was morally justifiable to expel Protestants prevailed.

By 1923, about 80 per cent of all rural tenants had become landowners; it was a massive transfer of land.[558] Post-independence, this was often presented as 'reversing Cromwell's policy'; Protestant farmers read this as a direct criticism of themselves,[559] given that many of them had Cromwellian ancestors and still owned a disproportionate percentage of the land. In 1926, almost 60 per cent of all employed men, and 45 per cent of Protestants, were involved in farming.[560] Although Protestants then composed just 8.4 per cent of the population, they owned 28 per cent of the farms exceeding 200 acres.[561] Between 1923 and 31 March 1932, the commission acquired and redistributed 330,825 acres, mostly in allotments of just under 20 acres, which was considered a standard holding at the time.[562] In 1989, Senator David Norris, from an Anglo-Irish background, recollected that people like his family 'did not always regard the Land Commission and its operations with unmixed admiration' but rather regarded it as 'like some rapacious wolf lying in wait until the proprietor became so feeble that they could be gobbled up'.[563]

Rachel says that while the Land Commission was not established to take land from Protestants per se, and while it also redistributed land that had been owned by Catholics, taking Protestant land was experienced as 'a joy' whereas redistributing Catholic land was 'just a day's work'. In theory, she says, the commission enabled many people to own their own land for the first time by taking unworked land from undeserving owners. In practice, in Rachel's locality, where some Protestant farmers had been murdered, many people who were 'working it perfectly well' had their land taken and were too frightened to make a strong protest. Local Protestant lore maintains that many relinquished their land because they were threatened or still frightened by recent events. Rachel describes the atmosphere after the killings as 'the silence', and as one in which bullies could flourish.

Rachel also relates the story of Sam Maguire, a Protestant who became involved in Gaelic games while he was living in London and working for the British civil service. A biography on Maguire gives a description of his family, 'Maguires may have been Protestant stock [...] but Maguires were very much part of the community they lived and worked in.'[564] The 'but' in the preceding quote is telling. When he left London, Maguire returned to his home area in Cork, where he died, in poverty, of tuberculosis. While he was ill, Rachel says, he was unable to work his land properly and the Land Commission took it in exchange for land bonds. Rachel believes that they would have been slower to take the farm from the GAA hero if he had not been Protestant.

In 1933, under the Fianna Fáil government, the Land Commission was given a 'freer hand' in buying untenanted land in order to relieve congestion and divide the land among suitable candidates. The change in the ruling on owners' consent, providing great scope for the compulsory purchase of land for redistribution to small landowners and former tenants, reflected various aspects of Fianna Fáil's policies for rural Ireland, including the aim that as many families as possible be 'rooted' in the soil. The party also promoted self-sufficiency, which meant producing more tillage and fewer cattle for export. Land was also awarded to IRA veterans.[565] From 1935, the Land Commission started offering ready-to-go farms in the much-more-fertile east to people with economically unviable farms in Irish-speaking areas.

Barney maintains that local Protestants who were planning to sell their farms and move away were forbidden from doing so; according to him, they were forced to sell to the Land Commission at a reduced rate so that the land could be redistributed to Catholics. Thanks to their positive relationship with their Catholic neighbours, his family was saved from this fate:

> And we had a farm up there [...] the Land Commission was on the brink, and it was only just by sheer chance, thankfully there was good Catholic farmers. You see, if they said that 'this man, even if he has young weans coming on, if he's not working this land, we can take it off him and give it to a Catholic man who's working it [...]' So, my father at that time [...] he hadn't a great way for labouring it and

that […] the good Catholic neighbours, they would take corn produce off that land and that covered him. Because they didn't say it
was them, it was him, you know. Only for that, the Land Commission
would have taken the land off us.

Stewart reports that when the local estate was divided among former estate
workers, his father 'did not qualify for a share' because he was Protestant.
Eadry says that her mother often talked about relatives who 'had a farm
taken from them' without their permission. Eadry's maternal grandfather
worked as a land agent for one of the big estates. When his uncle died, he
inherited a small farm, but the Land Commission took it. The family felt
that he had been treated extremely badly; he was poorly compensated, and
they were sure that, as a Protestant, he had been targeted. Whenever anyone
raised the topic of the land that had been taken, they were 'hushed, you
didn't talk about that'. Someone would say 'stop it!' Memories of their land
and how it was taken were often repressed, as people often found these topics painfully difficult to discuss. However, Eadry says that her grandfather's
belief that he had been victimised by the Land Commission because of
'what he was' was a motivating force for him. He was determined to own
land again and eventually managed to buy some, developing it into a successful market garden. Afterwards, stories were told about how the episode
with the Land Commission 'Gave them the determination to prove that
you could take it, but you weren't taking it from *us*.'

Samuel says that their area was dominated, in his parents' day, by large
estates often owned by absentee landlords, and that there 'weren't very many
what they would call strong farmers' (the group to which his own family
belonged). The Protestant community in his family's locality was always
very small. Although Protestant landowners tried to sell to other Protestants,
there weren't many Protestants to sell to, and most of them could not afford
to buy substantial amounts of land. Instead, the Land Commission 'hopped
in' and divided it up. While this benefitted many rural families that were
previously poor, it had the possibly unintended effect of leaving the small
local Protestant community with some difficulties. In a very small community, without the financial help of the landowners, many parishes became
unsustainable, and churches and parish halls closed. Samuel says that the impact on the Presbyterian community was particularly bad, because many

local Presbyterians were landless and worked in service positions on the big estates. Some remained in the area for several years after the Land Commission had done its work, but one by one, most of the small churches were boarded up. Church of Ireland churches closed too, because they were not viable without subsidies from the wealthy families.

Samuel says that people believed that the Land Commission was also very interested in acquiring ordinary Protestant farmers' land and that he grew up hearing stories about this. Problems would start if someone already had a farm and bought a little more land, 'The Roman Catholic neighbours would want it and there would be agitation.' Some of his relatives bought a little extra land to add on to their farm, which was large by local standards. The neighbours successfully endeavoured to have the Land Commission take it back so that it could be subdivided among them instead.

Doris remembers how local Protestant farmers disliked the Land Commission. She believes that there were no sectarian motives behind the way the land was selected for subdivision, but quite a few of the larger farmers in her area were Protestants, and, she says, 'You wouldn't be too popular if you had a fair bit of land.' Some of the larger farmers were inconsiderate with their neighbours, and issues and upsets regarding the Land Commission, whose land was taken, and how it happened, often related to hard feelings associated with past events. When Protestant farmers were involved, people would dislike them even more than they disliked a large Catholic farmer on bad terms with his neighbours. Whereas an unpopular Catholic farmer was assumed to speak only for himself, an unpopular Protestant farmer seemed to confirm negative stereotypes about Protestants in general. In Doris's childhood, when land was taken by the Land Commission, there was an understanding that this must *never* be talked about, but she overheard conversations about the Land Commission and redistribution of land, and realising how important they were, remembered them. In her parents' generation, memories of house burnings were still very fresh, and there was a great fear that if anyone 'made a fuss' about a perceived injustice relating to the land, the problems would return, 'They just wanted it to go and they just wanted us all to live peacefully and not to feel nervous about anything.'

Albert says that when local Protestant farmers wanted to sell their land, often their neighbours got together and made arrangements so that nobody would bid on it at auction. Thus, they could organise for the Land Commission to take the land and subdivide it so that plots could be acquired cheaply. He says that while some people felt that the Land Commission sometimes appeared to be targeting Protestant-owned land, the reality was that, on average, Protestant farmers tended to have bigger farms. He says, 'I wouldn't blame some of them agitating for a share of it […] I wouldn't hold that against them.'

Travers recalls his parents' upset about the compulsory purchase of land owned by a large local estate. His parents were small farmers, and many of their peers lost their jobs on the estate when the land was taken – the local Big House had already been burned down.[566] In this case, the land was not made available to local farmers but was purchased by a religious order that would not hire the Protestants who had lost their jobs. All the families that worked on the estate emigrated; their names remain in the area only in the local graveyard.

Thomas remembers one after another of the Protestant-owned farms in his area being acquired by the Land Commission after elderly bachelor farmers with no local heirs died. While he does not know if the Land Commission was more interested in 'Protestant land' than that owned by Catholics, he says that it 'looked that way' and that 'very few Protestant families now going back […] ever got any of the land that was divided'.

In actual fact, Catholic landowners with estates or large farms were just as likely to have land taken by the Land Commission,[567] and Protestant labourers or small farmers also got land from the commission. Although Protestant farmers may have felt disproportionately targeted by the Land Commission, and although there certainly were poor Protestant farmers with very little land, statistically they continued to own a disproportionately high amount of land – and poorer Protestants were not excluded from obtaining land from the commission. For example, Barbara, who traces her descent from a man brought from Scotland to work as a farm steward in about 1700, reports that her family finally became landowners when the Land Commission divided up the estate and they had the opportunity to buy some of it.

Hugh says that 'all Irish will kill for land' and cites the case of a local estate owned by absentee landlords who instructed their agent to sell it off in small plots and to try to sell it all to Protestants. The agent did as he was told, to the outrage of most locals. All the Protestant farmers who bought the land were boycotted, even by the local creamery, and they rapidly started to experience financial hardship. After this, the agent put the land on the open market, and some Catholic farmers bought parcels of land to add to their own properties. But by then there was a groundswell of indignation; the consensus was that the Land Commission should have come in from the start. Tempers got very high, and one of the Catholic farmers who had bought land was shot in the eye and blinded by an angry local.

Leary quotes a study carried out in the 1980s that cites great pleasure among rural Catholics when, through marriage or purchase, a farm passed into Catholic hands; the study also cites a Catholic curate saying that parishioners had commented on their pleasure at 'getting the land back'.[568]

Hugh recounts the private sale of another estate by the last member of a landowning family to a Catholic buyer. The topic of the sale arose at a public meeting, 'and out of the blue a man said, and I don't think he knew I was a Protestant [...] and he said, "Catholic at last!" He was delighted, because it had been Protestant for 300 years.' Hugh was upset but unsurprised. 'But it's how they feel', he says grimly. 'That's the way of it.' He maintains that many, if not most, Catholics in the area are still happy when Protestant land passes into Catholic hands, even if they are not always willing to say so aloud.

Ruane and Butler gathered similar material from an informant in Cork; the informant stated that 'the discussion going on inside in the pub was kind of, "Sure it's all ours again, we've only one more and it will be all ours."'[569] There are also various reports of locals, including priests, intervening in matters of land sale and purchase. Barton reports that the local priest 'went 'round the parish when a farm came up for sale. He said no Protestant was to be allowed to buy the land.'

Considering that selling one's land has often been considered an admission of defeat among rural people,[570] selling land to someone of 'the other sort' in a segregated society was often considered even more shameful. Violet recalls a family acquaintance, an elderly woman from a 'gentry' family, who was the last of her line and reduced to penury because of her refusal to sell any of her property to an 'RC', 'She was determined that she had to maintain the house and land. She didn't appear to spend anything on herself – didn't have a proper bathroom, was driven around in an ancient van [...] she refused to sell land to RCs!'

Mariah says that even in her childhood in the 1970s, Catholics sold land to Catholics whenever possible, and Protestants did likewise. Her area was, and remains, strongly republican. One result of this was that Protestant farmers often found it difficult to acquire more land. Pragmatically, one of her uncles took to sending his brother-in-law to auctions on his behalf, having learned that if he himself placed the winning bid in the auction, the land would hastily be withdrawn from sale to prevent it from going to a Protestant. As the brother-in-law lived far away, everyone assumed that he was Catholic and there was no barrier to him purchasing land.

Because Protestants often lived in proximity to one another, there was a sense, in some areas, that by selling land to Catholics, the whole community was being let down. Bob remembers how, in his father's day, the family lived in a Protestant enclave, 'we lived three or four miles from [the local town], and when [Dad] was a child he could go to [town] and not pass a Catholic farm!' In a context such as this, people who felt strongly about maintaining a distinct identity could place considerable social pressure on someone thinking of selling land.

Valerie reports that this kind of pressure is still apparent, to some degree, in her border area, 'Now, it can't be in any written form or anything, but sometimes I've heard where people might approach someone that is a Protestant to see if they would be interested in buying it first, before they put it on the open market.' She feels that this custom persists because of a lingering feeling that Protestants were 'downtrodden' in various ways, 'maybe through history they felt they were forced to do things […] things had happened to make the Protestant community smaller and things like that. They just liked to […] keep the Protestants together […] we don't want to be downtrodden, you know.'

Billy reports that this type of opportunism still happens in his area. He believes that some people are still interested in removing land from Protestant ownership because of old loyalties and resentments, and he explains that Protestants sometimes take measures to prevent this from happening. He has even heard of cases where the local Protestant church would 'step in and buy land' if land adjacent to the church became available. This was partly to ensure Protestant ownership of land adjoining Protestant sacred spaces and community buildings; it acted as a sort of physical bulwark against the Catholic space that Catholic-owned land, and most public spaces, represented. Joyce says that when she was young, both Protestants and Catholics vastly preferred to sell their land 'to one of their own', and that while this tradition has relaxed, 'there's a little bit there still'.

Richard remembers growing up with a strong sense of the land and 'the place' being very important, not just to him and his family but also to rural Protestants in general. His family had to sell their land out of economic necessity, but he married a woman with her own farm and is 'very glad that we have [it] and that we have land'. He feels that Protestants' relationship with land is distinctive – that it is quantitatively different to Catholics' and that, because Protestants in the past were more likely to own land and more likely to own large amounts of land, they have a particularly profound emotional relationship with the concept of land ownership. While his family did not feel strongly about selling their land to Protestants, he does know people 'who would want one of their own to have the land and one of their own would be either their own family' or 'if it wasn't someone in their family they would want another Protestant'. The reason for this was, 'they had maintained it, kept it, got it to the state it's in and don't want it to be messed about by someone else.' One acquaintance 'knew he was different to all his neighbours and he said, "I don't want any of *them* to get my land" and he was a bachelor. He had a cousin or something that was going to get it, but he was going to make sure that the land did not go to one of "them."' This sort of attitude, Richard says, 'is very much declining'.

Various official bodies worked to keep Protestants on the land. The Irish Land Finance Company was registered in 1910 to provide poor rural Protestants with financing for 'the acquisition, holding, improvement, working, and management of farms and lands in Ireland and generally to promote the material interests and welfare of members of the Church of Ireland'.[571] It was given an initial grant of ten thousand pounds by the Church of Ireland Representative Body and would work for more than seven decades to help poorer rural Protestant families to remain on the land. During its years of operation, it frequently encountered 'friction' with the Catholic Church.

Gurteen Agricultural College was founded in the late 1940s to provide agricultural education to young Protestant farmers – it had a Methodist 'ethos' but was open to Protestants of all denominations. It also worked to reduce the exodus of young rural Protestants. Enid's father was involved in establishing the college and she remembers that, from its earliest days,

Catholic farming families expressed an interest in sending their children there. However, 'There were senior officials in the Department of Agriculture, who were being very helpful and supportive about it, all said, "No, I don't think Ireland is ready for that."'[572] Apart from the religious aspect, Gurteen differed from other agricultural colleges in accepting female students, offering young women not just the chance to prepare for a life in the countryside but also the opportunity to meet a future spouse[573] – keeping both the family and the land 'Protestant'.

Struggle and Leaving the Land

One can understand resentment towards the very wealthy landowners, some of whose ancestors are recalled in local memory as the 'bad landlords' who sent people away to die on coffin ships. When Land Reform and other factors contributed to the break-up of estates, there were many consequences for lower-income Protestants. Many rural Protestants had worked for the big estates as servants, labourers, and gamekeepers. When their wealthy employers left, many became economic migrants to England and elsewhere.[574] Liz remembers that this was partly because of their reluctance to do rural jobs that were considered to have low social standing, 'Protestants emigrated sooner than become servants [...] No "decent" Protestants were scratchers in the local flax or corn mills; they left for England or America to find employment.' While vast numbers of Catholics also had to emigrate for economic reasons, this flight of working-class and lower-middle-class Protestants is sometimes remembered as a consequence of the wider community pushing them off the land.

Heather remembers the strong sense of place she experienced as a little girl. Her family owned two 'bits of land' about a mile apart, and they often had to walk cattle, or carry fodder for the animals, from one piece of land to another. 'All there was, was drudgery,' she says, 'and women often had the drudgery to do and walk the children with them because there was nobody else to look after them.' She describes accompanying her mother and dressing in a coat with a bit of baler twine around the middle, 'You'd be pulling the wellies and the muck would be coming up to the top of the wellies because the cattle would be treading on the ground and it's heavy clay soil.'

Heather and her mother often passed derelict houses and parcels of land that were once farmed by Protestants. These sights prompted storytelling

about the people who had once lived in this area and left, 'it was a continuous story of, "Oh, they sold up; they left; they went to England; they went
to Northern Ireland."' As it was a border area, there was a feeling among
the local Protestants (most of whom were small farmers with modest incomes) of being 'under siege' and of holding on to their land and their
meagre livelihoods through willpower and solidarity. While many local
Protestant families had been living there for centuries, most of them had
only become landowners after a large estate had been bought by the Land
Commission; Heather's own family was still making payments to the commission when she was a child. Many families had left in the early years of
independence and emigration continued throughout the twentieth century;
the abandoned cottages crumbling into the local landscape served as memorials to a diminishing community.

For many rural Protestants, closed, derelict, and repurposed churches are
a significant feature of the landscape. Doris lives near a village 'with one
pub and a Church of Ireland ruin' and describes how her son is involved in
work to stop the ruin from collapsing completely. Throughout her youth,
one Protestant church after another closed and people had to travel greater
and greater distances to attend church. Many of these buildings are now
derelict, or have become private homes or restaurants, and they still punc-
tuate both the physical and social landscape, prompting storytelling of days
long past. The church where she married is now only opened once a year,
although the local community maintains the building and grounds.

Travers recounts how the ruin of a little church near his farm was 'blown
up with gelignite' in the 1960s as it had become too dangerous to leave
standing. He remembers the destruction of the church as an upsetting incident, but he is pleased that the cemetery has been renovated in recent
years and that now one can see the gravestones that commemorate the
many Protestant families who used to live in the area. 'Mind you,' he says,
'there was a lot more of us at that stage'; many of the family names visible
in the graveyard are no longer represented locally.

Olive says that the sight of the church's 'beautiful buildings' in the surrounding landscape, and their state of dereliction often reminds her that 'We're
going to be wiped out'. She talks about the little church, now derelict, that
she and her family attended. The adjacent graveyard, which used to be all-
Protestant, was sold separately. The small plot was made into a community

graveyard and has been hugely expanded; the Protestant dead are now confined to one small corner. Attending a funeral in recent years, she found herself walking up the avenue that she used to cycle down every Sunday with her parents. She peered through a gap in the boarded-up window to look at the derelict church that was once at the heart of her community.

Cherishing the Land

For many years, the state's efforts to conserve the landscape, including its constructed elements, tended to overlook the heritage of Protestant communities, particularly the Big Houses that remained and were still inhabited by land-owning families. Many Protestants from this wealthy group have become involved in lobbying activities in areas such as agriculture, fishing, forestry, the environment, and the protection of built heritage, including stately homes and other buildings associated with 'gentry' families.

Karen Lysaght reports on the anger expressed by 'gentry' Protestants from West Cork during interviews she had conducted; they said that their heritage was 'devalued, seen as something that can be erased'.[575] While it may be tempting to see these comments as a reflection of self-interest, many Protestants, especially rural Protestants – not necessarily 'gentry' or wealthy – seem to share a sense that they are custodians of the land they own, the landscape, and its built heritage.

Declan Kiberd, commenting on writers of the Gaelic revival period, states that the writers from Roman Catholic backgrounds tended to obsess about history while Protestant writers knew that history 'could only be [...] a painful accusation against their own people' and therefore 'turned to geography in the attempt at patriotization'.[576] For Protestants, a sense of cherishing the land, of loving and caring for it, can sometimes be considered as a way of expressing their Irishness.

Mitchell comments that the Protestant relationship with both the built and the natural landscape was not quite the same as that of the Catholics, 'anybody [Protestant] who was interested in the field [...] whether it was antiquities or natural history [...] they sort of felt that they had an *ownership* of the heritage that was a different kind of ownership than the Catholics.' As a child, Oliver was always made very aware of sites of archaeological interest. His parents would explain what the site was, and what it meant. He contrasts this to the relationship he assumes that Catholics have with the heritage provided by the landscape, saying that they might have been more familiar with legends and fairy stories. When he was young, he was often told that he was not a 'real' Irish person. However, he says that he was raised in a way that made him feel 'intensely Irish', particularly as he was encouraged to share his grandfather's interest 'in everything Irish: the landscape, natural history and archaeology, the history', 'I grew up knowing the island, knowing the landscapes, knowing the natural history, being [...] taken up mountains and shown the megalithic tombs [...] all around the country [...] and being imbued with a strong personal sense of Irishness which was contradicted by [...] other people saying, "But you're not!"'

For Oliver, spending 'every spare minute' exploring the landscape was an important aspect of identity-building and a way to express a sense of Irishness that seemed congruent with his Protestant heritage. He believes that the difference between the Protestant and the Catholic relationship with the land is that Catholics interpret the land in a way that is rooted in narratives about historical and legendary happenings, and in recorded human experience, whereas Protestants (or at least, he clarifies, middle-class Protestants like him) have a 'romantic' and also a 'utilitarian' view of landscape. The 'utilitarian view' relates to the historic reality of Protestant planters who saw the landscape as a means to make money, and for whom legendary narratives had no resonance. He believes that Protestants both search for a 'sublime landscape' and explore it from a sense of 'academic or scientific curiosity'. He sees this as an important cultural difference between Protestants and Catholics, and he stresses how important it still is for him to 'find the sublime in nature'.

Myrtle makes a similar, if more succinct, comment on Protestants' interest in the archaeological landscape and how it contrasts with their avoidance of more recent history, 'Protestants [...] were keenly interested in Ireland's past and what they read about ringforts, old castles, etc. in the area. They avoided information on the struggle for independence.'

Friendship and the Land
While many of the stories related by the interviewees and respondents are about anxieties of one kind and another, there are also many stories about very positive neighbourly relationships. Especially among small farmers, cooperation was essential. Everyone helped everyone, and religion and cultural

heritage were irrelevant during crucial points of the agricultural year, or during some sort of an emergency.

Violet says, 'I remember one [of my farming cousins] saying that when a cow falls into a ditch you don't ask if it's Protestant or Catholic!' Aphra remembers that her family 'never overlooked our Church of Rome neighbours. We mingled together, helped one another at harvest, pig killing or animal in the drain, come what may.' Eunan grew up with an extremely close relationship with the neighbouring Catholic family, 'we shared everything including a common farmyard, shared pair of horses, creamery run and a deep and enduring friendship.' Honor remembers a wonderful sense of community. Eleanora remembers that Protestant and Catholic farmers helped one another as a matter of course, 'They would have shared horses at times, for ploughing or so on, and it moved along the community at harvesting and so forth.'

Sam's family could only afford one horse, and the Catholic family with the adjacent farm was in the same situation. Consequently, 'when it came to ploughing, tilling or reaping, when two horses were required, they co-operated and used both horses together'. Barbara's farm lay along a lane that gave onto three Catholic and two Protestant farms, and all the farmers co-operated with one another, 'I remember [...] putting in potatoes and binding the harvesting and the threshing and the five families came together with whatever help they had on the farm, and they all went around to each other, and that was a big day when you had, it was called a *meitheal*.' Mabel remembers that her family had 'no qualms' with their neighbours, working with them during all the busy times of the year:

> It was the horse and plough kind of thing [...] when it came to the threshing my mother would be feeding ten men along with ourselves and they were all Roman Catholic neighbours [...] And the men travelled round about; they might start at your house and worked round and round. We were together; that's how things were done. If you were going to the bog and needed hands, you got them. If you needed somebody, you got your neighbours.

Honora's grandparents had beloved Catholic friends on a nearby farm. 'When they had a threshing,' she says, 'my granny would do baking [...]

When they had Stations [Mass in somebody's house, to which all the neighbours and friends were invited] she would do likewise and lend her best
china and the silver teapot.' Gavin's family, from a border area, did not let
cultural or religious differences get in the way of friendship and collabora-
tion, 'My grandfather was a very senior Orangeman, but he had no hatred
of Roman Catholics. His best friend […] was an RC and they helped each
other regularly, particularly when "winning" the hay and harvesting the
spuds.' In Travers's area, each farmer traditionally provided a keg of beer to
all the neighbours who came to help with the threshing. A local Quaker
family was abstinent and provided apples instead (to general disgust).

Despite numerous stories about close friendships and co-operation in
rural areas, a few people also have memories of people being treated slightly
differently at busy times in the farming year. Cyril remembers Catholic and
Protestant farmers threshing together but being treated differently when
they stopped for a meal, 'Protestants were fed in the dining room with
lemonade […] and Roman Catholics ate in the kitchen with Guinness.'

Bob remembers a story his father told about a situation he observed during his own youth when a threshing was held at a Protestant house and the
men were segregated for meals, 'Protestants ate in one room, Catholics in another.' One man was a local Protestant farmer's son who had converted to
Catholicism upon marrying a Catholic 'kitchen girl'. Without thinking, he
went to eat with the Protestants, and he was stopped by the housewife, who
succinctly told him, 'If you sleep with them, you eat with them.' Normally,
he notes, 'more respect was shown, with Protestant housewives careful to cater
for Catholic farmers and workmen on meatless Fridays, for example'.

Sam remembers threshing in a mixed community on Fridays, when
Catholics did not eat meat, 'in a Protestant household we would have been
given something like beef stew, bacon, or mince, whilst Catholic neighbours
helping would have been given herring on a Friday or on fast days. In
Catholic households, both Protestant and Catholic workers would have
been given herring.'

Harvest Thanksgiving
Harvest Thanksgiving is a special event in the ecclesiastic calendar of the
Church of Ireland and the Methodist and the Presbyterian churches; it takes
place in the autumn, when the harvest has been gathered in. It was adopted

into formal religious practice in the mid-nineteenth century and remains an important fixture and expression of faith.[577] It is a colourful event – the church is decorated with actual fruits of the local harvest, and the faithful sing popular hymns like 'We Plough the Fields and Scatter', adapted from the original German ('We plough the fields and scatter / The good seed on the land / But it is fed and watered / By God's almighty hand').

For rural Protestants, Harvest Thanksgiving elevates everyday activities to the spiritual realm. Hope remembers, 'Harvest Thanksgiving was very big because it was a farming thing [...] Townspeople, I don't think, had quite the same feeling.' For many rural Protestants, Harvest Thanksgiving brought (and still brings) together various strands of their lives: faith, attachment to the land, and respect for and pride in the fruits of their labour (literally and metaphorically). It is also an opportunity for sometimes very scattered communities to socialise and display their collective identity, and a time to recall deceased loved ones. Evelyn remembers attending Harvest Thanksgiving at a family church, 'and as I sat there, I remembered all the generations [...] who had been there before me and the feeling of their presence was so real you could almost see and touch them'. Harvest Thanksgiving is even more important in her community because it is *their* festival, and a contrast to the much more numerous festivals celebrated by Catholics and the various festivals that they share with other forms of Christianity, such as Christmas and Easter.

Honora describes the event in her area as a 'big occasions with much preparation beforehand when farmers and gardeners would bring their best specimens of fruit, vegetables, flowers and grain to decorate the church'. There was often a guest preacher, and afterwards the community would enjoy tea, 'with sandwiches, scones, and beautiful cakes'. Ted remembers, 'We all loved to see all the red apples decorating the church windows, sheaves of oats, barley, and wheat, turnips, carrots, parsnips; holly, ivy, laurel, moss. All the veg. was taken up to a home [...] to feed the old.' Henry remembers Harvest Thanksgiving as a big event, 'there used to be a party in the Methodist Hall [...] with games and a bran tub and dances like "The Farmer Wants a Wife" and "The Waves of Tory."' Evelyn recalls:

Willie [...] the sexton decorated the church. Willie never allowed anyone to help [...] Willie used hydrangeas for decoration; he piled them everywhere, in the windows and the front of the pulpit and reading desk was covered completely with them. As well as the flowers, there was plenty of farm produce brought in by the parishioners, cabbage, turnip, carrots, parsnips and potatoes, etc. Stooks of corn, red hot pokers and dahlias were on every surface. The Harvest Thanksgiving was a really special occasion; people who paid their annual visit to church chose to come to the Harvest Thanksgiving on Friday night. Apart from the wonderful atmosphere, it was the time to display your new coat, hat, and gloves […] when some lucky people bought a new outfit for winter, it was always bought in time for the Harvest Thanksgiving. It was shown off at the Friday night service and hopefully was the envy of all.

In many rural areas, churches held their Harvest Thanksgiving services on different days so that people could attend as many as possible – in all the diverse Protestant denominations represented across quite a wide locality. Ed reports that clergymen were expected to visit every Harvest Thanksgiving within miles of their parish, and that the season was nicknamed 'The Autumn Manoeuvres'. Norm says, 'Any [Protestant] church in reasonable distance at all, everybody flocked in and you would pack the church.' Harvest Thanksgiving was an important social occasion as well as a religious one, with food and tea served afterwards, in a church hall or in someone's home. In rural communities where the opportunity to socialise was sometimes limited, this was a season that everybody looked forward to. Davina remembers:

Harvest Thanksgiving services were in September and invitations would be issued all around. They would always say 'DV' [Deo Volante, meaning 'God Willing']. We decorated the church. Some people would walk the fields to the church and some carried storm lanterns to the evening service. Some walked three or four miles. I liked harvest in the moonlight and it was good if we could have the service at a full moon because it was easier for the people to get home […] The Protestants were very ecumenical, and we went to special occasions in other churches [of diverse Protestant denominations].

Thomas remembers Harvest Thanksgiving as an opportunity for the members of the various Protestant denominations to express solidarity in his border area while also enjoying its social aspects. He describes the Harvest Thanksgiving season as 'all around' and he says that the local Methodists would put on 'one hell of a Harvest Thanksgiving' (he is Church of Ireland). People piled into horses and carts ('they'd be full of horses at that time') and often travelled great distances to attend each other's services and the tea and sandwiches afterwards.

Martha says that Harvest Thanksgiving was a huge event, with visiting preachers coming from different parts of the country to celebrate three services: two on Sunday – one in the morning and another in the evening – and one on Monday evening. The church was lavishly decorated with farm produce, and there was a lot of singing. William remembers Harvest Thanksgiving as 'always and always a highlight of the year' when everyone tried to bring in the best potatoes and other vegetables. It was very exciting for children; there was a special meal at the school after the service, which was attended by the whole community and their visitors. The children were taught special hymns, and everyone wore their best clothes and most carefully polished shoes.

Mariah says that Harvest Thanksgiving in her area was 'huge [...] we did the rounds. We went to Harvests here, there and everywhere.' Her family travelled to attend the Harvest Thanksgivings of the entire extended family, and each service was followed by a festive meal. Joyce says that Harvest Thanksgiving remains important in her rural community, and that people went to services and related events not just in their own parish but also in nearby parishes. Areas with church halls, which were used for social events connected with the parish, provided tea and food there, and some people put on supper and a dance, as it was a good opportunity to socialise among the broader community. May says that Harvest Thanksgiving remains a huge event in her area. Her mother still invites up to forty people back to her house after the religious service. As well as visitors from other Protestant parishes, Catholic friends and neighbours are now invited to the meal, which features abundant home-baked cakes.

Heather describes Harvest Thanksgiving where she grew up as an important event in various ways; significantly, it provided the opportunity for members of the different Protestant denominations to express a sense of solidarity. Her own family, although poor, always had a rose garden. Because their garden was well-stocked, they could provide flowers to anyone who needed them for their Harvest Thanksgiving festivities, 'My mother would have the most fantastic dahlias and they are fantastic at Harvest Thanksgiving and she would also give them to whoever asked from all the denominations, whoever decorated the churches.' Heather herself maintains this tradition to this day, 'If someone says, "I heard you got flowers," we say, "Come and I will give you whatever you want."' Adam remembers Harvest Thanksgiving as very important; his family provided the church with hydrangeas, apples, and other produce. He attributes the decline in importance of Harvest Thanksgiving in his area to the diminishment of rural heritage in general. He has never been very religious, but he experienced Harvest Thanksgiving as an aspect of a rural culture in which the emphasis was on self-sufficiency and one's relationship with the land.

In many rural (and, to a lesser extent, urban) parishes, Harvest Thanksgiving is still a highlight of the year. Its peripatetic aspects have some functional parallels with the traditions associated with holy wells in Catholic tradition, in both spiritual and territorial respects, and the festival is still cherished, even for many who are not very regular church-goers and despite growing secularism. It is also an occasion for Protestants to publicly perform their difference, as the festival does not have a direct counterpart in Catholic tradition. It offers Protestants the chance to show this colourful aspect of their worship and tradition to their Catholic friends and neighbours, who are not always familiar with it, and share their pleasure in it. 'They like the singing, oh they do, that's well known,' Eleanora says, '[Catholics] wouldn't have the tradition but they liked seeing the church decorated.'

Stories of Cities and Towns

Cities and towns can be many places at the same time. When there are several competing stories about a city's past, the city itself, its buildings, streets, and parks 'can be read as the topography of a collective memory in which buildings are mnemonic symbols which can reveal hidden and forgotten pasts'.[578] This certainly applies to all towns and cities of significant age. In urban areas in which the past is contested territory, the symbolic elements of the urban landscape are deeply compelling as they can be referred to in competing narratives about Ireland's past and the meaning of specific events.

In 1923, W.B. Yeats was asked what he felt about Nelson's Pillar in Dublin, which many already considered to be a controversial monument (and which was blown up by the IRA in 1966). He pointed out that for many Protestants the pillar represented the pride they had for the man who had been able to halt Napoleon, and he argued that it represented people who were 'part of our [Irish] tradition', adding that 'We should accept the past of this nation, and not pick and choose.'[579] But we all pick and choose which elements of our tradition to keep, and this applies to urban and rural landscapes alike. Despite the excising of various elements of English (and, by association, Protestant) history in Dublin,[580] even now the centre of Dublin, and many other cities and towns, is the physical legacy of the long period of British (and therefore Protestant) rule. This is one reason – maybe the main reason – why towns have historically been invoked much less often in imagery that is supposed to represent Ireland; postcards and publicity material have typically shown rural landscapes.[581]

The Protestant City

Although there had been a degree of urbanisation before the colonial period, notably in association with monasteries and ecclesiastical sites,[582] urban development expanded dramatically after Norman colonisation, with homes and businesses clustered around a protective castle in a mutually beneficial relationship.[583] In the later plantation, after the Reformation, a focused, planned approach to urbanisation occurred. Often an area that already had an urban settlement, such as a monastic centre or castle, was further developed. The colonial focus of early-seventeenth-century settlements is revealed in the fact that the official population tallies of urban areas refer to adult British males and generally discount the native Irish; another clear indication of this focus is the tendency for urban settlements to be clustered around a landlord's estate.[584]

By the late eighteenth century, landlords dominated political constituencies and nominated candidates for governmental office while doing nothing to encourage local, especially Catholic, involvement in issues relating to municipal governance. Towns tended to be filled with Protestant-owned properties and were ruled over by a Protestant upper class; they also tended to be economically very dependent on Britain.[585] From the mid-eighteenth century, the densest concentration of Protestants was in Dublin, where they occupied every socio-economic niche, from 'recognizable notables, pseudo-gentry and simple citizens to the unenfranchised and property-less'.[586]

Over time, the inner-city area became predominantly Catholic (77.1 per cent in 1861 and over 83 per cent in 1911)[587] and was the subject of philanthropic concern, with government policy aimed at improving living conditions. In Cork as in Dublin, affluent Protestants dominated commercial and economic life throughout the nineteenth century, despite a growing Catholic middle class. In 1881, Protestants held about 40 per cent of the professional jobs while representing about 15 per cent of the overall population.[588]

Many urban parks were constructed in the late nineteenth century, at least partly because of concerns about the 'physical and moral health of the urban poor' but also as a way of observing and maybe controlling them, as well as attempting to encourage or even enforce Protestant cultural norms. In Dublin, St Stephen's Green was opened to the public in 1880 amid the fears of the wealthy people who lived around it that it would become the site of public protests. In many public parks, playing sport on Sundays, which was generally frowned upon by Protestants but not Catholics, was forbidden, and many parks had statuary features and other aspects that reminded their users that they were in the British Empire[589] and that Catholics might be the majority but they were not in charge.

In the late nineteenth century, the nationalist movement increasingly used the 'cultural landscape' to further their aims,[590] and Dublin Corporation determinedly named and renamed the city's streets, with the new names (such as O'Connell Street, previously named Sackville Street) reflecting its increasingly nationalist agenda[591] and the claiming of the urban landscape for Catholic nationalism. After independence, the Free State repainted letterboxes, renamed streets, and erected monuments to nationalist heroes to remove as many traces of the former regime as possible. In cities and towns, memories incongruent with the new state's identity were removed or altered in a way that shows how important erasing or suppressing memory can be to the process of nation-building.[592] While many monuments were removed officially, others were the target of freelance vandalism and explosions (notably Nelson's Pillar).[593]

By the 1950s, many Protestants in cities, particularly Dublin, managed to inhabit a sort of parallel universe. They attended separate schools, often socialised in exclusively Protestant circles, and created a community maintained largely 'by the informal networks of charitable, social and cultural organisations' while living under a political ideology that saw them as quite unimportant. In response, many 'reduced [their] horizons to the size of their own community'[594] and became increasingly insular.

Suburban Protestant Life
Middle-class and wealthy Protestants in cities, especially Dublin, have traditionally inhabited areas with relatively high densities of Protestants, and where there are Protestant primary and secondary schools. For example, in 1926, 33 per cent of the inhabitants of Rathmines and Rathgar were Protestants, as were 24 per cent of those living in Dún Laoghaire and 22 per cent of those in Blackrock.[595] For suburban Protestants who preferred to remain apart from the majority population, it was easy to socialise and work almost entirely within Protestant circles and, in some cases, largely ignore the dramatic changes that had taken – and were taking – place. Craig remembers how his school reflected English concerns and his community felt closely aligned to Britain:

> In history, it was only English history which was taught. In English lessons, only English poets, and in geography only English geography and some of the continents. The headmaster [...] was a southern Protestant but very much in the mould of an Englishman, very orthodox in all matters [...] The Union Jack was flown on Empire Day in full view of the busy [...] road and the bus route (until local protest ended the practice). 'Land of Hope and Glory' was sung annually, the boys packed onto a balcony overlooking a garden where all the parents were gathered. There was the annual Remembrance ceremony in front of the school's War Memorial [...] in homes which had one of the new television sets, at least some Protestants were able to watch the Queen's speech on Christmas Day.

Craig says that the school was founded by a wealthy businessman who was a 'Cromwellian', and that at one stage they would have had pictures of King Billy on his horse on the walls; despite this fact, by 1966 it was celebrating the fiftieth anniversary of the 1916 rising. By now, he says, they have 'the proclamation written up with Padraig Pearse and all on the walls'. Nobody, he says, wants to recognise the historical fact that this school, and by exten-

sion much of the Dublin community, came into existence because of
'Cromwellians'.

Constance grew up in an affluent Dublin suburb with a large Protestant
population that kept itself strictly segregated. All the Protestant children went
to one school and all the Catholic children to another, and as she only met
Protestants, she had no concept as a child of belonging to a minority. She can
remember a little boy 'capering around the school yard saying "I'm a Roman
Catholic! I'm a Roman Catholic!"' and none of the other children knew
what a Roman Catholic was. Her area was home to many retired army men
who had served with the Royal Air Force in Britain, and most people she
knew had relatives who had fought in the Second or First World War, or both.
Because they only ever met other Protestants, she was unaware that many
people looked askance on those whom they considered 'West Brits'. Many
years passed before she became aware of being a member of a minority.

After independence, Roberta's business family continued as before, in-
teracting socially and professionally within an almost exclusively Protestant
and middle-class community. Having heard stories about the problems facing rural Protestants, they bought a house in Bristol so that they would have
somewhere to go if things got really bad. However, 'my grandmother said
no one was going to make her leave. [Dublin] was her city, and this was her
country and she was going to stay. So, they stayed.' There were many little
ways in which they continued to express a quite strongly British identity,
such as reading an English newspaper every day.

Roberta was vaguely aware as a child that the city was also home to
poor Protestants. Her mother and grandmother were actively involved in
several Protestant evangelical charities that helped the poor. She cites the
Bird's Nest, a children's home in Dún Laoghaire, as an example. The Bird's
Nest 'took children off the street' and cared for them, but it was often crit-
icised by Catholics and regarded with great suspicion for its evangelism.[596]
Roberta's mother was involved with the Marrowbone Lane Fund, established to address the dreadful poverty in the inner-city Coombe area; she
also served on the board of the Adelaide Hospital and was involved with
the Mount Street Club, which was a sort of co-operative for unemployed
men, providing them with a workshop and vegetable plots, and suits if they
needed one to wear for an interview.

While the 'Protestant charities' were not solely intended to help only poor Protestants, they had a strong Protestant ethos that was not necessarily welcomed by needy Catholics. Violet also mentions the charitable endeavours of her well-to-do professional family, who had what she remembers as a 'paternalistic attitude towards their RC neighbours'. Despite Protestant charities that catered largely to the Protestant poor and working classes, the class-based segregation in Dublin was such that many middle-class and wealthy Protestants were almost unaware of the small but resilient community of inner-city Protestants.

The Urban Protestant Working Class and the Inner-city
In cities and towns, businesses run by affluent Protestants were often easy to identify because of the name over the door. Another telltale sign was that they often preferentially hired Protestants, at least at management level. Just as the Big Houses of the rural landscape were often taken to represent rural Protestants as a whole, the great visibility of Protestant-owned businesses in the city and affluent suburbs with large numbers of Protestants threatened to erase awareness of poorer Protestants.

By the late nineteenth century, 44 per cent of employed Protestant men belonged to the working class. They tended to belong to militant strains of Protestantism and to be characterised by a 'sense of solidarity and social cohesion', and a distrust of the wealthier Protestants, whom they saw as excessively placatory.[597] They were 'an assertive and exuberantly sectarian Protestant working-class'.[598] The Protestant working classes of Dublin, who inhabited the same areas and shared many of the same concerns as working-class Catholics, were very vulnerable to economic downturns. In response to hardship, many believed that 'Protestant solidarity would guarantee Protestant employment',[599] and their staunch Protestantism, as well as an expression of faith, represented an effort to stick together in difficult times. They typically identified strongly as both Irish and Protestant. They did not see themselves as British, and even their unionism was incidental to their Protestantism.[600] While wealthier Protestants mostly inhabited the suburbs, there were working-class populations of Protestants in areas including the Coombe, Ringsend, the Liberties, and parts of the north and south inner-city.

Many of the middle-class Protestants knew little about poor inner-city Protestants,[601] and if they did, they were often quite uninterested in them. Many Catholics were also ignorant of the fact that there was a Protestant working class. Consequently, poor Protestants were left in a contested urban landscape that was still filled with physical reminders of a Protestant-dominated past, of which they were increasingly considered outsiders. Charitable organisations complained of the wealthy and middle-class Protestants' ignorance regarding the poverty in the inner-city, including the poverty experienced by Protestants.[602] Wealthy Protestants and Catholics alike tended to believe that the poor were somehow 'morally, intellectually and racially inferior', and that they could only by improved through training.[603] Charitable associations provided income to poor Protestants who were unable to work if they were 'of a decidedly pious character'. The Association for the Relief of Distressed Protestants, for example, had a series of questions to determine whether a poor Protestant family deserved help. The questions included, 'Does the applicant regularly attend divine service?'; 'Are the children sent regularly to weekday and Sunday School?'; and 'Is the applicant in the habit of daily family prayer and reading the Holy Scripture?' Those judged poor but unworthy were left to the mercies of the Poor Law, which could result in being sent to the workhouse and families being split up.[604]

In the late nineteenth century, the Dublin Conservative Workingmen's Club was founded to elicit greater involvement from working-class Protestants in conservative and unionist politics. The club did get involved in 'the excitement of mobilising the Protestant community'[605] and was politically active. Its membership was limited to 'Protestant men of good character holding constitutional and Conservative opinion',[606] and it offered social activities (which were sometimes also attended by Catholics). As well as offering moral and practical support to working-class men and their families, the club acted as a social venue, with copious alcohol consumption, gambling, and billiards.[607]

The inner-city became an increasingly unwelcoming place for Protestants. Seán O'Casey, the writer and playwright, was born into a working-class Protestant family, in Dublin, in 1880. His family was typical of working-class Dublin Protestants at the time: very proud, very staunch, and given to Bible- and sermon-reading. Of the relationship between his family and their Catholic neighbours, O'Casey said, 'It was not too difficult for Protestants to be on decent neighbourly terms with Catholics [...] while retaining a wholesome dread of what these same Catholics might do if they were mobilised to action by their priests.'[608]

In early independence, the number of urban working-class Protestants declined dramatically and rapidly – much more quickly than the decline in the number of rural Protestants[609] – although a distinctive working-class Protestant community was still discernible in the 1930s,[610] and it has still not entirely disappeared. The lack of awareness of this community was partly due to the lack of interest on the part of wealthier Protestants.[611] Various organisations involved in helping poor Protestants at this time, including the Protestant Orphan Society and the Association for the Relief of Poor Protestants, had to deal with the entrenched idea that Protestants were, almost by definition, at least well-to-do,[612] despite the lived reality of many working-class Protestants.

Brian Inglis remembers of his affluent childhood in Malahide in the early decades of independence that there were poor Protestants 'down the hill', but that people like his family 'had no contact with them except in connection with charitable enterprises, when some of them would join in helping to do the heavy work of preparation, discreetly effacing themselves on the actual day of the church fête, or whatever it might be.'[613] Poor Protestants were not just ignored by wealthier Protestants; they could also be distrusted or even disliked by Catholics. The author Frank O'Connor remembered his mother's assumption that the maid who worked in a neighbouring house was Catholic, 'Mother talked to her about the convent and about Mother Blessed Margaret, her favourite [...] but Betty hinted darkly that there was nothing she did not know about nuns and chaplains and the dark goings on in convents, and Mother realised, to her great astonishment, that Betty was a Protestant [...] Nobody had ever explained to Mother that Protestants could also be poor.'[614] Lily O'Shea, a memoirist, writes of her experience growing up in poverty in tenement accommodation in the 1930s and 40s,[615] and Edith Newman Devlin, from a somewhat better-off family, writes of her Protestant childhood in Dublin's city centre, 'There were many poor Protestants in our school, some with no shoes, even in winter; lips were blue with cold and trousers as likely to be attached with a rusty nail as with a button [...] two pupils lived in a caravan on waste ground on the way to Kilmainham.'[616]

As a boy, Gerald only encountered poor Protestants occasionally through Boys' Brigade events and felt 'superior' to them because of their inner-city accents; it was hard for him to understand that they were Protestants at all.

He became aware of working-class Protestants as an adult, at work and through fund-raising activities organised by the Masons. Craig remembers his first encounter with a working-class Protestant in the 1960s, 'It had never occurred to me that such a thing existed. I presumed there were no Protestants beneath the lower middle-class. He and I got on very well and often worked together, but there was no question of socialising together. I remember him saying to me, "You Protestants in your yacht clubs have never heard of us." He was right.'

Walter's family was relocated to a housing scheme outside the inner-city, but he remembers living in a tenement flat as a small child, 'I remember the flats were terrible [...] They were tenements! [...] It was dark corridors all the way up. I remember the water leaking in through the ceiling. They were that poor, like.' He also remembers the contrast between the way his family lived and popular assumptions about Dublin Protestants, 'This is the gas thing [...] They always were taught here, that Protestants were well-off [...] there was no such thing as poor Protestants, yet you have the Society for Distressed Protestants and you had the Protestant Aid, all these things were set up to help Protestants who were in poverty, living in these conditions.' Christopher remembers an inner-city childhood characterised by positive neighbourly relationships, 'We had many Catholic friends and religious differences never reared their ugly head'. All the people in his area were quite poor, 'Opposite our house [...] a row of tenements in pretty poor condition. We lived on the first floor of the Dutch-Billy [a characteristic building style of Dublin's inner-city] while my maternal grandmother and my unmarried aunt lived on the top floor. Our portion of the house had only two bedrooms, so my sister and I shared one, with a curtain acting as a partition. We had no bathroom, only an outside toilet.'

Natasha grew up hearing her mother's stories of her own childhood in a working-class area in Dublin. Her mother was born in the 1930s to a staunchly Protestant working-class couple. They lived in a two-up, two-down terraced house. Tensions with their largely Catholic neighbours were frequent, and the family still struggled to accept independence. Her father, an Orangeman who regularly travelled to Northern Ireland for parades, strictly observed the rule that there should be no work or play on Sunday and often got into fierce arguments with one of his neighbours, an ardent GAA fan, who played matches on the radio at full volume on Sundays. Her father worked for the Guinness factory, an important employer of Protestants in the city. When the primary school Natasha's mother attended announced that an optician was going to inspect the children's eyes, her father refused to let her be seen unless he could be guaranteed a Protestant optician. Consequently, an eye condition that could have been resolved in childhood went undiagnosed until it was too late.

Harry remembers an inner-city community that went to great efforts to socialise separately but which was on good terms with its Catholic neighbours. Looking back now, he questions the wisdom of the Protestant community's efforts to remain separate, 'Because if you had any sort of sickness or any trouble, where did you go? You had to go to your Roman Catholic friend, because there wasn't many Protestants to go to.' He also comments that he thinks that some of the neighbours were involved in the 1916 rising, and that his mother would never have reported them to the police out of a sense of loyalty to the community (inferring that she would, nonetheless, have been opposed to the rising itself).

Robert remembers the sense that the Protestant community of Limerick had been shrinking since before he was born, and that it continued to do so during his childhood. The Protestant-owned shops in the city closed, 'Families came to an end. There was nobody else to inherit it or members of the family had gone to America or gone to England. The family just sort of came to an end and so did the business.' Because his mother was widowed, the family was provided with accommodation in widows' alms houses in a poor part of the city. Working-class Protestants were typically employed in the city as housekeepers, maids, and shop assistants in Protestant shops. A problem that the Protestant working class in Limerick had to grapple with was the 'general feeling among Catholics that the Protestants were well-off because some Protestants were well-off'. However, Robert acknowledges that the local Protestant Orphan Society provided him with clothes, a good education, and support that might have been unavailable to Catholic children in similar circumstances.

Donald, who grew up in a northside inner-city area of Dublin, remembers his family as being very anti-social in their almost all-Catholic neighbourhood. While most children in the street went in and out of each other's houses, his parents preferred to stay by themselves. They liked to socialise within the family, but most of the family had emigrated and there were few relatives left. The children grew up keenly aware of their minority status and felt, he says, a 'great distance' between themselves and their Catholic neighbours. His mother encouraged them to maintain this sense of distance, 'I remember bringing a boy into the house who was the same age as I was. I can't remember exactly what mother said, but it was perfectly clear that he wasn't wanted.' As children, Donald and his siblings were shouted at in the street relatively often and they accepted this low-level abuse as a simple fact of life.

Harold, who grew up in social housing in Dublin, was frequently beaten by his classmates; they wanted to see his butler, because they thought that every Protestant had one. They found it hard to reconcile the fact that he was Protestant with the fact that he was poor and lived in social housing. 'The worst thing about it', he says, 'is that they probably had more money than we did because we had nothing.' Today, Harold lives in housing that belongs to one of the inner-city parishes; they were homes to a substantial number of extremely poor Protestants in the nineteenth century.[617] He is keenly aware of some lingering anger towards affluent Protestants in the city and the frequent failure to understand that not all Protestants are priv-ileged; he is also conscious of lingering tension between working-class Protestants and their neighbours. His parents quite often got into rows with people in their area, 'purely over religion', and he also knows of a Catholic family who were quite good friends of his parents until they found out they were Protestants, at which point they stopped talking to them. He says that the idea of 'looking after our own' is a historical legacy among working-class Protestants, some of whom still meet incredulity whenever someone learns that some Protestants need subsidised housing.

When she was a child, Shirley says, it was easier for her parents to so-cialise almost exclusively within their working-class Protestant community than to try to mix with Catholic neighbours, whose attitudes towards them ranged from curiosity to hostility. Her father attended an all-Protestant men's club, where he watched football and felt more comfortable cheering for the Glasgow Rangers, his favourite team. In his local pub, however, he was teased about being a Rangers fan, because Irish people are not supposed to support the Rangers. Most of the time, people in the pub called him 'blue nose'; it was done in a spirit of banter, but there was 'one fellow now, you'd know he was saying it with venom'. Her dad would try to avoid him, but when the man got drunk, he would 'come over'. Her father also played in an all-Protestant football league. For this inner-city Dublin family, their sense of difference was very important. They attended church every Sunday and sang in the choir, and they socialised mostly at Shirley's father's club. The club was very 'old-fashioned'; only Protestant men could become members. She has always found the idea that all Dublin Protestants are wealthy galling, as this is so different to her experience. She grew up in subsidised housing, with a communal garden and outdoors sanitary facilities; it was once exclusively for low-income Protestants, but by the time she was born, the population of working-class Protestants in Dublin had become so small that Catholics were living there too. The children who were so rude to her 'shouldn't even have *been* in the houses!'

Conclusion

As Ireland becomes progressively more secular and globalised, the religious landscape and the demographics of the nation's rural areas and its towns and cities are changing dramatically. Still, features in the natural and built landscape that are associated with particular periods in the past, or that have a strong resonance for people, can feature in storytelling and form the background to lived experience.

7. Conclusion: Gains, Losses, and the Future

Inevitably, many stories told by Protestants coalesce around the idea of loss, but many others focus on the ways in which things have improved in recent decades. Above all, attention is paid to the fact that Ireland is no longer a segregated country and is now home to many cultural minorities while the power of the Catholic Church has waned considerably.

Fewer People and Loss of Influence
Many Protestants, especially in rural and inner-city parishes, talk about the steadily dwindling physical infrastructure of their community. Donald remembers the churches and community halls of his childhood closing, one by one:

> The first [local church in the city to close] was St Mathias, Adelaide Road [...] The church was demolished [...] St Peter's was demolished [...] St Luke's was reduced to ruin, St Mary's is a pub [...] St Catherine's Church [...] bits started to fall off and the church was rather abruptly closed [...] St James's [...] closed, St Jude's [...] closed and the building removed [...] and then St Andrew's was closed and the chapel of St Brendan's Hospital and St Mary's, which is now a pub, and St Paul's, which became a centre for industrial incubation units.

Morris has a similar account, '[The town] had three churches of the Protestant faith. One was a Methodist church, now a pub. One was a Church of Ireland, now knocked and is a housing estate. The third was Presbyterian, now a museum. Of course there was other reasons [for the decline of the local Protestant community] ... but *Ne Temere* did the rest.' To avoid tax, those responsible for the buildings frequently removed their roofs and they rapidly deteriorated. In consequence, the people who stayed in the area found themselves passing decaying buildings: physical reminders of their own collective decline in numbers and influence.

By the mid–1950s, many Protestants seem to have felt increasingly irrelevant. In 1954, Hubert Butler wrote, 'We Protestants [...] are no longer very interesting to anyone but ourselves', and that while a generation before many had seen them as 'imperialistic bloodsuckers' or, conversely, 'the last champions of civilisation in an abandoned island', now they 'merely exist and that with increasing unobtrusiveness'.[618] In about 1959, the great Dublin writer Seán O'Casey, a Protestant, wrote scathingly of the Protestants to his friend Risteárd Ó Glaisne, a Protestant and Irish language enthusiast. 'What are they', he said, 'but miserable specimens travelling the country with but an apology in their snouts for being alive, and with no desire to speak a word which would make anybody anxious or angry or surprised: they lack magic.'[619]

Despite gradual liberalisation, 'ethno–religious' nationalism[620] lingered. When commemorations for 1916 were held on its fiftieth anniversary, arrangements were made for a special ceremony at which the Catholic Archbishop of Dublin would bless the new Gardens of Remembrance. Representatives from all the major minority faiths were invited, and the invitations were accepted by the Church of Ireland and the Presbyterians. However, when the Protestant representatives arrived, the gate had already been locked, leading to the embarrassing situation of their being excluded from what everyone agreed was an important moment for the nation.[621]

While stories about loss are common across the socio-economic spectrum, they seem to resonate most among Protestant families and communities that have experienced economic hardship. Many recount stories about how the wealthier members of their communities dominated vestry meetings and other parish and community organisations. Now those wealthy people have gone, they have left the cost of the upkeep of local Protestant infrastructure to those who cannot afford it, leading to yet more closures – the large churches once attended by dispersed rural parishes are now too big for the diminished Protestant communities to heat and maintain.

Feelings of upset about having 'let the side down' can be expressed in more isolated parishes. William volunteers as sexton at the tiny local church, cutting the grass around the graves and doing his best to ensure that the building does not succumb completely to damp. He remembers that his family 'were very respected people' who served as sextons since the days of his great-grandfather, at least. Now, he says, 'I am doing it, and that is a long family tradition, and it upsets me [...] when I think of [the tradition dying with me].' In one study carried out in Donegal, a large proportion of correspondents were very worried about a perceived decline in numbers and its impact on community life and identity. This concern is often held even when numbers of observant Protestants have ceased to decline, and sometimes even when numbers have grown.[622]

Although Ireland steadily became a much more comfortable place in which to belong to a religious minority, the 'old' Protestants continued to lose ground, demographically and culturally. Writing in 2001, Marcus Tanner describes Protestants as 'a very petty people, almost entirely confined to the Dublin-Kildare-Wicklow area, with a few outposts in Wexford, Kilkenny and the holiday-cum-retirement home of Kerry'. He also states, 'It may be that Protestants in the South have fallen below the threshold of a sustainable community in the long term.'[623]

Acceptance and Friendship

After the Second Vatican Council, from 1962–65, one of the biggest differences between the Protestant faiths and Catholicism – the use of the vernacular during religious ceremonies – had disappeared, and the Catholic Church had softened its views on Protestants. They were now 'defined as separated brethren possessing part of the truth, albeit less than Catholics'.[624] New opportunities emerged for everyone, facilitating participation in shared gatherings of faith and social events, making it easier for Protestants to participate in public life and to identify with it.[625]

Robert recalls, 'We [Protestants] took great pride in [Vatican Two] because suddenly the Catholics were becoming Protestantised.' He describes how dramatic the change was. Suddenly, the Catholics were saying Mass in their own language. This, he says, removed one of the things that 'we'd always looked down our long noses at'; they had seemed so 'superstitious' sitting in church saying the rosary in Latin and not understanding a word of it. The Protestants had considered this an example of 'vain incantations'. Catholics also started to sing in church. This made them seem more like the Protestants, for whom singing in church was routine, and made some feel that the Catholics were tacitly admitting that the Protestants had been right all this time. 'Mixed' marriages were increasingly referred to as 'inter-faith', and Catholic publications even started publishing appreciative articles about Martin Luther, citing his Marian devotion.[626]

Basil remembers the first party that he and his wife held as newlyweds at around the time of Vatican Two; he recalls the party as a major event and one of the first local occasions in which Protestants and Catholics socialised together. For his generation, everything was beginning to change dramatically, partly because of Vatican Two, but also because of a general trend towards more liberal views:

> We had a famous party here three years after we were married, and we had what you might call an eclectic mix of guests [...] Which wasn't usual, I mean, the rector and one of the local priests that we knew very well because of Macra na Feirme [an organisation for young farmers] [...] everybody was sort of milling around. It was quite a big party and [...] that was a watershed.

In 1964, Bishop Lucey of Cork and Ross advised that the Catholic Irish should see their Protestant neighbours 'not as descendants of landlords, planters and the rest, but as Irishmen like ourselves' whose religion was only slightly different.[627] Among churchmen, ecumenism became fashionable, and many who had previously been inclined to look within their community for friendship and social contact felt more open towards friendships outside the group. From 1966, the rules dictated by the Irish Catholic hierarchy instructed that Catholics were free to attend the baptisms, weddings, and funerals of Protestant friends, even participating as a bridesmaid or best man; mixed marriages, too, could now occur in a Catholic church with the usual rites and blessings.[628] While many Catholics and Protestants had already enjoyed close friendships, and worked together on farms and in businesses all over the country, these changes helped the remaining social barriers to erode.

In 1972, Article 44 in the constitution, which stated that the Catholic Church had a 'special position' in Ireland, was repealed. The same year saw the resignation of Archbishop John Charles McQuaid,[629] whom many Protestants loathed and identified as a significant barrier to their integration; Hugo remembers, 'He used to give me the creeps because he kept this

country back for generations [...] he was so negative and a bit like de Valera.'
Roberta remembers that, from this time, successive governments relaxed
and became more accepting of the country's largest minority, which was
also feeling more at ease with itself. A whole generation of Protestants had
been born and reached middle age since the foundation of the Free State,
and their attitude towards their country was often very different to that of
their parents. They were in a better position to get civil service jobs because
Protestant schools were teaching Irish to a higher standard, and they stopped
looking for work exclusively with 'Protestant' employers. With Ireland's
membership of the European Economic Community looming, middle-
aged and younger Protestants felt more confident that they were no longer
seen as outsiders. Relationships between Protestants and Catholics continued to improve, with lower levels of segregation at work and mixed marriages becoming ever-more frequent.[630]

In recent years, Aphra's border community has participated in cross-bor-
der initiatives that have been regarded as very positive by all concerned, and
that have included commemorations of the centenary of 1916 and the
events of the First World War; the historical lectures that were organised
have opened the eyes of people from both sides of the border and all religious communities to the 'bias' in the versions of history that they knew.
Huge gains have been made in the area of community building, even in
border areas where the tensions of the North had a great impact. Simon
points out that a potent symbol of positive change can be seen in the fact
that, in the border areas where the Orange Order is active, Orange bands
are increasingly invited to participate in events such as St Patrick's Day parades, and they are increasingly likely to accept.

This greatly increased acceptance of Protestantism in Ireland, or of
Protestants as truly Irish, is recognised as a good thing in many ways, and
many state their joy and relief that their children or grandchildren are growing up in a much more relaxed environment than they did themselves, freely
socialising with whomever they choose. Problems around mixing and bullying in schools and in the community have receded to vanishing point.

Horace expresses his relief that things are 'hugely more relaxed' than
they were in his day. Andrew discusses the positive changes he has witnessed
in just the past twenty years with the acceptance of Protestants in Ireland,
'Today I feel I can mention to my work colleagues – those I've known for

a while, at least – what my religious upbringing was, whereas, twenty years ago I would do all I could to avoid the subject and hope that no-one would notice my odd surname and guess my religion.' Stewart comments on the many improvements in community relations that he has witnessed in the course of his life, 'We [Protestants] now have more confidence, we do not feel bullied as 60 years ago, & we feel that with the *Ne Temere* decree gone […] a more level playing field exists re. mixed marriages, which is good.'

While many Protestants frequently felt themselves to be a community and a cultural minority 'under siege', there is growing awareness that this feeling was determined not just by the many well-known, much-discussed extrinsic factors (such as *Ne Temere*, the policies of de Valera, the influence of McQuaid, and so on) but also by intrinsic factors. While one can understand, for example, the anger that the egregiously unfair *Ne Temere* roused, Protestant families themselves often chose to react to the mixed marriages of loved ones – often at least partly in response to community pressure – with anger and anguish rather than pragmatism or acceptance. While the Irish state often unfairly prioritised Catholicism and Catholic interests, many rural Protestants participated actively, and sometimes even eagerly, in excluding themselves from community events. Today, everything is different.

The Future

Research into the future of the Irish Protestant demographic tends to focus on numbers going to church rather than on Protestants as a cultural group. Immigration has led to a vast increase in the number of minority religions in Ireland, including an array of evangelical Protestant faiths.[631] D'Alton points out that the census figures in the early twenty-first century pointed to a Protestant minority that was thriving relative to what doom-mongers had predicted for them as recently as the 1980s; at that time, it seemed as though their numbers were terminally dwindling, while more Catholic children were being sent to Protestant fee-paying schools.[632] To a great extent, cultural differences have been eroded. D'Alton describes this as the convergence of narratives, and 'the conflation of mindsets in which Catholics have become more secular, Protestants a little less so; Catholics less assertive, Protestants more so'.[633]

Today, many Protestants report that a sense of Protestant cultural distinctiveness has greatly retreated. Some embrace this change, while others resent it; many people's feelings on the matter encompass both emotions. Andrew comments that very few of his former classmates in a Protestant school – 'only one out of perhaps 30' – are still active in either a Protestant faith or Protestant cultural life; he sees this as inevitable. Henry compares Irish identity to a brand name and says, 'The Irish Catholic, if it was a brand name, it is such a strong global brand, it's up there with Coca-Cola and MacDonald's.' By contrast, Protestants are 'down with some Mickey Mouse brand'. The result, he says, is that most Protestants do not try to maintain their heritage and identity, 'They have given up [...] have nothing to link themselves to anymore [...] They are ashamed of being Protestant [...] They just can't take it anymore [...] It's the brand image of Irish nationalist re-publicanism [...] Britain always being the baddie and people here always being the downtrodden. It's irresistible.' This is very upsetting for him, and he believes that it's also a 'really bad thing' for the whole country. 'I can't stress it strongly enough.' Of the future, he says, 'there will be plenty of Protestants in Ireland, but they will not be what I would call culturally Protestant for much longer [...] when you're up against one of the strongest brands in the world it's very hard not to change over to it, if not religiously then in everything else.'

Peter comments that 'The Protestant identity has changed out of all recognition in my lifetime. The abandonment of a separate social identity will soon be the end of the Protestant community.' Heather feels that Irish Protestants are 'definitely dying away' as a cultural group. People of her generation do not engage much with either the church or the rituals, social and otherwise, that once bound together rural Protestant communities like hers. So many, including herself, have married outside the community that their faith and secular traditions are 'diluted' and the sense of being culturally distinct has waned. 'The Irish Protestant identity was a very low-key affair [...] Now the number of Protestants is so few that their identity is mean-ingless,' says Morris. A few Protestants tell stories about couples resisting the trend towards the increasing 'dilution' of the Protestants of Ireland, having very large families specifically to address the issue of declining numbers in their community; this was far from the norm, however. Some Protestants cling to the current education system, which is still largely organised along denominational lines, although the student bodies have become increasingly mixed.[634]

Donald comments on the impact of Ireland's continuing trend towards secularism. Fewer children are confirmed every year, and fewer marriages and funerals take place in a church setting. In the process, most are likely to drift away from the cultural aspects of their background until there is simply nothing left that can be considered culturally distinctive. Samuel says that there are so few Protestants in his area that they have had no choice but to integrate and that, as their numbers are so much smaller, they are the ones who have the most to lose. He comments on a rector who spoke at Mass in Knock (an important site for Catholic pilgrims), and of another church man who plays traditional Irish music. For him, this is a symbol of how much things have changed for Protestants.

Mabel says the Protestant community in her home area has shrunk to an unsustainable level. Where once there were three clergymen serving a reasonably big population, there is now one. Although the community is 'fighting hard to survive', she sees no future for Protestants in the longer term and is annoyed with what she sees as the passive acceptance, and even facilitation, of the steady erosion of their people as a discrete group. Eadry states her view that the 'old' Protestant community of Ireland is 'dying out' except for a few areas with pockets of engaged community members. She thinks that it is an 'awful pity', because there's 'a lot of good in it', not just in terms of the religious observation, which she considers 'very respectful', but also in terms of the role it played, as a cultural group, in challenging norms and expectations. Letitia says that the Protestant community in her area, which has always been small, is getting even smaller. She herself, although once active in the community and in the church, is increasingly disengaged. She feels that her parish authorities are mostly interested in their congregation for their money, because it is in constant need of funds for repairing church buildings. The infrastructure and buildings were built for a much larger population, and the few, mostly elderly, people who are active in the community are under constant, unremitting financial pressure to provide for their upkeep.

Today, most people can accept the new reality of a more secular society and the necessity of 'mixed marriages', but seeing their cultural distinctiveness diminish – and sometimes their actual community decline – can be hard. To some Protestants, it can seem as though their heritage is deliberately ignored by a government and dominant majority that is going through its own debate about what religion means for its cultural identity. The visit of US President Barack Obama in 2011 is identified by Priscilla, Martha, Vivienne, and Olive as typical of mainstream attitudes towards their group today. Obama's remote ancestor, Falmouth Kearny, from the small village of Moneygall, was a Protestant who emigrated in the mid-nineteenth century. The connection was unearthed by the local rector. In the ensuing celebrations, they lamented that the Protestant aspect of Obama's Irish heritage was hardly mentioned. Politicians and local dignitaries lined up to have their photographs taken with the illustrious visitor and proudly claimed him as Irish without acknowledging that he was descended from a group that has become a tiny minority in the area. Heather also discusses this apparent oversight. 'It was on purpose *to be sure*,' she says. 'All the experiences I've come through [...] there's something important like that didn't just get forgotten about [...] you start to question what's going on. Where's the fairness in society?'

Harold says that the arrival of a wide range of immigrants in recent years has 'taken the heat off' Protestants, who are seen as much more similar to the majority population now that there are so many more minorities who are 'different' in other, often more obvious, ways, 'the influx of foreigners who have such different skin and stuff has probably taken the heat off the whole thing because, apart from anything else [...] it's the same God and you're Christians, and "right, you can speak English and you have the same skin colour."' Simon also notes that, in the multi-cultural Ireland of today, few people care anymore about Irish people's religious and cultural background. But he also comments, with some irritation, that 'nobody' was interested in diversity until immigrants started to arrive from far away and debates started about whether or not it was appropriate to have holy statues and other religious signifiers in public places such as hospitals:

> Like now, by degrees, people are starting to value diversity [...] it's interesting that now we have debates [...] about whether or not there should be a statue of the Virgin Mary in the hospital [...] What about the Protestants that have lived [...] from the foundation of the state to now? [...] Is it only if you're from Nigeria that it's an issue, or if you're from Syria, or something? Does that then make you have a right? What about the rights [of the Protestants who were always there]?

Vivienne's parish is struggling to stay active, as younger people are no longer interested in religion or their Protestant cultural heritage. She says that in twenty years there will be more Muslims than Protestants, more mosques than Protestant churches, and that 'we'll all be observing Friday instead of Sunday'. 'That will be a *fact*', she finishes, very firmly.

Roberta feels that younger generations of Protestants are probably quite ambivalent about their identity. Unlike Protestants in her youth, they are completely integrated into mainstream society, and their professional and recreational lives are completely unsegregated. However, she says, the fact that so many of them still prefer to send their children, when they can, to schools under Protestant management means that they do still have a lingering sense of separateness, even while 'they are proud and pleased to be members of a pluralist society'.

Heather states that 'we are under threat. It can be very difficult, very challenging to be Protestant and remain true to your own belief system and precepts.' She also refers to the difficulty of maintaining the infrastructures associated with her community when their numbers are so small, and she describes the ongoing impact of mixed marriage on the community, constantly drawing people away not just from church but also from shared traditions and history.

Trephina provides a different, more positive interpretation of the same situation, 'Protestant identity has changed considerably since independence. Younger Protestants have no hesitation in identifying themselves as Irish and are less likely to need a separate "culture."' Bob welcomes the erosion of cultural difference, saying that 'the isolation of the past has broken down. No longer do Protestants rely on their own community for social contact, marriage partners and entertainment, and in many ways are now a barely visible strand of a modern secular society.'

Some are hopeful that growing disillusionment with the Catholic Church will cause Protestant congregations to swell. Ian expects this to become a trend, and Penelope says her own community is being enlarged by disaffected former Catholics. However, these new members do not have the same set of shared folk memories and histories. Richard, who lives in an area with a fairly high Protestant population, cautiously opines that the future of the community is 'healthier than it has been' and partly attributes this to the growing disillusionment of many Catholics, who see Protestants as 'people with integrity' whose values have not been 'undermined from within'.

Protestant cultural integration is increasingly the status quo. For older people, who can remember when life as an indigenous minority in Ireland was much more complicated than it is today, this reality can give rise to a complex blend of shame and pride: shame in having failed to assert a sense of cultural difference that is valued, and pride in making the pragmatic decision to relinquish many of the behaviours, traditions, and even shared memories that once made them unique for the sake of harmony and integration. However, for Protestants, Ireland's tendency towards secularism impacts on their cultural identity in a particular way. The Protestant who drifts away from their religious identity also drifts away from their community's traditions and shared memories. It is hard to avoid the conclusion that the story of the Protestants of independent Ireland as a cultural, if not a religious, minority is drawing to a close. In light of this, hearing the stories of those who still remember a time of marked cultural distinctiveness is important.

Appendix: Interview Subjects and Questionnaire Respondents

Interviewees

Interviews were carried out between 2013 and 2018. The questionnaires were collected from a period starting in June 2016, with the last questionnaire material submitted in early 2018. Where the same name appears in both lists, this indicates that the person in question provided information in both interview and questionnaire format. Most of the interview subjects and questionnaire respondents requested anonymity, and all of them are identified here by pseudonyms. Biographical information provided by the interviewees reflects what they felt comfortable revealing about themselves.

'Adam', born 1950s, grew up in in the south-west in a business and farming family.

'Albert', born 1940s, is a farmer from the west.

'Amy', born 1940s, is from a farming background in a border area.

'Barbara', born 1940s, is a farmer from a border area.

'Barney', born 1950s, is a farmer from the north-west.

'Barton', born 1920s, is a retired shopkeeper from the midlands. Barton also provided a written response to the questionnaire.

'Basil', born 1940s, is a retired farmer from the south-west.

'Ben', born 1950s, is from a farming background in the north-east.

'Bob', born 1950s, is a retired teacher from the east. He also provided a written response to the questionnaire.

'Cedric', born 1960s, is a farmer in the south-east.

'Celeste', born 1940s, grew up in a 'trade' family and did clerical work.

'Clement', born 1950s, is from an inner-city Dublin background.

'Constance', born 1940s, is from Dublin and worked in a professional area.

'Daphne', born 1940s, grew up in Dublin and works in a creative field.

'Donald', born 1950s, grew up in Dublin and works in a religious capacity.

'Doris', born 1930s, comes from a farming background in the south-east.

'Eadry', born 1940s, is from Dublin and worked in healthcare.

'Edward', born 1960s, is from the south-east and works in a professional area.

'Edwin', born 1940s, is from the south-west and worked in a technical profession. Edwin also provided a written response to the question-naire.

'Eleanora', born 1940s, is a professional from a rural background in the west.

'Enid', born 1930s, in Northern Ireland, spent most of her working life in healthcare in the midlands.

'Everett', born 1960s, is from a rural area in the west and comes from a labouring background.

'Flora', born 1930s, is from a farming and business background in the east.

'Frank', born 1920s, grew up in a rural border area. He worked in a secu-rity field in the UK before returning to farm.

'Freddie', born 1940s, is from a farming background in the west.

'Gerald', born 1930s, is from the Dublin area and is a retired businessman.

'Grace', born 1940s, is from the south-east and is retired.

'Harold', born 1960s, comes from a working-class inner-city background.

'Harry', born 1920s, grew up in inner-city Dublin and became involved in ministry late in life.

'Heather', born 1960s, grew up on a small farm in a border area.

'Helen', born 1940s, grew up in the Dublin area.

'Henry', born 1960s, grew up in the Dublin area and works in a profes-sional capacity.

'Hillis', born 1950s, has roots in the east and west, and he works in the maritime industry.

'Honor', born 1960s, works in a professional area.

'Hope', born 1940s, is from a farming background in the south-east.

'Horace', born 1950s, is from a farming background in the west.

'Hubert', born 1930s, grew up in the south-east and is a retired business-man.

'Hugh', born 1920s, is from the south-west and is a retired businessman.

'Hugo', born 1950s, is a retired businessman from the south-west.

'Ian', born 1960s, is from a farming background in the midlands and works in a professional area.

'Iris', born 1940s, is from the midlands and worked in healthcare.

'Ivy', born 1940s, grew up in the midlands and is a retired farmer's wife.

'John', born 1940s, grew up and lives in Dublin. He worked in an academic area.

'Jonathan', born 1950s, is a Dubliner who works in a creative profession.

'Joyce', born 1940s, is from a farming background in the south-east.

'June', born 1950s, grew up in a rural area of the north-west and works in education.

'Kate', born 1950s, grew up in a rural part of the east and works in education. Kate also provided a written response to the questionnaire.

'Katherine', born 1920s, grew up in England with Irish parents, returning to Ireland in adulthood.

'Letitia', born 1970s, is from the south-east and works in education.

'Lily', born 1960s, is from a small farming background in the midlands.

'Lisa', born 1920s, is from the east and worked in healthcare. Lisa also provided a written response to the questionnaire.

'Lizzie', born 1930s, grew up in an urban area in the west.

'Mabel', born 1940s, grew up on a small farm in the west.

'Mariah', born 1960s, is a business woman and farmer in the south-east.

'Marigold', born 1950s, is from an urban area in the northeast.

'Marion', born 1930s, is from the east and worked in education.

'Marcus', born 1950s, is from the Dublin area and lives in the south-west. He works in a professional area.

'Mark', born 1940s, is a retired farmer from the north-west.

'Martha', born 1940s, is a retired farmer from the midlands.

'Matthew', born 1920s, is a retired member of the clergy from the south-west.

'May', born 1960s, is a farmer from the south.

'Millie', born 1940s, is from the midlands and worked in education. Millie also provided a written response to the questionnaire.

'Miriam', born 1940s, is from the east and worked in healthcare.

'Mitchell', born 1940s, is from the Dublin area and worked in an academic field.

'Myrtle', born 1940s, grew up in a shop-keeping family in the south-west. Myrtle also provided a written response to the questionnaire.

'Nancy', born 1940s, has roots in both the Republic of Ireland and Northern Ireland, and she worked in education.
'Natasha', born 1970s, is from a rural area and works in education.
'Neil', born 1940s, is from the east and worked in a religious capacity. Neil also provided a written response to the questionnaire.
'Norm', born 1940s, is from a small farming background.
'Olive', born 1930s, is from a rural background in the west.
'Oliver', born 1950s, is a professional from the Dublin area.
'Pamela', born 1940s, is from the midlands and worked in retail.
'Peter', born 1940s, grew up in Dublin and now lives in the south-east.
'Philippa', born 1990s, is from the Dublin area.
'Priscilla', born 1940s, is from a farming background in the west.
'Prudence', born 1940s, grew up in the west and worked in healthcare.
'Quentin', born 1940s, grew up in the Dublin area and worked in a caring profession. Quentin also provided a written response to the questionnaire.
'Rachel', born 1960s, is from a farming background in the south-west and works in education.
'Reggie', born 1950s, is from a border area and works in retail.
'Richard', born 1940s, grew up in the south-east and worked in education.
'Robert', born 1940s, is from the south-east and worked in education.
'Roberta', born 1930s, is from the Dublin area and worked in an academic field.
'Roger', born 1930s, is from a border area and is a retired farmer.
'Samuel', born 1930s, is from a farming background in the west.
'Shirley', born 1960s, grew up in an inner-city family from Dublin.
'Simon', born 1960s, grew up in the north-west and works in a professional area.
'Sylvia', born 1940s, is from a border area and worked in education.
'Thomas', born 1920s, is from a farming background in a border area.
'Tilly', born 1940s, is from a farming background in the east.
'Timothy', born 1950s, grew up in Dublin and works in a professional area.
'Travers', born 1940s, is from the south-east and is a retired farmer.
'Trevor', born 1930s, is from a shop-keeping family in the west.

'Ursula', born 1930s, is from the south-east and worked in education.

'Valerie', born 1960s, is from a border county and works in retail.

'Vivian', born 1930s, has roots in the Republic of Ireland and Northern Ireland, and he worked in an academic field.

'Vivienne', born 1950s, is from a farming background in the east.

'Walter', born 1940s, is from an inner-city Dublin background and worked in a trade profession.

'William', born 1950s, is from a small farming background in the west.

'Willy', born 1940s, is from a landed background in the south-west.

Questionnaire Respondents

'Andrew', born 1960s, grew up in a farming family in the midlands.

'Andy', born 1930s, grew up in the south-west and worked in education.

'Aphra', born 1940s, is from a border area and worked in wholesale.

'Archie', born 1940s, is from the Dublin area and worked in education.

'Arthur', born 1940s, grew up in the south-west and emigrated in the 1970s.

'Astra', born 1940s, is from Dublin. She was the child of a mixed marriage and raised Protestant.

'Barton', born 1920s, is a retired shopkeeper from the midlands. He also participated in a recorded interview.

'Betty', born 1970s, grew up in a rural area of the east.

'Bob', born 1950s, is from the east and worked in education. He also participated in a recorded interview.

'Candide', born 1940s, is from the east and worked in healthcare.

'Charlotte', born 1930s, grew up on a farm in the east and was a farmer's wife in the midlands.

'Christopher', born 1940s, is from Dublin. He worked in the technical industry.

'Clara', born 1980s, is from a border area and works in the professional sector.

'Clive', born 1950s, grew up in the midlands and works in education.

'Colin', born 1930s, grew up in a farming family and has remained in farming.

'Craig', born 1940s, is from the Dublin area and worked in education.

'Cyril', born 1940s, grew up in the midlands and emigrated to work in education.

'Dave', born 1930s, is from the west and worked in education.

'Davina', born 1920s, is from a border area.

'Don', born 1930s, is from the midlands area and worked in engineering.

'Ed', born 1940s, grew up in the south-west and worked in the church.

'Edwin', born 1940s, grew up in the south-west and worked in a technical profession. He also provided a recorded interview.

'Eileen', born 1940s, grew up on a small farm in the east.

'Elsie', born 1950s, to Irish parents overseas. She grew up in the south Dublin area and works in a creative profession.

'Emma', born 1930s, grew up in a rural part of the south-west and is a homemaker.

'Eric', born 1930s, is a retired farmer from the midlands

'Esther', born 1940s, is from a Big House background in the south-east.

'Ethel', born 1940s, is from the east.

'Eunan', born 1950s, is from the south-west and works in the farming sector.

'Eustace', born 1940s, grew up in a clerical family and works in the fields of academia and management.

'Evelyn', born 1930s, is from a farming background in the north-west.

'Florrie', born 1970s, is from the south-east and works in education.

'Frances', born 1930s, is from the Dublin area and grew up in a clerical home.

'Francis', born 1920s, is a retired farmer from the midlands.

'Gavin', born 1960s, grew up in a rural area of the north-west and works in a professional field.

'Gay', born 1940s, is from Dublin and worked in administration.

'George', born 1920s, is from the Dublin area and worked in education.

'Gerald', born 1930s, is a retired businessman from Dublin.

'Gregory', born 1930s, is from the east of the country.

'Hannah', born 1930s, grew up in the Dublin area and settled in the south-east.

'Hazel', born 1940s, grew up in a border area.

'Honora', born 1930s, is a farmer's daughter in the south.

'James', born 1940s, grew up in a clerical family in the south-west and worked in education and in the professional sector.

'Jim', born 1930s, grew up in a small town in the south-east.

'Jennie', born 1940s, grew up in the Dublin area.

'Joan', born 1950s, grew up in the west and works in the professional sector.

'Joe', born 1930s, grew up in the Dublin area and worked in insurance.

'Juliet', born 1930s, is from a farming background in the east.

'Kate', born 1950s, grew up in a farming family in the east and works in education. She also participated in a recorded interview.

'Laura', born 1907, was recorded in the 1980s by her daughter, 'Gay', who participated in the current research. Laura was a nurse.

'Lisa', born 1920s, is from the east and worked in healthcare in Dublin. Lisa also participated in a recorded interview.

'Liza', born 1940s, is a shopkeeper and farmer's daughter from a border area.

'Lucy', born 1930s, was born into a farming family.

'Luke', born 1950s, was born to a 'mixed' couple, grew up in the Dublin area, and worked in the civil service.

'Lynne', born 1920s, is a landowner from the midlands.

'Mike', born 1940s, grew up in a shop-keeping family in the midlands and worked in banking.

'Millie', born 1940s, is from the midlands and worked in education. She also participated in a recorded interview.

'Morris', born 1940s, is a businessman from the south-west.

'Myrtle', born 1940s, grew up in a shop-keeping family in the south-west. Myrtle also participated in a recorded interview.

'Neil', born 1940s, grew up in the south-east and worked in a religious capacity. Neil also participated in a recorded interview.

'Pat', born 1930s, grew up in south Dublin and worked in business.

'Percival', born 1940, grew up in a midlands farming family and worked in farming.

'Quentin', born 1940s, grew up in the Dublin area and worked in a caring profession. He also participated in a recorded interview.

'Rebecca', born 1930s, is from the south-east and worked in education.

'Sam', born 1940s, is from the north-west and worked in farming.

'Sidney', born 1940s, is from the Dublin area and is retired.

'Stewart', born 1940s, is from the midlands and has a background in agriculture.

'Ted', born 1930s, grew up in a farming family and is a farmer.

'Tim', born 1940s, is from the Dublin area and worked in law.

'Tom', born 1940s, is from the Dublin area and worked in the legal sector.

'Trephina', born 1970s, is from a border area and is an office worker.

'Trev', born 1920s, is a retired civil engineer from the Dublin area.

'Violet', born 1940s, has had a musical career in Ireland and abroad.

'Wallace', born 1940s, grew up in a clerical family in the south-west and worked in education.

'Winnie', born 1930s, is a farmer's wife from the south-east.

BIBLIOGRAPHY

Almqvist, B., 'The Irish Folklore Commission: Achievement and Legacy' in A. Dundes (ed.), *Folklore: Critical Concepts in Literary and Cultural Studies* (Abingdon-on-Thames: Routledge, 2005).

Alver, B., 'Folkloristics: The Science about Tradition and Society' in A. Dundes (ed.), *Folklore: Critical Concepts in Literary and Cultural Studies* (Abingdon-on-Thames: Routledge, 2005).

Arensberg, C.M. and S.T. Kimball, *Family and Community in Ireland* (Ennis: Clasp Press, 2001).

Assman, J. and J. Czaplicka, 'Collective Memory and Cultural Identity', *New German Critique*, 65 (1995), 125–33.

Association for the Relief of Distressed Protestants. Report of the Managing Committee for the year 1837.

Banjeglav, T., 'Conflicting Memories, Competing Narratives and Contested Histories in Croatia's Post-war Commemorative Practices', *Politicka Misao: Croatian Political Science Review*, 49, 5 (2012), 7–31.

Bardwell, L., *A Restless Life* (Dublin: Liberties Press, 2008).

Barkley, J.M., *A Short History of the Presbyterian Church in Ireland* (Belfast: Publications Board, Presbyterian Church in England, 1959).

Barnard, T., *A New Anatomy of Ireland: The Irish Protestants, 1649–1770* (New Haven and London: Yale University Press, 2003).

Barnard, T., *Improving Ireland?: Projectors, Prophets and Profiteers, 1641–1786* (Dublin: Four Courts Press, 2008).

Barnard, T., 'Protestantism, Ethnicity and Irish Identities, 1660–1960' in T. Claydon and I. McBride (eds), *Protestantism and National Identity: Britain and Ireland, c.1650–c.1840* (Cambridge: Cambridge University Press, 1998).

Barnard, T., 'Scholars and Antiquarians' in T. Barnard and W.G. Neely (eds), *The Clergy of the Church of Ireland, 1000–2000: Messengers, Watchmen and Stewards* (Dublin: Four Courts Press, 2006).

Barnard, T.C., 'The Uses of 23 October 1641 and Irish Protestant Celebrations', *English Historical Review*, 106, 421 (1991), 889–920.

Barth, F., *Ethnic Groups and Boundaries: The Social Organisation of Culture Difference* (Illinois: Waveland Press, 1998).

Bauman, R., 'Differential Identity and the Social Base of Folklore', *Toward New Perspectives in Folklore Studies*, 84, 331 (1972), 31–41.

Beiner, G., 'Disremembering 1798?', *History Memory*, 25, 1 (2013), 9–50.

Beiner, G., *Remembering the Year of the French: Irish Folk History and Social Memory* (Madison: The University of Wisconsin Press, 2007).

Bew, P., *Ireland: The Politics of Enmity* (Oxford: Oxford University Press, 2007).

Bielenberg, A., 'Exodus: The Emigration of Southern Irish Protestants During the Irish War of Independence and the Civil War', *Past and Present*, 218, 1 (2013), 199–233.

Biagini, E.F., 'The Protestant Minority in Southern Ireland', *The Historical Journal*, 55, 4 (2012), 1161–84.

Blank, T.J. and R.G. Howard, *Tradition in the Twenty-first Century: Locating the Role of the Past in the Present* (Logan: Utah State University Press, 2013).

Blume, H., 'Some Geographical Aspects of the Palatine Settlement in Ireland', *Geographical Society of Ireland*, 2, 4 (1952), 172–9.

Bondeson, J., *Freaks: The Pig-Faced Lady of Manchester Square & Other Medical Marvels* (Stroud: Tempus Publishing, 2003).

Bowen, D., *History and the Shaping of Irish Protestantism (Irish Studies)* (Oxford: Peter Lang, 1995).

Bowen, E., *Seven Winters* (Dublin: The Cuala Press, 1942).

Bowen, K., *Protestants in a Catholic State: Ireland's Privileged Minority* (Dublin: McGill-Queen's University Press, 1983).

Boyce, D.G., '"No Lack of Ghosts": Memory, Commemoration, and the State in Ireland' in I. McBride (ed.), *History and Memory in Modern Ireland* (Cambridge: Cambridge University Press, 2001).

Boyd, A. 'The Orange Order', *History Today*, 45, 9 (1995), 16–23.

Bramsbäck, B., 'William Butler Yeats and Folklore Material', *Béaloideas*, 39, 41 (1971–73), 56–68.

Briody, M., '"Dead Clay and Living Clay": Máirtín O'Cadhain's criticisms of the work of the Irish Folklore Commission', *Approaching Religion*, 4, 1 (2014), 55–65.

Briody, M., *The Irish Folklore Commission 1935–1970: History, Ideology, Methodology* (Helsinki: Finnish Literature Society, 2007).

Broderick, E., *The Boycott at Fethard-on-Sea, 1957: A Study in Catholic-Protestant Relations in Modern Ireland* (Newcastle: Cambridge Scholars Publishing, 2011).

Brown, T., *Ireland: A Social and Cultural History 1922–2002* (London: Harper Perennial, 2004).

Brown, T., *The Whole Protestant Community: The Making of a Historical Myth (A Field Day Pamphlet)* (Derry: Field Day Publications, 1985).

Browne, N., *Against the Tide* (Dublin: Gill and Macmillan, 1986).

Browne, N., 'Church and State in Modern Ireland' in T. Murphy and P. Twomey (eds), *Ireland's Evolving Constitution, 1937–1997: Collected Essays* (Oxford: Hart Publishing, 1998).

Brück, J., 'Landscapes of Desire: Parks, Colonialism, and Identity in Victorian and Edwardian Ireland', *International Journal of Historical Archaeology*, 17, 1 (2013), 196–223.

Buck, J., 'The Role of Ne Temere in the Decline of an Irish Custom Regarding the Religious Affiliation of the Children of Mixed Marriages', *The Australasian Journal of Irish Studies*, 11 (2011), 28–43.

Burke, P., 'History as Social Memory' in T. Butler (ed.), *Memory: History, Culture and the Mind (Wolfson College Lectures)* (Hoboken: Blackwell Publishers, 1989).

Burn-Murdoch, B., *What's So Special About Huntingdonshire?* (St Ives: Friends of the Norris Museum, 1997).

Bury, R., *Buried Lives: The Protestants of Southern Ireland* (Dublin: The History Press Ireland, 2017).

Busteed, M., 'Ascendency Insecurities: Cross Pressures on an Eighteenth-Century Improving Landlord' in M. Busteed, F. Neal and J. Tonge (eds), *Irish Protestant Identities* (Manchester and New York: Manchester University Press, 2008).

Butler, D. and R. Joseph, 'Identity, Difference and Community in Southern Irish Protestantism: The Protestants of West Cork', *National Identities*, 11, 1 (2009), 73–86.

Butler, H., 'Boycott Village' in H. Butler (ed.), *Independent Spirit* (New York: Farrar, Strauss and Giroux, 1985).

Butler, H., *Escape from the Anthill* (Mullingar: The Lilliput Press, 1985).

Butler, H., 'Postscript 1' in H. Butler (ed.), *Escape from the Anthill* (Mullingar: The Lilliput Press, 1985).

Butler, T., 'Memory: A Mixed Blessing' in T. Butler (ed.), *Memory: History, Culture and the Mind (Wolfson College Lectures)* (Hoboken: Blackwell Publishers, 1989).

Byrne, A., R. Edmondson and T. Varley, 'Arensberg and Kimball and Anthropological Research in Ireland: Introduction to the Third Edition' in C.M. Arensberg and S.T. Kimball (eds), *Family and Community in Ireland* (Ennis: CLASP, 2001).

Caird, D.A.R., 'Protestantism and National Identity' in J. McLoon (ed.), *Being Protestant in Ireland: Co-operation North, in Association with the Social Study Conference. Summer School St. Kieran's College, 1984* (Belfast and Galway: Co-operation North, 1984).

Caldicott, C.E.J., H. Gough and J.P. Pittion, *The Huguenots and Ireland: Anatomy of an Emigration* (Dun Laoghaire: The Glendale Press, 1987).

Carty, J., *A Class-book of Irish History with Maps and Illustrations. Book IV: From the Act of Union to the Present Day* (London: Macmillan and Co. Limited, 1951).

Casserley, D., *History of Ireland: Part I. Earliest Times to the Flight of the Earls* (Dublin and Cork: The Talbot Press, 1941).

Central Protestant Defence Association, *Address to the Protestants of Ireland of all Denominations* (Dublin: Porteous and Gibbs Printers, 1868).

Christiansen, R.T., *The Migratory Legends: A Proposed List of Types with a Systematic Catalogue of the Norwegian Variants* (Helsinki: Suomalainen Tiedeakatemia, 1958).

Clark, G., *Everyday Violence in the Civil War* (Cambridge: Cambridge University Press, 2014).

Coakley, J., 'Religion, Ethnic Identity and the Protestant Minority in the Republic' in W. Crotty and D.E. Schmitt (eds), *Ireland and the Politics of Change* (London and New York: Longman, 1998).

Connerton, P., *How Societies Remember* (Cambridge: Cambridge University Press, 1989).

Connolly, S., *Religion and Society in Nineteenth Century Ireland* (Dundalk: Dundalgan Press, 1985).

Cooney, J., *John Charles McQuaid: Ruler of Catholic Ireland* (Dublin: The O'Brien Press, 1999).

Corkey, Rev. W.M., *The McCann Mixed Marriage Case* (Edinburgh: The Knox Club, 1912).

Crawford, H.K., *Outside the Glow: Protestants and Irishness in Independent Ireland* (Dublin: University College Dublin Press, 2010).

Cruise O'Brien, C., 'The Protestant Minority: Within and Without', *The Crane Bag Book of Irish Studies*, 5, 1 (1981), 786–9.

Cubitt, G., *History and Memory* (Manchester and New York: Manchester University Press, 2007).

Cunningham, N., 'Troubled Geographies: A Historical GIS of Religion, Society and Conflict in Ireland since the Great Famine' in I.N. Gregory and A. Geddes (eds), *Toward Spatial Humanities: Historical GIS and Spatial History* (Bloomington: Indiana University Press, 2014).

Curtis, M., *A Challenge to Democracy: Militant Catholicism in Modern Ireland* (Dublin: The History Press Ireland, 2010).

Cusack, T., 'A "Countryside Bright with Cosy Homesteads": Irish Nationalism and the Cottage Landscape', *National Identities*, 3, 3 (2001), 221–38.

D'Alton, I., 'A Vestigial Population? Perspectives on Southern Irish Protestants in the Twentieth Century', *Eire-Ireland*, 44, 3 & 4 (2009), 9–42.

D'Alton, I., 'Educating for Ireland? The Urban Protestant Elite and the Early Years of Cork Grammar School, 1880–1914', *Éire-Ireland*, 46, 3 & 4 (2011), 201–226.

Dalton, K. and P. Semple, *'That Could Never Be': A Memoir* (Dublin: The Columba Press, 2003).

Daly, E., *Religion, Law and the Irish State* (Dublin: Clarus Press, 2012).

Daly, M., 'Late Nineteenth and Early Twentieth Century Dublin' in D. Harkness and M. O'Dowd (eds), *The Town in Ireland* (Dublin: Appletree Press, 1981).

Danaher, K., *The Year in Ireland: Irish Calendar Customs* (Cork: Mercier Press, 1972).

Dawson, G., 'The 'Ulster'-Irish Border, Protestant Imaginative Geography and Cultural Memory in the Irish Troubles' in M. Ascari and A. Corrado (eds), *Sites of Exchange: European Crossroads and Faultlines* (Amsterdam and New York: RODOPI, 2006).

Derry and Raphoe Action, *Protestants in Community Life: Findings from a Co.*

Donegal Survey (Newtownstewart: Derry and Raphoe Action, 2001).

Dickinson, P.L., *The Dublin of Yesterday* (London: Methuen and Co Ltd, 1929).

Dingley, J., 'Religion, Protestants and National Identity: A Response to the March 2009 Issue', *National Identities*, 15, 2 (2013), 101–24.

Doherty, G., 'National Identity and the Study of Irish History', *The English Historical Review*, 111, 441 (1996), 324–49.

Dooley, T., *The Decline of the Big House in Ireland: A Study of Irish Landed Families 1860–1960* (Dublin: Wolfhound Press, 2001).

Dooley, T., *'The Land for the People': The Land Question in Independent Ireland* (Dublin: University College Dublin Press, 2004).

Dooley, T., *The Plight of Monaghan Protestants, 1912–26. Maynooth Studies in Irish Local History* (Dublin: Irish Academic Press, 2000).

Donnelly, J.S., 'Big House Burnings in County Cork during the Irish Revolution, 1921–22', *Éire-Ireland*, 47, 3 (2012), 141–97.

Dundes, A., 'A Study of Ethnic Slurs: The Jew and the Polack in the United States', *The Journal of American Folklore*, 84, 332 (1971), 186–203.

Dundes, A., *Cracking Jokes: Studies of Sick Humor Cycles and Stereotypes* (Berkeley: Ten Speed Press, 1987).

Dundes, A., *Interpreting Folklore* (Bloomington: Indiana University Press, 1980).

Dunleavy, J.E. and G.W. Dunleavy, *Douglas Hyde: A Maker of Modern Ireland* (Oakland: University of California Press, 1991).

Dunne, T., *Rebellions: Memoir, Memory and 1798* (Dublin: The Lilliput Press, 2004).

Edgeworth, B., 'Rural Radicalism Restrained: The Irish Land Commission and the Courts (1933–39)', *Irish Jurist*, 42, 7 (2007), 1–28.

Elliott, M., *When God Took Sides: Religion and Identity in Ireland* (Oxford: Oxford University Press, 2009).

Ervine, St J., *Mixed Marriage: A Play in Four Acts* (Dublin: Maunsel & Company Ltd, 1911).

Fallon, B., *An Age of Innocence: Irish Culture, 1930–1960* (Dublin: Gill and MacMillan, 1999).

Fanning, T., *The Fethard-on-Sea Boycott* (Cork: The Collins Press, 2010).

Farmar, T., *Privileged Lives: A Social History of Middle-class Ireland, 1882–1989* (Dublin: A&A Farmar, 2010).

Farrell Moran, S., 'History, Memory and Education: Teaching the Irish Story' in L.W. McBride (ed.), *Reading Irish Histories: Texts, Context and Memory in Modern Ireland* (Dublin: Four Courts Press, 2003).

Fealy, G.M., *The Adelaide Hospital School of Nursing, 1859–2009* (Dublin: The Columba Press, 2009).

Fernihough, A., C. Ó Gráda and B.M. Walsh, 'Intermarriage in a Divided Society: Ireland a Century Ago', *Explorations in Economic History*, 56, 4 (2015), 1–14.

Ferriter, D., *Ambiguous Republic: Ireland in the 1970s* (London: Profile Books, 2013).

Finney, P., 'The Ubiquitous Presence of the Past? Collective Memory and International History', *International History Review*, 36, 3 (2014), 443–72.

Fitzpatrick, D., 'Protestant Depopulation and the Irish Revolution', *Irish Historical Studies*, 38, 152 (2013), 643–70.

Fitzpatrick, D., 'The Futility of History: A Failed Experiment in Irish Education' in C. Brady and I. Berend (eds), *Historical Studies XVII, Ideology and the Historians: Papers Read before the Irish Conference of Historians Held at Trinity College, Dublin, 8–10 June 1989* (Dublin: The Lilliput Press, 1991).

Fitzpatrick, D., *Descendancy: Irish Protestant Histories since 1795* (Cambridge: Cambridge University Press, 2014).

Fitzsimon, N., *Child of the Irish Border: A Memoir and Family History* (Bantry: Somerville Press, 2010).

Fleming, L., *Head or Harp* (London: Barrie and Rockliff, 1965).

Fletcher, Reverend Canon, *The Decree Ne Temere* (Church of Ireland Printing Co., 1947).

Foster, R.F., *Modern Ireland, 1600–1972* (London: Allen Lane, 1988).

Foster, R.F., *Paddy and Mr Punch: Connections in Irish and English History* (London and New York: Allen Lane and The Penguin Press, 1993).

Foster, R.F., 'Remembering 1798' in I. McBride (ed.), *History and Memory in Modern Ireland* (Cambridge: Cambridge University Press, 2001).

Foster, R.F., *The Irish Story: Telling Tales and Making It Up in Ireland* (London: Allen Lane, 2001).

Foster, R.F., 'Varieties of Irishness' in M. Crozier (ed.), *Proceedings of the Cultural Traditions Group Conference, 3–4 March, 1989* (Belfast: Institute of

Irish Studies, The Queen's University of Belfast, 1989).

Foster, R.F., *Vivid Faces: The Revolutionary Generation in Ireland 1890–1923* (London: Allen Lane, 2014).

French, B., 'Ethnography and "Postconflict" Violence in the Irish Free State', *American Anthropologist*, 115, 2 (2013), 160–74.

Gahan, D., 'The Scullabogue Massacre 1798', *History Ireland*, 4, 3 (1996), 27–31.

Gahan, D.J., 'New Ross, Scullabogue and the 1798 Rebellion in Southwestern Wexford', *The Past: The Organ of the Uí Cinsealaigh Historical Society*, 21 (1998), 3–33.

Gardiner, M., 'Folklore's Timeless Past, Ireland's Present Past, and the Perception of Rural Houses in Early Historic Ireland', *International Journal of Historical Archaeology*, 15, 4 (2011), 707–24.

Garvin, T., *The Evolution of Irish Nationalist Politics* (Dublin: Gill and Macmillan, 1981).

Garvin, T., *Preventing the Future: Why Was Ireland So Poor for So Long?* (Dublin: Gill and Macmillan, 2004).

Geertz, C., *The Interpretation of Cultures: Selected Essays* (New York: Basic Books, 2000).

Gibbon, M., '"Am I Irish?" A Sense of Nation' in M.P. Hederman and R. Kearney (eds), *The Crane Bag Book of Irish Studies 1977–1981* (Dublin: Blackwater Press, 1982).

Gibney, J., 'The Memory of 1641 and Protestant Identity in Restoration and Jacobite England' in M. Busteed, F. Neal and J. Tonge (eds), *Irish Protestant Identities* (Manchester: Manchester University Press, 2008).

Gibney, J., 'Protestant Interests? The 1641 Rebellion and State Formation in Early Modern Ireland', *Historical Research*, 84, 223 (2011), 67–86.

Gillmor, D.A., 'Changing Religions in the Republic of Ireland, 1991–2002', *Irish Geography*, 39, 2 (2006), 111–28.

Goldberg, T., B.B. Schwarz and D. Porat, 'Living and Dormant Collective Memories as Contexts of History Learning', *Learning and Instruction*, 18, 3 (2008), 223–37.

Golden, J., 'Irishness, Foreignness, and National Identity. Apostolic Succession in Disestablishment Historiography' in M. Empey, A. Ford, and M. Moffitt (eds), *The Church of Ireland and Its Past: History, Interpretation, and Identity* (Dublin: Four Courts Press, 2017).

Graham, B.J., 'Ireland and Irishness: Place, Culture and Identity' in Brian J. Graham (ed.), *In Search of Ireland: A Cultural Geography* (New York and London: Routledge Psychology Press, 1997).

Graham, B.J., 'The Imagining of Place: Representation and Identity in Contemporary Ireland' in B.J. Graham (ed.), *In Search of Ireland: A Cultural Geography* (New York and London: Routledge Psychology Press, 1997).

Greaves, R.L., *God's Other Children: Protestant Nonconformists and the Emergence of Denominational Churches in Ireland, 1660–1700* (Stanford: Stanford University Press, 1997).

Gregg, Rev. J.A.F., *The 'Ne Temere' Decree. A Lecture Delivered Before the Members of the Church of Ireland Cork Young Men's Association on March 17th, 1911* (Dublin: Association for Promoting Christian Knowledge, 1943).

Gregory, I.N. and N.A. Cunningham, '"The Judgement of God on an Indolent and Unself-reliant People"? The Impact of the Great Irish Famine on Ireland's Religious Demography', *Journal of Historical Geography*, 51 (2016), 76–87.

Griffin, V.G.B., *Anglican and Irish: What We Believe* (Berkeley: Anglican Province of Christ the King, 1976).

Griffin, V.G.B., *Enough Religion to Make Us Hate: Reflections on Religion and Politics* (Dublin: The Columba Press, 2002).

Guinnane, T.W., *The Vanishing Irish: Households, Migration and the Rural Economy in Ireland, 1850–1914* (Princeton: Princeton University Press, 1997).

Halbwachs, M., *On Collective Memory* (Chicago: The University of Chicago Press, 1992).

Hale, H., 'Explaining Ethnicity', *Comparative Political Studies*, 37, 4 (2004), 458–85.

Harkness, D. and M. O'Dowd, *The Town in Ireland (Historical Studies XIII): Papers Read Before the Irish Conference of Historians 1979* (Belfast: Appletree Press, 1981).

Hart, P., 'The Protestant Experience of Revolution in Southern Ireland' in R. English and G. Walker (eds), *Unionism in Modern Ireland* (London: Palgrave Macmillan, 1996).

Hart, P., *The I.R.A. and Its Enemies: Violence and Community in Cork, 1916–1923* (Oxford: Oxford University Press, 1998).

Hayes, B.C. and T. Fahey, 'Protestants and Politics in the Republic of Ireland: Is Integration Complete?' in M. Busteed, F. Neal and J. Tonge (eds), *Irish*

Protestant Identities (Manchester: Manchester University Press, 2008).

Hechter, M., *Internal Colonialism: The Celtic Fringe in British National Development 1536–1966* (London: Routledge and Kegan Paul, 1975).

Hick, V., 'The Palatine Settlement in Ireland: The Early Years', *Eighteenth-Century Ireland Society / Iris an dá chultúr*, 4 (1989), 113–31.

Higgins, R., *Transforming 1916: Meaning, Memory and the Fiftieth Anniversary of the Easter Rising* (Cork: Cork University Press, 2012).

Horgan, J., *Noel Browne: Passionate Outsider* (Dublin: Gill and Macmillan, 2000).

Howe, S., 'Killings in Cork and the Historians', *History Workshop Journal*, 77, 1 (2014), 160–86.

Hunter, R.J., 'Ulster Plantation Towns' in D. Harkness and M. O'Dowd (eds), *The Town in Ireland* (Dublin: Appletree Press, 1981).

Hynes, E., 'The Construction of Insiders as Outsiders: Catholic Accounts of Protestant Converts in Pre-Famine Western Ireland', *Cultural and Social History: The Journal of the Social History Society*, 6, 2 (2009), 195–209.

Inglis, B., *West Briton* (London: Faber and Faber, 1962).

Irwin, Rev. H., *A Sermon Preached in Saint Werburgh's Church, on Sunday, February 11th, 1838* (Dublin: Milliken and Son, 1838).

Jackson, A., *Home Rule: A History 1800–2000* (London: Phoenix Press, 2004).

Jameson, D., 'The Religious Upbringing of Children in "Mixed Marriages": The Evolution of Irish Law', *New Hibernia Review*, 18, 2 (2014), 65–83.

Janmaat, J.G., 'History and National Identity Construction: The Great Famine in Irish and Ukrainian History Textbooks', *History of Education*, 35, 3 (2006), 345–68.

Johnston, R.H.W., *Century of Endeavour: A Biographical and Autobiographical View of the Twentieth Century in Ireland* (Dublin: Tyndall Publications in Association with the Lilliput Press, 2003).

Jones, S. and L. Russell, 'Archaeology, Memory and Oral Tradition: An Introduction', *International Journal of Historical Archaeology*, 16, 2 (2012), 267–83.

Jones, V., *A Gaelic Experiment: The Preparatory System 1926–61 and Coláiste Moibhí* (Dublin: The Woodfield Press, 2006).

Jones, V., *Rebel Prods: The Forgotten Story of Protestant Radical Nationalists and the 1916 Rising* (Dublin: Ashfield Press, 2016).

Jupp, P., 'Urban Politics in Ireland 1801–1831' in D. Harkness and M. O'Dowd (eds), *The Town in Ireland* (Dublin: Appletree Press, 1981).

Kearney, H.F., *Ireland: Contested Ideas of Nationalism and History* (Cork: Cork University Press, 2007).

Kearney, R., *Postnationalist Ireland: Politics, Culture, Philosophy* (London and New York: Routledge, 1997).

Kehoe, E., 'Daughters of Ireland: Maud Gonne McBride, Dr Kathleen Lynn and Dorothy McArdle' in E. Biagini and D. Mulhall (eds), *The Shaping of Modern Ireland: A Centenary Assessment* (Dublin: Irish Academic Press, 2016).

Kenny, M., *Goodbye to Catholic Ireland* (Dublin: New Island Books, 2000).

Kiberd, D., *Inventing Ireland* (London: Jonathan Cape, 1995).

Larkin, E.J., *The Historical Dimensions of Irish Catholicism* (Dublin: Four Courts Press, 1997).

Leckey, W.E.H., W.E.G. Lloyd and F. Cruise O'Brien, *Clerical Influences: An Essay on Irish Sectarianism and English Government* (Dublin: Maunsel and Co., 1911).

Leonard, J., 'The Twinge of Memory: Armistice Day and Remembrance Sunday in Dublin since 1919' in R. English and G. Walker (eds), *Unionism in Modern Ireland: New Perspectives on Politics and Culture* (Basingstoke: Gill and Macmillan, 1996).

Leonard, M., 'Echoes from the Past: Intergenerational Memories in Cyprus', *Children and Society*, 28, 1 (2014), 66–76.

Limond, D., '[Re]moving Statues', *History Ireland*, 18, 2 (2010), 10–11.

Locus Management and K. Walsh, *Border Protestant Perspectives: A Study of the Attitudes and Experiences of Protestants Living in the Southern Border Counties* (Belfast: Locus Management, 2005).

Lyons, F.S.L., *Ireland Since the Famine* (London: Weidenfeld and Nicolson, 1971).

Lyons, F.S.L., 'The Minority Problem in the 26 counties' in F. MacManus (ed.), *The Years of the Great Test, 1926–39* (Cork: Mercier Press, 1967).

Lysaght, K., 'Living in a Nation, a State or a Place? The Protestant Gentry of County Cork', *National Identities*, 11, 9 (2009), 59–71.

Lysaght, P., *The Banshee: The Irish Death Messenger* (New York: Roberts Rinehart, 1997).

Macourt, M., *Counting the People of God: The Census of Population and the*

Church of Ireland (Dublin: Church of Ireland Publishing, 2008).

Maguire, M., '"Our people": The Church of Ireland and the Culture of Community in Dublin since Disestablishment' in R. Gillespie and W.G. Neely (eds), *The Laity and the Church of Ireland, 1000–2000: All Sorts and Conditions* (Dublin: Four Courts Press, 2002).

Maguire, M., 'Sources for Researching the Protestant Working-class in the Archives of the Church of Ireland', *Journal of the Irish Society for Archives*, 21 (2014), 23–30.

Maguire, M., 'The Church of Ireland and the Problem of the Protestant Working-class of Dublin, 1870s–1930s' in A. Ford, J.I. McGuire and K. Milne (eds), *As by Law Established: The Church of Ireland since the Reformation* (Dublin: The Lilliput Press, 1995).

Maguire, M., 'The Organisation and Activism of Dublin's Protestant Working-class, 1883–1935', *Irish Historical Studies*, 29, 113 (1994), 65–87.

Malcolm, E., 'A New Age or Just the Same Old Cycle of Extirpation? Massacre and the 1798 Irish Rebellion', *Journal of Genocide Research*, 15, 2 (2013), 151–66.

Markey, A., 'The Discovery of Irish Folklore', *New Hibernia Review*, 10, 4 (2006), 21–43.

Martin, G., 'Plantation Boroughs in Medieval Ireland' in D. Harkness and M. O'Dowd (eds), *The Town in Ireland* (Dublin: Appletree Press, 1981).

Maume, P., 'Douglas Hyde' in E. Biagini and D. Mulhall (eds), *The Shaping of Modern Ireland: A Centenary Assessment* (Dublin: Irish Academic Press, 2016).

Maxton, H., *Waking: An Irish Protestant Upbringing* (Derry: Lagan Press, 1997).

McBride, I., 'The Common Name of Irishman' in T. Claydon and I. McBride (eds), *Protestantism and National Identity: Britain and Ireland c. 1650–c. 1840* (Cambridge: Cambridge University Press, 1998).

McBride, I., 'Introduction: Memory and National Identity in Modern Ireland' in Ian McBride (ed.), *History and Memory in Modern Ireland* (Cambridge: Cambridge University Press, 2001).

McBride, L.W., 'Young Readers and the Learning and Teaching of Irish History, 1870–1922' in L.W. McBride (ed.), *Reading Irish Histories: Texts, Context and Memory in Modern Ireland* (Dublin: Four Courts Press, 2003).

McDermott, R.P. and D.A. Webb, *Irish Protestantism Today and Tomorrow: A*

Demographic Study (Dublin: Association for Promoting Christian Knowledge, 1938).

McDowell, R.B., *Crisis and Decline: The Fate of Southern Unionists* (Dublin: The Lilliput Press, 1997).

Megahey, A., *The Irish Protestant Churches in the Twentieth Century* (Basingstoke: MacMillan Press, 2000).

Middleton, D. and D. Edwards (eds), *Collective Remembering* (London: Sage Publications, 1990).

Milne, I., '"The Jersey is all that Matters, Not Your Church.": Protestants and the GAA in the Rural Republic' in I. d'Alton and I. Milne (eds), *Protestant and Irish: the Minority's Search for Place in Independent Ireland* (Cork: Cork University Press, 2019).

Milne, K., 'Disestablishment and the Lay Response' in R. Gillespie and W.G. Neely (eds), *The Laity and the Church of Ireland, 1000–2000: All Sorts and Conditions* (Dublin: Four Courts Press, 2002).

Milne, K., 'The Protestant Churches in Independent Ireland' in J.P. Mackey and E. McDonagh (eds), *Religion and Politics in Ireland at the Turn of the Millennium* (Dublin: The Columba Press, 2003).

Misztal, B.A., *Theories of Social Remembering* (Maidenhead and Philadelphia: Open University Press, 2003).

Mitchell, G., *Deeds Not Words: The Life and Work of Muriel Gahan, Champion of Rural Women and Craft-workers* (Dublin: Town House, 1997).

Moffett, F., *I Also Am of Ireland* (Bath: Chivers Press, 1986).

Moffitt, M., 'Identity Issues: What the Sources Show', *Journal of the Irish Society for Archives* (2014), 12–22.

Moffitt, M., *Soupers and Jumpers: The Protestant Missions in Connemara, 1948–1937* (Dublin: Nonsuch Publishing, 2008).

Moffitt, M., *The Church of Ireland Community of Killala and Achonry, 1870–1940. Maynooth Studies in Local History, no. 24* (Dublin: Irish Academic Press, 1999).

Moffitt, M., *The Society for Irish Church Missions to the Roman Catholics, 1849–1950* (New York: Manchester University Press, 2010).

Murphy, C., '"The Destruction of the Protestant Church and Dismemberment of The Empire": Charlotte Elizabeth, Evangelical Anglican in Pre Famine Ireland', *Women's Studies: An Interdisciplinary Journal*, 30, 6 (2001), 741–61.

Murphy, C. and L. Adair, *Untold Stories: Protestants in the Republic of Ireland, 1922–2002* (Dublin: The Liffey Press, 2002).

Murphy, G., *The Year of Disappearances: Political Killings in Cork, 1921–1922* (Dublin: Gill and MacMillan, 2010).

Murray, P., *Oracles of God: The Roman Catholic Church and Irish Politics, 1922–37* (Dublin: University College Dublin Press, 2000).

Nagel, J., 'Constructing Ethnicity: Creating and Recreating Ethnic Identity', *Social Problems* 41, 1 (1994), 152–76.

Nagle, S., 'Confessional Identity as National Boundary in National Historical Narratives: Ireland and Germany Compared', *Studies in Ethnicity and Nationalism*, 13, 1 (2013), 38–56.

Nagle, S., 'Historians for Britain vs. Historians for Europe', *History Ireland*, 23, 4 (2015), 10–11.

Nash, C., *Of Irish Descent: Origin Stories, Genealogy and the Politics of Belonging* (Syracuse: Syracuse University Press, 2008).

Newman Devlin, E., *Speaking Volumes: A Dublin Childhood* (Dublin: The Blackstaff Press, 2000).

Ní Dhuibhne, É., '"The Old Woman as Hare", Structure and Meaning in an Irish Legend', *Folklore*, 104 (1993), 77–85.

Ní Fhloinn, B., 'The Role of the Postal Questionnaire in the Collection of Irish Folklore' in S. Ó Catháin (ed.), *Northern Lights: Following Folklore in North-Western Europe: Essays in Honour of Bo Almqvist* (Dublin: University College Dublin Press, 2001).

Ní Ghiobúin, M., *Dugort, Achill Island, 1931–1861: The Rise and Fall of a Missionary Community. (Maynooth Studies in Irish Local History, no. 39.)* (Dublin and Portland: Irish Academic Press, 2001).

Nic Néill, M., 'Wayside Death Cairns in Ireland', *Béaloideas*, 16, 1/2 (1946), 49–63.

O'Callaghan, M., 'Language, Nationality and Cultural Identity in the Irish Free State, 1922–7: The "Irish Statesman" and the "Catholic Bulletin" Reappraised'. *Irish Historical Studies*, 24, 94 (1984), 226–245.

O'Carroll, P., 'Re-membering 1798' in E. Slater and M. Peillon (eds), *Memoirs of the Present: A Sociological Chronicle of Ireland, 1997–1998* (Dublin: Institute of Public Administration, 2000).

Ó Catháin, S., '"Institiuid Bhealoideas Eireann 1930–1935" [Irish Folklore Institute 1930–1935]', *Bealoideas*, 73 (2005), 85–110.

Ó Catháin, S., 'Súil siar ar Scéim na Scol, 1937–8', *Sinsear*, 5 (1988), 19–30.

O'Connor, C., 'Mixed Marriage, "A Grave Injury to Our Church": An Account of the 1957 Fethard-on-Sea Boycott', *The History of the Family*, 13, 4 (2008), 395–401.

O'Connor, C., 'The Church of Ireland Diocese of Ferns, 1945–65: A Female Perspective' in M. Busteed, F. Neal and J. Tonge (eds), *Irish Protestant Identities* (Manchester and New York: Manchester University Press, 2008).

O'Connor, Lily, *Can Lily O'Shea Come Out to Play?* (Dingle: Brandon, 2000).

Ó Corráin, D., *Rendering to God and Caesar: The Irish Churches and the Two States in Ireland, 1949–73* (Manchester and New York: Manchester University Press, 2006).

Ó Cróinín, D., 'J.H. Todd and the Life of St Patrick' in M. Empey, A. Ford and M. Moffitt (eds), *The Church of Ireland and Its Past: History, Interpretation, and Identity* (Dublin: Four Courts Press, 2017).

O'Giolláin, D., 'An Béaloideas agus An Stát', *Béaloideas*, 57 (1989), 151–163.

O'Giolláin, D., *Locating Irish Folklore: Tradition, Modernity, Identity* (Cork: Cork University Press, 2000).

Ó Glaisne, R., 'An Irish Protestant Culture' in J. McLoone (ed.), *On Being Protestant in Ireland: Co-operation North, in Association with the Social Study Conference* (Galway: Social Study Conference, 1985).

Ó Glaisne, R., 'Irish and the Protestant Tradition' in M.P. Hederman and R. Kearney (eds), *The Crane Bag Book of Irish Studies, 1977–1981* (Dublin: Blackwater Press, 1983).

Ó Glaisne, R., *The Irish Language: A Protestant Speaks to his Co-Religionists* (Longford: Nua-Eire, 1965).

Ó Glaisne, R., *To Irish Protestants* (Dublin: Ara, 1991).

Ó Gráda, C., *Black '47 and Beyond: The Great Irish Famine in History, Economy, and Memory* (Princeton: Princeton University Press, 1999).

O'Leary, R., 'Religious Intermarriage in Dublin: The Importance of Status Boundaries between Religious Groups', *Review of Religious Research*, 41, 4 (2000), 471–87.

O'Leary, R., 'Modernization and Religious Intermarriage in the Republic of Ireland', *British Journal of Sociology*, 52, 4 (2001), 647–65.

'One of Them', *The Case of the Irish Protestants in Relation to Home Rule: Stated by One of Them* (Dublin: William McGee, 1886).

'One of Themselves', *Disendowment: Is it Safe? – Is it Expedient? – Is it Right? An Appeal to Irish Protestants. By One of Themselves* (Dublin: Moffat and Co., 1869).

O'Toole, F., *Black Hole, Green Card: The Disappearance of Ireland* (Dublin: New Island Books, 1994).

O'Toole, F. *The Ex-Isle of Erin: Images of a Global Ireland* (Dublin: New Island Books, 1997).

Patton, H.E., *Fifty Years of Disestablishment: A Sketch* (Dublin: Association for Promoting Christian Knowledge, 1922).

Petrie, G., *The Ecclesiastical Architecture of Ireland: An Essay on the Origin and Uses of the Round Towers of Ireland* (Dublin: Hodges and Smith, 1845).

Pine, E., *The Politics of Irish Memory: Performing Remembrance in Contemporary Irish Culture* (Basingstoke and New York: Palgrave Macmillan, 2011).

Poole, M.A., 'In Search of Ethnicity in Ireland' in B. Graham (ed.), *In Search of Ireland: A Cultural Geography* (London: Routledge, 1997).

Potterton, H., *Rathcormick: A Childhood Recalled* (Dublin: New Island Books, 2001).

Power, B., 'Religion and the Irish Boys' Brigade, 1888–1914' in M. Hatfield, J. Kruse and R. McGonagle (eds), *Historical Perspectives on Parenthood and Childhood in Ireland* (Dublin: Arlen House, 2018).

Preston, M., 'Discourse and Hegemony: Race and Class in the Language of Charity in Nineteenth-Century Dublin' in T. Foley and S. Ryder (eds), *Ideology and Ireland in the Nineteenth Century* (Dublin and Portland: Four Courts Press, 1998).

Pringle, D.G., *One Island, Two Nations?: A Political Geographical Analysis of the National Conflict in Ireland* (Letchworth and New York: Research Studies Press, 1985).

Rafferty, O.P., 'Embedded Memory and the Churches in Ireland', *The Heythrop Journal*, 55, 3 (2014), 409–21.

Rast, M., '"Ireland's Sister Nations": Internationalism and Sectarianism in the Irish Struggle for Independence, 1916–1921', *Journal of Global History*, 10, 3 (2015), 479–501.

Reilly, T., 'Cromwell: the Irish Question', *History Today*, 62, 9 (2012).

Repina, L., 'Historical Memory and Contemporary Historical Scholarship.' *Russian Studies in History*, 49, 1 (2010), 8–25.

Roulston, R., 'Reassessing the Church of Ireland's Relationship with the

Irish State in Education: An Archival Approach', *Journal of the Irish Society for Archives*, 21 (2014), 51–63.

Ruane, J., 'Ethnicité, Religion et Religiosité: Les Protestants dans la République Irlandaise' *Ethnologie Française*, 41 (2011), 271–278.

Ruane, J., 'Ethnicity, Religion and Peoplehood: Protestants in France and in Ireland', *Ethnopolitics*, 9, 1 (2010), 121–135.

Ruane, J. and D. Butler, 'Southern Irish Protestants: An Example of De-ethnicisation?' *Nations and Nationalism*, 13, 4 (2007), 619–35.

Ruddock, N., *The Rambling Rector* (Dublin: The Columba Press, 2005).

Scholes, A., *The Church of Ireland and the Third Home Rule Bill* (Dublin: Irish Academic Press, 2010).

Schwartz, B., 'The Social Context of Commemoration: A Study in Collective Memory', *Social Forces*, 61, 2 (1982), 374–402.

Semple, P., *The Rector Who Wouldn't Pray for Rain* (Cork: Mercier Press, 2007).

Simms, A., 'The Origin of Irish Towns' in A. Simms and J.H. Andrews (eds), *Irish Country Towns: The Thomas Davis Lecture Series* (Cork: Mercier Press, 1994).

Smith, A., 'Mapped Landscapes: The Politics of Metaphor, Knowledge, and Representation on Nineteenth-Century Irish Ordnance Survey Maps', *Historical Archaeology*, 41, 1 (2007), 81–91.

Smith, A.D., *Myths and Memories of the Nation* (Oxford: Oxford University Press, 1999).

Smyth, W.J., *Map-making, Landscape, and Memory: A Geography of Colonial and Early Modern Ireland, c.1530–1750* (Cork: Cork University Press, 2006).

'Some Clergymen of the Church of Ireland', *A Brief Historical Catechism Concerning Ireland and her Church* (Dublin: James Charles and Son, 1885).

Somerville-Large, P., *An Irish Childhood* (London: Constable and Robinson Ltd, 2002).

Tanner, M., *Ireland's Holy Wars: The Struggle for a Nation's Soul* (New Haven: Yale University Press, 2001).

Temple, Sir J. and W. King, *The Irish Rebellion: Or, a History of the Beginnings and First Progress of the General Rebellion Raised within the Kingdom of Ireland upon the three and twentieth Day of October in the Year 1641. Together with the Barbarous Cruelties and Bloody Massacres which Ensued Thereupon. To Which is Added The Stated of the Protestants of Ireland Under the Late*

King James's Government (Dublin: Patrick Campbell, 1713).

Tobin, R., *The Minority Voice: Hubert Butler and Southern Irish Protestantism, 1900–1991* (Oxford: Oxford University Press, 2012).

Tobin, R., '"Tracing Again the Tiny Snail Track": Southern Protestant Memoir Since 1950', *The Yearbook of English Studies*, 35 (2005), 171–85.

Todd, J., N. Rougier, T. O'Keefe and L.C. Bottos, 'Does Being Protestant Matter? Protestants, Minorities and the Re-making of Ethnoreligious Identity After the Good Friday Agreement', *National Identities*, 11, 1 (2009), 87–99.

Tracy, R., *The Unappeasable Host: Studies in Irish Identities* (Dublin: University College Dublin Press, 1998).

Wallace, V., *Mrs Alexander: A Life of the Hymn-writer* (Dublin: The Lilliput Press, 1995).

Walsh, B.M., 'Religion and Demographic Behaviour in Ireland', *ESRI General Research Series*, 55 (1970).

Walsh, B.M., 'Trends in Religious Composition of Population in Republic of Ireland 1946–71', *Economic and Social Review*, 6, 4 (1975), 543–55.

Walsh, M., *Sam Maguire: The Enigmatic Man Behind Ireland's Most Prestigious Trophy* (Ballineen: Kenneigh Tower Publications, 2003).

Walsh, O., *Anglican Women in Dublin: Philanthropy, Politics and Education in the Early Twentieth Century* (Dublin: University College Dublin Press, 2005).

Walsh, P., 'Education and the "Universalist" Idiom of Empire: Irish National School Books in Ireland and Ontario'. *History of Education*, 37, 5 (2008), 645–60.

Walsham, A., 'Sacred Topography and Social Memory: Religious Change and the Landscape in Early Modern Britain and Ireland', *Journal of Religious History*, 36, 1 (2012).

Walsham, A., *The Reformation of Landscape: Religion, Identity and Memory in Early Modern Britain and Ireland* (Oxford: Oxford University Press, 2011).

Wertsch, J.V., 'Deep Memory and Narrative Templates: Conservative Forces in Collective Memory' in A. Assmann and L. Shortt (eds), *Memory and Political Change* (Basingstoke: Palgrave Macmillan, 2012).

Wertsch, J.V., *Voices of Collective Remembering* (Cambridge: Cambridge University Press, 2002).

Whelan, I., 'The Stigma of Souperism' in C. Póirtéir (ed.), *The Great Irish*

Famine (Cork and Dublin: Mercier Press, 1995).

Whelan, Y., 'Decoding Symbolic Spaces of Dublin: A Photographic Essay', *The Canadian Journal of Irish Studies*, 28/29, 1/2 (2002–2003), 46–73.

Whelan, Y., *Reinventing Modern Dublin: Streetscape, Iconography and the Politics of Identity* (Dublin: University College Dublin Press, 2003).

White, J., *Minority Report: The Protestant Community in the Irish Republic* (Dublin: Gill and Macmillan, 1975).

White, R., *Remembering Ahanagran: Storytelling in a Family's Past* (Cork: Cork University Press, 1999).

Wigham, M.J., *The Irish Quakers: A Short History of the Religious Society of Friends in Ireland* (Dublin: Historical Committee of the Religious Society of Friends in Ireland, 1992).

Wilde, J.F. ('Speranza'), *Ancient Legends, Mystic Charms and Superstitions of Ireland with sketches of the Irish past, by Lady Wilde ('Speranza'). To which is appended a chapter on 'the Ancient Race of Ireland' by the late Sir William Wilde* (London: Ward and Downey, 1887).

Yeats, W.B., *Fairy and Folktales of the Irish Peasantry* (London: Walter Scott Publishers, 1888).

Zerubavel, E., *Time Maps: Collective Memory and the Social Shape of the Past* (Chicago: The University of Chicago Press, 2003).

ENDNOTES

1. Burke, 1989, 98; Wertsch, 2002, 7.
2. Nagle, 2015, 10.
3. Zerubavel, 2003, 2.
4. Akeson, 1975, 109.
5. O'Leary, 2000, 474.
6. Tobin, 2012, 6.
7. All informants have been given pseudonyms, and brief non-identifying biographic material is provided in an appendix.
8. Bielenberg, 2013, 227.
9. Tanner, 2003, 313.
10. Megahey, 2000, 141.
11. Hart, 1996, 83.
12. Ó Glaisne, 1991, 91; Cunningham, 2014, 74.
13. Coakley, 1998, 91.
14. Fitzpatrick, 2013, 644.
15. Cunningham, 2014, 70.
16. McDowell, 1997, 164.
17. Macourt, 2008, 67.
18. McDowell, 1997, 164.
19. McDermott and Webb, 1938, 1.
20. Lyons, 1967, 95.
21. Cooney, 1999, 201.
22. Akeson, 1975, 133.
23. Macourt, 2008, 144.
24. Cunningham, 2014, 70.
25. Central Statistics Office, www.cso.ie.
26. Locus Management and Walsh, 2005, 13.
27. Dundes, 1980, 4.
28. O'Giolláin, 2000, 94.
29. Wilde, 1887.
30. Yeats, 1888.
31. Alver, 2005, 45.
32. O'Giolláin, 2000, 63.
33. O'Giolláin, 1989, 151–63.
34. Briody, 2007, 69.
35. Still published to this day, now by the National Folklore Collection.
36. Briody, 2014, 57.

37 Ó Catháin, 2005, 85 ff.
38 Gardiner, 2011, 711.
39 Brown, 2004, 136; Markey, 2006, 23.
40 Ó Catháin, 1998, 17–30; Ní Fhloinn, 2001, 217.
41 Briody, 2007, 261–3.
42 See in particular 'Churches of Other Persuasions', p. 156; 'The Irish People', p. 545; and Chapter 12, 'Religious Tradition', pp. 548–54. Ó Súillabháin, 1942, 156.
43 Briody, 2007, 447.
44 Ms. 421 Protestant storyteller Charley Walshe, An Tulach Mhór, Ardara, Co. Donegal. 17th November 1936, pp. 247–8, with a description of him from pp. 261–5. With thanks to Lilis Ó'Laoire for this note and reference.
45 Byrne, Edmondson and Varley, 2001.
46 Arensberg and Kimball, 2001; French, 2013, 164.
47 Briody, 2014, 61.
48 White, 1999, 45.
49 In 1971, the commission was re-established at University College Dublin as an academic department of Irish Folklore. Almqvist, 2005, 130–1.
50 Beiner, 2007, 42.
51 O'Giolláin, 2000, 15.
52 Hale, 2004, 458.
53 Nagel, 1994, 154.
54 Barth, 1998, 9–10.
55 Todd et al., 2009, 88.
56 Tobin, 2012, 85.
57 Guinnane, 1997, 75.
58 Brown, 2004, 97.
59 Fitzpatrick, 2014, 3.
60 Biagini, 2012, 1163–4.
61 Maguire, 2014, 23.
62 Stith Thompson, cited in Bramsbäck, 1971–73, 58.
63 Blank and Howard, 2013, 2.
64 Assmann, 1995, 130; Butler, 1989, 4.
65 Albert, for example, says that he is often able to identify Protestants, especially Protestant men, at sight, and says that even in the case of people who were born into mixed marriages and raised as Catholics, 'You'd nearly see it coming through'.
66 'The performance of folklore', as discussed by Bauman, 1972, 34.
67 White, 1999, 27.
68 Foster, 1993, 19.
69 Burke, 1989, 98.
70 Connerton, 1989, 17.
71 Jones and Russell, 2012, 271.
72 Cubitt, 2007, 187.
73 McBride, 2001, 6; Leonard, 2014, 66; Middleton and Edwards, 1990, 3. Rafferty provides the example of the 'forgetting' (by Catholics and Protestants) of the Catholics who supported William of Orange at the iconic Battle of the Boyne because they believed, at the time, the line that his victory would protect religious and civil liberties. Rafferty, 2014, 413.

74 Halbwachs, 1992, 51.
75 Cubitt, 2007, 224.
76 White, 1999, 35.
77 Halbwachs, 1992, 182–3.
78 Misztal, 2003, 2013.
79 Finney, 2014, 459.
80 Barthes, 1993.
81 Boyce, 2001, 265.
82 Assman, cited in Wertsch, 2012, 174. See also Geertz, 2000, 239.
83 Tobin, 2012, 3.
84 Pine, 2011, 7.
85 Banjeglav, 2012, 8.
86 The National Folklore Commission, founded in 1935, was the predecessor of the Department of Irish Folklore, founded in 1971, and the National Folklore Collection as it is today; it used questionnaires as an element of folklore collecting from its early days, having learned from the Swedish approach to the academic study of folklore. Ní Fhloinn, 2001, 215–28.
87 Biagini, 2012, 1172.
88 Cruise O'Brien, 1981, 786.
89 Ní Eigeartaigh, 2006, 216; Kearney, 1997, 107.
90 Tobin, 2012, 12.
91 Tanner, 2001, 76; 89.
92 Barnard, 2008, 14.
93 Busteed et al., 2008, 1.
94 Barkley, 1959, 3.
95 Ibid. 123.
96 Tanner, 2001, 127.
97 Graves, 1997, 9.
98 Patton, 1922, 2; 15.
99 Barnard, 1998, 230. It was given further impetus by work carried out in the nineteenth century by James Todd and R. Steele Nicholson, (Ó Cróinín, 2017, 118–23), and Alfred Lee (Golden, 2017, 149).
100 Hill, 1988, 103.
101 Barnard, 1998, 230.
102 Foster, 1993, 4.
103 Patton, 1922, 70.
104 Elliott, 2009, 100.
105 Ibid. 100.
106 'Some Clergymen of the Church of Ireland', 1885, preface (unnumbered) 8–13; 19; 22.
107 Murphy, 2001, 747.
108 Connolly, 1985, 25.
109 Barkley, 1959, 1.
110 Ibid. 101.
111 Elliott, 2009, 101.
112 Griffin, 1976, 8.
113 Moffitt, 2014, 17.

[114] de Valera in the *Irish Independent,* 19 March 1935. Cited in Pringle, 1985, 42.

[115] Zerubavel, 2003, 105.

[116] Somerville-Large, 2002, 103.

[117] About 25 per cent of all the country's Big Houses (of which there were 2,000) were destroyed (Bury, 2017, 85) and some more modest homes were also targeted. This topic is discussed in more detail in Chapter Three.

[118] Hart, 1998.

[119] Ruane and Butler, 2007, 624.

[120] Nash, 2008, 7.

[121] Most historians accept that there was a massacre at Drogheda and, afterwards, in Wexford, but some dissenting voices such as Reilly (2012) question this view.

[122] Exceptions to this 'distancing' can be found in counties such as Cavan and Monaghan, along the border with the 'six counties', where the Protestant population is higher and there are links to cultural artefacts such as Orangeism. (The Orange Order, founded in the late eighteenth century and discussed in Chapter Three, celebrates the victory of William of Orange at the Battle of the Boyne and is characterised by particular cultural, historical, and musical traditions, and sectarian views.) These counties also carry more entrenched links to unionist communities in Northern Ireland, where some take an almost defiant pride in being descendants of the Plantation of Ulster despite what they consider to be the Irish state's desire to write them out of history.

[123] Macourt, 2008, 61.

[124] Blume, 1952, 172; Hick, 1989, 119.

[125] Hick, 1989, 119–21.

[126] http://www.irishpalatines.org.

[127] Caldicott et al., 1987.

[128] Wigham, 1992, 85.

[129] Greaves, 1997, 34.

[130] Sakaranaho, 2011, 136.

[131] Schwartz, 1982, 375.

[132] Elliott, 2009, 2.

[133] Wertsch, 2002, 71.

[134] Repina, 2010, 11.

[135] Sakaranaho, 2011, 139.

[136] Repina, 2010, 15.

[137] Farrell Moran, 2003, 215–16.

[138] Goldberg et al., 2008, 224.

[139] Lysaght, 2009, 64.

[140] Zerubavel, 2003, 53.

[141] Doherty, 1996, 326.

[142] Foster, 2001, *The Irish Story,* 41.

[143] Doherty, 1996, 328.

[144] Walsh, 2008, 655–6.

[145] Fitzpatrick, 1991, 171–2.

[146] McDowell, 1997, 21.

[147] McBride, 2003, 88. As both the Catholic Church and the Church of Ireland claimed direct descent from St Patrick (as discussed in Chapter One), symbols of Ireland's an-

cient Christian past resonated with both groups.

[148] Petrie, 1845, v.

[149] Walsh, 2008, 658.

[150] Fitzpatrick, 1991, 169–70.

[151] Brown, 1985, 6–7.

[152] McBride, 2003, 101.

[153] Doherty, 1996, 342.

[154] Walsh, 2008, 659.

[155] Elliott, 2009, 10.

[156] Casserley, 1941, 53.

[157] Roulston, 2014, 53; 55.

[158] Carty, 1951.

[159] Janmaat, 2006, 365–6.

[160] Elliott, 2009, 64.

[161] Ibid.

[162] Gibney, 2011, 68.

[163] Ruane and Butler, 2007, 623.

[164] Gibney, 2008, 19; Elliott, 2009, 65.

[165] McBride, 1998, 239.

[166] Barnard, 1991, 890; 915.

[167] Barnard, 1991, 889.

[168] McBride, 1998, 239.

[169] Temple, 1713, 1; 34.

[170] Temple, 1713, 38; 78; 113; 223–5.

[171] Gibney, 2011, 69.

[172] Tanner, 2001, 134.

[173] Barkley, 1959, 9.

[174] Barnard, 2008, 47; 19.

[175] Nagle, 2013, 39–40.

[176] Tait et al., 2007, 9.

[177] Tanner, 2001, 145.

[178] Busteed, 2008, 28.

[179] Ó Glaisne, 1965, 5.

[180] Barnard, 2003, 115.

[181] Barkley, 1959, 38.

[182] Malcolm, 2013, 154; 159; 160.

[183] Foster, 2001, 'Remembering 1798', 72–3.

[184] Beiner, 2013, 11.

[185] Barkley, 1959, 39.

[186] Fanning, 2010, 21.

[187] Gahan, 1996, 27.

[188] Malcolm, 2013, 161–2.

[189] Gahan, 1996, 22; 30; 28.

[190] Dunne, 2004, 198.

[191] Ibid. 264.

[192] Malcolm, 2013, 151–2.

[193] Dunne, 2004, 102–3.

194 Beiner, 2007, 307–8.
195 O'Carroll, 2000, 18.
196 Foster, 2001, *The Irish Story* 228.
197 O'Carroll, 2000, 17.
198 Gahan, 1998, 17.
199 Dunne, 2004, 6.
200 Foster, 2001, *The Irish Story,* 228.
201 Foster, 2001, *The Irish Story,* 88.
202 Dunne, 2004, 128.
203 Casserley, 1941, 85.
204 Hynes, 2009, 196. The first Irish translation of the Anglican Book of Common Prayer was published in 1608. Ó Glaisne, 1983, 865.
205 Whelan, 1995, 139.
206 Ní Ghiobúin, 2001, 3.
207 Moffitt, 2008, 18.
208 Gregory and Cunningham, 2016, 77.
209 Connolly, 1985, 3.
210 Guinnane, 1997, 67.
211 Ó Gráda, 1999, 86.
212 Gregory and Cunningham, 2016, 81.
213 Whelan, 1995, 146.
214 White, 1975, 47.
215 O Ciosáin, 2004, 227–8.
216 Whelan, 1995, 140.
217 Hynes, 2009, 200–3.
218 Corporaal, 2009, 143.
219 Bowen, 1995, 314.
220 O Ciosáin, 2004, 228.
221 Moffitt, 2008, 181–2.
222 Elliott, 2009, 80.
223 Whelan, 1995, 135.
224 Nic Néill, 1946, 57.
225 Irwin, 1838, 21.
226 Tanner, 2001, 204; 207; 217; 218.
227 Ibid. 222.
228 Central Protestant Defence Association, 1868, 3.
229 Tanner, 2001, 227.
230 'One of Themselves', 1869, 4.
231 Lloyd and Cruise O'Brien, 1911, 11.
232 Scholes, 2010, 7.
233 Griffin, 2002, 41.
234 Patton, 1922, 10.
235 Lyons, 1971, 133.
236 Elliott, 2009, 96–7.
237 Patton, 1922, 66.
238 Lloyd and Cruise O'Brien, 1911, 4.
239 Wallace, 1995, 153.

[240] Elliott, 2009, 112.
[241] Wallace, 1995, 153.
[242] Lyons, 1971, 137.
[243] Jackson, 2004, 5.
[244] Tanner, 2001, 163–4.
[245] 'One of Them', 1886, 14.
[246] Fitzpatrick, 2014, 13.
[247] Milne, 2003, 65–6.
[248] White, 1975, 76.
[249] Maguire, 2002, 285.
[250] The Boys' Brigade was founded in Glasgow in 1883, and the first branch was established in Dublin in 1891. Power, 2018, 154.
[251] Moffett, 1985, 147.
[252] Tanner, 2001, 283.
[253] Nagle, 2013, 49.
[254] He is referring to the Ulster Volunteers, a militia organisation (known as the Ulster Volunteer Force from 1913) that was founded in 1912 to fight against self-government for Ireland.
[255] Tanner, 2001, 284.
[256] Tanner, 2001, 312.
[257] Tanner, 2001, 292.
[258] Brown, 2004, 95–6.
[259] Rast, 2015, 481–2.
[260] Dooley, 2000, 44–5.
[261] Maxton, 1997, 144.
[262] Hart, 1996, 92.
[263] Bielenberg, 2013, 204.
[264] Clark, 2014, 90.
[265] Donnelly, 2012, 5.
[266] Dooley, 2001, 184–5.
[267] Howe, 2014, 160.
[268] Bowen, 1983, 23.
[269] Murphy, 2010, 72–6.
[270] Hart, 1996, 89.
[271] Clark, 2014, 41.
[272] Hart, 1998, 277.
[273] Murphy, 2010, 73.
[274] Clark, 2014, 48–50.
[275] There are varying opinions about the prime motivations for the killings. A major (and controversial) book about the episode was published in 1999 (Hart, 1999).
[276] The brothers Mariah mentions were Richard and Abraham Pearson, who were killed by the IRA. While a TV documentary told their story as one of straightforward sectarian violence, there was also a political element in that the Pearsons had previously attacked an IRA road-blocking party. There are also unsubstantiated reports that they were linked to a secret loyalist organisation and that they were informers. Howe, 2014, 177.
[277] Hart, 1996, 85.

[278] Fitzpatrick, 2014, 161.
[279] Butler and Ruane, 2009, 82
[280] Tanner, 2001, 293.
[281] Ibid. 291.
[282] Griffin, 2002, 44.
[283] Brown, 2004, 98.
[284] Akeson, 1975, 113.
[285] Caird, 1984, 60.
[286] Clark, 2014, 19; 21; 89.
[287] Ibid. 148.
[288] Hayes and Fahey, 2008, 71.
[289] D'Alton, 2009, 14.
[290] McDowell, 1997, 165–6.
[291] Murray, 2000, 262.
[292] Curtis, 2010, 46.
[293] Kenny, 2000, 137.
[294] Farmar, 2010, 181.
[295] Browne, 1998, 46.
[296] Murray, 2000, 263.
[297] Fallon, 1999, 195; Kenny, 2000, 138.
[298] Fallon, 1999, 195.
[299] Farmar, 2010, 184.
[300] Barnard, 2006, 256–7.
[301] Garvin, 1981, 188.
[302] Tobin, 2012, 115.
[303] Dawson, 2006, 239.
[304] Ferriter, 2013, 139.
[305] Ruane, 2010, 128.
[306] McDowell, 1997, 168–9.
[307] *Rebel Prods* by Valerie Jones (Ashleaf, 2016) is an excellent work of the role of Protestant nationalists in Ireland's independence movement; she notes that those who converted to Catholicism, like Markievicz, have tended to be commemorated, while others have been allowed to sink into obscurity.
[308] Maume, 2016, 42.
[309] Foster, 1988, 459.
[310] Larkin, 1997, 91.
[311] O'Toole, 1997, 15.
[312] Barnard, 1998, 213.
[313] Moffitt, 2014, 13.
[314] Dingley, 2013, 109.
[315] Murray, 2000, 260.
[316] Foster, 1988, 544.
[317] Fleming, 1965, 161.
[318] Murphy and Adair, 2002, 35.
[319] Fleming, 1965, 163.
[320] Fleming, 1965, 91.
[321] Inglis, 1962, 12; 15.

322 Bardwell, 2008, 29.

323 Lyons, 1967, 100.

324 McDowell, 1997, 163.

325 Megahey, 2000, 109.

326 O'Connor, 2000, 77.

327 Boyce, 2001, 255.

328 Ruane and Butler, 2007, 628.

329 A memorial day intended to be a day of remembrance and gratitude for the soldiers who died in the First World War (1914–1918), as well as a way to raise money for former soldiers; it was known as Armistice Day before the Second World War.

330 Hart, 1996, 85.

331 Ruane and Butler, 2007, 626.

332 Foster, 2014, 72.

333 Gibbon, 1982, 113–14.

334 And cultural artefacts associated with it, such as the Irish language, in which so many important narratives and other aspects of folk tradition were manifested.

335 At that point, the Irish language had only ever been taught at Trinity with the aim of providing Protestant missionaries with an important tool towards their goal of converting Irish peasants in the west to Protestantism. Tracy, 1998, 137.

336 Bowen, 1942, 10.

337 On the other hand, she also comments that her family did use the services of local healers who had 'the cure' and would never 'seat thirteen people down to table', as this was considered 'a very risky thing to do'.

338 As Adam was from a well-to-do family, the idea of 'the others' may be regarded in terms of economic and social issues as much as, or more than, denominational or cultural difference.

339 Although these ideas around the bonfire night celebrated in the west are not in general circulation, in folklorist Kevin Danaher's *The Year in Ireland*, embedded in an interesting discussion on a wide range of traditions relating to the midsummer bonfire tradition, he reports a snippet from an edition of *Ulster Folklore*. The piece reports that in 1950 a group of children provided as an explanation for their fire that they were 'burning the Protestants' bones'. Danaher, 1972, 139. With thanks to Fiachra MacGabhann for pointing out the reference.

340 Billy sees a direct link between older beliefs around holy wells and the phenomenon of 'moving statues' in the 1980s; this was a phenomenon that was greeted by equal amounts of enthusiasm and scepticism, seen by a popular bishop of the time as a cry from the heart, on the part of Irish Catholics, for 'a religion which will encompass all of one's life' when 'we [Irish] demonstrated ourselves to the world as being so naïve' (Comisky, 1988, 563).

341 For a complete discussion of this tradition, see Lysaght, 1997.

342 The National Folklore Collection has many references to the fairy tree. See, for example, The Schools' Collection, Vol. 29, p. 308. Retrieved from Duchas.ie.

343 The National Folklore Collection has many references to the fairy forts. See, for example, The Schools' Collection, Vol. 904, p. 113. Retrieved from Duchas.ie.

344 The National Folklore Collection has many references to customs and beliefs associated with May Day. See, for example, the Schools' Collection, Vol. 46, p. 319.

345 A reference to Migratory Legend 3056, 'The Old Woman as Hare', according to the

system proposed by folklorist Reidar Thoralf Christiansen (1958). For a full discussion of this legend type, see Ní Dhuibhne, 1993, 77–85.

346 A similar account can be seen in the National Folklore Collection. The Schools' Collection, vol. 856, p. 164.

347 This is a local variant of a relatively common legend. A version was also written up, in ballad form, in the novel *Uncle Silas*, which was written by the Dublin gothic writer Joseph Sheridan Le Fanu. The earliest known variants are found in printed sources from early-seventeenth-century London, which describe a pig-faced woman who was born that way after her mother turned away a beggar woman who cursed her and said that her child would be born with a pig's head. A version was also told about Griselda Steevens, a sister of the Dublin doctor who left money to found Steevens' Hospital, which is part of the Health Service Executive today. Griselda had to wear a veil over her face because of a medical condition, as was said of the pig-faced women known from the common legend. This presumably led to the rumour that she too had a pig's head. The rumour was given credence by a Dublin pub that hung a supposed picture of her with a pig's head and a trough she was supposed to eat from. Peep shows that travelled around the country also showed engravings supposed to show Griselda eating from her trough. Bondeson, 2006, 29; 83–7.

348 She gives several examples, 'When I was about eight years old, I had the mumps and my mother took me to our neighbour [...] who was supposed to have the cure. Apparently, a pair of donkey's 'winkers' was put on your head and you were led to the nearest river or stream by the reins and had to put your head in the water [...] When my husband's youngest brother was about three years old, he was badly scalded by hot water [...] they didn't send for the doctor but for a man who was known to have the cure for burns. He arrived immediately started to lick the little boy all over every inch of his body. The child settled and in a short time stopped crying and fell asleep. The child recovered quickly without a single scar on his body. This man supposedly got the cure by finding and licking the belly of an "ashleaf" or newt.'

349 This sparks a discussion about the many processions that Catholics had during the year, such as Corpus Christi, when all the Catholic families would put little altars outside their homes with statues and flowers, and people paraded the streets. These were not festivities that had any direct counterpoint in the small Protestant community, but they would come out and 'take a look' at the Catholics. It was a day out in a rural area in which those were often hard to come by.

350 *Encyclopaedia Britannia*, vol. 4, 1911, 339.

351 Jokes are an element of folk tradition and, of course, this includes jokes that may be racist or otherwise bigoted. See Dundes, 1987, for a discussion of the role of jokes in tradition and Dundes, 1971, for an exploration of the role of jokes embodying ethnic slurs in the American context.

352 Boyd, 1995, 16–17.

353 Although this music was very important to the local Protestant community, they were aware of being 'less musical' than the Catholics they knew, 'if you got a hundred Catholics together, forty of them would play an instrument. With the same number of Prods, it'd be very hard to get two or three.'

354 As for other traditions regarded as specific to the Protestant community in border areas, Andy remembers that some of the Protestant families in his area lit bonfires on 5 November to celebrate Guy Fawkes' Night, and he states, 'I cannot remember that

any controversy or triumphalist feelings arose from this.' Also, in parts of the north-west, mumming was a tradition found in Protestant communities. Gavin recalls, 'Some Protestants were "mummers" at Christmas, or was it Halloween, singing in houses with masks on, but not many did this – only one family as I recall it.'

355 Griffin, 2002, 10.

356 While many informants reported resistance and hostility to the GAA, there were also Protestants who participated actively. This topic is discussed in Chapter Five, and it is covered in detail by Ida Milne – see Milne, 2019, 171–90.

357 White, 1975, 97.

358 Patton, 1922, 271.

359 Dooley, 2001, 122.

360 Patton, 1922, 271.

361 Leonard, 1996, 102–3; Milne, 2002, 228.

362 White, 1975, 97.

363 Leonard, 1996, 102.

364 Gerry Fitt was a founder and the first leader of the Social Democratic and Labour Party (SDLP) in Northern Ireland, a social democratic and Irish nationalist party that later joined the House of Lords in the UK.

365 Mitchell, 1997, 14; 17.

366 Walsh, 1970, 25.

367 Fleming, 1965, 36–9.

368 Noël Browne is famous for having championed the cause of free maternity care for all women and free healthcare for all children up to the age of sixteen; it was a move that was rigorously opposed by the Catholic hierarchy of the time, as they felt it was a communistic idea. Browne, 1998, 41.

369 Horgan, 2000, 141; 33.

370 Browne, 1986, 142.

371 Butler, 1985, 115.

372 Prayers for the British monarch were removed from the Church of Ireland Book of Common Prayer in 1949 – when the Republic of Ireland left the British common-wealth – to the distress of some members of the Church. Moffitt, 2014, 19.

373 Gregg, 1943, 3.

374 Buck, 2011, 3–5.

375 Buck, 2011, 2.

376 Bowen, 1983, 43.

377 Fletcher, 1947, 11.

378 http://www.vatican.va/holy_father/paul_vi/motu_proprio/documents/hf_p-vi_motu-proprio_19700331_matrimonia-mixta_en.html.

379 Tobin, 2012, 232.

380 Ibid. 172.

381 Corkey, 1912, 6.

382 Fernihough et al., 2015, 4.

383 Ibid. 7–8.

384 Ibid. 22–3.

385 Ervine, 1911, 15; 32; 55.

386 Buck, 2011, 6.

387 Tanner, 2001, 313.

[388] Fernihough et al., 2015, 11–12.

[389] Tanner, 2001, 317.

[390] Guinnane, 1997, 218.

[391] Kenny, 2000, 175.

[392] Fletcher, 1947, 18.

[393] Tobin, 2012, 172.

[394] O'Connor, 2008, 'Mixed Marriage, "A Grave Injury to our Church"', 395–8.

[395] Tobin, 2012, 173.

[396] *Clontarf Parish Magazine*, quoted in Maguire, 2002, 277.

[397] Given the age profile of most informants, the stories discussed here refer primarily to the period 1930–70.

[398] Ruddock, 2005, 17–18.

[399] Walsh, 1975, 14; 544–7.

[400] Cruise O'Brien, 1981, 786.

[401] Lyons, 1967, 100.

[402] O'Leary, 2001, 652; 660.

[403] Broderick, 2011.

[404] Fanning, 2010, 72.

[405] O'Connor, 2008, 'The Church of Ireland Diocese of Ferns, 1945–65: A Female Perspective', 114.

[406] Butler, 1985, 136.

[407] Broderick, 2011, 12–17.

[408] O'Connor, 2008, 'Mixed Marriage', 398.

[409] Tobin, 2012, 175.

[410] Butler, 1985, 137.

[411] Ruddock, 2005, 62.

[412] Tobin, 2012, 175.

[413] Butler, 1985, 141.

[414] Tobin, 2012, 174.

[415] Butler, 1985, 139.

[416] O'Connor, 2008, 'Mixed Marriage', 397.

[417] Megahey, 2000, 118.

[418] Ruddock, 2005, 58–9.

[419] Browne, 1998, 46.

[420] O'Connor, 2008, 'Mixed Marriage', 397; Jameson, 2014, 79.

[421] Lyons, 1971, 671; Jameson, 2014, 72.

[422] O'Connor, 2008, 'Mixed Marriage', 399.

[423] Butler, 1985, 137.

[424] Ursula reports that in her community, not far away, the local parish priest responded to the boycott by instructing his parishioners not to attend the annual Protestant parish fête. However, led by a prominent local family, the parish decided to go against his order and attended it *en masse* to show that they did not intend to be influenced by him – a suggestion that the events in Fethard, while deeply distressing, were not necessarily typical of all small communities.

[425] Broderick, 2011, 103.

[426] Ruddock, 2005, 65–6.

[427] *A Love Divided*, directed by Sidney Macartney and released in 1999.

[428] Maxton, 1997, 151.

[429] Dalton, 2003, 93.

[430] Coakley, 1998, 90.

[431] Ó Glaisne, 1991, 105–6.

[432] Gillmore, 2006, 125.

[433] Poole, 1997, 138.

[434] Smith, 1999, 197.

[435] Poole, 1997, 139.

[436] McDowell, 1997, 165.

[437] Maxton, 1997, 88.

[438] Bowen, 1942, 52.

[439] Newman Devlin, 2000, 114.

[440] Kenny is an Irish journalist, based in the UK, who has written for a wide range of Irish and British newspapers.

[441] Akeson, 1988, 120.

[442] Connolly, 1985, 27.

[443] Akeson, 1988, 122–3.

[444] Moffitt, 1999, 41; Roulston, 2014, 52.

[445] Akeson, 1975, 3.

[446] Garvin, 1981, 192.

[447] Dingley, 2013, 109.

[448] Connolly, 1985, 35.

[449] O'Toole, 1994, 126.

[450] Kearney, 2007, 43.

[451] Browne, 1998, 44–5.

[452] Garvin, 2004, 129.

[453] Browne, 1998, 49.

[454] Lang, 1995, 422.

[455] Ó Corráin, 2006, 78–9.

[456] Foster, 2014, 31.

[457] Akeson, 1988, 117.

[458] Akeson, 1975, 116–18.

[459] Ó Corráin, 2006, 80.

[460] Moffitt, 1999, 15.

[461] Ó Corráin, 2006, 87.

[462] Akeson, 1975, 147; Crawford, 2010, 34.

[463] Daly, 2012, 275.

[464] Johnson, 2003, 60.

[465] Moffitt, 2010, 250–1.

[466] Akeson, 1988, 116.

[467] Newman Devlin, 2000, 112.

[468] In its early days, many prominent members of the Church of Ireland, such as Douglas Hyde, were active in the Gaelic League and found it to be a way to express their sense of Irishness 'without being Catholic or separatist'. Foster, 1989, 18.

[469] Kenny, 2000, 24.

[470] Garvin, 1981, 102.

[471] Just 16 per cent in 1921. Hechter, 1975, 269.

[472] O'Callaghan, 1984, 229.

[473] Graham, 1997, 197.

[474] Scholes, 2010, 8.

[475] Akeson, 1975, 122–3.

[476] White, 1975, 98.

[477] Dickinson, 1929, 2–3.

[478] Jones, 2006, 182.

[479] Bielenberg, 2013, 225.

[480] Akeson, 1975, 127.

[481] Bowen, 1983, 158.

[482] Caird, 1984, 62.

[483] O'Callaghan, 1984, 242.

[484] Kearney, 2007, 141.

[485] Akeson, 1975, 121.

[486] Bowen, 1983, 156; Foster, 1988, 518.

[487] Foster, 1988, 518.

[488] Akeson, 1975, 41; 46–8.

[489] Fitzsimons, 2010, 125.

[490] Kearney, 2007, 45.

[491] Foster, 2014, 52.

[492] Jones, 2006, 68; 178.

[493] Jones, 2006, 181.

[494] Ó Glaisne, 1965, 1.

[495] Sam Maguire was a Protestant from Cork.

[496] Akeson, 1975, 111.

[497] Dunleavy and Dunleavy, 1991, 434.

[498] Foster, 2001, *The Irish Story*, 81.

[499] Tobin, 2012, 151.

[500] Conversely, in his memoir, Peter Somerville-Large remembers his grandfather, a cleric, writing down anecdotes 'about saving dying people from priests and returning them to the true Protestant faith'. Somerville-Large, 2002, 40.

[501] Walsh, 2005, 15.

[502] Farmar, 2010, 80.

[503] Bardwell, 2008, 31; 105.

[504] Pringle, 1985, 226.

[505] Moffitt, 1999, 11.

[506] White, 1975, 101.

[507] Lang, 1995, 396.

[508] Moffitt, 1999, 11.

[509] Pringle, 1985, 227.

[510] O'Connor, 2000, 180.

[511] Tanner, 2001, 337.

[512] In mitigation of the Adelaide's deeply discriminatory practice, it should be pointed out that, certainly in earlier years, Protestant doctors and medical institutions had had to deal with a lot of opposition, particularly during the career of Archbishop Mc-Quaid. Archbishop McQuaid even fought against the doctor Kathleen Lynn and her work to reduce Ireland's appalling infant mortality statistics because she was a Protes-

tant. With the help of the Knights of Columbanus, who spied on the Protestant medical body and reported back to McQuaid, the Archbishop strove to reduce the influence of Protestants in the field of medicine. Kehoe, 2016, 150. Gerald remembers that, at the Adelaide's social events, 'God Save the King' was still sung in the 1940s; Peter remembers that 'if you went out with a girl, an Adelaide nurse, you knew you were on the right side of the fence, you see.'

[513] Dalton, 2003, 74–85.

[514] Murphy and Adair, 2002, 18.

[515] Although this perception lingered, by the 1960s it seems that there was no anti-Protestant discrimination in the public sector, and the number of Protestants employed roughly mirrored the percentage of the population that they represented. Ó Corráin, 2006, 88.

[516] Megahey, 2000, 149,

[517] Guinnane, 1997, 76.

[518] Barkley, 1959, 23–4.

[519] Tobin, 2005, 176.

[520] Some are at pains to point out that not all the 'Big House' people were Protestants at all, despite the stereotype. For instance, Ted comments that his own farming family 'did not mix too freely with the RC family in the big house as they were top class', and he notes that the family in question had lost a son who was fighting for the British in the Second World War.

[521] Dalton, 2003, 37.

[522] Irish farmers were encouraged to grow sugar beet as part of a general effort to make Ireland self-reliant, and the sugar beet crop became very important to the Irish rural economy; the sugar company even published a regular magazine for farming families, including a children's page ostensibly written by a friendly sugar beet called Bo. The importance of the sugar company events would have been considerable in rural Ireland at the time.

[523] Ruddock, 2005, 13; 23.

[524] At a time of great urban poverty in Dublin, the hospital was founded to 'give to the poor Protestant (often a person fallen from the ranks of respectable society) an asylum in illness' and to provide them with pastoral support as well as medical care. Fealy, 2009, 14–16.

[525] Fealy, 2009, 17; 20–2

[526] Walsham, 2012, 33.

[527] Cubitt, 2007, 195.

[528] Misztal, 2003, 16.

[529] Smyth, 2006, 4.

[530] Walsham, 2012, 40. This sort of behaviour can be identified all over the world whenever one population conquers another. The same recognition of the 'mnemonic significance of place' was, for example, behind the decision of the Spaniards to essentially destroy the great Aztec city of Tenochtitlán before building Mexico City in the same spot. Zerubavel, 2003, 90.

[531] Walsham, 2012, 40.

[532] Walsham, 2011, 146.

[533] Foster, 1988, 7.

[534] Smyth, 2006, 12. It's interesting to note that historical archaeology, which researches

(among other things) homes built and inhabited during the historical period, got off to a late start in Ireland because of the nationalist sentiment that it was a bad idea to study the activities of the people involved in the plantation of Ireland, despite this being a matter of historical record. Gardiner, 2011, 715.

[535] D'Alton, 2009, 58.

[536] Smyth, 2006, 25; 175; 55.

[537] Smyth, 2006, 17.

[538] Said, 1994, 273.

[539] Smith, 2007, 83.

[540] O'Giolláin, 2000, 42.

[541] Petrie, 1845, x.

[542] Halbwachs, 1992, 65–6.

[543] Crawford, 2010, 20.

[544] Lysaght, 2009, 60.

[545] Graham, 1997, 4.

[546] Crawford, 2010, 22.

[547] Bielenberg, 2013, 207.

[548] Dooley, 2001, 172.

[549] Clark, 2014, 75–7; 92.

[550] Dooley, 2001, 177.

[551] Bielenberg, 2013, 207–8.

[552] Austin Clark's poem 'The Planter's Daughter' refers to the house of the planter being 'known by the trees'.

[553] Cusack, 2001, 230.

[554] Cusack, 2001, 232.

[555] Guinnane, 1997, 66.

[556] Edgeworth, 2007, 1.

[557] Dooley, 2004, 40–5.

[558] Edgeworth, 2007, 4.

[559] Dooley, 2004, 3; 38.

[560] Bowen, 1983, 81.

[561] Dooley, 2004, 45.

[562] Bew, 2007, 445.

[563] Dooley, 2004, 224. Norris went on to say that he now sees it as a 'useful historical instrument'.

[564] Walsh, 2003, 13. Ed reports that years after Maguire's death, some of the locals proposed that he be disinterred from the Protestant graveyard and reburied in the Catholic one, as he was really 'one of our own'.

[565] Edgeworth, 2007, 6; 10.

[566] Dooley, 2004, 41.

[567] Ibid. 220.

[568] O'Leary, 2001, 660.

[569] Ruane and Butler, 2007, 631.

[570] Dooley, 2004, 4.

[571] Original document provided by David Bird.

[572] However, in the early 1960s, when Enid's husband became involved, a few Catholic students were accepted. Some members of the local Protestant community were in-

clined to see the students as potential spouses for their own children and they were invited to Protestant socials, but by the 1960s, young people had become much more liberal than their parents, and Enid recalls that the students refused to attend their socials unless their Catholic friends could come too – so nobody went.

[573] Prudence and her sister were sent there by their parents after they had been caught escaping down the drainpipe to meet Catholic boyfriends one time too many. Her parents thought they would be safe there, among Protestant boys. 'It really backfired', she comments.

[574] Bielenberg, 2013, 206.

[575] Lysaght, 2009, 64.

[576] Kiberd, 1995, 107.

[577] Burn-Murdoch, 1996, 24.

[578] Misztal, 2003, 16.

[579] Higgins, 2012, 133.

[580] Limond, 2010, 10.

[581] Simms, 1994, 11.

[582] Harkness and O'Dowd, 1981, 1,

[583] Martin, 1981, 28–9.

[584] Hunter, 1981, 55; 61.

[585] Jupp, 1981, 110–11.

[586] Barnard, 2003, 15.

[587] Daly, 1981, 227.

[588] D'Alton, 2011, 203.

[589] Brück, 2013, 199; 209; 214,

[590] Whelan, 2002–3, 'Decoding Symbolic Spaces of Dublin', 48.

[591] Whelan, 2003, *Reinventing Modern Dublin*, 101.

[592] Whelan, 2002–3, 'Decoding Symbolic Spaces', 48; 69.

[593] Whelan, *Reinventing*, 194–6.

[594] Maguire, 2002, 278; 287,

[595] White, 1975, 11.

[596] In the late nineteenth century, the Bird's Nest had been identified by Catholics opposing proselytism, and the Catholic Archbishop of Dublin, William Walshe, had established the Sacred Heart Home in Drumcondra and the Catholic Boy's Home in Abbey Street; the latter institution was for Catholic children who had been 'rescued' from Protestant homes. Protestant children's homes, with their missionising aspect, had been identified as one aspect of proselytism that was 'a perpetual running sore on the Catholic body'. Moffitt, 2010, 220. The Bird's Nest was the orphanage in which Mr Tilson, whose case is discussed briefly in Chapter Four, deposited his children when his marriage broke up.

[597] Maguire, 1995, 195.

[598] Maguire, 1994, 65.

[599] Maguire, 1995, 196.

[600] Maguire, 1994, 75.

[601] Maguire, 1995, 198.

[602] Walsh, 2005, 95.

[603] Preston, 1998, 101.

[604] Maguire, 2014, 27.

605 Maguire, 2002, 280.
606 Maguire, 1994, 65–7.
607 Maguire, 1994, 73–4; Maguire, 2014, 29.
608 White, 1975, 57.
609 Maguire, 1995, 202.
610 Tobin, 2012, 3.
611 Crawford, 2010, 83.
612 Higgins, 2012, 74; Clark, 2014, 37.
613 Inglis, 1982, 24.
614 O'Connor, cited in Walsh, 2005, 152.
615 O'Connor, 2000.
616 Murphy and Adair, 2002, 67.
617 Maguire, 1995, 198.
618 Tobin, 2005, 171.
619 Ó Glaisne, 1985, 74.
620 Kearney, 2007, 35.
621 Higgins, 2012, 43.
622 Derry and Raphoe Action, 2001, 9.
623 Tanner, 2001, 421.
624 Butler and Ruane, 2009, 78
625 Ruane, 2010, 130.
626 Kenny, 2000, 211–13.
627 Tanner, 2001, 359.
628 Kenny, 2000, 216.
629 Tobin, 2012, 223.
630 Ruane, 2011, 6.
631 Gillnor, 2006, 112.
632 D'Alton, 2009, 11.
633 D'Alton, 2009, 40–1.
634 Crawford, 2010, 26–7.

INDEX

INDEX